AD WOMEN

JULIANN SIVULKA

AD WOMEN

HOW THEY IMPACT
WHAT WE NEED, WANT, AND BUY

659
.1082
S642a

9/09
Prometheus Books

59 John Glenn Drive
Amherst, New York 14228–2119

Published 2009 by Prometheus Books

Inquiries should be addressed to
Prometheus Books
59 John Glenn Drive
Amherst, New York 14228–2119
VOICE: 716–691–0133, ext. 210
FAX: 716–691–0137
WWW.PROMETHEUSBOOKS.COM

13 12 11 10 09   5 4 3 2 1

Library of Congress Cataloging-in-Publication Data

Sivulka, Juliann.
    Ad women : how they impact what we need, want, and buy / by Juliann Sivulka.
        p. cm.
    ISBN 978–1–59102–672–3 (hardcover)
    1. Women in the advertising industry—United States—History. 2. Women in marketing—United States—History. 3. Businesswomen—United States—History. 4. Advertising industry—United States—History. 5. Consumers—United States—History. 6. Social change—United States—History. I. Title.

HF5805.S58 2008
659.1082'0973—dc22

                                                                2008032726

Every attempt has been made to trace accurate ownership of copyrighted material in this book. Errors and omissions will be corrected in subsequent editions, provided that notification is sent to the publisher.

Printed in the United States of America on acid-free paper

They talk about a woman's sphere,
As though it had a limit;
There's not a place in earth or heaven,
There's not a task to mankind given,
There's not a blessing or woe,
There's not a whisper, Yes, or No,
There's not a life, or death, or birth,
That has a feather's weight of worth,
Without a woman in it.

     —Frances E. Willard, *Occupations for Women*, 1897

CONTENTS

ACKNOWLEDGMENTS

This study of women in the advertising profession is a part of a larger study of the making of consumer culture. It began as an examination of how advertising grew in America, how products and brands were produced and promoted, and how manufacturers used advertising in ever more sophisticated ways to convince Americans, especially women, that buying their products would improve their lives. But I continually returned to a 1903 issue of *Profitable Advertising* that published a fifty-five-page feature titled "Women Workers in Publicity," which appeared at a time when women increasingly claimed a public role once reserved for men. Finally, I took on the challenging task of exploring women's contributions to the advertising profession and the making of modern American consumer culture.

I spent nearly ten years researching and developing the ideas in this book. During the years, I received generous support from the Josephine Abney Faculty Fellowship for Research in Women's Studies at the University of South Carolina. Smith College assisted me through the Margaret Storrs Grierson Scholars-in-Residence Fellowship to work in the Sophia Smith Collection and Smith Archives. The Hartman Center of Marketing, Advertising, and Sales History provided a travel grant to work in their extensive archives at Duke University. Waseda University assisted me through its Faculty Research Awards Program to complete the final stages of research and writing.

A number of people read and commented on the entire manuscript and encouraged my research. David Katzman has actively supported this book since it was only a grant proposal for research—and gave wonderful comments and criticism on several drafts of the manuscript. I am grateful to many more people who have shared insights from their own work and talked with me about women's work, marketing, advertising, and consumer culture throughout the years, so I want to thank Bonnie Drewniany, Olga Khomenko, Marilyn Motz, Carrie A. Z. Smith, Laura Woliver, and the students in my Gender and Consumer Culture seminar. I am also grateful to Jacqueline Reid and her staff at the Hartman Center for Marketing, Advertising, and Sales History at Duke University and Sherrill Redmon and her staff at the Sophia Smith Collection at Smith College Library for their invaluable help during my years of research. I am also grateful to the staffs of the Hagley Museum and Library, Harvard Business School Baker Library, the Library of Congress, the Mass Communications History Collection at the Wisconsin Historical Society, the New York Business Library, the Schlesinger Library, and the Smithsonian National Museum of American History.

Once the book was done, my agent, Neil Salkind, found the perfect publisher. I am grateful to my editor at Prometheus Books, Steven L. Mitchell, who also saw the value of this book. Last I wish to thank others at Prometheus—Christine Kramer, Julia DeGraf, Mark Hall, and Jill Maxick—for their contributions in rendering this work into final shape.

INTRODUCTION

WOMEN, THE BODY AND SOUL
OF ADVERTISING

For most of the twentieth century, advertising has portrayed women in narrow roles—as dim-witted sex objects, as perky young things in search of a man, or as one-dimensional homemakers eager to serve their husbands. These popular images projected in the national media of Mrs. Consumer—who is born to shop—were also born at this time, into an unreal world created by the image makers, the ad men. In fact, one of advertising's most enduring clichés is the male executive who tries to defend his proposal by saying: "My wife thinks . . ." And so the story goes, it is the ad man, acting from his peculiar, limited masculine ideas of female character, who responded to what he believed were the aspirations and lifestyle of the typical homemaker. But for all of men's efforts in this new industrial economy, it has been women who were involved not only as consumers but in a myriad of commercial practices.

Women, not men, had been responsible for the increasing amount of women-centered advertising, for such products as soap, fashion, food, and housewares. They encouraged consumption as part of women's concerns with nutrition, health, and household efficiency. Other women worked for manufacturers to promote standardized goods and sanitary packaging under the guise of good domestic practice. In department stores, they wrote reams of copy. Many women also played pivotal roles as editors of newspapers and magazine service departments. They promoted new inventions and styles, cooperated with advertisers, mentioned brand names in recipes and advertising columns, conducted market investigations, and even put their names on products. In broadcasting, women also worked as information brokers, interlocutors, and tastemakers, as they wrote advertising spots, acted as spokespersons, and produced commercials.

In the process, women have transformed the body and soul of advertising that is the subject of this book. From Mathilde C. Weil in 1867 to Mary Wells and Charlotte Beers in the twenty-first century, *Ad Women* tells the story of how women have risen to the top of the advertising profession. With each wave of the feminist movement, women took up reform, overcame barriers, and carved out a niche in advertising agencies and the new mass-market industries over the course of the twentieth century. Now women make up nearly 60 percent of the workers in advertising and public relations today, as well as countless organizations in industry, media, retail, and fashion. Women account for more than one half of account managers in agencies. Women also outnumber men in journalism, communications, and advertising higher education programs. And every year, more women enter the ad business. Because they now hold key marketing and advertising positions, they have shaped the basic promotional appeal of accounts more than ever before in history.[1]

How did the advertising business go from a handful of women in a man's world to women working in virtually every mass-consumer goods industry in America in the space of the twentieth century? How did these women impact the promotional appeal of almost every consumer product in America over the last century, continuing to do so today? And how does their work influence future practices? Unfortunately, these women left few records of their professional life. But articles in trade journals, account files, personnel records, and personal papers provide some insight into these ad women who worked hard to ascertain customer preferences and to find customers for their product. Although these sources are fragmentary—for the most part limited to white middle-class women—they do open a window to how ad women working in mass-consumer industries closely collaborated with publishers, mass media, manufacturers, and retailers. Around the turn of the twentieth century, the singular recognition of women as primary consumers resulted not only in agencies but in other mass-consumer industries to hire a new ensemble of businesswomen to promote their products aimed at the women's market. Manufacturers emphasized color, fashion, and style, while advertising embraced a new language of persuasion: *If you are selling to women, nothing succeeds like a woman's viewpoint.*

What is distinct about this book as opposed to other books on advertising history and consumer culture is its focus on women's pivotal contributions to the evolution of our nation's economic development and American consumer culture. Although books on advertising history examine representations of gender, advertising history is a gendered narrative reflecting mostly men's rather than women's experience in advertising. Based on rich and diverse archival sources, this book is filled with stories of women who succeeded in traditionally feminine occupations as well as those who challenged these limited social roles. *Ad Women* places these figures in the larger context of business and economic development, the entry of women in the professions, and women's history. Finally, it examines the fact that women were actually a part of the story. It also conveys the radical nature of that view—not an adjustment of the existing story but rather the creation of an entirely new narrative.[2]

⊰⊱⊰⊱

To retell the history of advertising and the making of American consumer culture, I emphasize that women took their place alongside men and played an important role in the development of the American economy as both consumers and ad women. By the 1890s, advertisers and manufacturers had begun to recognize that women not only bought beauty products but also most of the mass-produced household food, clothing, and other goods. As most of the goods sold at retail were marketed to women, it made sense that if women followed their instincts, they should come close to knowing what to say in advertisements to other women. And what she did not buy, she influenced through her father and brothers, her husband and sons.

In the new consumer industries and services, a small group of professional and managerial women positioned themselves as offering the woman's viewpoint in the new mass-market industry. Women wrote reams of persuasive copy for agencies, department stores, and mail-order firms. They also managed corporate advertising activities, ran publicity campaigns, and coordinated fashion shows. Others worked as "outside" consultants in merchandising, in marketing research, and as home economists. Still, other women worked as commercial artists, product designers, and photographers. By the 1930s, women gained both a presence and a degree of power in consumer advertising, which complicates the notion that advertising was a man's world. Enterprising ad women then cultivated and expanded this thriving area of women-centered business throughout the twentieth century. Others would strike out in new directions, moving well beyond the arena of women's business and going where they recognized opportunity.

A second area of retelling this history is to understand Mathilde C. Weil's experience as just one of the many ad women whose entry into advertising should also be seen as a larger part of the professionalization that occurred between the late nineteenth century and the early twentieth century. Similar to women in law, medicine, and architecture, the entry of women into the advertising profession also needs to be understood in terms of identity, as women's work was redefined for their own purpose.

Simply put, the stories of these ad women reveal at once the unique opportunities and limits that women, unlike their male counterparts, shared, as the persistence of traditional ideas forced them to balance two worlds. As a woman, she was dependent and her place was in the home, but as a businesswoman, she had to be independent and work outside the home. These conflicting roles created a unique and enduring dilemma: how to be at once a woman and a businesswoman. Paradoxically, femininity and domesticity uniquely prepared women to offer their insights on marketing consumer goods and services, while it also excluded them from entering male-dominated careers by all the contrivances of professionalization. At the start of the twentieth century, professional schools, licensing procedures, and trade organizations emerged in which men took firmer control over various occupations as the profession matured. At the same time, they faced the same challenges—legal and institutional discrimination, cultural limitations, and motherhood—that confronted all women who have strived for a meaningful career outside the home. From this perspective, the stories of these women are the stories of America's women.

Finally, women's entry into the advertising profession didn't build steadily and slowly; rather, it happened in waves. The study begins in the 1880s, when an entirely new business in America, the advertising agency, began to take form and open up professional opportunities for women, which continue to the present day. Over this time, there are three key periods in the history of advertising that are deeply entwined with economics, politics, and women's history in modern America. First, 1880–1920 marks the key period in which the modern consumer economy emerged parallel with the rise of the advertising industry and the suffrage movement. The second and third eras, the 1920s and 1970s, represent times of major social change for women. In any case, sexual, racial, and ethnic discrimination were persistent themes in women's history. Something else clearly played a role in reversing women's subordinate position and helping them overcome barriers in the marketing and advertising business.

The most intriguing explanation for that "something else" was that each generation of women created new opportunities for the next generation of ad women. First-wave suffragists fought for women's citizenship and challenged traditional patriarchies, but only the rare professional women advanced as rapidly as men, while other women settled for positions far below their talents and training. Second-wave feminists then questioned nearly everything, transformed much of American culture, and expanded the idea of democracy to include women's right to pursue professional careers and to achieve personal success. Their greatest accomplishment was to change the terms of the debate so that women mattered. A third wave of new feminists have drawn attention to the underlying drives that contribute to women's buying actions and developed campaigns that establish emotional connections with consumers by insisting that advertising for women had to include the realities of women's lives. This new breed of workingwomen—the university-educated, professional, middle-class career woman who first emerged in the 1970s—then gradually assumed many key marketing and advertising positions.

These three characteristics—one, the woman's viewpoint; two, professionalization; and three, the fact that the history of advertising is deeply entwined with feminism—are the same principles that explain over the last century how the number of women in the advertising profession increased from a handful selling newspaper space to thousands impacting the basic promotional appeal of almost every consumer product in America.

Of the three, the third characteristic—the impact of each wave of the feminist movement on advertising—is the most important because it makes sense of the first two, permitting the greatest insight into why modern American consumer culture is the way it is today. Over the course of the twentieth century, the woman's viewpoint had become a dynamic aspect of modern consumerism, stimulating the buying and selling of brand-name packaged goods and services. Virtually every widely accepted product had been promoted through advertising. Advertising's financial support of newspapers and magazines also powered the publishing and later, broadcast industries—our primary sources of ideas, news, and entertainment.

⋞⋰⋟

With that said, in this study the term *marketing* refers to the product conception, pricing, promotion (including advertising), and distribution of ideas, goods, or services. The blend of these four areas of decision making is often referred to as the *marketing mix*, whereas *advertising* is just one of the primary tools an organization uses to communicate to a target audience the value a brand has to offer. An *advertising campaign* is a series of coordinated advertisements and other promotional efforts that communicate essentially a singular theme. I will argue that the ad makers did not create national advertising campaigns out of thin air; rather, the process evolved as a business science—some would say art—as marketing applied new theories of economics, sociology, and psychology to the complexity of advertising. As a result, advertising expanded beyond simple brand identification to incorporate consumer research and targeting, competitive analysis, media planning, and creative strategies to get messages across to consumers about products, brands, and corporate images.

The first step in an advertising strategy is to identify the prospective customers and then assess how to communicate with them. In the language of advertising, a *target audience* is a group of potential consumers singled out for an advertisement or advertising campaign. Because of the mediating process between producers of advertising and consumers, ad makers could only imagine consumers—in the sense that they did not have direct contact with one another but had a general sense of what the other was like. Of course, most audience interpretations were not completely off base, either. Most of the ad makers designed advertising messages based on their interpretation of the currents of culture and marketing research, asking women what they thought and what they wanted. In shaping their sales message, they made assumptions about the gendered nature of their audience, stereotyping them around characteristics of age, sex, class, race, and nationality, using these aspects to create advertisements. By producing a selling message that makes sense to potential consumers, serves their needs, and fits their personal history with a product category and brand to appeal to each specific group, advertisers could sell things much more effectively than by simply emphasizing qualities like practicality and price. Consequently, American attitudes toward the ideal roles for men and women in society can be easily marked by the changing nature of the popular stereotypes associated with them.

This study, then, makes a special contribution by situating the work of ad women as *cultural mediators* within the context of encouraging consumption as both a material and a cultural process, as defined by Richard Campbell in *Mass Media and Culture*. These *translators* facilitated communications between consumers and producers, working as researchers, copywriters, designers, and media buyers, among other professionals who influenced the buying decisions. As American women became increasingly involved in the design, marketing, and advertising of commodities, they also had a significant influence on shaping lifestyles, perpetuating stereotypes, and engendering the practice of consumption as a feminine pursuit.[3]

As researchers, women worked hard to find buyers for their products, to ascertain consumer preferences, and to connect with consumers. After all, the firm's profitability depended upon its ability to interpret the meanings that individuals and groups attach to products and to create markets for them. Advertisers and publicists then tried to educate and convince consumers to prefer one product to another. In the other direction, marketers, buyers, and designers offered products that consumers would want to buy. Despite the enormous efforts made to control the production process, each person who participated in the activities also brought a process of selection and interpretation. A key part was the ad maker's concept of prevailing ideals of masculinity and femininity that shaped the advertising campaigns, which ad makers researched, strategized, and executed. Consequently, there was a constant interplay between consumers and producers, and advertising facilitated communications. As markets and consumer identities changed, popular stereotypes, marketing strategies, and advertising messages shifted. In an ongoing cycle, producers designed, priced, distributed, and advertised products and services for markets. In turn, consumers used these products to create identities and lifestyles through their consumption practices.

Yet, it is this border area where marketing and advertising intersects with the consumer side that is key to understanding those messages, their providers, and the complex motivations of consumers. The case studies of ad women and their work described in the following chapters do just that. For example, this study shows how advertisers of housekeeping products perpetuated the stereotype of the woman as the apron-clad homemaker, while cosmetics and underwear marketers dismantled women's stereotypes to create an entirely new type of empowered consumer. By identifying these ad women by their activities and roles as producers, entrepreneurs, and managers, this work will show to what extent individual women defined and redefined their roles in the new profession of advertising to suit their own talents and capabilities.

What difference does it make to retell the history of American consumption as a gendered story? One of the dominant stories told and retold, researched and written about, is the ascendancy of the United States in the twentieth century. Friend and foe alike seek to understand the impact of America as a major power and an open power. All recognize and debate the meaning of factors uniquely associated with the United States, nearly all associated with the middle class: from white-collar work to mass education, from homeownership to automobiles, from passbook savings to widespread stock ownership, argues historian David Katzman. Despite the inequality of income, wealth, and the persistence of poverty, what distinguishes modern American society was that the rise of the middle class increasingly elevated men's work for wages outside the home, while most women continued to perform unpaid labor in the home. Middle-class Americans also idealized the nuclear family, respectability, education, and clean or physically undemanding work.[4]

Only recently have feminist scholars, historians, and cultural theorists attempted to understand the central importance of gender in shaping American business and the rise of a consumer culture. In particular, the work of Angel Kwolek-Folland's *Engendering Business* (1994) has influenced this approach to business history, as it begins with the assumption that gender has been tied to the production of marketing, advertising, and consumption from the start. Gender is an ideological and cultural construction, a complex of cultural ideals and ideas tied to fundamental classifications of the meaning and experience of *male* and *female*. Masculinity and femininity are socially constructed and historically contingent. They reflect (and reinforce) power relations in society. They change over the course of time. They are political as well as cultural issues. It is also important to remember that people's ideas about gender, like ideas about other aspects of culture, differ. And gender conventions are neither simple nor one-dimensional; there are many people who by necessity or by personal inclination resist or cross gender expectations. To understand advertising and gender in history we have to look at how both masculine and feminine roles have been represented at given times and places.[5]

Analytical tools from both the history of technology and gender studies have also provided insight into how the production of advertising and consumption became bound together. The essays in both *The Sex of Things: Gender and Consumption in Historical Perspective* and *His and Hers: Gender, Consumption, and Technology* have also influenced this work, as they consider how cultural ideals of what is appropriate for men and women have shaped the way goods and services are manufactured, marketed, and advertised. In particular, Steven Lubar's "Men/Women/Production/Consumption" essay suggests some more interesting ways to study the connections betweeen gender, production, and markets. By focusing on these issues, he suggests that a historian might ask: "How have women defined their femininity in relation to selling, buying, and using things? How have men defined their masculinity in relation to using, buying, and selling things? And how have the two fit together?"[6] In doing so, this work looks at both sides of the history of advertising by examining some of the ways in which cultural ideals of gender have influenced advertising and the course of American consumer culture. How has advertising reflected, constructed, and reinforced ideas about gender? And how did the very business of advertising change to reflect the gendered ideas that shaped it?

To answer these questions, the stories in this book touch on various aspects of business connected by gender and specifically by the ways that participants in advertising used gender to give us a window into the ideas, experiences, and expressions of ad women over the twentieth century. These examples are intended to suggest that patterns of consumption may have changed a great deal since the days of the Civil War, yet the importance of gender and the role of women in consumption culture have persisted in the sex-typing of material objects and gender-based advertising, which consumers often associate with the prevailing ideas of masculinity and femininity. But the making of American consumer culture was a complicated, interactive process that meshed information and demands from buyers and other data on consumer preferences to production, marketing, and advertising. There was a constant interplay between them and a wide area of both interaction and connection.

⋘⋙

Ad Women introduces the reader, then, to the professional women who worked in marketing, advertising, retailing, publishing, and public relations. It highlights the pioneers, well-known personalities, and not-so-well-known women who made it happen. Those featured were selected for their impact on the industry and audiences, for their influence in advancing other women, and for a distinct vision of the future.

Finally, this study is intended as an interdisciplinary history in business and social history; it is not meant to be a definitive study of women in business or the advertising profession in twentieth-century America. For historians, I address the study of the central importance of the role of gender in the rise of modern advertising and American consumer culture. For sociologists, I attempt to introduce historical elements too often absent from the sociology of work and consumer culture. In any case, it is primarily the evidence of women's work in the profession of advertising that is represented in the book, illuminating how women's roles and consumer culture were changed during the past one hundred years. For women experiencing these changes, images of women in advertising became a source for conflicts over female autonomy and social roles, while the advertising profession itself created opportunities for women to gain a presence and a degree of power in the new, mass-consumer goods and service industries.

Further individual case studies built on women's agency in the advertising, public relations, and sales promotion fields, particularly in the nineteenth century, must be undertaken before firm, higher-order generalizations can be constructed. Also, studies of women's roles in modern retailing, real estate, insurance, and women's professional organizations, as well as their role as consumer activists in the twentieth century, should be done. We also need to be more attentive to how gender has informed and mediated not only the images of women but also of men projected in the mass media. What of the marketing and advertising activities of women that targeted the male consumers? How have women used the *feminine* as a cultural resource in order to more effectively sell products and services to the men's market? How have they reinforced and exploited stereotypical images of men while advancing their professional identity? A look at these four areas where women have gained both a presence and a degree of power—beauty and personal care products, fashion, food, and furnishings—suggests how an analysis of gender might further complicate the gendered narrative of advertising history. My hope is that this book will encourage scholars to explore women's impact on the making of American consumer culture.

To put the stories of these ad women in a larger context, I first will provide a broad overview of the circumstances that gave rise to modern marketing before introducing the first generation of ad women to enter the advertising profession during the late nineteenth and early twentieth century. I'll explore the new developments in marketing and advertising thought, as well as the second generation of women who came to the fore in advertising from 1900 to 1930. I'll talk about how retail and radio work provided women the best opportunities, even in the hard times of the Depression. I'll take the reader through the 1950s, a decade of domesticity with a sexual underside that led to an increased use of sexual appeals in advertising despite the conservative social fabric. Finally, I'll discuss the legacy of the forces of feminism and multiculturalism, as these trends that began in the late nineteenth century continue into the twenty-first century. Eventually, women no longer expressed their identity simply through consumption, but also modern men increasingly defined their masculinity in terms of buying, using, and selling things.

The aim of all this is to shed light on the impact that women, as both producers and consumers, had on the making of American consumer culture and the images of Mr. and Mrs. Consumer. The power of those commercial images and the vigorous critique against them obscures the many forces and the agency of women—a complex network of cultural mediators, consumer rituals, and female institutions—that gave form to American consumer culture. The rise of advertising, then, also tells a rich history of women's ambition, self-fulfillment, and reform. It is the story of the possibilities and limits of the American dream. It is also America's story of the rise of the middle class and a mass-consumer society. And it is the story of how women took up reform, overcame barriers, and carved out a niche in the new profession of advertising over the course of the late nineteenth and twentieth centuries.

NOTES

1. US Department of Labor, US Bureau of Statistics, 2006.

2. The major histories on advertising show women as having a limited influence in advertising. Daniel Pope's *The Making of Modern Advertising* (1983), Stephen Fox's *Mirror Makers* (1983), Roland Marchand's *Advertising the American Dream* (1985), and Jackson Lears's *Fables of Abundance* (1994) all have this bias. Only recently have scholars explored the diversity of women's experiences in the profession. At a basic level, Ed Applegate's encyclopedic account of *Ad Men and Women: A Biographical Dictionary of Advertising* (1994) demonstrates the presence of women in advertising without addressing the larger issues of gender and consumption, whereas Jennifer Scanlon's *Inarticulate Longings* (1995) devotes an entire chapter to the contributions of a cadre of ad women at the J. Walter Thompson agency during the early twentieth century.

3. Richard Campbell, *Mass Media and Culture* (New York: St. Martin's, 1997).

4. On the middle class, see Mary Beth Norton et al., *A People and a Nation: A History of the United States*, 6th edition (Boston: Houghton Mifflin, 2006), pp. 317–21.

5. On gender, business history, and consumer culture, see Angel Kwolek-Folland, *Engendering Business: Men and Women in the Corporate Office, 1870–1930* (Baltimore: Johns Hopkins University Press, 1994); Jennifer Scanlon, ed., *Gender and Consumer Culture Reader* (New York: New York University Press, 2000).

6. On gender and production, see Victoria de Grazia with Ellen Furlough, eds., *The Sex of Things: Gender and Consumption in a Historical Perspective* (Berkeley: University of California, 1996); Roger Horowitz with Arwen Mohun, eds., *His and Hers: Gender, Consumption, and Technology* (Charlottesville: University of Virginia Press, 1998); Steven Lubar, "Men/Women/Production/Consumption," in Horowitz and Mohun, *His and Hers*.

CHAPTER 1

CUSTOMERS BECOME CONSUMERS

THE EVOLUTION OF MARKETING, ADVERTISING, AND AMERICAN CONSUMER CULTURE

Mathilde C. Weil came to this country from Germany in the 1870s. Her life dramatically changed when her husband died suddenly. She found work as a translator in New York City, being proficient in many languages, and added to her income with newspaper and magazine writing. When Weil volunteered to secure advertising for a German society paper owned by the brother of her friend Meta Volkman, one of the accounts she first solicited was Sozodont toothpaste. Although the advertising manager could not offer any advertising for her publication, he could favor an order for another New York newspaper. Knowing nothing of the business, she offered the Sozodont order to the New York paper with the question "How will you recompense me for the same?"[1]

For the next two decades, Weil was not simply a widow, she was the first known ad woman in America, buying and selling media space in the new industrial age. Weil immediately proved her business ability and soon established valuable contracts with other firms. By this time, she realized that there was a better living in selling advertising space for newspapers and magazines than writing for them, and in partnership with Volkman, she established a general advertising agency in 1880—the M. C. Weil Agency. Weil divided the work into departments in order to systemize the work: while she devoted herself to running the general business and soliciting proprietary medicine firms that sold drugs without prescriptions, Volkman took charge of entertainment advertising, and later Mary Compton specialized in schools and colleges. They, too, recognized that the profession was a fine career choice for women. The work was agreeable, paid well, and did not entail a great expenditure of physical strength, explained Volkman in 1899. "Generally those who give it up find something better to do or something best to do, which is to get married." So did she. She eventually married and gave up agency work. But Weil continued to work until her death in 1903, leaving behind a large estate. Among her possessions were many jewels, as she had also become regarded as an expert in the valuation of diamonds and other precious stones.[2]

The opening of Weil's agency also coincided with a broad movement of women gaining access to higher education and entry into the professions. Because of special circumstances, the advertising profession became known as a field where savvy women like Weil could succeed. Central to Weil's success and the integration of women in advertising was the expansion of industrialization and consumption after the Civil War, combined with changes in the legal climate. In the emerging advertising industry, women might hope to fill any open positions, since the profession was not yet divided into male and female accounts and jobs. "To work in advertising demanded no particular knowledge of copy or design or the product being celebrated," wrote historian Stephen Fox. "Instead it required an acquaintance with the periodicals in any given territory, some sense of the going advertising rates, and—in particular—a rare gift of haggling."[3]

In addition, some of the legal codes that restricted women's rights and entry into business had crumbled. By the 1880s, state after state modified laws to give many women like Mathilde C. Weil the right to their own wages during marriage, while others enjoyed more freedom to enter into business partnerships and sign contracts. By the early twentieth century, women's roles as consumers and as ad women became all the more important in the emerging consumer society.

Younger women who entered advertising felt confident that they would have a fair and equal chance to prove their ability and succeed in the profession. Some women achieved success as copywriters or in positions as clerks, solicitors, commercial artists, or in related fields. But their gains were modest, not monumental in these early years.

To put the story of the first ad women in context, this chapter will explore the circumstances that gave rise to the modern marketing era and advertising as a profession, as well as look at the tensions that developed between consumption and gender identity.

EVOLUTION OF THE MARKETING PROCESS

The history of the first generation of ad women is also part of the evolution of the modern marketing era, which marks the beginning of widespread efforts to distribute, promote, and sell mass-produced products to nearly all of society. The period began with the start of the Industrial Revolution in Britain in the 1770s, which succeeded because production and marketing worked together to cultivate large-scale demands for inexpensive products. Among the pioneers of mass production, British-based Matthew Boulton manufactured artistic objects in metal, and Josiah Wedgwood specialized in ceramics; but their energetic style of marketing was just as influential and frequently imitated. They promoted vigorously, targeted promising groups of buyers for special attention, and designed products primarily to appeal to potential buyers. They used sophisticated techniques considered to be mid-twentieth-century American innovations: market segmentation, product differentiation, prestige pricing, style obsolescence, advertising and direct mail campaigns, and testimonials, among others. These activities characterize modern marketing.[4]

Mass Production and Mass Marketing

When the Industrial Revolution began in England in the 1770s, the colonial American economy looked quite different than the British economy. Early America was an overwhelmingly rural, undeveloped land with seaports serving as commercial centers for colonial American traders, while farming filled almost all of the backcountry between the Appalachian Mountains and the Atlantic Ocean. Most of the nation's households made a living from farms, growing and making nearly everything they needed.

With a sparse, predominantly rural population and without efficient transportation, communication, and financial infrastructures, however, the country had neither the need nor the means to support coordinated national advertising campaigns. Manufacturers rarely produced branded consumer goods for sale in wider markets, and for the most part, advertising was almost entirely local. Their advertising aimed to give the location, business, and service of a store or to acquaint the public with any unusual changes occurring in the life of the firm. Furthermore, cheap reading matter was a rarity in 1765, and the impending American Revolution made the chronic paper shortage even more acute, which led to limited copies of many major city newspapers. In the case of advertising, publishers crammed more type into less space and restricted paid announcements to separate sections. The densely packed small ads looked similar to classified advertising today. And so, advertising changed little over the next seventy years.

Starting in America around 1830 and continuing until about 1870, the pervasiveness and impact of marketing increased. Improvements in production and transportation coupled with a massive migration of the rural population to urban areas, which were no longer self-sufficient and relied on manufactured goods, provided the potential for a mass market and eventually national advertising.

The emergence of steam power, interchangeable parts, assembly lines, and factories in the production process enabled manufacturers to turn out a stream of goods at both a low cost and a uniform quality. Soon a network of roads and canals were being built to deliver goods, and steamships transported raw materials and manufactured goods, whereas an intricate distribution system of wholesalers, jobbers, and other middlemen bought large lots of commodities and sold them in smaller ones. But it was the key development of the railroads that made it possible to move raw materials and finished goods coast to coast swiftly and cheaply, thereby reducing both production and distribution costs. In turn, the savings enabled manufacturers to deliver low-priced goods to distant markets and encouraged thousands of traveling salesmen to go on the road to market everything from underwear to coats, from curtains to furniture. For the first time, it cost people less to buy a product than to make it themselves. The completion of the telegraph network and postal service further unified the continent into a national mass market. With the broad development of transportation and communication infrastructure spanning the continent, territories began being settled west of the Allegheny Mountains, which created new markets for manufactured products.[5]

The rapidly expanding urban markets also led to some *dailies*, as newspapers were then called, selling papers at a low price and relying on a large volume of advertising to subsidize the paper's operation. A new generation of *weeklies*, or weekly magazines, also depended on a new class of subscribers—the middle-class readers who were largely concentrated in urban areas, enjoyed regular wages from factory jobs, and had the economic means to buy more than necessities. These periodicals gave Americans current events, opinion pieces, photographs, fashions, and a sense of community. Still another group of *class* magazines, or the genteel monthlies intended for family consumption, serialized novels and aimed their substantial reading matter at an affluent, literate readership but limited advertising to a few pages in the back of the issues. The pre–Civil War era also saw the emergence of women's magazines, such as *Ladies' Home Journal*, *Peterson's Magazine*, and *Godey's Lady's Book* (figure 1.1). They covered fashion and decorative arts as well as printed the popular fiction of the time; they also established a format that women's service magazines have followed to this day.[6]

But it was the Civil War that spurred mass communications, changed manufacturing, and gave rise to a consumer culture. The demand for war news stimulated innovations in publishing, including new methods of illustration, improved printing techniques, and advances in papermaking. A decade later in the 1870s, publishers eventually recognized that retailers and other advertisers were willing to spend a lot of money to attract attention and eventually gave them the freedom to create larger ads that spanned two columns and eventually the full page.[7]

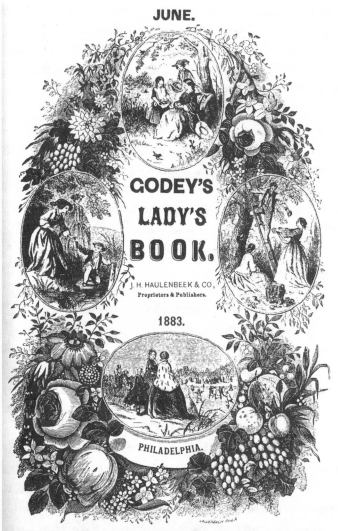

Publication Office, 1006 Chestnut Street, Philadelphia, P℈

Figure 1.1. June 1883 cover, *Godey's Lady's Book*. Sarah Jessica Hale was editor 1837–1877. Reproduced from Frank Rowesome Jr., *They Laughed When I Sat Down: An Informal History of Advertising in Words and Pictures* (New York: McGraw-Hill Company, 1959).

Furthermore, the Civil War introduced a whole new generation of customers to canned foods, bakery-baked bread, and ready-made clothing. Previously, people bought food and dry goods shipped, stored, and sold in bulk. With the onset of the war, the need to feed thousands of soldiers sometimes in remote locales led to innovations in packaging and food preservation, such as the can opener, which removed a troublesome obstacle to the widespread use of canned vegetables, fruits, and condensed milk. In addition, the need for thousands of soldiers' uniforms, underwear, and shoes brought the sewing machine into wider use, while ready-made clothing evolved into a big business. Finally, the adoption of a national currency in 1863, based on banks' holding of US securities, facilitated trade between individuals and businesses in different parts of the country, rather than individual state banks issuing their own currencies.

After the war, these purchasing trends continued. When many people left the farms to work in the new urban factories, they came to rely less on their own production and more on the purchase of affordable, mass-produced goods. They simply could not match the variety, attractiveness, and, particularly, the prices of the goods produced by American manufacturers—from clothing and furniture to food and drink. Around the twentieth century, the signs of a consumer society began to appear everywhere, as formerly self-sustaining households purchased soap, bread, clothes, and other necessities instead of making their own. Thus, markets composed of masses of urban people came to depend on these mass-produced goods from distant sources.

What is interesting is that branded standardized products came to represent new systems of production, distribution, and advertising that brought people the things they used. In an ongoing cycle, manufacturers designed, priced, distributed, and advertised products and services for markets. In turn, people made fewer things and bought more goods that manufacturers sold, as consumption became a major part of household work. It was this interplay between society and business, between producers and consumers—not simply one or the other—that brought forth change. "Formerly *customers*, purchasing the objects of everyday life from familiar craftspeople and storekeepers, Americans became *consumers*," explains Susan Strasser.[8]

Era of Institutional Development

Through the end of the 1920s, the institutionalization of the marketing process accelerated. During this period, factory-produced and packaged merchandise largely replaced locally produced goods sold in bulk, while better physical distribution and more responsive wholesaling also helped circulate products quickly and extensively. But the first national marketers of manufactured consumer goods faced a larger task: convincing consumers to buy more standardized brand-name goods and to make fewer things themselves.

Companies also learned that the success of selling standardized, small-packaged goods depended on a *brand name*. To distinguish one product from another, marketers advertised both a specific brand name and a graphic image or symbol for visual identification, called a *trademark*, which identified the source of the goods in trade. Packaging, too, provided an effective medium to display the brand and trademark and to explain why the product was superior. This identity differentiated the product from others in the market and enabled buyers to appraise the value of the merchandise before buying. With a memorable brand name and attractive packaging, manufacturers could charge a higher price for goods; in turn, they urged consumers to accept no substitutes (figure 1.2).

The lead in generating demand for packaged goods was often taken by producers, who were largely motivated by their dissatisfaction with the merchant wholesalers who had dominated marketing. These producers often felt that wholesalers did not give special attention to their newly branded goods and could no longer supply market information to meet their increased needs. As a number of manufacturers had realized unprecedented scales of economy, they began to take charge of their own distribution efforts, from market analysis through distribution, promotion, and pricing. New national organizations of managers, distributors, salesmen, and buyers developed, while hierarchies of responsibility also made possible corporate structures that managed administration, manufacturing, and marketing. This enormous market power forced many retailers into distributing products without any price breaks.

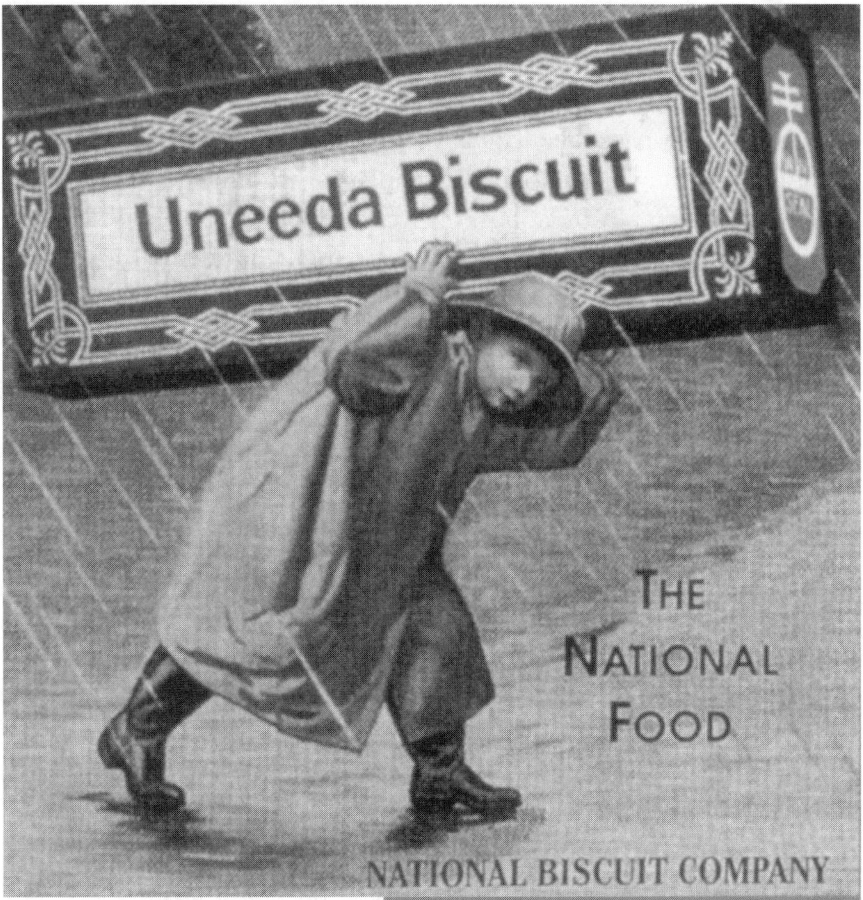

Figure 1.2. In 1900, Uneeda Biscuit (pronounced You-need-a) and its trademark slicker boy symbol set the standard for multimillion-dollar advertising campaigns. With an appealing name, the soda crackers came in a distinctive octagonal shape and were packaged in airtight, wax-paper-lined packages to preserve freshness.

With so many new consumer products, the marketing objective became the recruiting of new sellers and buyers as well as inducing current buyers to purchase more packaged goods. The initial effort to find new buyers for packaged goods often involved finding new sellers, according to Strasser. For most companies, moving to new regions involved creating new relationships with wholesalers. They also had to choose new authorized dealers and make sure that every grocer, hardware store, or druggist carried the product. In an attempt to expand the field, manufacturers created national sales forces to increase contact with retailers and chain stores. Their efforts resulted in the use of the store's market research to strengthen the producer's marketing efforts. They also helped retailers with sales training, window displays, literature, advertising, and demonstrations for customers.[9]

Organizing new distribution often involved assigning a product a new position with respect to competition or to groups of consumers, a practice called *positioning*. For example, Asa Candler purchased a headache remedy, sold it to soda fountain owners as syrup mixed with carbonated water, and promoted it as a pleasant, refreshing beverage called Coca-Cola. A change in packaging could also reposition a product, as evidenced in the case of Henry Parson Crowell, who packaged raw oats in a cardboard box printed with the picture of a Quaker man and a recipe for cooking oatmeal. To exploit a defined market, many companies went a step further. They provided consumers with suggestions for product uses that they may have not thought of before. Companies gave out booklets suggesting dozens of possible uses for their products, such as Procter & Gamble recommending Ivory Soap for cleaning brass, freeing plants from insect pests, and even removing ink stains from carpets. Thanks in part to the home economics movement, which encouraged home cooking by the book, manufacturers' compilations of recipes proved the most popular form of promotional material intended to increase the market share, giving people more ideas for how to use various foodstuffs, from Sunkist oranges to Baker's chocolate and coconut. In addition, heavy advertising could encourage people, who were already buying certain products perceived as seasonal, to buy more year-round. Finally, marketers also promoted their products with persistent sample campaigns, sponsored contests, and employed other ingenious methods to engage the public.

Even when a product was successfully positioned, most successful companies did not rely on offering only one in a competitive market. Instead they worked simultaneously on a family of products, or *line extensions*, based on new flavors, styles, or models. For example, Heinz, Libby, McNeill & Libby, and Campbell's continually introduced new food products under their brand names, while other manufacturers used line extensions to reach consumers along a broad range of prices. Nevertheless, companies with so many products could not necessarily afford to advertise them all, so firms chose to concentrate almost solely on one product or rotated the products featured in the advertising.

Yet, the historical significance of this market creation lies in the attention of manufacturers and retailers to buyers' needs. Relying on the notion that a single product did not satisfy everyone, producers widely practiced segmentation of the mass market. By the turn of the century, most manufacturers divided consumers by gender and had a conception of the class base of their products based on firsthand observations, which influenced their choice of promotional plans. Variations in consumption patterns based on what a person could afford, rather than by what he or she preferred, generally explained what type of consumer would be the most profitable to advertise to for its most constant source of sales. Over time, some manufacturers became more explicit about the relationship between quality and price in their lines, packaging goods in different grades and using different color schemes and descriptions on labels to differentiate them. More often, packaged goods companies produced another version of an existing brand, gave it a new name, and advertised it to a different market segment, but they did not promote it in ways to detract from the existing brands. More important, marketers had a choice: they could create standardized products that might be sold to both sexes and to all regions, classes, and nationalities, or they could exploit their differences in tastes. They also had the choice to not only design the products but also the advertising copy to take regional, class, and ethnic variations into consideration.[10]

Moreover, new retail institutions made the products readily available and enticing to buyers. After the Civil War, a new breed of merchandiser brought the European ideas of large retail shops—or *department stores*—to America. Among them, A. T. Stewart, R. H. Macy, Lord & Taylor in New York, John Wanamaker in Philadelphia, and Marshall Field in Chicago set up department stores, offering customers elegant surroundings, selection, and service. In rural America, though, mounting dissatisfaction with high prices and limited selection, coupled with the introduction of free delivery service, eventually led to the idea of shopping by mail. The great expansion of mail-order houses by Montgomery Ward and Sears then demonstrated the possibilities for sales on a national scale.

The next major step in modern retailing came with *chain stores* that shared the same brand name and sold similar merchandise. Instead of the individual stores, central management placed large orders at low prices, established low profit margins, and made money through volume. For example, Woolworth's Five-and-Dime and Kresge's offered a number of useful items at low prices, while J. C. Penney's clothing outlets grew rapidly. At the same time, A & P and Piggly Wiggly established the foundation for self-service supermarket chains. Other national firms like Avon and Fuller Brush created systems of training and distribution that proved enormously successful in selling packaged goods door-to-door across the country.[11]

Product development, pricing strategies, and distribution emerged as only one aspect of a national marketing effort. Businesses began to recognize that advertising could do more than reduce overall production costs by increasing sales. It could also create desires—desires that could fuel a consumer economy. People bought articles that they did not know they wanted until advertising showed them the product's benefits and told them why they couldn't live without it. In this period, many small businesses quickly became large-scale ventures with annual advertising expenditures skyrocketing from several thousand dollars a year to multimillion-dollar sums in the following decades.

Thus, rational and efficient management was a hallmark of these new institutions in the modern marketing era. Firms quickly recognized the advantages of controlling production and centralizing management, as well as assuming marketing and purchasing activities. A wave of mergers consolidated independent firms to form large-scale corporations, which wielded much more capital and typically possessed large shares of the market in which they operated. Eventually the promotion needs of these large national marketers reshaped mass-circulation newspapers and magazines to function as advertising vehicles largely supported by ad revenue rather than subscription.

Newspapers following the lead of Joseph Pulitzer and William Randolph Hearst sought an even broader audience, readers of all classes. These newspapers gradually converted millions of people to the daily reading habit, as they competed for the public with their features, pictures, and comics, as well for advertising. Likewise, many middle-class magazines changed their policy and began to offer advertisers full pages. But it was Boston advertising solicitor Cyrus H. Curtis who conceived of *Ladies' Home Journal* as an advertising vehicle to reach the middle-class reader in terms of not just price but also content (figure 1.3). By accepting only high-grade advertising, Curtis could set subscriptions at a low price, fifty cents per year, compared to *Godey's Lady's Book*, until then the leading American women's magazine, which cost six times as much. Within five years the *Journal* displayed over twice the amount of advertising than any other women's magazine. The *Journal* offered the right mix of abundant reading on decorating tips, needlework patterns, fiction, and plenty of romance. In 1903, the *Journal* became the first American magazine to reach a circulation of one million.

Still, it was only with the emergence of such large publishing firms and manufacturing enterprises capable of packaging food, drinks, and nearly everything else for vast national markets that the need for a modern advertising industry arose, with its special agencies, sophisticated market research, and complex million-dollar campaigns.[12]

THE ADVERTISING AGENT, A NEW OCCUPATION

Advertising as a profession did not exist in the mid-1800s. There were no copywriters, art directors, account executives, or marketing profes-

Now For Sale on All News=stands: The Easter Number of

THE
LADIES' HOME JOURNAL

Figure 1.3. The *Ladies' Home Journal* reached the middle-class women not only in terms of price but also content, April 1895. Reproduced from Frank Rowesome Jr., *They Laughed When I Sat Down: An Informal History of Advertising in Words and Pictures* (New York: McGraw-Hill Company, 1959).

APRIL 1895   TEN CENTS

The · Curtis Publishing · Company · Philadelphia

sionals. As long as advertising was aimed only at local readers, manufacturers had little need for outside assistance to buy advertising space in newspapers and magazines, and they dealt directly with the media. When manufacturers began to distribute their goods coast to coast and overseas, they often found that the media arrangements needed to print their announcements involved a myriad of details and time-consuming tasks: identifying effective newspapers, negotiating rates, directing the printer, confirming the insertion, and sending in payment. So the new complexities of business created a need for an intermediary to specialize in the placing of advertisements by shopkeepers and manufacturers, and, later, to solicit business among those who might have occasion to advertise in newspapers.[13]

The newspapers themselves supplied the first advertising agents who attained prominence in the United States, thereby giving birth to an entirely new business, the advertising agency. Some of these employees soon perceived it was more profitable to solicit orders for several publications than for one, and they could make a great deal more money working on a commission basis than by working for a single paper. The earliest known advertising agents in America were Volney B. Palmer, who started in Boston in 1841 and soon opened offices in New York and Philadelphia, and John Hooper, who set up shop in New York. The agents offered to buy a certain number of column inches per month in newspapers all over the country and guaranteed cash payment up front. Once they agreed on a price with the publishers, they went to merchants and firms, offering to show that their announcements ran in a certain number of papers, a certain number of times, for a certain amount of money.[14]

With the rise of national advertisers and the advent of new media in the late nineteenth century, advertising agencies soon multiplied in size and number. They changed to meet the demands of American businesses and began to specialize in preparing, placing, and distributing advertising messages. Whereas general agencies learned how to create advertising campaigns and plan marketing strategies, some agents specialized to form bill-posting companies, which erected their own boards and leased space. Others organized streetcar, religious and farm papers, and magazine advertising on a national basis. These efforts solved many of the staggering problems that entrepreneurs faced when they set out to advertise beyond their communities. The selling of newspaper space alone became increasingly complex with thousands of dailies in circulation.

By 1890, about fifteen advertising agents exclusively represented newspapers, while others worked for religious or farm papers. Plus, another fifty professionals worked as general advertising agents in the United States. Like the M. C. Weil agency, the majority were located in New York City, and the nation's leading city in domestic and foreign trade emerged as the center of advertising. In particular, the borough of Manhattan, particularly Madison Avenue, became identified with the advertising industry after a number of major agencies opened up shops there. A number of other agents also established businesses in Chicago, while the remaining few worked in Boston, Cincinnati, Philadelphia, Pittsburgh, Baltimore, Newmarket (New Jersey), and Wilmington (Delaware). In this era, the major agencies included N. W. Ayer & Son (1869); J. Walter Thompson (1871); Lord & Thomas, later Foote, Cone & Belding (1871); George Batten Company, later BBDO and now known as Omnicom Group (1891); and Bates Agency (1893). And in 1899, J. Walter Thompson opened its London office, possibly the first international office of an advertising agency. This enterprise also led to the launch of a number of trade journals that dispensed information on methods of advertising, cultivated economic interests, and provided an industry.

Agencies made other significant changes in their organization and the way they did business. Among them, the most important areas included compensation, ad preparation, and research. Traditionally agencies were compensated for their services by paying for the media space and time and then billing the advertisers at a higher price. When George P. Rowell first opened a Boston office in 1865, he followed advertising agents Palmer and Hooper's example and wholesaled newspaper space, but he standardized his commission at 25 percent. Rowell later moved on to New York, and in 1869, published the *American Newspaper Directory*, which provided advertisers and agencies with the first sound basis for estimating a fair value for media space. The directory listed more than five thousand newspapers in the United States and Canada and rated the accuracy of the circulation estimates. But Rowell outraged newspaper publishers who had tended to inflate circulation numbers up to five times more than their actual figures to justify their high advertising rates. Whereas Rowell's directory forced many newspapers to reform their deceptive reporting practices, Francis W. Ayer added another strong selling point for his agency—the open contract. Other agents had kept advertising rates strictly confidential, so that the customer never knew the net publication prices. Ayer, however, fixed his commission at 15 percent, giving the advertiser the benefit of all discounts and even shrewd bargaining. This practice has since become standard in the industry. Nevertheless, market research proved slower in getting started than skilled copywriting, layout, and account management, since the quality of the ads the agency prepared became one of the agencies' prime methods of attracting clients.[15]

The demand for skilled advertisement preparation first came from the department stores and the manufacturers of brand-name consumer goods, who frequently mounted extensive national promotions. The placement of the all-important product name, package, trademark, and slogans became a significant part of the advertisement, so the art, copy, and layout also had to be carefully considered to reflect the broader marketing strategy of product image, pricing, and distribution. In response, some agencies began to offer services other than space brokerage to justify their media commissions. One of the earliest major agencies to hire a full-time copywriter was N. W. Ayer in 1892. The Bates Agency had an art department, the first one in the business. And when Albert D. Lasker started working at the Chicago agency of Lord & Thomas, he hired both a copywriter and a commercial artist. By 1900, copy preparation had become a standard practice of the agency practice, and ad preparation soon followed.

From humble media brokering in the mid-nineteenth century, advertising agencies had by 1910 become leaders in devising and encouraging the use of market research, customer-oriented product design, and enticing packaging. Some also conducted experimental research into the psychology of advertising to measure the effectiveness of media and copy appeals, as well as different type styles and colors. This incessant demand stimulation also had its effect: consumption rose, and "aggressive consumption" spread to almost all of society.[16]

CONSUMPTION AND GENDER IDENTITY

Advertising in America developed within a culture that distinguished between men and women, masculine and feminine, on almost every issue imaginable. Consumption was no exception. From the early Victorian household manuals popular among the middle class in the nineteenth century to the mass national market targeted by advertisers in the twentieth century, the ideal consumer has always been female and consumption a feminine activity, with shopping perceived as a frivolous form of leisure. "From the philosopher's standpoint, woman is an incidental helpmeet to man; from the standpoint of the wise advertiser she is queen of the nether world, mistress of the privy purse, keeper of the rolls, the hounds, and the exchequer [financial resources]," heralded James Collins in 1901.[17]

With this advice, Collins articulated the idea of consumption as a feminine pursuit that was not shaped by supply and demand but by energetic marketers and advertisers who understood that the women's market could be developed. Techniques like market segmentation and targeted promotion emerged in tandem with this conception of the consumer as largely female, whereas women's service magazines particularly helped to both define and shape the women's market. Through stylized portrayals of characters, objects, and images, advertisements contributed to our understanding of what it is to be masculine and feminine and influenced our conception of gender identity.

Among the middle- and upper-class households, men, in theory, earned wages outside of the home, while women transformed these earnings into well-decorated homes, fashionable bodies, appetizing meals, and well-developed children. As the ideal, a *family wage* was an income earned by the man, a handsome enough sum of money to support his wife and children. When the consumer economy expanded, the job of shopping for household needs multiplied, and women took over most of that task, serving as the household's purchasing agent and budget expert. For middle-class women, then, consumption became a job—the other side of the paycheck. If the model ignored women's rising labor-force participation, however, it did capture the essence of consumption as women's work, argues economist Viviana A. Zelizer. It stigmatized women's earnings as supplementary household income, or *pin money*, more frivolous and less serious than a man's income.[18]

On the other hand, marketers generally considered workingwomen the worst economic prospect for consumer purchases around the turn of the twentieth century. From 1870 to 1900, women made up only 15 percent of American paid workers. African American women and immigrant women were most likely to do paid work. With the exception of African Americans, these female workers were almost all young and unmarried, earning no more than half the wage of a male worker for the same job. They also turned over most of their wages to their family, so they did not have discretionary income to spend on products other than necessities. Everyone assumed that men would work, but women's employment aroused controversy. Some insisted that women work just for pin money, while others argued women's work took away from a man's wage, whereas still others thought a workingwoman would never be respectable. The national advertisers then would not cultivate the workingwoman as a profitable market for cigarettes, cosmetics, fashion, and magazines until the 1920s.

What most divided the upper classes from the lower classes living on the minimum required for subsistence was the waste of money on "conspicuous consumption" to display a higher social position, explains Thorstein Veblen in his 1899 book, *The Theory of the Leisure Class*. For example, the leisure class used silver utensils at meals, even though utensils made of cheaper material worked just as well or, in some cases, better. In Veblen's view, demand consisted of more than simple purchasing power or the need to increase physical comfort. It reflected the desire to display a higher status than others as well as the ability to purchase. Similar ideas on social stratification appear in the early work of social analyst George Simmel, who first proposed the "trickle-down theory" to explain the fashion system in 1904. Simmel argued that people in the upper-class groups responded to the attempts of the lower class to impersonate or emulate them by adopting even newer fashions. Together these two processes described by Simmel and Veblen created a self-perpetuating cycle of change that drove fashion. Hence, women's choices also reflected their families' social standing.[19]

Although American women gained increasing power as consumers, they were legally "dead" throughout most of history. Whether in the farming villages or commercial seaports, women's lives were tied to and dependent on their husband's economic ventures with little ability to work independently. Under English common law, single women (*feme sole*) who reached their majority age could make contracts, buy and sell, and control a business enterprise, but they lost all these rights upon marriage. Class status, racial background, and ethnicity also shaped the fields open to women. And no woman, single or unmarried, could vote. Nonetheless, it was not unusual for wives whose husbands were absent from the farm or seaport due to their work, military or political service, or death to fulfill their husband's role and stand in his place. However, a married woman (*feme covert*) could not own real estate or personal property, and whatever she brought into marriage became her husband's, unless they used an antenuptial agreement. Their status also limited many women from issuing any legal document without permission of some male member of the family. When a man died without having made a will, his wife was entitled to a minimum share of his estate, but the statutes otherwise favored the eldest son.[20]

Over the course of the nineteenth century, the balance of power between the sexes shifted as women entered high schools and colleges, took up careers and sports, entered the workforce, and formed organizations for reform. By the end of the 1880s, many states modified the legal codes that restricted women. This gave women the right to their own wages during marriage and control over their inherited property, though some states continued to prohibit women from entering business partnerships or signing contracts without the consent of their husbands. Consequently these women gained some measure of economic independence but not necessarily the political clout or power to change perceptions about gender and money. At every turn, they faced the same legal and institutional discrimination, cultural restrictions, and burdens of work and family life that confronted all professional women well into the twentieth century.[21]

Inevitably, women adopted certain strategies for career management, as they moved out of the home and into the workforce. They attempted to create separate communities or women's departments, where they could offer opportunities for advancement and train future generations of women. They also built up women's authority until even men came to believe: *It takes a woman to sell a woman.* Thus, the conception of the female as consumer not only underscored the growing power of commercialism and consumerism, it also symbolized the emergence of a freer, more independent American woman engaged in business activities in the late nineteenth century.

NOTES

1. Obituary of M. C. Weil, *New York Times*, July 28, 1903. See also Mary Morrow Craig, "Ad Men and Women from 1887," letter to J. George Frederick (n.d.), Advertising Women of New York Collection, box 2, folder 4, Schlesinger Library, Radcliffe Institute, Harvard University. Hereafter, Schlesinger Library.

2. "Women in Advertising," *Printers' Ink*, February 9, 1899, p. 3. Obituary of Mrs. M. C. Weil, *New York Times*, July 29, 1903. Dorothy Dignam, "Some Women Have Made Good in Advertising, but as to Others," *Printers' Ink*, April 27, 1939, p. 16.

3. Stephen Fox, *The Mirror Makers: A History of American Advertising and Its Creators* (New York: Vintage Books, 1984), pp. 14, 285–86.

4. Ronald A. Fullerton, "How Modern Is Modern Marketing? Marketing's Evolution and the Myth of the 'Production Era,'" *Journal of Marketing* 52 (January 1988): 108–25. See also Neil McKendrick, John Brewer, and J. H. Plumb, *Birth of a Consumer Society: The Commercialization of Eighteenth-Century England* (Bloomington: Indiana University Press, 1982).

5. Richard Tedlow, *New and Improved: The Story of Mass Marketing in America* (New York: Basic Books, 1990).

6. On newspapers, see Frank L. Mott, *American Journalism: A History, 1690–1960*, 3rd edition (New York: Macmillan, 1962). On magazines, see Amy Janello and Brennon Jones, *The American Magazine* (New York: HNA, 1991), pp. 230–37. John Tebbel and Mary Ellen Zuckerman, *The Magazine in America, 1741–1990* (New York: Oxford University Press, 1991).

7. On sources for early American advertising, see Henry Sampson, *A History of Advertising from the Earliest Times* (1874; repr. Detroit: Gale Research, 1974). Frank Presbrey, *The History and Development of Advertising* (Garden City, NY: Doubleday, Doran & Company, 1929). James P. Wood, *Story of Advertising* (New York: Ronald Press, 1958). Poyntz Tyler, *Advertising in America* (New York: H. W. Wilson, 1959).

8. Susan Strasser, *Satisfaction Guaranteed: The Making of the American Mass Market* (New York: Pantheon, 1989), p. 15.

9. On generating demand and organizing distribution, see Strasser, *Satisfaction Guaranteed*, pp. 58–88. Pamela Laird, *Advertising Progress: American Business and the Rise of Consumer Marketing* (Baltimore: Johns Hopkins University Press, 1998), pp. 193–200. See also Richard Tedlow, *New and Improved*, for case studies on soft drink and automobile industries and grocery and general merchandising retailing.

10. On designing markets, see Strasser, *Satisfaction Guaranteed*, pp. 124–62.

11. On department stores, see William R. Leach, *Land of Desire: Merchants, Power, and the Rise of a New American Culture* (New York: Vintage Books, 1984). On mail order, see Tedlow, *New and Improved*, pp. 259–343. On general merchandise, drugstores, and grocery retailing, see Tedlow, *New and Improved*, pp. 182–258. Frank Seaman, Inc., *The Chain Store* (March 1928), Hagley Library. James J. Mayo, *The American Grocery Store* (Connecticut: Greenwood Press, 1993). Kim Humphrey, *Shelf Life: Supermarkets and the Changing Cultures of Consumption* (New York: Cambridge University Press, 1998).

12. Daniel Pope, *Making of Modern Advertising* (New York: Basic Books, 1983), pp. 18–61.

13. Fox, *Mirror Makers*, pp. 9–39.

14. Ibid., pp. 14–22.

15. On agency practice, see Fox, *Mirror Makers*, pp. 13–15. Laird, *Advertising Progress*, pp. 155–82.

16. McKendrick et al., *Birth of a Consumer Society*, p. 315.

17. Quoted in Jackson Lears, *Fables of Abundance: A Cultural History of American Advertising* (New York: Basic Books, 1995), p. 209.

18. Viviana A. Zelizer, *The Social Meaning of Money* (Princeton, NJ: Princeton University Press, 1997), pp. 36–70.

19. Thorstein Veblen, *Theory of the Leisure Class* (New York: Macmillan, 1899). George Simmel, "Fashion," in *George Simmel*, ed. D. Levine (1904; repr., Chicago: University of Chicago Press, 1971), pp. 294–323.

20. During the colonial era, Elisabeth Anthony Dexter estimates that between 10 to 25 percent of the female population engaged in some entrepreneurial venture. See *Colonial Women of Affairs: Women in Business and the Professions in America before 1776* (1931; repr., Clifton, NJ: Augustus M. Kelley, 1972), p. 139. On the legal and economic status of women, see Barbara Irene Kreps, "The Paradox of Women: The Legal Position of Early Modern Wives and Thomas Dekker's *The Honest Whore*," *ELH* 69, no. 1 (Spring 2002): 83–102. Angel Kwolek-Folland, *Incorporating Women: A History of Women and Business in the United States* (New York: Palgrave, 2002).

21. On women entrepreneurs, see Kwolek-Folland, *Incorporating Women*. Mary Yaegar, ed., *Women in Business* (London: Edward Elgar Press, 1999). Kathy Peiss, *Hope in a Jar: The Making of America's Beauty Culture* (New York: Owl Books, 1999). Virginia G. Drachman, *Enterprising Women: 250 Years of American Business* (Chapel Hill: University of North Carolina Press, 2004).

CHAPTER 2

THE ENTERING WEDGE

THE WOMAN'S VIEWPOINT AND ADVERTISING

There were many ways for women to become advertising professionals, just as there were ways for them to practice advertising. When author Frances E. Willard, head of the Women's Christian Temperance Union, wrote *Occupations for Women* in 1897, she included a chapter titled "Women in Advertising." She observed that there were four types of ad women. First, newspaper and magazine writers or literary types added to their income by producing articles and advertisements calling attention to the virtues of new food products, patent medicines, fabrics, appliances, and other novel inventions created to meet a newly discovered need. A second type, the researcher, interviewed men and women who used a certain product. A third category worked as stenographers, and in the course of time, some moved up to manage the company's promotion program. Once a woman settled on an area of the profession, Willard advised her to make *the feminine* a central part of her professional strategy. Never let them forget: "The world likes a womanly woman, and this you can be, no matter how far afield you go in the world of personal endeavor."[1]

Willard's advice was representative of turn-of-the-century occupational advisers and female commentators in a transitional era.

Whether drawn from the nineteenth-century notions of a woman's place in the home or the more public orientation of the Progressive Era's *New Woman*, the aspiring ad woman was to maintain both cultural and domestic standards of womanhood within the workplace. In this way, women in offices could show men that they were good potential wives, explains Angel Kwolek-Folland. "She was still associated with a sense of duty, a willingness to subsume self into work, an unflinching devotion to her boss and his business, and an inherent difference from men."[2]

The advertising business emerged during the insurgence of the late-nineteenth-century struggle for women's rights, which included education, training, and employment as well as suffrage. In a period that both celebrated and feared the white, middle-class woman's entry into the public world of the workplace, college, and politics, society also emphasized the social and economic importance of advertising work to women. Women's involvement with the arts, writing, and philanthropy in the nineteenth century helped them develop organizational skills and confidence that could then be used not only for suffrage work but also in the new profession of advertising. When suffrage activity was heating up, women were encouraged to become involved with advertising as "safe activities to distract them from political activities." Some firms even advocated a form of feminism by making an effort to train women in the advertising trade and to offer them gainful employment, thereby shaping a new generation of both professionals and consumers.[3]

Moreover, the efforts of these early ad women also enlarged our sense of the scope of middle-class women's activities in nineteenth- and twentieth-century America, placing them outside the home and in business. Women not only worked in business for wages, as labor historians have shown, but also the activity was empowering. They turned the cultural basis of their exclusion from the general pursuit of business—their femininity, a sign of fashion, beauty, and domesticity—into a resource for entrepreneurship, economic independence, and self-fulfillment. Thus, the first generation of women entered the new profession of advertising as agents buying and selling space, copywriters, commercial artists, and advertising managers for large firms and department stores, among others. Who were these pioneers?

What kind of work did they do? And why a career in advertising? Answering these questions requires us to first look back at the strange world of patent medicines to consider how the feminine offered women an entering wedge in the new profession of advertising.

ADVERTISING A NEW OCCUPATION FOR WOMEN

Although few nineteenth-century women achieved the level of independence necessary to support themselves without assistance from their parents, husband, or other family members, the fact that Mary Morrow Craig chose gainful, career-oriented employment is significant, especially since single women's employment was strictly something that led up to marriage, never a substitution for it.

When Morrow began her fifty-year professional career in 1887, Mathilde C. Weil, Meta Volkman, and Mary Compton had already paved the way at the M. C. Weil Agency. Morrow entered the business first as an advertising representative through newspaper work and later moved on to the National Advertising Company, one of the large New York agencies. She later worked with Weil as a media representative, and they became friends. Upon Weil's death in 1903, Morrow inherited the office and built up a "good" business. Though Morrow made all the contracts, she continued to carry the name M. C. Weil Agency out of respect. Two months prior she married Mr. R. A. Craig, and "he very much opposed my taking up such reins," wrote Morrow. "But this determined dame had her way."[4]

Nostrums—cure-alls and elixirs—provided the "backbone" of the M. C. Weil Agency, as it did for many other advertising agencies during the nineteenth century. There was a great deal of money to be made in buying and selling advertising space in newspapers and magazines for patent medicine companies, then reselling it for a profit. This enormous activity also opened up many of the earliest opportunities for women in the advertising profession. "There were a number of women working for advertising concerns but few held other positions than that of stenographer, typist, bookkeeper [or] checking-clerk, later some few women solicitors on newspapers," recalled Craig.[5]

At the time, the biomedical industry in this country was still in its infancy, and medicine was ill equipped to deal with most diseases. An army of enterprising advertisers, evangelists, peddlers, and respected doctors and druggists were prepared to step in and alleviate the suffering with their advertised products, pitching promises of instant relief. When the Civil War came, the United States government introduced these remedies to soldiers who had not yet heard of patent medicines. One of the most popular brands was the catarrhal tonic Peruna, a pleasantly flavored elixir containing about 28 percent drinking alcohol, making it stronger than wine. Ads for Peruna maintained that the tonic cured cough, colds, and inflammation. Indeed, it improved the soldiers' sense of well-being and soothed many of their aches as advertised. When the war was over, Peruna was introduced to the general public accompanied by pictures of bosomy women, apparently to attract men's attention, but it actually sold four or five times more to women than to men. The possible reason might have been that the high alcoholic content gave women an opportunity for an unwitting secret tipple at a time when women were not permitted to go to the corner saloon. The manufacturers maintained that the alcohol was necessary to preserve the roots and medicinal bitters.[6]

What was actually in these postwar remedies? Anywhere from 20 to 40 percent flavored ethyl alcohol with innocuous roots and herbs, sometimes cocaine or opium. Among them, Lydia E. Pinkham's Vegetable Compound made advertising history. On her kitchen stove, Pinkham brewed a folk remedy for "female complaints" and for years shared it just with her friends. In the hard times after the 1873 depression, however, her sons Dan and Bill persuaded her to bottle the remedy for sale and promote it in a pamphlet. Sales took off when the family decided to include Lydia's face in the advertisements (figure 2.1). The ads stressed that "woman can sympathize with woman"; the copy assured the reader that the compound was "pleasant to the taste, effective, and immediate in its effect"—that is, a sure cure for everything from "female weakness" to menstrual problems to a prolapsed uterus. It was also a socially acceptable form of alcohol for women. Pinkham also urged ailing women to write her for answers about their most intimate health problems, suggesting that men didn't under-

Figure 2.1. When Lydia Pinkham's picture appeared in the ads with the caption "Woman can sympathize with woman," sales for the remedy took off. Reproduced from Frank Rowesome Jr., *They Laughed When I Sat Down: An Informal History of Advertising in Words and Pictures* (New York: McGraw-Hill Company, 1959).

stand. Orders and letters poured in, and Lydia, an early feminist, employed young women to answer the letters. Later her huge factory was run almost entirely by local girls both in the front office and on the production line. Although Pinkham died in 1883, her famous face continued to appear in newspapers and magazines, on billboards, and in streetcar ads. In 1890, however, the Pinkhams slashed advertising expenditures, and annual sales tumbled by nearly 80 percent. In response, the family resumed heavy advertising over the next decade and succeeded in increasing their annual sales by 2,500 percent. The campaign effectively demonstrated to businesspeople a simple principle: it pays to advertise.[7]

Sales of nostrums soared from an annual $3.5 million before the Civil War to $75 million after by the turn of the century and accounted for one-third of American publishers' revenues. This enormous activity required not only independent advertising agents like

Weil but also women who could work as in-house managers, preparing ads, buying media, and coordinating large-scale advertising activities for companies. As early as 1870, for example, Mary Compton placed advertising for Vapo-Cresolene, one of the first big patent medicine accounts promised to cure whooping cough and diphtheria. Peruna also had a female advertising manager. And, to get the diuretic Kilmer's Swamp Root in circulation, advertising manager Beatrice Conklin exchanged two dollars' worth of the elixir to newspapers for one dollar's worth of advertising space. In turn, the newspaper resold the Swamp Root to the local drugstores. However, increasing revelations about the most extreme patent medicines showed that many of the so-called remedies were genuine threats to the health of the community, which, by the end of the century, led to federal and state laws about truth-in-labeling and governmental pure food and drug inspection and control.[8]

The growth of women in publishing and advertising occurred during this period of large-scale advertising of nostrums. The needs of the industry for advertising vehicles increased enormously and created new opportunities for women to earn a living as writers and advertising solicitors. Notably, Sarah Jessica Hale took charge of *Godey's Lady's Book*, and a number of women followed in her wake. Among them, Susan C. Vogel made a success of the magazine *Woman's Journal* by persuading firms and services to buy advertising space in the issues. Other women took another path. For example, Ella L. Breedlove started her career as a high school teacher and came into advertising in connection with a church paper. Her first week's business totaled only thirteen dollars, but Breedlove persisted until she mastered the ins and outs of securing advertising for church publications, culinary magazines, and other class periodicals. Eventually she succeeded, and in 1899, she joined the well-known advertising agency Pettengill & Company as a solicitor.[9]

In the advertising business, more than two hundred advertising trade journals had been launched since 1888, providing how-to-do-it articles, reviews of current campaigns, and other summaries of the field. But fifteen years later, in 1903, perhaps only thirty remained listed in the *American Newspaper Directory*—among them the most successful being George P. Rowell's *Printers' Ink* and Kate Griswold's *Profitable Advertising*.

As publisher and editor of the trade journal, Griswold became one of the most respected women in turn-of-the-century advertising (figure 2.2). Born in West Hartford, Connecticut, Griswold began her business career by managing a poultry farm followed by work in the executive offices of the National Trotting Association. In 1891 she accepted editorship of *Profitable Advertising*, which was founded as a house organ for C. F. David Advertising Agency. When the agency went out of business in 1895, Griswold took over ownership and gradually built the business journal into a successful monthly, filling a tangible need in the advertising world. The journal later absorbed Charles Austin Bates's *Current Advertising* together with the San Francisco *Returns*, and finally evolved into *Advertising and Selling* magazine. Griswold encouraged women to enter a business where her viewpoint provided "certain advantages." If a woman had ability, the place to gain invaluable experience in general publicity would be work as the associate of an advertising manager, which invariably would give her experience, while retail-advertising operations would bring her into closer touch with readers.[10]

Occasionally, George Rowell's *Printers' Ink* showcased a few ad women as they made their way into the world of advertising. When Rowell presented such articles, they somehow appeared more curious than serious. For example, one article featured society matron Harriet Hubbard Ayer, who survived a divorce and complete financial ruin when her former husband, an iron manufacturer, filed for bankruptcy. Three years after her divorce was finalized, she restored her lost family fortune by launching a successful cosmetics business that came to be known as the Recamier Manufacturing Company. She started from a $50,000 loan from a wealthy Wall Street investor and pioneered selling cosmetics in the United States through extensive advertising in the newspapers. Although the article lauded Ayer for succeeding in doing a "man's" job, conspicuously absent were the specifics of how the widow accomplished this turnaround in business. Nevertheless, it made the point that the feminine was central to her professional strategy. "I can't tell much about Mrs. Ayer's career," *Printers' Ink* wrote in 1892, "partly

Figure 2.2. Kate E. Griswold, editor of *Profitable Advertising*, from *Printers' Ink*, February 4, 1903.

because I don't know it, and partly, because I don't have the space." But there was "something pre-eminently feminine about Ayer," from her rose corsage to a vase of flowers on her desk.[11]

THE FEMININE POINT OF VIEW FINDS A VOICE

During this era, the traditional view of women's place in the home and their natural instincts appeared to put them in a unique position to offer what came to be called the *woman's viewpoint*. Consequently, the role of ad women expanded as feminine insights became a statement to manufacturers about what they should produce and how they should advertise.

The Woman's Viewpoint

When advertising agencies and retailers recruited women writers from newspapers and magazines in the 1890s, the viewpoint necessary for reaching the women's market had already been articulated. Publishers had long recognized women as potential readers and welcomed contributions by women writers. The period saw a proliferation of articles about fashion, women's clubs, cooking, and housekeeping interspersed with full-page advertisements devoted to promoting food, fashion, cosmetics, housewares, and home furnishings. For the most part, though, the articles, like most advertisers, correctly assumed that married women kept house, and a large percentage of magazines reached women who relied on the publications for fashion, recipes, and new ideas on household management.

By the 1890s, advertisers and manufacturers had begun to recognize that women not only bought beauty products but also mass-produced food, clothing, and other goods for the home. As early as 1891, Nathaniel C. Fowler, author of *Fowler's Publicity*, wrote that "the principle of advertising to the women to reach men will generally bring more business than by advertising to reach the men by advertising to men." Numerous other articles similarly advanced that females simply possessed more knowledge of human nature, which uniquely qualified them for a place in the advertising profession. "As most of the goods sold at retail are sold to women it follows that women ought to come pretty close to knowing what to say to other women in advertisements," explained James F. Gibson in 1898. "Consequently the store advertising business ought to be one for which women are peculiarly adapted, if they follow their instincts."[12]

Women of the same era echoed similar notions that a woman's point of view—her *natural* home building, fashion, or aesthetic instincts—could be a help rather than a hindrance to the advertising business. To a certain extent, women's writings exploited gender differences to their own advantage. In 1898, for example, Alice Grimley provided three reasons why women as ad writers make the better advertiser: One advantage women had was that an advertising department could secure their talent for a smaller salary. In addition, women also had finer perceptions; as a woman, she would naturally know how to appeal to women, who after all did most of the buying in the world. Finally, what buying they did not do, they influenced through husbands, fathers, and brothers. Certainly women could do better work than men, "who could not be expected to write alluringly about lace petticoats and bonnets," emphasized copywriter Edith R. Gerry, then assistant advertising manager of the Siegel Siegel-Cooper Company's New York store.[13]

Consequently, the new profession of advertising gradually took shape along these prevailing notions of gender roles and work identities. Women came to write reams of copy as they entered corporate advertising departments, retail advertising, and agencies. Among these early ad writers was the former journalist Carmelita Beckwith, who specialized in the electrical field, writing for the General Electric Company and the Elmer Morris Electric Company. Another newspaperwoman, E. S. Leonard of the J. A. Richards Company, New York, developed a large share of the business in booklet and catalog writing. Such office work offered new opportunities for both social and economic mobility. For example, Helen Mar Shaw, editor of the women's department of the *Boston Daily Journal*, moved to Chicago where she took charge of the advertising for a paint manufacturing house, occupied a similar position with Rand, McNally & Company, and in 1898 accepted a better offer from James B. Clow & Sons appliances.[14]

Other women brought years of experience in magazine advertising for housewares as well as buyers of household goods. When M. B. Caffin, formerly advertising manager of the *American Kitchen*, and M. C. Mahl, from the advertising department of the *Hartford Post*, founded the Sherwood Advertising Company of New York in 1901, the agency was composed entirely of women. Thereby the feminine became a central part of their strategy. "The service we offer is copy that is written from the woman's standpoint, by women, to women, and that avoids a woman's prejudices," according to Caffin. "Such copy is the best substitute for a saleswoman."[15]

Yet this notion of the woman's viewpoint was a double-edged sword. Although popular ideas about gender allowed women entry into the male-dominated profession of advertising, the industry also used them to explain and justify limiting women's roles in business and in work in general. Industry executives and agents recognized the increasingly gendered nature of their markets and aimed their products differently at male and female customers. Consequently, women seemed ideal advertising writers for women-centered products, such as food, fashion, cosmetics and beauty aids, and furnishings. As purveyors for middle-class culture and domesticity, working in the public interest and officially or unofficially in public service, they seemed to instinctively know what would please and influence women.

It was disturbing, however, that these deep-seated notions about work identities grew out of the same biological laws that deemed women's minds were weak and the Victorian doctrine that governed relations between the sexes. Since the 1830s, many of the medical advice books, as well as etiquette and beauty manuals, viewed the life-cycles of puberty, menstruation, childbirth, and menopause as difficult and draining experiences for women. The scientific community concurred with these medical theories, adding that on the basis of height, weight, and cranial measurements, woman was the weaker sex. One of the most influential attacks on higher education for women was Boston physician Dr. Edward Clark's *Sex Education in America: Or, a Fair Chance for the Girls* (1872), in which the author argued that the rigors of higher education would endanger women's health because they needed rest during menstruation. In the best-selling *Man and Woman* (1894), British physician Henry Havelock Ellis also raised concerns about the fitness of women for business positions, because he felt their menstrual cycle affected their self-control. Even Charlotte Perkins Gilman, the most radical feminist thinker of these decades, believed in biologically based differences between male and female minds and defined women's primary role as mother and homemaker.[16]

Using these ideas on sex differences and gender roles, employers and workers defined particular jobs or positions as more suited to manhood or womanhood as *natural*, or biological, serving the public interest in twentieth-century society. Such ideas about the nature of men's and women's work and their relationship to job skills were important in forming a male managerial force and a female clerical staff, since the gender hierarchy gave men more privileges, status, and economic value than women. These inequities were reflected in different access to position and privilege, pay scales, and promotional tracks for men and women. Women working in factories earned little more than half of the wages earned by men, and in service jobs, women earned even less. Clerical work often offered the best promise, even to those women with college degrees.[17]

With the enormous success of the women's pages in newspapers, women's magazines, and Lydia Pinkham's Vegetable Compound, many businesses and advertising agencies began to recognize female authority and woman-to-woman advice as a crucial sales strategy for selling beauty products, housewares, and other consumer goods. Although the feminine offered women an entering wedge into the new profession of advertising, the woman's viewpoint also provided women—and men—a cultural resource for business strategies. Over the course of the twentieth century, these strategies became increasingly significant to the economy.

Feminization of the Workforce

The rise of these new opportunities in the advertising profession coincided with the larger modernization of American business that occurred during the period of 1880 through 1930. One outcome was the gender coding of managerial and job rules that kept women out of the highest-paying jobs and opened the way for the feminization of clerical and personnel work. White, native-born females filled specialized, white-collar office positions as clerks, jobs previously held by men, while new populations of immigrants played an important role working in the new factories. Furthermore, the shifts in new technologies were also changing the nature of women's work, explains Angel Kwolek-Folland. "The increasing use of the typewriter, the increasing specialization of office work, and the fact that women would work for less than men all made the lower echelons of office labor less attractive to white-male workers."[18]

Still, most of these office jobs did not lead to managerial positions for women in this early period. On the other hand, the growth of white-collar work provided new opportunities in business fields previously closed to women even as it reinforced differences between men and women. In 1870 female office workers numbered ten thousand. By 1900, their numbers increased to four hundred thousand, and by 1920, they numbered two million. Women also entered jobs in the department stores, in the telephone industry, and in the domestic science industry. Chain stores also employed large numbers of women. Another significant change in women's employment opportunities concerned the employment of married women, which doubled between 1900 and 1930. Although the numbers remained small, the social stigma attached to middle-class women's paid employment did not disappear, especially in the pages of homemaking magazines. Articles in magazines and dozens of vocational advice books provided lessons for middle-class women on how to assess careers and enter the workforce. From experience, many women knew the hardships of the Civil War, and the changing economy left little room for widows and maiden aunts at home.

One issue of *Woman's World* in 1896, for example, addressed advertising as a career. A good ad writer was one who possessed a fair knowledge of character and human nature, some literary skill, and ideas. When writing, they must have the capacity to put themselves in the place of the purchaser and consider what reasons or arguments would appeal to the buyer. The article continued with this step-by-step plan:

> . . . the woman who has been interested in this article should study the advertisements in *Woman's World*; let her also study the announcements in her daily paper. This study will give her more insight into advertising than a volume of suggestions. Let her remember that each article has some distinctive merit that is to be harped on constantly until it is burned into the public mind in connection with the article; let her remember that brevity is always necessary; let her study the journals devoted to the subject. Then, when she feels she is able to make an attempt, let her make it, and send it to the advertiser. Perhaps he will send it back. He will surely

do so unless it is exceptionally brilliant, for other people are supplying him with good work. If success appears to crown the woman's
efforts, she can apply to the advertising agencies for work.[19]

The article went on to say that remuneration for writing advertisements varied greatly. Some newspaper ads paid writers as little as one
dollar, while a large illustrated advertisement for which the ad writer
engaged an artist paid in excess of a hundred dollars. Over the next
four years, *Printers' Ink* had so many inquiries from women asking
how to enter the advertising world that the trade journal reprinted the
Woman's World article in 1900.

What is key here is that early vocational advice magazines like
Frances Willard's *Occupations for Women*, the popular press, trade journals, and ad women themselves emphasized that the reason these
women ultimately succeeded was because they capitalized on gender
conventions, rather than emulating men in dress or manner. This
became the accepted argument as the years went by. If women had to
work, and it seemed that more and more of them needed the money and
enjoyed the freedom, they could work in advertising and promote
women's consumption. Ironically, the promotion of the feminine did
open up opportunities for women, albeit limited, in the new mass-
consumer culture, but they had more challenges to overcome than men.

GETTING A FOOT IN THE DOOR

Women in general, and women in the business world particularly,
heard conflicting messages about their chances for their enterprise,
career, and capabilities in business. As the advertising profession
matured and gained prestige, educated, native-born middle-class men
took firmer control and made the field more their own, which isolated
women yet ironically also opened up new opportunities for them. The
specialized positions in the advertising profession came to demand
training in certain areas, such as writing, typesetting, and engraving,
as well as clerical and managerial skills beyond what women were nor-
mally exposed to as homemakers, wives, and mothers.

Women's entry into advertising also coincided with a broad movement among nineteenth-century women to gain access to higher education and professional training. In the years following the Civil War, several women's colleges opened in the Northeast, including Vassar, Wellesley, Smith, and Bryn Mawr, while new universities in the Midwest were open to both men and women. By 1890, over 60 percent of the colleges were either coeducational or open to women only, which created a new generation of highly trained women. Still, it would be another two decades before institutions of higher learning such as Harvard University, New York University, Boston University, Northwestern University, and the University of Missouri began to take advertising seriously enough to include it in their business curricula, but they were reluctant to admit women.[20]

By then some educational institutions and numerous correspondence schools like the Alexander Hamilton Institute and the International Correspondence Schools began to offer courses in advertising techniques. In 1901, for example, *Printers' Ink* carried this announcement for the Ad-School:

WANTS WOMEN AS WRITERS

Women read nine-tenths of the advertisements; women purchased nine-tenths of the merchandise advertised (or the purchaser is influenced by women), and it is women who should know best how to appeal to her sex. With her keen perception of feminine attire, who but a woman to interest other women on millinery, silks, dress goods, ribbons, notions and lingerie? Doesn't the field for ad-women, in their distinctive lines, appear full of hope and promise?—*Ad-School.*[21]

What became of these ad school graduates?

Printers' Ink suggested that women in particular wasted a great deal of money and time on such programs as the Ad-School. In a 1902 article titled "Schools in Advertising," ad men Artemas Ward and Charles Austin Bates forcibly argued that correspondence schools teaching advertising were a waste of money and that the discipline could be taken up at no charge. They contended that writing could be learned by practice and study of books like Arlo Bates's *Talks on Writing English* or a concise text on rhetoric. Type display could be learned in a printing office or from ads, while the theories of advertising were far more advanced in the advertising journals than the literature of advertising schools. *Printers' Ink* also had the same bias. In another issue, the trade journal featured the case of Ann Greer, who on "the day on which she succumbed to the slick statements and assurances of the ad school advertisement marked the beginning of a wild goose chase." Why? Because simply by reading the trade journal *Printer's Ink*, any person with ability to become an "advertising man" could learn the principles of publicity. It cost less than ten cents a week, and the course could be completed without the "slightest interference" with your present work.[22]

The movement of women in advertising made for great copy, and the media soon responded with a mixture of excitement, bemusement, and condescension. Few businesswomen could forget, for example, how Kate Griswold devoted fifty-five pages to "Women Workers in Publicity" in *Profitable Advertising* in 1903, featuring career sketches of twenty-five women in almost every branch of advertising work, embracing writing, art, and business. These women, however, were the exceptional elite. "The women who have wandered into the advertising field, and who have succeeded are worthy to be classed among the brightest women of the world," wrote Griswold. "Advertising, in any and all of its phases, is a business that demands ability and persistence—an art that requires skill. Therefore, those who win success in such a vocation must be liberally endowed with mental gifts and artistic tastes."[23]

The accomplishments of these women set the standard and fostered the image of women as remarkable professionals, when in fact most ad women made much more modest gains. Among them, Dr. Ellen C. Gage of Chicago practiced medicine for ten years when opportunities for women doctors were declining. She eventually succeeded by becoming a copywriter of promotional booklets, catalogs, and advertisements for women's apparel and other household goods. Her clients included Nutro-Crisp Cereal, the White Sewing Machine,

Libby Glass Company, and Cream of Wheat, among others (figures 2.3, 2.4). Other women achieved success as commercial artists; some examples include Mrs. Crosby-Buck (first name unknown), who became vice president of the Barnes-Crosby Engraving Company in Chicago; illustrator Anna Burnham, who drew pictures of graceful women figures for advertisements; and B. Ostertag, who applied her ideas on art to advertising posters. Still other women, like L. Gertrude Irving, who worked for a large wholesale grocery firm, planned campaigns as advertising managers. Finally, women worked as advertising representatives, soliciting contracts for newspaper and magazines: Lilian Whitney Babcock in Boston, as well as A. B. Barnes and Yetta

Figure 2.3. Dr. Ellen C. Gage, medical doctor turned copywriter, from *Profitable Advertising*, February 1903.

Figure 2.4. Food adver-tisement written by copywriter Dr. Ellen C. Gage, from *Profitable Advertising*, February 1903.

Small Folk have such a lot to learn, and such a lot to grow — to do either well, they MUST BE PROPERLY FED. Proper food, means food that *tastes* good, *looks* good, *is* good—that gives vitality, and has muscle-making properties.

is an appetizing, pre-digested, thoroughly cooked food, READY TO EAT. It is not mushy, but requires chewing — so it's *good for the teeth*; AND CHILDREN LIKE IT. Made only by

The Hygienic Food Company, St. Joseph, Michigan

Schmidt in New York City. These profiles represented not only the diverse types of advertising work but also Griswold's serious desire for more women to join the small numbers of ad women. Immigrant daughters, reformers, part-timers and full-timers, married and unmarried, and even society women all appeared to have a place in the advertising and new mass-consumer industries.[24]

Most women understood that men had a better chance to succeed in advertising, because of the stark reality that prejudice against women held them back from succeeding as equals. One only has to take a look at the help-wanted announcements in trade journals like *Printers' Ink* or newspapers like the *New York Herald Tribune* to see that advertising was a man's world. Typical of the time, the gendered language reinforced the notion of what was appropriate *men's work* and *women's work*. In *Printers' Ink*, for example, the classified ads called for "salaried men," "advertising man," and "young man," or the generic "advertising manager," "advertising writer," or "clerks." But on a rare occasion the ad called for women instead of men. In the June 24, 1903, issue, for example, a help-wanted ad specifically asked for a "forelady" for the subscription department of an established leading agricultural publication in the Midwest. And in the October 19, 1904, issue, another ad for the Harvie Company in New York read: "Reliable men and women wanted in all parts of the country; exclusive territory; one hundred percent profit; no risk." Still, ads specifically asking for women workers were rare. Nevertheless, *Printers' Ink* encouraged both young male and female job seekers to use its classifieds to advertise their services, since every week it reached more people employing advertising workers than any other trade publication in the United States.

Over a ten-year period from 1900 to 1910, the classified columns of *Printers' Ink* showed only a handful of job seekers who clearly identified themselves as females. The first known announcement by an identifiable woman appeared in an August 27, 1902, edition. It read: "A young woman experienced in newspaper work, country and city, desires position. Good proofreader. M.Ed. care Printers' Ink." Then, two women advertised for a position, highlighting the fact that they were ad school graduates. In the October 14, 1903, issue, one woman announced: "Ambitious young woman, ad school graduate, desires position with agency." The second graduate placed her ad nearly two years later: "Ad writer, woman (24) capable of doing first class work. Page-Davis graduate with some experience, desires position as assistant to Advertising Manager in Department Store." Regretfully, there is no record of the actual number of female job seekers, let alone the responses to their notices, because they often hid their marital status and gender.

Many women retained their maiden name after they married for several reasons. First, traditionalists considered any measure of independence achieved by married women as a threat to the traditional family. Ellen Key, for example, urged mature women to devote themselves full-time to motherhood in her influential *A Century of Childhood* (1900). The modern woman, however, considered work in the public arena as a path to respectability for women in general, whether she worked for wages or went unpaid. In the middle ground, others found it acceptable for a woman to work until her husband attained a level of income that would allow her to quit her job. So an ad woman typically built her reputation working as a single woman before getting married, referring to herself as a "business girl," which summed up her real life, for she was a woman and a worker. When working-women married, they continued to refer to themselves as "girls" to justify their work, since social convention prescribed that middle-class married women work in the home rather than in public.

The common practice of women hiding their gender or marital status can also be seen as an influence on language, which has been viewed by some as imbued with sexism. By using *Miss* (and later *Ms.*) to refer to both married and unmarried businesswomen in place of *Mrs.* or *Madame*, where the marital status is known, women promoted equal and respectful treatment. For example, Miss Carro M. Clark formed the C. M. Clark Publishing Company of Boston in 1901. Although she achieved success as "Miss Clark" in her business life, in her private life she was Mrs. Charles F. Atkinson of Beacon Street. Some female ad writers and illustrators also used male pen names or their initials to ensure that their works were accepted by publishers or taken seriously by the public. Certainly this area should be further explored to better understand the scope of women's contributions to nineteenth- and early twentieth-century business.[25]

THE CASE OF ADELE MacGILL

Almost uniformly, articles in the popular press or vocational advice literature painted a rosy picture of multiple opportunities and luxurious salaries for women with ability. On occasion the trade press published practical advice about career and job training opportunities for young women or success stories of their accomplishments in the work world, while often warning that the business was highly competitive. From the scattered evidence available, I will build a picture of what it was like for an aspiring young ad woman in 1904, as suggested by a *Printers' Ink* story on Adele MacGill.

When MacGill began to study advertising through the Powell Correspondence School, she already was working as the director of an Industrial Club for Working Girls in Saratoga, New York, earning an annual salary of five hundred dollars, around the same wages as a fac-

tory worker but half of the average pay for clerical work in this period
(figure 2.5). But MacGill felt the need to change her job to one that
would provide more room for advancement, express her individuality,
and earn more money. She chose the Powell program because it
offered the "woman's reason"—that is, "because I liked his [Mr.
Powell's] face." The tuition was thirty dollars, paid in three monthly
installments. Lesson plans came once a week, two lessons in each.
There were fifty lessons in all, which took MacGill about eight
months to finish, working perhaps one hour a day in her spare time.
Almost the entire course consisted of analyzing ads of different businesses and improving on them. The work was sent back to Mr. Powell
each week and always returned with comments.[26]

Unlike many other students, however, MacGill brought a solid
foundation to the correspondence course. She was a high school graduate with two years special literary work in college; this at a time
when the average man had no more than an eighth-grade education.
Also, she possessed a diploma from Kindergarten Training Program
and had two years practice teaching. Plus, her father owned a daily
paper, and one of her brothers managed the printing office, so she had
some familiarity with the actual work of setting up ads. "If, on the
other hand, I had had little education and been without previous
training, I doubt if I should have thought that my course in the correspondence school fitted me to become a successful advertisement
writer," recalled MacGill.[27]

After completing the courses, MacGill went to New York City
with samples of the work she'd done for local merchants, determined
to make a success as an ad writer. She placed three advertisements in
the *Herald Tribune* and answered other position-wanted announcements that she found in the newspapers. Although she had no
response from her notices for a position wanted, she did receive two
replies from those to whom she had written. The first came from a
large mail-order house, but she lost the job to a man with ten years'
experience. She did accept the second venture as solicitor for a series
of church papers. After she did not secure a single contract, she then
narrowed her search only to those who wanted advertisements
written. She visited nearly every agency in New York City, besides

Figure 2.5. Adele MacGill, aspiring ad woman, from *Printers' Ink*, February 4, 1903.

numerous firms with advertising to place. But being a fairly attractive young woman was both a help and a detriment. MacGill found it easy enough to secure an appointment from most businessmen; she also found that they often prolonged the interview and sometimes were even glad to have her call again. "On the other hand it is hard to get them, most of them, to give proper consideration to my writing; a blush and a smile, which I can't help, seeming to prove to them that I am not capable of doing serious work," lamented MacGill. "Two leading agencies refused to give me a desk where there was work to be done, and they even said I could not do it. 'Because the men smoke, and it is no place for a woman.'" Finally, the first real help came from another female Powell graduate, who sent her some leads that eventually resulted in work. Each order then brought in others, and samples became useful in obtaining more work.[28]

MacGill succeeded not out of sheer luck or from a fierce struggle for advancement, but she seemingly had some "feminine" ability that made her noticeable. Whatever the case, it is significant that the *Printers' Ink* article concluded with MacGill achieving success in the advertising business rather than escaping to her home. For single women, a career would be an appropriate goal in itself. Clearly the Adeles of the world could look to such experiences to legitimize and encourage their ambitions, yet women's involvement in women's networks emerged as another one of the most persistent aspects of their business dealings. Still, *Printers' Ink* responded with platitudes about hard work, persistence, and women's insights while sidestepping the gender issue in the advertising industry. They were not alone.

Actually, there was little room for advancement within the segregated female job sector, white-collar or otherwise, regardless of what the career books promised. Women's work became just that—work done solely by women—and was hence less prestigious and less profitable by definition. In the advertising profession, men filled the training programs and worked through various departments in search of the right job for them. Women started lower, however, as stenographers, researchers, or occasionally as space buyers, while they struggled to get noticed as copywriters to work on products deemed "ladylike" and to be paid a lower salary than the male writers. Still, women account representatives and art directors were generally unknown at this time, since such *contact* or *outside* jobs required face-to-face inter-action with manufacturer representatives. Some women were more hopeful, but most of them understood the reality that prejudice against women prevented them from succeeding as equals.

THE NEW WOMAN AND
TURN-OF-THE-CENTURY ADVERTISING

In many respects, these early ad women embodied the ideals of the New Woman, successive generations of women who prevailed against Victorian strictures and demanded career and public roles. The first generation attended the new women-only and coed colleges in the 1870s and 1880s, and they flourished professionally between the 1880s and the First World War as evidenced in the advertising field. In the mass media, Charles Dana Gibson's "Gibson Girl" symbolized the hopeful changes of the age for the white, middle-class woman between 1895 and World War I: the new movement of women into higher education and the workforce, the new freedom of behavior. She might have gone to college; she might work as a stenographer if financially pressed. Romance and marriage remained the central pur-pose of her life. With both men and women now working and earning money, it became possible to choose a mate based on attraction and on compatibility. However, exactly how these natural women would adjust to the strictures of marriage was never explained in the senti-mentalized and fantasized scenes of life.

Frequently unmarried, the New Women often aligned them-selves with members of their own sex (in partnerships that were not necessarily romantic) rather than in conventional marriages. They were not simply rebelling against their fathers or husbands but more significantly against the role that women were traditionally sup-posed to follow. What characterized them was a new self-reliance and vigor, as well as a desire for independence and pleasure that flew in the face of Victorians' canons of purity, submissiveness, piety, and domesticity. Many were outspoken feminists, addressing issues of industrialization, race, sexual justice at home, and promoting world peace.

The New Woman included a variety of types drawn from the spectrum of American class structure. She could be associated with the settlement house movement, educational and political reform, the medical and legal professions, journalism, the arts, and literature. Others worked as teachers, social workers, physicians, nurses, and businesswomen who supported themselves and lived independently. Though some women had a college education, typified by the New Woman, more had a high school education, working in mills, shops, or retail, even though they did ultimately marry. At the turn of the century, working-class women, too, turned their attention away from men to spend their leisure time in dance halls, amusement parks, and movie theaters.[29]

It was also a time when work done by married or widowed women was difficult for society, at least for the middle class, to accept. Throughout American history, women were excluded from the nation's largest and most powerful industries, institutions of higher learning, and professionalization. When women did succeed in industry or launched enterprises, on their own or with a husband, they typically developed businesses geared to women. It was a successful and familiar strategy for women who sought careers in traditionally male-dominated professions, such as medicine, law, publishing, and retailing. Still, women had few options, and, as a result, their successes in the professions were apt to be treated as one-of-a-kind stories typified by such figures as Rose Markward Knox, an important transitional figure in this era of the New Woman, and Jane Johnston Martin, who symbolized the possibilities.

Rose Markward Knox, Advertising Director

What connects ad women Mathilde Weil and marketer Rose Markward Knox is an accident of their private lives: widowhood transformed them from wives to entrepreneurs. Women who owned traditionally male businesses often inherited rather than initiated their enterprises, at least until the turn of the twenty-first century.

When Charles Knox watched his wife, Rose Markward, prepare homemade gelatin, he decided that there could be a market for prepared gelatin. In 1890 he set up business in Johnstown, New York. "I spent all that first summer writing out my own favorite gelatine recipes for him," recalled Markward. "I thought I had a tremendous number of them, but when the book came out it was so tiny I almost shed tears." In the years that followed, she created more recipes, and in 1896, her recipe book, *Dainty Desserts for Dainty People*, appeared in

Figure 2.6. Rose Markward Knox, director of advertising for Charles Knox Gelatine Company, from *Printers' Ink*, February 1919.

print. Her recipes reached millions of people, bringing fame to Charles Knox as the largest manufacturer of unflavored gelatin in the world (figure 2.6).

Upon Charles's death in 1908, Markward had to decide whether to run the business herself or employ a manager. "If I did the latter," she reasoned, "by the time my boys came of age the business would belong to the manager." So she took over management of the firm. From the start, Markward ran the Knox Gelatine Company in what she called "a woman's way." Since it was unthinkable at this time for a woman to be active in commerce, she sent messengers in black-bordered cars to her husband's customers and associates, announcing his death and declaring their son Charles would take over his father's responsibilities. (In truth, Charles was still in school.) As a business-woman, she also always wore a hat, in her office or in her test kitchen, to differentiate her from subordinates and unhatted secretaries.[30]

But while Markward is remembered for always being ladylike, she was an astute, resourceful, and successful businesswoman as well. Thanks to her efforts, sales for the Knox enterprise increased a remark-able 300 percent in a ten-year period, from 1909 to 1919. In an age of the rise of advertising, she played a major role in advertising as well as product development. Prior to this time, her husband had spent large amounts of money on the "old style publicity" to keep the Knox name in front of the public: a blimp with the Knox name that toured the nation, big signs on horseless carriages, and even a string of racing horses named *Gelatine Lad* and *Gelatine Queen*. Markward completely revamped the sales campaign and directed her advertising to women; showing attractive dishes made with gelatin and writing copy that emphasized the purity, cleanliness, and convenience of the product. Markward next launched a campaign in a number of women's magazines that empha-sized the fact that this was a business of, by, and for women with the headline: "Mrs. Knox Says," followed by a personal statement about the attractive dishes made with Knox Gelatine. Newspaper columns headed "Mrs. Knox Says" also offered practical advice for homemakers. Mark-ward also established research kitchens and an information bureau that provided advice on practical domestic problems, and she endowed research at the Mellon Institute to find new uses for gelatin.[31]

What is important here is that Markward made her homemaking instincts a help rather than a hindrance to her business career. Although she did a *man's job*, she placed an emphasis on the presentation of herself as a woman.

Jane Johnston Martin, the "New Woman"

Perhaps more than anyone else, it was Jane Johnston Martin who typified the first generation of the New Woman in advertising: outspoken feminist (figure 2.7). Unlike Mathilde Weil and Rose Markward Knox, she never married, nor did she inherit an enterprise. Instead, she rose to prominence as the advertising manager for Sperry & Hutchinson (purveyors of S & H Green Stamps), as she sought white-collar work, economic independence, and fulfillment from a career outside the home. In the process, Martin carved out a niche by specializing in the woman's viewpoint, while she claimed to understand women's needs and desires to sell to the female consumer market.

Martin began her business career in a large lace and embroidery concern around 1890 after high school, starting at ten dollars per week as a stenographer. After three months, she was asked to ready a page advertisement for the *Delineator*, a women's fashion magazine. This she did, and it was accepted. So began Martin's advertising career. Martin's experience continued with Scott & Bowne, manufacturers of Scott's Emulsion, where she worked as secretary to Mr. Scott, who frequently went abroad and left the advertising work for Martin to handle. Ten years later, she left this concern, having had her own secretary and signing letters over the title of assistant

Figure 2.7. Jane J. Martin, advertising manager for Sperry & Hutchinson, from *Printers' Ink*, February 1919.

advertising manager. Her salary had reached the amount of $30 a week, a luxurious amount at that time.[32]

In 1901 Martin joined the Alfred E. Rose Special Advertising Agency, earning $50 a week as an advertising manager. While at the agency, she edited a magazine called *Trained Motherhood* and *The Silver Cross*, the national publication of the King's Daughter, an organization of Christian men and women. And she has been credited with placing the first color advertisement on the front page of a newspaper: an ad for the celebrated H & O's Force cereal campaign that featured Sunny Jim. Three years later, in 1904, she joined the advertising department of the Sperry & Hutchinson Company, as assistant advertising manager, and in 1915, she was promoted to advertising manager. Martin also had a seat on the executive committee of the Advertising Clubs of the World in 1919 and 1920, the first woman to be elected to this position. When she resigned from Sperry & Hutchinson due to illness in 1922, Martin was reputed to have earned a salary of $10,000 a year, about eight times the average annual salary in 1925.[33]

Although the New Woman symbolized by Jane Martin expanded the definitions of women's place in business, it did not ultimately break the widespread acceptance of separate male and female arenas. Gender differences complicated the world of work in industrial America, being, in part, the product of men's and women's struggles over meaning and identities.

Advertising Managers, Illustrators, and Photographers

Following a similar path as Jane Martin, a handful of other women rose to prominence in the advertising field, despite the conservative climate between the 1880s and 1910s. Women who worked as advertising managers had responsibilities not only in the larger duties of the office, but they also bought space, lithography, posters, and printing. In 1899 the top salary for ad women like Persis Pomeroy, who handled the advertising for Warner, one of the biggest corset companies in the country, averaged about $6,000 a year, a princely sum at the time. Pomeroy had bought corsets in the market for years, so she brought knowledge of the market as well as the trade side to the concern. She not only made decisions on the advertising appropriations, but she also wrote all of the corset advertisements and supervised the artist's work illustrating her goods. Other prominent advertising managers included Ida Sharpe of Scott and Bowne, Dora Miller of the American Lead Company, and Mary G. Webber of the Fisk Rubber Company.[34]

A number of women also entered advertising as illustrators. There were those who initially knew nothing of the advertising field but were drawn in by a family member. When feminist Charlotte Perkins Gilman was sixteen, she designed trade cards with traditional visions of womanhood for at least four soap companies to help support her family (figure 2.8). She later wrote advertisements for manufacturers in her magazine, *The Forerunner*. The work of Nellie (sometimes spelled Nelly) Littlehale Umbstaetter stands out, her signature "N. L. U." appearing on many striking and effective advertising designs for Malta Vita breakfast cereal, Fast Black Diamond Dye, and Durkee Salad Dressing. She first drew these images for the Black Cat books published by her first husband, H. D. Umbstaetter, and advertisers later used them in other mediums (figure 2.9). Finally, to fully

Figure 2.8. As a young woman, feminist Charlotte Perkins Gilman designed trade cards for Kendall Manufacturing, circa 1876–1880.

appreciate the professional commitment of this new generation, one need only look to the Hoffman sisters. The creative writing of Celeste turned her sister Clara's drawing into a magazine ad for Diamond Soups. Their effort brought them more business, and in 1901, they opened their own studio in Chicago, turning out illustrated ads for national companies, such as Heinz, Swift & Company, and Pearline Soap. Nevertheless, Celeste found that solicitation work could be discouraging. At times, "it takes all the grit that one can summon," she recalled. "Sometimes, I meet with direct snubs and only the other day I was received by a man who kept his hat on and puffed smoke almost in my face" (figures 2.10, 2.11).[35]

In contrast, other women came into commercial art with extensive training in fine art and design. For example, Elizabeth B. Humphrey worked as a staff illustrator for Louis Prang and Company, which used

Figure 2.9. Nellie Littlehale Umbstaetter created striking advertising designs with her signature Black Cat, from *Profitable Advertising*, February 1903.

Figure 2.10. Celeste A. Hoffman (left), writer, and her sister Clara E. Hoffman, artist, from *Printers' Ink*, December 3, 1902.

the chromolithographic process to reproduce her work in greeting cards and gift books. A versatile artist, she had training at the Cooper Union School of Design in Philadelphia. Maud Humphrey Bogart designed artwork for Prang and did illustrations for *Harper's* and *Century* magazines; later, she was the art director for the fashion magazine *Delineator*. Elizabeth Shippen Green, Jessica Wilcox Smith, and Violet Oakley were students of illustrator Howard Pyle at the Drexel Institute in Philadelphia (1894–1900); the three became close friends and shared studios for many years. Another Drexel student, Sarah Stilwell Weber, illustrated advertisements for Wamsutta Mills, H-O Oats, Rit Dyes, and Scranton Lace Company. Among these female illustrators, Jessica Wilcox Smith earned the most, with an estimated annual income of $12,000 in 1910; that figure rose in the following years. In fact, Smith received between $1,500 and $1,800 for each of the nearly

I know that it isn't a recipe book
That makes my son's wife such a fine pastry cook;
Although she knows recipes off by the yard.
This proves that she uses

Swift's Silver Leaf Lard

Figure 2.11. The Hoffman sisters created a distinctive look for Swift & Company's Silver Leaf Lard, from *Printers' Ink,* December 3, 1902.

two hundred *Good Housekeeping* covers that she illustrated between 1917 and 1933, earning more than a quarter million dollars from this magazine alone.[36]

Not only were women distinguishing themselves with their work before the camera, they made a name for themselves behind the camera as well. "Pictorial advertising itself had only then begun to attract the attention of advertisers, while the application of the camera to the production of designs and pictorial features for purposes of publicity was practically unheard of," noted *Profitable Advertising* in 1903. It also celebrated the achievements of the "Mistress of the Camera," Beatrice Tonnesen, the pioneering Chicago-based photographer who, in the early 1890s, created the novel idea of producing illustrations and designs for advertisers through the use of photography. Beatrice joined with her sister Clara, who managed the business, to form the enormously successful Tonnesen Sisters (Inc.), which became one of the nation's first professional modeling agencies (figure 2.12). Such control over their modeling labor gave the Tonnesen Sisters a competitive edge over other commercial photographic establishments. By 1903, Tonnesen Sisters (Inc.) was the largest photographic printing establishment in America.[37]

Thus, this first generation of advertising women advanced the pro-

Figure 2.12. Beatrice Tonnesen, photographer, from *Profitable Advertising*, February 1903.

fession with an outlook more influential in businesses and services selling beauty products, fashion, housewares, and other consumer products marketed to women. Over the following decades, this female niche exploded into a thriving area of the advertising profession, as fashion, beauty, and packaged goods became important consumer industries.

NOTES

1. Frances E. Willard, *Occupations for Women* (Cooper Union, NY: Success Co., 1897), p. 154.

2. Sources for earliest vocational guidance for women: Virginia Penny, *The Employments of Women: A Cyclopedia of Woman's Work* (Boston: Walker, Wise & Co., 1863). See also Gertrude de Aguirre, *Women in the Business World; or, Hints and Helps to Prosperity* (Boston, Arena Publishing Company, 1894). Irene Hartt, *How to Make Money although a Woman* (New York: J. S. Ogilvie, 1895). On standards of womanhood within workplace, see Angel Kwolek-Folland, *Incorporating Women: A History of Women and Business in the United States* (New York: Palgrave, 2002), p. 67.

3. Karen Anderson, *Changing Women: A History of Racial Ethnic Women in Modern America* (New York: Oxford University Press, 1996), pp. 142–43.

4. Mary Morrow Craig, letter to J. George Frederick (n.d.), Advertising Women of New York Collection, box 2, folder 4, Schlesinger Library, Radcliffe Institute, Harvard University. Hereafter, Schlesinger Library.

5. Ibid.

6. History of patent medicines: James Harvey Young, *The Toadstool Millionaire: A Social History of Patent Medicines in America before Federal Regulation* (Princeton, NJ: Princeton University Press, 1961), pp. 220–21. Barbara Hodgson, *In the Arms of Morpheus: The Tragic History of Laudanum, Morphine, and Patent Medicines* (Buffalo, NY: Firefly Books, 2001).

7. "Lydia Pinkham," *Printers' Ink*, February 12, 1902. Sarah Stage, *Female Complaints and the Business of Women's Medicines* (New York: Norton, 1981).

8. Sales of nostrums: Young, *Toadstool Millionaire*, p. 110. Opportunities for women: "Places for Women of Ability," *Printers' Ink*, February 18, 1903. See also "The Rise of Advertising Women," speech, September 1938, box 12, folder 4, Advertising Women in New York Collection, Schlesinger Library.

9. *Profitable Advertising*, February 1903, p. 756.

10. "An Esteemed Contemporary," *Printers' Ink*, February 4, 1903, pp. 20–22.

11. Harriet Hubbard Ayer: "A Woman Advertiser," *Printers' Ink*, January 6, 1892, pp. 20–21. For other representative profiles of early ad women, see *Printers' Ink*, January 6, 1893, pp. 20–21; October 26, 1898, p. 6; October 29, 1902, p. 44; and December 2, 1902, pp. 2–6.

12. "Advertising for Women," *Printers' Ink*, August 26, 1891, p. 174. "Women as Advertiser," *Printers' Ink*, August 3, 1898, pp. 3–5.

13. "Women as Adwriters" and "Women as Advertiser," *Printers' Ink*, August 3, 1898, pp. 3–5.

14. *Profitable Advertising*, February 1903; Beckwith, p. 734; Leonard, pp. 733–35; and Shaw, pp. 727–29.

15. "A Woman's Advertising Agency," *Profitable Advertising*, July 1902, p. 130.

16. Henry Havelock Ellis, *Man and Woman* (1894; repr., New York: Arno, 1974). Charlotte Perkins Gilman, *Women and Economics* (1898; repr., Mineola, NY: Dover, 1994). See also Charlotte Perkins Gilman, *The Yellow Wallpaper* (1899; repr., Mineola, NY: Dover, 1997).

17. Nancy Cott, *The Grounding of Modern Feminism* (New Haven, CT: Yale University Press, 1987), p. 130.

18. Kwolek-Folland, *Incorporating Women*, p. 76.

19. How-to article from *Woman's World* reproduced in *Printer's Ink*, June 6, 1900, p. 31.

20. Barbara Miller Solomon, *In the Company of Educated Women: A History of Women and Higher Education in America* (New Haven, CT: Yale University Press, 1985), p. 44.

21. *Printers' Ink*, July 13, 1901, p. 43.

22. Artemas Ward and Charles Austin Bates, "Schools of Advertising," *Printers' Ink*, January 1, 1902, pp. 3–5. Ann Greer, *Printers' Ink*, November 4, 1903, pp. 6–8.

23. *Profitable Advertising*, February 1903, p. 723.

24. Ibid.

25. Arthur T. Vanderbilt II, *The Making of a Best Seller: From Author to Reader* (Jefferson, NC: McFarland & Company, 1999), pp. 124–25.

26. Adele MacGill, "Experiences and Conclusions of a Female Ad-School Grad," *Printers' Ink*, November 30, 1904, pp. 8–11. Wages: The annual income for industrial work was $486 in 1890 and $630 in 1910, while the clerical worker earned $848 in 1890 and $1,156 in 1910. See Mary Beth Norton et al., *A People and a Nation*, 6th ed. (Boston: Houghton Mifflin, 2001), pp. 505–506. Education of average man: "What Is the Level of the Buyer's Intelligence," *Advertising & Selling*, September 1923, p. 26.

27. MacGill, "Experiences and Conclusions of a Female Ad-School Grad."

28. Ibid.

29. On the "Gibson Girl," see Lois W. Banner, *American Beauty* (Chicago: University of Chicago Press, 1984), pp. 157–66. On the "New Woman," see Banner, *American Beauty*. See also Cott, *Grounding of Modern Feminism*. Kathy Peiss, *Cheap Amusements: Working Women and Leisure in Turn-of-the-Century New York* (Philadelphia: Temple University Press, 1986).

30. "How One Man Trained His Wife to Take Care of Herself," *American Magazine*, October 1921; "Women in Business," *Fortune*, September 1935; and "Grand Old Lady of Johnstown," *Collier's*, January 1, 1949. *New York Times*, May 23, 1937.

31. "Woman Advertiser and Manufacture," *Printers' Ink*, February 20, 1919.

32. Jane J. Martin: Advertising Women of New York Collection, box 2, folder 17: 2, Schlesinger Library.

33. Ibid. In 1925 the average annual salary was about $1,236, and only about 40 percent of the population earned $2,000 or more.

34. On Warner's corset advertising, see Frank Presbrey, *The History and Development of Advertising* (Garden City, NY: Doubleday Doran, 1929), p. 403. Advertising managers: "Women as Advertiser," *Printers' Ink*, August 3, 1898.

35. See, for instance, Fels-Naptha Soap, Holeproof Hosiery, and Moore's fountain pen advertisements written and signed "C. P. G." for Charlotte Perkins Gilman, *Forerunner*, November 1909 and December 1909. Umbstaetter: *Charles Austin Bates Criticisms*, advertising periodical, May 1898, p. 511. Hoffman sisters: "Two Chicago Women Who Make Advertising," *Printers' Ink*, December 3, 1902, p. 56. *Profitable Advertising*, February 1903, pp. 745–46.

36. On illustrators, see Walt Reed, *The Illustrator in America, 1860–2000* (New York: HarperCollins, 2001). On Jessie Wilcox Smith, see Carolyn Kitch, *Girl on the Magazine Cover* (Chapel Hill: University of North Carolina Press, 2004), p. 14. *Profitable Advertising*, April 1907, p. 1272.

37. "Mistress of the Camera," *Profitable Advertising*, December 1903.

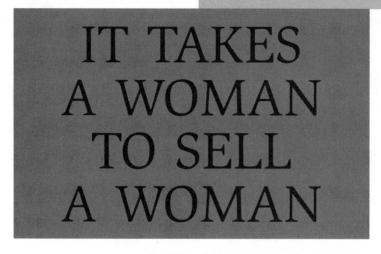

CHAPTER 3

IT TAKES A WOMAN TO SELL A WOMAN

DESIGNING MRS. CONSUMER

The single most important discovery about the "mass mind" goes back to a World War I finding from intelligence tests prepared for the draftees in the army. In addition to this data, Dr. Harry L. Hollingworth, a Columbia psychologist, conducted thousands more similar intelligence tests of men and women in order to draw a composite portrait of the "average man": he was superstitious, had an eighth-grade education, and possessed the mind of a fourteen-year-old. He was likely to drift into the skilled trades, marry at an early age, have three to five children, and earn not more than $1,000 a year. Such scientific characterizations of average or typical Americans were a striking phenomenon of the new century.[1]

Hollingworth's studies of the "average" American also represent corporate, educational, and media fascination with statistical normality, as is evident in the sheer range of enterprises devoted to quantifying and sorting all aspects of American life in the years before

World War I. To answer the demand of an advanced industrial society for ways to order a diverse and swelling population, intelligence measurement, social science investigations, and modern market research all began in earnest. But it was not obvious that the assembled answers were trustworthy or true. Even those who would benefit from such data gathering were not all convinced of its value in the 1910s and 1920s. It took considerable work to persuade business owners that collecting information about their customers' buying habits was worthwhile, and the media led the way.

By the end of the 1920s, the media had formed a lucrative business in supplying information; it also purported to offer national advertisers well-developed advertising vehicles that addressed different segments of the mass market. Over the interwar period, this appetite for detailed surveys and social data about mainstream America would especially give more weight to the working-class and other minority markets, which had earlier been considered the worst economic prospects among consumers. Such market investigations and surveys became responsible for shaping and expanding mass markets, as will be shown in the next two chapters. First, I will explore the impact and the limitations this new knowledge about the *average man* and the *average woman* had on the mass media, marketing, and advertising, as well as the gendering of the professions. The subsequent chapter then focuses on those professional women who brought progressive reform and scientific thinking to their work in advertising.

EVOLUTION OF MARKETING RESEARCH

The American business scene changed dramatically at the turn of the century. A wave of mergers reshaped thousands of independent firms into large-scale corporations. Between 1900 and 1930, the firms that succeeded incorporated the general reform movement known as progressivism. Scientific management underlies this movement to identify and define marketing opportunities and problems by generating, refining, and evaluating marketing actions as well as monitoring marketing performance to improve the process. In this way, firms created new marketing research institutions and practices that resulted in new conceptions of consumers, media, and advertising appeals. This research proved essential to link the consumer, customer, and the public to the marketer.

In this era, the development took place over three decades: Prior to 1910, researchers explored methods of firsthand observation through economics, sociology, and psychology that found useful information. Around 1910, the practice of marketing research began when quantitative analysis and social science showed new, more scientific ways of knowing modern Americans. Then, the period of 1920–1930 saw the introduction of new products, growth of new types of marketing establishments, and the uncertainty of consumer buying habits that led to the extensive use of surveys in marketing research and new analyses of consumers in developing sales messages.

Scientific Investigations

Early marketing thought and market research studies gradually began to replace advertisers' intuition about who the audiences were, what they wanted, and how best to reach them. Gradually, ad makers began to apply the science of general psychology to the five main problems of advertising: (1) To whom may the product be sold? (2) By what appeals may it be sold? (3) How may the appeals be most effectively presented? (4) What media should be used to present the appeals to reach the people to whom the product is to be sold? (5) What is a reasonable expenditure for promoting the sale of a product?[2]

With a focus on solving these basic business problems, the scientific literature on advertising and selling increasingly emphasized the use of psychological concepts, shifting from structuralism and functionalism to behaviorism as the development of psychological thought progressed in America. These new ideas began with William James's *Principles of Psychology* (1890), which laid the foundation for such concepts as consciousness, emotions, and habit. During the next decade, Hugo Munsterberg's writings about the application of psychology to industry, law, and other professions began to appear in magazines, while the theories of Viennese psychoanalyst Sigmund Freud and

Swiss psychiatrist Carl Jung circulated. But it would be Walter Dill Scott who first attempted to apply the principles of psychology to advertising in a series of articles titled "The Psychology of Advertising." This series first appeared in *Mahin's Magazine* in 1903, was reprinted in *Atlantic Monthly*, and was eventually published as a book. Daniel Starch then applied his work in educational applied psychology to advertising in his landmark *Advertising: Its Principles, Practices, and Techniques*. Collectively, their findings advanced the understanding of motivation, the process of learning, and communication.[3]

The first group of findings related concepts of psychology to motivation and, in turn, to sales appeals. The acknowledgment of the *unconscious* mind was derived from the new science of psychology. It played a significant role in determining the actions of an individual, which are often more powerful than those of the conscious mind. A successful ad works because it creates a connection between the product being advertised and some need or desire that the audience feels. These links, called "appeals," fall into two categories: logical and emotional. Logical (or rational) appeals base selling pitches on either the product's performance features or its ability to solve a problem. In contrast, *soft sell* (or emotional) appeals base selling pitches on the satisfaction that comes from purchasing the product and then owning it or making a gift of it. An extremely strong appeal tells the consumer: This is *the* product that will meet your needs or fulfill your desires. Although fundamental to advertising today, these ideas seemed novel and revolutionary in 1905, especially the idea that skillful use of emotional appeals could move products faster than any other approach. While these concepts of appeals developed, a second group of findings applied ideas of psychology to the learning process—attention, interest, desire, and action—to advertising, in other words, a paid, mass-mediated attempt to persuade.

As a result, two fundamental schools of advertising theory emerged—the hard sell and the soft sell—that still provide the foundation for contemporary campaigns. The effectiveness of the style depended on the product being advertised. The hard-sell copy style gave concrete reasons why to buy the product and worked best for small, inexpensive, frequently purchased items that could be cheaply offered as samples and sent through the mail, such as cigarettes, toothpaste, and soap. The soft-sell style built prestige for large, expensive items bought infrequently and seldom on impulse, like pianos and automobiles. But suggestive copy was just the surface of the campaign. It had to convey a certain look with similar appeals to gender and social status.

At this time, Claude Hopkins emerged as one of the most influential "reason-why" copywriters. Instead of focusing advertising copy on simple brand identification that sold the product name to the public, he created lengthy sales arguments designed to overcome any resistance. From this perspective, advertising served as business news on brand features, price, and availability through distribution. Rather than offering tired superlatives or founder's portraits, Hopkins guided consumers through sensible, long arguments with specific reasons for why the advertised product was worth buying. In order to make a generic claim stronger, however, Hopkins searched for *preemptive claim* in the manufacturing processes to establish the product's uniqueness. For example, Hopkins impressed the public with the purity of Schlitz beer by building the advertising around this single selling point and giving readers scores of reasons and countless numerical facts to support this claim (figure 3.1). Hopkins later added mail-order selling techniques to his copy approach, including such devices as free or inexpensive samples, premiums, coupons, hard-selling arguments, and functional illustrations with informative captions.[4]

But the "reason-why" copy approach had been oversold, insisted psychologist Walter Dill Scott, since the consumer interest was subordinate. From Scott's perspective, the psychological factors were an essential force in advertising. Customers might on occasion be directly persuaded, but more often they bought because of a suggestion at the right psychological moment, what today is called *image building*. The soft-sell strategy employed opulent art and suggestive sales pitches that mainly revolved around appeals to class and gender, as opposed to making an argument on price or utility. The text, illustration, and historical allusions with words such as *aristocratic, exclusive*, and *distinguished* made a subtle appeal to the feminine sentiment or class distinctions. Such appeals to consumers' yearning for social

Figure 3.1. Copywriter Claude Hopkins used the "preemptive" technique to establish the supposed uniqueness of Schlitz beer. *Harper's Bazaar*, July 1902.

status were especially appropriate in a society geared toward social mobility.[5]

For ad makers like Ernest Elmo Calkins, advertising psychology only justified and elaborated on what they were already doing. If an ad had the "look," it would stop a reader from turning the page. For example, Calkins anticipated that depictions of attractive men in advertising could attract the attention of women, as evidenced in his ads for Arrow Collars and Shirts. In 1905, Calkins hired illustrator Joseph Leyendecker, known for *Saturday Evening Post* covers, to paint the first stylish young Arrow Collar Man surrounded by opulent possessions, instead of depicting the collar by itself. The Arrow Collar Man would set the standard for masculine looks and demeanor for almost twenty-five years; and when a new face appeared in the ads, women wrote thousands of letters to the model in care of Cluett Peabody & Company (figure 3.2).[6]

Finally, ad makers applied concepts of general psychology to how advertising works as means of communication. To provide a rough idea of consumer preferences for advertising appeals and types of media, mail-order testing emerged as the major research tool. One popular method used coded advertisements with slightly different addresses and ran coupons, which readers could cut out and return for information, product samples, booklets, or premiums. In test cities, identical ads appeared in different magazines and the results were compared, or *split runs* related different versions of the same ads in the same edition. From these studies agencies identified the best medium or media and appeals for advertising a given product.

After the general application of scientific research to basic business market problems, the concept that markets are measurable unfolded. By this time, many newspapers and magazines had already compiled lists of subscribers by different markets, and some even sent out questionnaires to them, with prizes to those who responded, asking them their occupations and what brands they bought. The measurement of these markets served to guide manufacturers, sales managers, advertising agencies, publishers, and others for whom understanding markets is important. Using methods derived from the survey movement in sociology, the analysis mainly consisted of

Figure 3.2. The stylish, young Arrow Collar Man as conceived by J. C. Leyendecker in 1913.

securing data by questionnaire—in other words, the market survey. These studies attempted to examine different dimensions of a society, such as inequality and class structure and changes in population size or type.

Perhaps the most comprehensive study in the service of reform was Paul Kellogg's *Pittsburgh Survey* of 1909–1914. Kellogg, editor of the New York–based journal *Charities and Commons*, some seventy social science investigators, a documentary photographer, and an artist collaborated to describe the urban conditions of the city of Pittsburgh, Pennsylvania, then considered America's prototypical industrial city. The Pittsburgh researchers first published their findings in *Collier's* magazine and later in a series of six books, which included *The Steel Workers*, *Homestead: The Households of a Mill Town*, and *Wage-Earning Pittsburgh*. The study found the city of Pittsburgh home to an exploited labor force, a degraded environment, and corrupt institutions. But the immigrants from eastern and southern Europe endured it not because they wanted to become Americans but because the majority viewed it as an opportunity to realize their life goal: to make enough money to move into the middle class of the *heimat*, the peasant society of their European villages.[7]

Although this information-gathering project became a classic of twentieth-century social history, it also provided marketers and advertisers new insights into working-class and immigrant life in industrial cities throughout the nation. Moreover, the Pittsburgh research served as a model for the systematic gathering, recording, and analyzing of data about the conditions of work and life in a region. When enough information was combined—on geographic, demographic, psychographic, and behavioral variables—it created a clear picture of a typical member of a group of customers (or market segment). With quantitative social science research as a model, advertising agencies employed commercial research firms in an attempt to put advertising on a more scientific basis and to assure clients that their money had been well spent on advertising in these areas.

Marketing and Advertising Research

Historians have generally marked the beginning of market research in America to around 1910 and have attributed the practice to Charles Coolidge Parlin. Initially, these studies focused on identifying distribution outlets. In 1911, for example, Parlin undertook *Commercial Research*, a 460-page investigation of the agricultural implement industry, which many consider the first formal marketing research study. Another early scientific market investigation was the 1912 study *Population and Its Distribution* published by the J. Walter

Thompson agency, the first book in which demographics from the census and economic data from the Curtis Publishing Company were related to advertising planning. It listed virtually every retail outlet by category and by state. These studies laid the foundation for market research.[8]

In the following decade, the theoretical foundation and a number of methods were worked out to analyze markets. One of the first writers to deal with the concept of market analysis was A. W. Shaw in 1916. Shaw believed that markets were made up of *strata*, or segments, distinguished by geographical distributions of customers, mental attitudes, climate, racial characteristics, density of population, and so on. Analysis of the market was made by careful consideration of these factors for the purpose of determining who bought where, how often they purchased, how much they were willing to spend, and the most effective media by which those consumers could be reached.[9]

Generally, marketers and agencies then determined which groups had the greatest buying power and market potential based on their income and whether they could afford the product. This method was used rather than segmenting the market in terms of both their income, occupation, and social standing in the community. For example, manufacturers of clothing, watches, talking machines, hand tools, and a long list of other products had long recognized the existence of market segments by putting out their products in two or more grades, according to Shaw. In their understanding of the consumer market, they specified five basic segments based on annual income, taste, and potential for spending: A level ($5,000 to $10,000 income per year), BB ($3,000 to $5,000), B ($2,000 to $3,000), C ($1,000 to $2,000), and D (less than $1,000). This classification continued to be used from the Progressive Era through World War II. "In most cases, advertisers catered to the comparatively fewer families in the upper BB and B brackets, even though by most calculations, the majority of Americans lived at best at the B level or above," explains historian Charles F. McGovern.[10]

Around the same time, scholars also published the results of their university investigations and experiments into the application of psychology to advertising. The work of Edward K. Strong at Columbia

University, G. L. Hollingworth at Columbia University, and Henry F. Adams at the University of Michigan typified scholars working in applied psychology. In 1911, for example, Strong published findings from a study to determine whether psychological tests could be employed to estimate the value of advertisements before they were actually used, investigating topics such as recall, recognition, comprehension, repetition, ad location, and the effects of different type styles and colors. He concluded that such an investigation would be valuable, citing the studies of Walter Dill Scott, Harlow Gale, and G. L. Hollingworth. In the same year Hollingworth also presented his scientific analyses to a weekly series of roundtable discussions with advertising men in New York City. The trade press reported similar forays, and occasionally an advertising textbook featured an entire chapter on psychology with references to "reason-why copy," "salesmanship in print," and "copy appeals."[11]

In the advertising industry, the J. Walter Thompson Company established the first formal research department within an American advertising agency. In 1916 the agency president, Stanley Resor, who was the first major agency executive with a college background, hired as director of research Paul T. Cherington, who had taught at Harvard Business School and served as editor of several business trade publications. For him, the real task of business was to understand buying motives since advertising was a means to bring together the article and the consumer. They rang doorbells, surveyed prospective customers, and worked as advertising solicitors, retail clerks in stores, or salespeople on the road to meet the buying public face-to-face. In addition to motivational studies, the agency also used scientific and medical findings as the basis for copy; and in 1920, John B. Watson, a psychologist, joined the agency to promote the application of behavioral theory to advertising. The agency also formed the Consumer Panel, composed of families whose buying habits were analyzed, and the findings were applied to advertising for clients. Finally, Resor hired a talent pool that included artists, writers, sociologists, scientists, lawyers, marketers, photographers, dress designers, home economists, and even technicians, all headquartered in elaborate New York City offices. As early as the mid-1920s, Resor proudly promoted a staff that included 105 college graduates, including five PhDs, reinforcing the claim to professional status. Thus, marketing research had begun to take hold as an attempt to put advertising on a more scientific basis.[12]

By the 1920s, the theory and practice of advertising had matured. General works on advertising appeared, integrating principles of marketing research and psychology that established the structure of thought for years to come. These works include Daniel Starch's *Principles of Advertising* (1923) and Otto Kleppner's *Advertising Procedure* (1925). In particular, Starch offered a method to measure the readership in advertisements that has basically remained unchanged since the book's publication, except for the changes that technology has brought in the techniques used to collect data. A basic assumption underlying Starch's recall measure studies is that the advertisement leaves a memory trace after a person has been exposed to it; similar assumptions apply to those studies conducted by Walter Dill Scott. He began the process by identifying a statistical sample of people who had read a particular magazine and he found stable results with sample sizes of approximately two hundred. The target audience for the magazine determined the gender of the reader and samples were collected from twenty to thirty different areas of the United States. Once a respondent was identified, an interviewer turned the pages of the magazine to assist recall, waiting for the respondent to indicate if he or she had seen the ad. If a respondent responded favorably, the interviewer probed the depth to which the respondent read the advertisement, recording scores for the ad itself, major visuals, and the advertisement signature. The tremendously successful book earned more income for Starch than his salary as professor at Harvard Business School, which gave him the impetus to form the Daniel Starch and Staff Research Company that specialized in studying magazine and newspaper circulation as well as the new media of radio.[13]

There also continued the social science quest to characterize *normal* American opinions and behavior—what we thought, what we believe, how we will vote, how we behave—which gradually gained acceptance as a more scientific way of knowing modern America. Eventually Hollingworth's intelligence studies filtered down to the trade and popular press. "What Is the Level of the Buyer's Intelligence?" asked *Advertising and Selling* in 1923. It reported that out of the great mass of the buyers in the United States, 110 million people had the mind of an adolescent. Still, there was only a relatively meager amount of information available on possible class differences between farmer and city dweller, laborer and capitalist, and other various social strata until the publication of Robert and Helen Lynd's *Middletown* studies. In the first 1924 study, the Lynds conducted an in-depth field study of the small urban center Muncie, Indiana, to study American culture and social change, and in 1935, they returned for a follow-up study during the Depression.[14]

Such interaction between surveys and those surveyed not only helped to culturally construct a mass society, but the wonderfully rich information gradually shaped the media and changed national advertisers' conceptions of consumers. The practice of segmentation using variables of gender, race, class, and lifestyle would continue to narrow and reflect news insight into consumer needs, especially their most important customer—the woman, who controlled the major share of household spending.

THE MASS MEDIA AND THE MASS MARKETS

As an industry, marketers were bent on bonding with women, and with good reason. Women handled from 80 to 85 percent of the forty billion dollars that went to make up the nation's retail sales, observed *Ladies' Home Journal* in 1929. Women bought food, household goods, clothing, beauty aids, and furnishings. On the whole, they also bought huge volumes of men's clothing, accessories, toiletries, and luxury goods for husbands, fathers, and sons; and what they did not buy, they influenced the purchase. Whatever they had to sell, it appeared that the mass marketers and retailers aimed their message at the American woman. During the decade, the total amount of advertising expenditures skyrocketed from $2.2 billion in 1919 to $3.4 billion in 1929; the food and beverage, drug and toilet goods, and automobile industries led the way. And in 1926, the volume of advertising in magazines for women's products alone totaled $61.5 million.

But advertising faced a different audience than it had known. Women enjoyed a far different role and prosperity than their grandmothers a half century before. Economic prosperity had extended to a large segment of the population. Women's wages now amounted to more than pin money or pocket change, and so families had extra money to spend on *wants* rather than just *needs*. By 1925 about 40 percent of the population earned a middle-class salary of $2,000 or more, and the number of women working outside the home reached 30 percent. Women made up half the financial community's employees and 90 percent of all clerks and typists. They also found new opportunities in the expanding mass-consumer goods industries, department stores, and service departments of magazines, as well as in new technologies, such as motion pictures and radio.

As American women changed, magazine editors helped marketers reconceptualize the women's market. By the 1920s there were well-developed advertising vehicles that addressed two levels of a highly stratified society. One was the upper and middle class who read *Vogue, Bazaar, Ladies' Home Journal,* and *Good Housekeeping* magazines; the second was the bottom two tiers, or the working class, who favored *McCall's, True Story,* or *Photoplay.* These *women's service magazines,* as they are now known, exerted a significant influence to reach the white female population, purporting to offer their readers a service in the form of fashion and homemaking advice. The increased volume of advertising also began to impact the publication's bottom line, and the influence of advertisers grew on the publications themselves. Eventually, manufacturers, retailers, and advertising agencies would directly influence the content of editorials, the choice of news features, and even magazine layouts.

With new insights into the average intelligence of Americans and class differences, many publishers and marketers now shifted their strategy to the broad market of young working-class women who had plenty of money to spend on products like clothing, cosmetics, and toiletries. Publishers then sought to develop new genres of publications that connected with the average American and also served as advertising vehicles defining this segment, or target market—tabloid newspapers, confession books, and fan magazines.

Following publication of the *Illustrated Daily News* in 1919, the tabloid newspaper quickly gained widespread circulation. Moreover, the concept of *tabloid copy for tabloid minds* gained credibility. Although smaller in size than normal newspapers, the lively tabloids had something for everyone—advice for the lovelorn, outrageous scandals, gruesome murders, and sensational stories. Photographs dominated the news presentations and left little to the imagination; the accompanying text provided fast-paced titillation. Thus, the term *tabloid audience* came to characterize the reading tastes of average men and women.[15]

Like the tabloids, a new genre of inexpensive pulp fiction called *confession magazines* also attracted a vast audience. One of the first was *True Story*, which Bernarr MacFadden launched in 1919. When the editors of MacFadden's *Physical Culture* health and science magazine had been flooded with unsolicited letters recounting intimate experiences, they decided to publish them as first-person confessional stories aimed at young workingwomen, offering dramatic personal accounts of tragic adventures, temptations, and romantic triangles, with such titles as "Perhaps It Should Be a Secret . . . But I'll Tell You How I Won a Husband," "I Thought My Home Was BARRED Against Her," and "Starved [for Affection]." The primary appeal of such periodicals was the intimate stories built around "a homely human interest situation," told in a first-person narrative style with short words and shorter sentences, and illustrated with compelling photographs. In addition to *True Story*, MacFadden went on to publish *True Romances*, *True Experiences*, and *True Mysteries*. By the late 1920s, this group of magazines along with *Physical Culture* built MacFadden a fortune of over $30 million (figures 3.3, 3.4).[16]

In response to the success of the tabloids and confession magazines, some of the high-grade publications changed their editorial formula to reach the "modern mind" and raise their circulation. Instead of the topics of suffrage, leisure, and culture, the editors shifted to articles with themes of happiness, marriage, and morals to fill glossy magazines—the high-grade publications intended for general family reading. Twenty years earlier, literary magazines such as *Scribner's* and *Harper's* featured genteel articles for the reader's betterment, such as

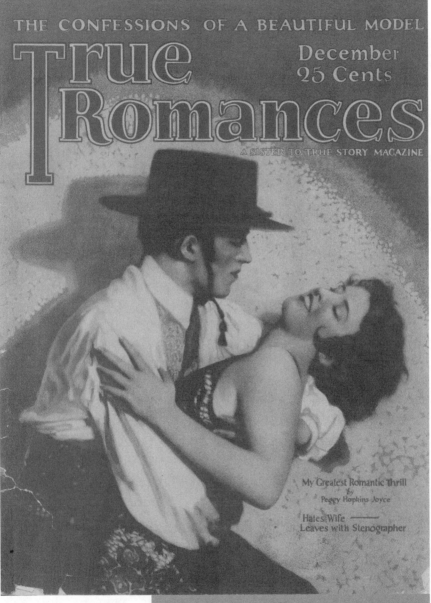

Figure 3.3. Cover of *True Romances* magazine,
December 1923.

Figure 3.4. "The Confessions of a Beautiful Model," a typical story in *True Romances*, December 1923.

"Indiana Idyll," "My Summer in Japan," "Leaves from a Flower Lover's Notebook," and "Little Old Miss Lavender." But by 1930, the sentimental tone had given way to an entirely different set of appeals to reach the "mass mind": "Psychiatry and the Confessional," "The Speakeasy as a Cultural Asset," "Must We Scrap the Family?" and "Moral Racketeering in the Movies." Even the *Saturday Evening Post* made similar changes to its editorial formula to be more accessible and reach a larger audience.[17]

Like the popular press, motion pictures and film magazines also reflected a similar emotional era but were preoccupied with sheiks, vamps, and sex goddesses. Movies with titles like "Cheap Kisses," "Soiled," and "Sinners in Silk" attracted large numbers of patrons. Films were often seen to be advocating values that were too different from the conservative, white middle class; for the working girl, the movie house offered recreation, sexuality, and social aspiration. Hollywood film stars embodied ideals of femininity and masculinity, which were presented to the nation through the movies and reinforced by a myriad of magazine articles, photographs, and advertisements featuring handsome models and pinup girls. Among them, one of first film magazines, *Photoplay*, was founded in 1911, followed by a similar magazine titled *Motion Picture Story*. These short-fiction magazines were concerned mostly with the plots and characters of the films at the time; they also were used as a promotional tool for those films. But it was the creation of *Photoplay*'s format by editors Julian Johnson and James Quirk that set a precedent for celebrity media that followed and was fueled by the public's ever-increasing interest in the private lives of celebrities.

Women readers often identified with *True Story* or *Photoplay*, which featured as a role model the virtuous working girl or the screen actress, in particular, women who had risen from the ranks of the poor, since they were not always content with emulating the practices of middle-class patrons or socialites. By 1926, *True Story* confession magazine reached a circulation of almost two million, a remarkable achievement considering that the mainstream *Saturday Evening Post* enjoyed a circulation of about three million in the mid-1930s. The popularity of these confession and fan magazines, tabloid newspapers, and Hollywood movies, in part, responded to women's sense of entitlement to sexual pleasure, at least within marriage, that was beginning to be recognized in the early twentieth century.[18]

Elaboration of Segments

The fiercely competitive periodicals now reclassified other consumer groups and shaped the editorial material to help marketers develop new markets. Even a woman's age and marital status had become significant segmenting factors. The female audience could be single, married, and even be children, as well as belonging to different social classes. By the mid-1920s, however, a distinctive children's consumer culture emerged that replicated many of the same class, racial, and gender stratifications of the wider American society. The demographics had shifted considerably, and magazine marketing began to target the child—white, urban, middle-class, and somewhere between the ages of nine and nineteen—as a consumer group, while working-class children drew little attention.

Before this time, advertising to children was quite limited and mostly done to imprint lasting impressions on future adult buyers. Advertisers had seen children as collectors with a great desire to accumulate, and they constituted a ripe market for the promotional material offered with a wide range of goods. Marketers also produced trade cards intended as paper dolls or puzzles with children's themes, issued booklets with nursery rhymes and moving pictures, and imprinted toys with trademarks. This broad shift in the conceptualization of the child consumer appeared in all forms and texts—in literature, advertising, art, advice columns, and industry trade presses.

Advertisers' interest in developing children's markets stemmed in part from the recognition that modern childhood itself had become organized around peer activities at schools and youth organizations such as the Boy Scouts, Girl Scouts, and the Camp Fire Girls, all of which published their own magazines supported by advertising. Reaching a predominantly white, middle- and upper-class juvenile audience, magazines like *St. Nicholas*, *American Boy*, *American Girl*, *Boys' Life*, and *Youth's Companion* enjoyed circulations that ranged from eighty thousand to five hundred thousand and attracted accounts for nationally advertised brand goods.

When national advertisers and merchants explored the possibility of directly selling to children and their influence on the purchase behavior of their parents, they also portrayed a consumerism that countered traditional visions of women. Because the realm of consumption was traditionally coded as female, advertisers took special care to associate consumer goods with manly enthusiasm for business endeavors, technological invocation, and modernity. Hence, they showed boys as connoisseurs, progressive and modernist consumers, who educated their whole families in taste and brand preferences. By contrast, national advertisers invoked stereotypical notions of the female consumer when addressing the adolescent girl. They also continued to project a mythical, middle America populated by white people.[19]

There were no so-called black products, services, features, or advertisements in the national magazines aimed at the white audience until well into the mid-twentieth century. In the South, for example, blacks could trade among themselves, but tensions from Jim

Crow laws during this time limited African Americans' efforts to sell to or buy from whites. Instead the national media remained completely segregated in terms of the general press—publications aimed at the general populace dominated by white Americans, and magazines aimed at African American readers. Among the most popular newspapers read by blacks, the *Chicago Defender*, the *Pittsburgh Courier*, the *Virginia Journal and Guide*, and the *Baltimore Afro-American* had a strong mass appeal. For the middle-class readers devoted to the "higher culture," the *Colored American* magazine brought the fashion columns of Madame Rumford, while *Half-Century* magazine modeled itself on *Ladies' Home Journal*.[20]

The first records of African Americans advertising to black consumers on a national scale do not appear until the early twentieth century. One of the most striking examples of such enterprise in the African American mass market can be found in the personal care field. In *Hope in a Jar*, Kathy Peiss writes of the black enterprises of Madam C. J. Walker, Poro, Overton Hygienic, and Kashmir Chemical, which conducted a nationwide business in soaps, cosmetics, and hair care systems. There were, of course, large white manufacturers also doing limited business with African Americans, but few mounted national advertising campaigns aimed at black consumers. Little would change until the civil rights movement in the 1950s and 1960s (see chapter 9).[21]

SELLING FASHION, COLOR, AND STYLE

When American manufacturers shifted away from the manufacture of capital goods to the production of new consumer goods in the 1920s, the sophistication of color, fashion, and style set these goods apart from prewar efforts. In this era, American manufacturers developed products for a clearly defined group of customers based not only on income but also on appeals to lifestyle and status. This concept would become known as a *marketing strategy*.

Automakers dominated this era of product styling. Perhaps no invention would change the pattern of American living more than the automobile. Roads improved, traffic lights appeared, painted lines marked parking spaces, and gasoline service stations popped up. Other urban rapid-transit systems such as trains, buses, and subways also kept Americans on the move. With this new mobility people could live in one town and work in another or travel to nearby cities for shopping and events. Although people had purchased autos for transportation, they now increasingly bought a car to reward themselves or impress their neighbors. To capture this market, Detroit-based General Motors, under chairman Alfred Sloane's leadership, advanced a three-point strategy to capture the mass marketplace, from farm boys to corporate executives: "A car for every purse and purpose" to appeal to every income and lifestyle of the mass market, and all available on the "convenient GMAC payment plan." This strategy distinctly linked social class with product development: you start with a Chevrolet, trade up to an Oldsmobile, and when you arrived—a Cadillac.

The idea that appearance might affect sales ripened into a styling strategy called *planned obsolescence.* Sloane wanted a production automobile that was as beautiful as the custom cars of the period, so he hired Harley Earl to execute the concept. GM's newly created Art and Color Section, under Earl's direction, emphasized styling and deluxe interiors and introduced colored body styles in a palette of Duco lacquer finishes for the 1927 Chevrolet (figure 3.5). From this division emerged the source of all the styling clichés that Americans came to take for granted: chrome, two-tone paint, tail fins, hardtops, wraparound windshields. To sell Americans on the necessity of owning an up-to-date car, ad makers glorified each annual model change so that owners became dissatisfied with their current model and purchased what appeared to be the superior car. For the first time, in 1928, a GM model—the stylish and colorful Chevrolet—outsold a Ford Model T, the nation's first choice for transportation ("It's available in any color you want, as long it is black"). Yet, how could people afford to buy an automobile, let alone a new model, every few years?

A combination of higher wages and the availability of credit increased the American consumer's ability to purchase new goods. Initially, only a few items like Singer sewing machines could be bought by installment payments, but that quickly changed. As early

CHEVROLET

The Most **Beautiful** CHEVROLET *in Chevrolet History*

Brilliant in their modish new colors—alluring in their distinguished smartness, the new Chevrolet models disclose that individuality and perfection of silhouette you would expect to find only in the costliest of custom-built creations.

One of the most revolutionary advancements ever made in the development of the low-priced motor car, the Most Beautiful Chevrolet introduces marvelous new bodies by Fisher with their beauty emphasized by bullet-type lamps and one-piece full-crown fenders. In addition, longer life and better operation are assured by a host of

mechanical improvements, including an oil filter and an air cleaner.

Thus, for the first time there are available at such low prices both that extraordinary ease of handling and that elusive something which women of discrimination have always demanded in a motor car.

Plan to visit the nearest Chevrolet dealer. There a single inspection will reveal how successfully the world's largest builder of gearshift automobiles is maintaining leadership with new models of delightful beauty and amazing value!

CHEVROLET MOTOR COMPANY, DETROIT, MICHIGAN
Division of General Motors Corporation

The Coach

QUALITY AT LOW COST

Figure 3.5. With "modish new colors," Chevrolet became America's choice for cars emphasizing styling and colors. *House and Garden*, February 1927.

as 1912 dealers offered to sell cars on credit, and soon it became commonplace to buy a new car, drive for thousands of miles, and then trade the car in for a newer model—without having fully paid for the old car. By 1925 dealers sold three-fourths of all cars on installment plans. Ever since, anxious shoppers have asked, "What's the monthly payment?" rather than "What does it cost?" By the end of the 1920s, vendors of home appliances, powerboats, and fur coats also trumpeted: "Enjoy now, pay later." As a result, Americans bought over 60 percent of their cars, radios, and furniture with some form of credit.[22]

GM's newly created Art and Color Section is also representative of a larger trend in selling color, fashion, and style. The design, or *the look*—such as color, line, and shape—took a central place in the manufacture of a vast range of merchandise. The style factor had affected the making of expensive jewelry, hats, dresses, inexpensive tableware and glassware, furniture, washing machines, automobiles, and other machine-made goods. But greater investment in merchandising also required specialized skills, so managers of fashion and style began to populate the field. By 1930, hardly an item was left untouched by them.

As the merchandising trend accelerated, agencies and consulting firms mushroomed to supply merchants with fashion resources and counsel to showcase the style factor. Display people and stylists grouped nearly everything into little units of merchandise accompanied by related goods to create an entirely different appeal to consumers and to promote impulsive ensemble buying. Now model rooms could be found in nearly every major department store, from kitchens to boudoirs. Merchants enlisted experts to make certain that there were close connections with the strategies for the advertising, window dressing, and store display of each department. Thus department stores mounted elaborate efforts to persuade consumers to follow their fashion lead, as advertisements, catalogs, magazines, fashion shows, and seasonal special events became early staples of department life. Street lighting in retail districts and extensive pre-Christmas parades for adults and children spread throughout the country, and since 1924 Macy's has given us a Thanksgiving Day parade, which both celebrates America and calls forth Christmas.[23]

For manufacturers, retailers, and merchandisers, changing fashions held the prospect of higher sales volume and larger profits, because the impression was forced on consumers that the last season's petticoat, costume, or hat was irretrievably out of date, thus creating demand for the business catering to the merchandise. This tremendous amount of activity opened up unprecedented new opportunities for women in the expanding mass-consumer goods industries, department stores, and service departments of magazines, as well as in new technologies, such as motion pictures and radio. But the tension between gender and professional identity and of achieving sexual equality challenged ad women to redefine the advertising field and create new solutions.

THE GENDERING OF THE PROFESSIONS

As women left the home for education and employment, what historians call "masculinization" in office work occurred. In almost every category of work, skills were divided into men's work and women's work. This limited women to subsidiary positions, and so different career tracks appeared. In the case of the teaching profession, women clustered in grade schools and high schools, while men dominated administration in such organizations as well as in universities. In social science and public careers, men became sociologists and research scientists, while women became social workers and psychologists in schools and welfare agencies. The "male" professions had more status and paid more than women's work. Women who had formerly worked as doctors and lawyers earlier in the nineteenth century now found themselves increasingly excluded by all the contrivances of professionalization, such as professional schools, licensing procedures, and trade organizations. "After 1910, discrimination had become a hallmark of the professions," explains historian Sharon H. Strom.[24]

Ad women who enjoyed, for a time, a range of opportunities in the advertising profession also found themselves barred from many new advertising clubs and trade organizations. Denied these vital sources of contacts, trade gossip, and networks, women started losing ground in the field. In response to their increasing exclusion from men's organizations, women defensively organized their own associations and took up reform. For example, the League of Advertising Women of New York encouraged other women to develop and utilize networks of women, followed by similar groups in Boston, Philadelphia, Chicago, St. Louis, and Los Angeles. Businesswomen also organized associations in the fashion trade, merchandising, and media. These groups, useful as expressions of solidarity and support, nonetheless further separated women in a separate but unequal arena of their own. Although the gender line had been firmly drawn in advertising clubs in major cities like New York and in national associations, local advertising in less prominent cities such as Hartford, Kansas City, Portland, and Fort Worth did welcome women to their programs.

These discriminatory practices existed alongside a social conservatism that influenced even social reformers. The opening of colleges to women had sparked heated controversy. By 1910, nearly 40 percent of all college students were women, and a decade later, the number increased to 47 percent of all students in four-year colleges. Advocates of women's education, like psychologist Leta Stetter Hollingworth, claimed that "women are competent intellectually as men are, to undertake any and all human vocations." But competence, intelligence, and dedication could get women only so far. Other progressive intellectuals feared higher education would encourage large numbers of women to leave the home for the workplace, causing a breakdown in the institutions of marriage and family. The possibility of coeducation led them to employ the prevailing theory that women were biologically inferior to men and could not withstand the rigors of scientific thought. Consequently, a significant number of women would find the doors closed to business education, training, and the experience required to move up into major positions until after World War II.[25]

Moreover, the process of professionalization had also changed the business curriculum at such schools as Ohio State University in the 1910s, which expanded from a handful of courses on distribution, credit, and salesmanship to a professional curriculum in the 1920s, including new courses in business communication, marketing, advertising, advertising practice, and research in marketing, among others. The traditionalists then used quota techniques to exclude the increasing number of college-bound women and minorities from obtaining the college-level degrees and advanced professional training beyond secretarial schools and liberal arts programs. When Columbia University started a full-time business program in 1913, for example, it clearly separated female students into a one-year clerical program and guided male students into the professional-degree curriculum that offered courses in distribution of product, commercial credit, and salesmanship. The Wharton School did not admit women until 1938, and for the next fifteen years, the Harvard School of Business Administration continued to bar women. Even when advertising became a subject in the curriculum at Harvard University, New York University, Boston University, Northwestern University, and the University of Missouri in the 1910s, women found themselves barred from these programs. Finally, the gender line in education became even more apparent in 1918, as the Commission on the Reorganization of Secondary Education recommended gender-based vocational education rather than a college-prep curriculum, requiring even young women who were college-bound to take domestic science or home economics and sending young men in another arena.[26]

Despite these obstacles, white middle-class women enrolled in business courses in large numbers through vocational business colleges, correspondence schools, and four-year coeducational institutions, though administrators and educators frequently steered them to take typing and stenography courses to qualify for work after they graduated. As a result, white middle-class women, especially the college-educated, found their aspirations for a high-paying executive position diffused and more readily accepted the emerging lower-level opportunities in business.[27]

A turning point came when new employment bureaus for college women began to appear in most major cities around 1910, which attempted to place women in professions other than teaching. From the perspective of educators and vocational advisers, advertising made a fine career choice. After all, they reasoned that most of the purchasing power of the world is with women, and who better to sell women? Similar to the educators' guidance, the bureaus also advised women that they should start on the clerical side in an advertising department of a manufacturer, in an agency, or on a publication. As early as 1911, the Women's Educational and Industrial Union of Boston bureau published promotional material with titles like "Advertising as a Vocation for Women."[28]

Among the new employment bureaus, the "Intercollegiate Bureau of Occupations" emerged as one of the most influential of the new employment bureaus for college women. The New York alumnae of the "Seven Sisters" colleges—Mount Holyoke, Vassar, Smith, Bryn Mawr, Barnard, Wellesley, and Radcliffe—plus those of Cornell formed the employment bureau in 1911, which provided up-to-date information on appropriate careers for women and how they could obtain training. The bureau later codified a broad list of appropriate occupations for women in the "Classified List of Vocations for Trained Women" (1917), including nine office jobs in advertising as follows: Advertising Artists, Advertising Managers, Clerks, Copywriters, Proofreaders, Research Workers, Secretaries, Solicitors, and Statisticians. As for salary, an experienced advertising manager could expect to earn far more than the average man in the skilled trades.[29]

When the United States entered World War I in 1917, advertising fell into step with the war effort, creating opportunities for women to participate in fostering patriotism, selling bonds, and recruiting soldiers. Wartime employment shortages also opened up lower-level managerial jobs and administrative positions in government and business, bringing many women to employment outside the home for the first time. After the national crisis had abated, however, many of those women chose to keep their jobs or, if fired to make way for returning soldiers, sought employment elsewhere. Still, most women found themselves closed out of upper management, where hostility to women and the feminine continued to persist. Since discrimination guaranteed a large pool of capable, educated women who could be hired as secretaries, research assistants, and clerks and enabled firms to keep wages relatively low, the practice may have contributed to the gendering of the office labor force.[30]

ADVERTISING PROFESSION IN THE INTERWAR PERIOD

After women won the constitutional right to vote in 1919, the suffrage movement scattered, as they went to work on a variety of different issues from child labor protection to world peace. Progressive as they may have been in their own time, the women of the previous generation were still rooted in the values of social purity that condemned the behavior of a new generation. For these women, life essentially remained the same: they cooked, cleaned, raised families, and managed households.

On the other hand, a new generation of women questioned the conservative attitudes of the mothers of the suffrage movement, the *Old Feminists* as they were known in the 1920s. In their zeal, legions of young women asserted themselves by their dress, their dancing, and their romances. The central figure was the *flapper*, then a term interchangeable with the *New Woman, New Feminist*, or *New Girl*. This modern woman posed a challenge to gender roles; women strongly believed that they should now strive for feminist goals other than economic independence. That desire included developing a different morality and tradition of feminism, one in which all persons had the right to pleasure, love, and care, as well as economic independence. And so they made it clear in many ways that they wanted the same freedoms that men enjoyed both at home and in the workplace.

When the expanding mass-consumer industries generated new job opportunities for women, college-educated women increasingly moved into the advertising profession and came together to create women's departments, programs to educate women, and women's organizations during the interwar period. This was in part a defensive response to their exclusion from traditional male professions and networks. A 1924 survey of forty-seven New York agencies reported that experienced ad women accounted for 10 percent of the specialized positions beyond clerical, secretarial, and stenographic work. Beginners with no previous work experience could enter the field as reception clerks, telephone operators, and file clerks who hoped to advance to *checkers*—workers who confirmed the appearance of insertions ordered in magazines and newspapers. A checker, once familiar with accounts and copy of the agency, could advance to the media or space-buying department or field research doing statistical work. With regard to research and investigation, some agencies found that women could more easily gain entrée into homes for house-to-house investigations, chat with women about domestic problems, and get them to open up. Thus, those college graduates who entered in the media department for advancement to space buyer or assistant copywriter might advance to copywriter or account executive. Those with special knowledge of engraving or printing might enter into mechanical production.[31]

When college women found their opportunities for advancement limited in advertising agency work, they capitalized on their experience from executive and semi-executive positions to advance into copywriting or publicity in other mass-consumer industries that offered more opportunities. After they gained more business background, some returned to agency work at a more mature age with a wider background, often at increased salaries with more opportunities.

There were successful women at New York agencies, such as Lillian Eichler Watson, a Ruthrauff and Ryan copywriter who sold over one million copies of her best-selling *The Book of Etiquette* (1921). Dorothy Barstow, backed by Florence Richards and Margaret Jessup, created campaigns for Pacific ("Twenty-Mule Team") Borax and Cheseborough's Vaseline at McCann-Erickson in New York. At Blackman (later Compton Advertising in New York), Mary Shomier, assisted by a group of women, created campaigns for Ivory Soap, Crisco, and other brands for Procter & Gamble. Laura Hobson joined George Batten Company (latter BBDO) to write copy for the American Greeting Card Association. In Chicago, Berta Hendrick worked at Blackett-Sample, while Tracy Samuels and Mary Lasker Foreman were at Lord & Thomas (though Foreman had forced her way into her father Albert Lasker's agency against his wishes at a pittance of eight dollars a week). Dorothy Dignam wrote for Chicago-based Vanderhoof and Company as well as for McJunkin Advertising Company before she joined N. W. Ayer in Philadelphia. And in St. Louis, Erma Proetz of the Gardner Agency created a Pet Milk test kitchen, developed recipes, and created advertising campaigns. Her work won the famed Harvard Award in 1924 and 1925 for the most effective illustration in advertising, and in 1927, for the best planned and executed national advertising campaign (figure 3.6).

Other women found doors to advancement in agencies closed to them and entered into the vast segments of the trade: the staffs of retail and local advertisers, the space buyers and media representatives, agency personnel engaged in research, creating or gaining approval for advertising content, as well as mail-order advertising,

Figure 3.6. Erma Proetz's award-winning campaign for Pet Milk appeared in *Ladies' Home Journal*, May 1927.

industrial advertising directed at businesses, and domestic science experts working with businesses. Ad women also went on to edit top women's magazines and home journals or worked as editors of the service departments, where they assisted manufacturers and advertisers in conducting market research and determining style trends. At this time, Mabel Hill, a copywriter from N. W. Ayer, started her own agency in New York, in partnership with Harry Winston, sales manager of Wooltex. Later, as Mabel Hill Souvaine, she became editor-in-chief of *Woman's Day*. Elizabeth Woody joined the copy department of the George Batten Company, and, some years later she went on to become an editor of *McCall's* magazine. An even larger number of women worked in local agencies and the advertising staffs of manufacturers, wholesalers, or mail-order firms. Others earned five-figure incomes, extravagant sums at the time, including Beatrice Hastings, who earned $25,000 or more per year in commissions soliciting ads for a dry goods trade paper. As these ad women circulated from post to post, they expanded their influence and strengthened the foundation of women's institutions.[32]

For all appearances, progressive educators, industry professionals, and ad women themselves had succeeded in delivering a rosy message to women: advertising was a place for women of ability to succeed, albeit circumscribed, and their entering wedge was the woman's viewpoint.

NOTES

1. "What Is the Level of the Buyer's Intelligence?" *Advertising & Selling*, September 26, 1923, p. 26. John Carson, "Army, Alpha, Army Brass, and the Search for Army Intelligence," *Isis* 84 (1993): 278–309. See also Sarah E. Igo, *The Averaged American: Surveys, Citizens, and the Making of a Mass Public* (Cambridge, MA: Harvard University Press, 2007).

2. Typical of the principles of advertising textbooks in the 1920s, the introduction to Daniel Starch's textbook sums up the broad problems of advertising in business. See Daniel Starch, *Principles of Advertising* (Boston: Harvard University Press, 1923).

3. Works by Walter Dill Scott: *Psychology of Advertising* (Boston: Small, Maynard, 1908) and *Influencing Men in Business* (New York: Ronald Press, 1911). See also Daniel

Starch, *Advertising: Its Principles, Practices, and Techniques* (Chicago: Scott, Foresman, 1914).

4. Works by Claude Hopkins: *Scientific Advertising* (1923; repr., Lincolnwood, IL: National Textbook, 1987) and *My Life in Scientific Advertising* (1927; repr., Lincolnwood, IL: National Textbook, 1987).

5. Although men were open to class appeals, it was essentially a feminine appeal. "The natural instinct of women makes them study the dress and appointment of those they admire or envy and either imitate or strive to surpass and excel them," explained one advertising manager. See *Printers' Ink*, July 12, 1912, p. 64.

6. Ernest Elmo Calkins and Ralph Holden, *Modern Advertising* (New York: D. Appleton & Company, 1905). Calkins, *The Business of Advertising* (New York: D. Appleton & Company, 1925).

7. Eva Morawska, "From Myth to Reality," in *Pittsburgh Surveyed: Social Science and Social Reform in the Early Twentieth Century* by Maurine W. Greenwald and Margo Anderson (Pittsburgh: University of Pittsburgh Press, 1996).

8. Robert Bartels, *The History of Marketing Thought* (University of Missouri, 1976), originally published by Richard D. Irwin as *The Development of Marketing Thought* in 1962.

9. A. W. Shaw, *Approach to Business Problems* (Cambridge, MA: Harvard University Press, 1916), p. 225.

10. Charles F. McGovern, *Sold American: Consumption and Citizenship, 1890–1944* (Chapel Hill: University of North Carolina Press, 2006).

11. Representative articles, include "Advertising and Psychology," *Printers' Ink*, March 2, 1904. "Advertising to the Mind," *Judicious Advertising*, October 1906; "Suggestion as Power in Advertising," in *Profitable Advertising*, September 1907; and "Psychology and the Market," *Advertising and Selling*, December 1909. Representative textbooks include Paul T. Cherington, *Advertising as a Business Force* (New York: Doubleday Page & Co., 1913).

12. Stephen Fox, *The Mirror Makers: A History of American Advertising and Its Creators* (New York: Vintage Books), p. 84.

13. Otto Kleppner, *Advertising Procedure* (New York: Prentice Hall, 1925). E. K. Strong, *The Psychology of Advertising and Selling* (New York: McGraw-Hill, 1925). See also Albert T. Poffenberger's *Psychology in Advertising* (Chicago and New York: A. W. Shaw, 1925). Daniel Starch, *Principles of Advertising* (Chicago: A. W. Shaw, 1923).

14. "What Is the Level of the Buyer's Intelligence?" *Advertising & Selling*, September 26, 1923. Sarah E. Igo, *The Averaged American*. Robert Lynd and Helen Lynd, *Middletown: A Study in American Culture* (New York: Harcourt, Brace & Company, 1929). Lynd and Lynd, *Middletown in Transition: A Study in Cultural Conflicts* (New York: Harcourt, Brace & Company, 1937).

15. Roland Marchand, *Advertising the American Dream: Making Way for Modernity, 1920–1940* (Berkeley: University of California Press, 1985), pp. 52–61.

16. Born Bernard Adolphus McFadden, he later changed his name to Bernarr MacFadden. "The True Story of Bernarr McFadden," *American Heritage Magazine*, no. 1, December 1981, p. 33.

17. On *Scribner's* and *Harper's*, see "General Talk on Copy," J. Walter Thompson Company Staff Meetings, September 30, 1930, Minutes of Representatives, p. 7, box

3, J. Walter Thompson Company, Hartman Center for Marketing, Sales, and Advertising History, in the Rare Book, Manuscript, and Special Collections Library, Duke University, hereafter JWT. On *Saturday Evening Post*, see "Fourth of a Series of Talks on Copy," J. Walter Thompson Company, February 7, 1931, Minutes of Representatives, p. 10, box 3, JWT.

18. Amy Janello and Brennon Jones, *The American Magazine* (New York: HNA, 1991), p. 62. Circulation: *True Story* advertisement in *Printers' Ink*, May 2, 1929.

19. Lisa Jacobson, "Manly Boys and Enterprising Dreamers: Business Ideology and the Construction of the Boy Consumer, 1910–1930," *Enterprise and Society* 2 (2001): 225–58. See also Lisa Jacobson, *Raising Consumers: Children and the American Mass Market in the Early Twentieth Century* (New York: Columbia University Press, 2004).

20. Black newspapers: Henry Lewis Suggs, *The Black Press in the South, 1865–1979* (Westport, CT: Greenwood Press, 1983); Armistead S. Pride and Clint C. Wilson, *A History of the Black Press* (Washington, DC: Howard University Press, 1987).

21. Juliet E. K. Walker, *The History of Black Business in America* (New York: Macmillan, 1998), especially chapter 7, "Golden Age of Black Business, 1900–1930," pp. 184–224.

22. H. J. Bass et al., *America and Americans*, vol. 2 (Morristown, NJ: Silver Burdett), p. 63.

23. Macy's did not originate the Thanksgiving Day parade. For years, Gimbels in Philadelphia and Eaton's Department Store in Toronto had been moving in this direction for years. William R. Leach, *Land of Desire: Merchants, Power, and the Rise of a New American Culture* (New York: Vintage Books, 1984), pp. 331–38.

24. Sharon Hartman Strom, *Beyond the Typewriter: Gender, Class, and the Origins of Modern Office Work* (Urbana: University of Illinois Press, 1992), p. 327. See also Virginia G. Drachman, *Sisters-in-Law* (Cambridge, MA: Harvard University Press, 1998). Penina Migdal Glazer and Miriam Slater, *Unequal Colleagues* (New Brunswick, NJ: Rutgers University Press, 1987). Angel Kwolek-Folland, *Incorporating Women: A History of Women and Business in the United States* (New York: Palgrave, 2002), pp. 84–127.

25. "Is Woman Biologically Barred from Success?" *New York Times Magazine*, September 19, 1915. Women Position and Progress Collection, box 1, folder 1, Sophia Smith Collection.

26. Higher education: Willis J. Winn, *Business Education in the United States* (New York: Newcomen Society, 1964). June B. Schmidt, *Chronology of Business Education in the U.S.* (Reston, VA: National Business Education Association, 1990). Thurman W. Van Metre, *A History of the Graduate School of Business, Columbia University* (New York: Columbia University Press, 1954). Secondary education: Sarah Stage and Virginia B. Vincenti, eds., *Rethinking Home Economics: Women and the History of a Profession* (Ithaca, NY: Cornell University Press, 1997), pp. 87–88.

27. On the history of the business profession, see Strom, *Beyond the Typewriter*, pp. 63–108. See also Virginia Drachman, *Sisters-in-Law*; Glazer and Slater, *Unequal Colleagues*; and Kwolek-Folland, *Incorporating Women*, pp. 84–127.

28. "Advertising as a Vocation for Women," booklet (1911), box 1, folder 9, B-8, Women's Educational and Industrial Union of Boston Papers, Schlesinger Library.

29. "Advertising as a Vocation for Women," pamphlet (1911), and "Business Advertising," Women in Industry Lecture no. 12, January 1916, Intercollegiate Bureau of Occupations, Bureau of Vocational Information Records, 1908–1932, reel 1, Sophia Smith Collection. On salary of average man in skilled trades, see "What Is the Level of the Buyer's Intelligence?"

30. Angel Kwolek-Folland argues that the growth of the financial and banking industries rested on the same dynamics that reshaped nineteenth-century manufacturing and the need for industry leaders to keep wages low. This appears to be the same case for the advertising industry. Kwolek-Folland, *Engendering Business: Men and Women in the Corporate Office, 1870–1930* (Baltimore: Johns Hopkins University Press, 1998), p. 20.

31. "Women in Advertising in New York Agencies," Young Women's Christian Association in the City of New York Study, 1924, Women's History Collection, Employment, box 20, folder: Advertising Booklet, Sophia Smith Collection.

32. "Women Wage Earners with Five Figure Incomes," *New York Herald Magazines and Books*, February 6, 1921, pp. 7–10, Advertising Women of New York Collection, volume 4, Manuscripts and Archives, State Historical Society of Wisconsin, Madison, Wisconsin. For profiles of twelve other women, see "Women Who Have Made a Success in the Busy Field of Advertising," *New Success*, vol. 4, September 1920, in Advertising Women of New York Collection, State Historical Society of Wisconsin.

CHAPTER 4

THE BUSINESS OF FEMININITY

SELLING MRS. CONSUMER

"The proper study of mankind is man," declared *Printers' Ink* in 1929, echoing Alexander Pope, but the proper study of markets is woman. This singular recognition of the importance of Mrs. Consumer resulted in not only agencies but in other mass-consumer industries hiring a new ensemble of business-women—product designers, merchandisers, fashion and beauty experts, editors, publicists, and home economists—to promote their goods aimed at the women's market. To "cash in on the women's sphere," manufacturers emphasized color, fashion, and style, while advertising embraced a new language of persuasion. Through close collaboration with magazine publishers, mass media, and retailers, they successfully wove mass commerce in consumer goods into women's reading, shopping, housework, and leisure activities—the web of women's daily lives and minds. Thus this "business of femininity," as *Fortune* magazine called it in 1935, intensified women's connection to consumer culture and the mass-market industries.[1]

The second generation of the New Woman came to the fore of advertising in this era and proved their value by advancing, with some ambivalence, the woman's viewpoint in the new mass-market industries and services. These women were educated and flourished professionally in the years immediately before and after World War I and, just as a more self-conscious notion of the woman consumer took hold, they sought to negotiate and even redefine what it meant to be a modern woman in a consumer society. They placed emphasis on self-fulfillment, less on societal service, and a great deal more on the flamboyant presentation of self than had their predecessors. Moving easily within the bohemian world of Paris to New York City, they strived to appear as successful and political as men.

Among the most prominent national figures in the 1910s and 1920s were copywriter Helen Lansdowne Resor, account executive Helen Woodward, and home efficiency expert Christine McCaffey Frederick. They knew that their place in an industry dominated by men rested on the authority of female consumers. They understood how to appeal to other women, how to convey that the advertised products would make them more beautiful and well liked, and that housekeeping was the greatest business in the world. In their private lives, they balanced marriage with career. These women set the standard and nourished the image of the successful new ad woman.

HELEN WOODWARD:
COPYWRITER, ACCOUNT EXECUTIVE, AND CRITIC

During the Progressive Era, Helen Rosen Woodward exemplified a pocket of ad women who campaigned for needed reforms in the advertising industry. Woodward made a name for herself at the Frank Presbrey Agency as one of the first female copywriters and as the first female account executive at a major agency, working in advertising for over twenty years before her retirement at the age of forty-two in 1925. She was one of the highest-paid women in advertising at the time.

When Woodward was nineteen in 1901, she began to look for a job. She could read French and Latin, had excellent math skills, and learned quickly. But she found that these assets did not make an inexperienced job seeker highly valuable. "I went through nine of the most heart-breaking months that a woman could experience," recalled Woodward. Her first two jobs, as a bookkeeper and a librarian, ended abruptly, and later she took a job demonstrating type-writers. When the routine of addressing envelopes became unbear-able, Woodward secured a job with the Merrill and Baker agency, which advertised books and household furnishings. For the next eighteen months, Woodward moved beyond stenographic work to writing advertising, as well as managing the mail subscription depart-ment. When poor management caused the agency to close, Woodward began working for the Hampton advertising agency but found herself in the wrong position, one similar to a modern-day traffic manager—a coordinator for all the jobs in progress to ensure deadlines are met. Although her six weeks at Hampton were a "disaster among chaos," her experience there convinced her that she wanted to be a copy-writer and earn a higher wage.[2]

Still only twenty-one, Woodward moved on to the J. A. Hill Com-pany, a mail-order publishing house, as an assistant to advertising manager W. E. Woodward, whom she married many years later. At the Hill Company, she wrote advertising as well as managed a staff that wrote and mailed promotional material about books. For mail-order advertising, Woodward perfected a persuasive, heroic style inspired by the writings of Rudyard Kipling and prospered by selling beautiful editions of classics by authors such as Robert Louis Stevenson, O. Henry, and Alexander Dumas. Using what seemed an unimportant device at the time, she gave a brief outline of the story to arouse the reader's curiosity of how it ended (figure 4.1). She also wrote adver-tising for *Review of Reviews* that sold hundreds of thousands of sets of the Brady Civil War photographs and later for Robert Lanier's elabo-rate series *The History of the Civil War.*

During her spare time, Woodward did freelance work as well as work for the *Woman's Home Companion,* overseeing the sales of sub-scriptions through women's clubs; she later started one for *Pictorial Review.* Although literary writing came easily, Woodward found her-self twisting her prose to construct a more overwritten and senti-mental style aimed at the women's market. First, she tried to imitate the editorial columns of *Woman's Home Companion,* but it was too

Die, Thou Villain!

He had thought of being a great Indian Chief, or a soldier—but the biggest idea of all had come to him. He would be a Pirate! ¶ Now his future lay before him. His name would fill the world and make people shudder. And, at the zenith of his fame, how he would suddenly appear at the old village and stalk into church, brown and weather-beaten, in his black velvet doublet and trunks, his great jack-boots, his crimson sash, his belt bristling with horse-pistols, his crime-rusted cutlass at his side, his slouch hat with waving plumes, his black flag unfurled, with the skull and crossbones on it! His career was determined.

Remember the days when you dreamt of being a Pirate?—When you thought you would be a black avenger of the Spanish Main? ¶ Get back the glamour of that splendid joyousness of youth. Read once more of Tom Sawyer, the best loved boy in the world; of Huck, that precious little rascal; of all the small folks and the grown folks that made Mark Twain so dear to the hearts of men and women and boys and girls in every civilized country on the face of the globe.

MARK TWAIN

Out of the generous West came Mark Twain, giving widely and freely to the world such laughter as men had never seen.

There seems to be no end to the things that Mark Twain could do well. When he wrote history, it was a kind of history unlike any other except in its accuracy. When he wrote books of travel, it was an event. He did many things—stories, novels, travel, history, essays, humor—but behind each was the force of the great, earnest, powerful personality that dominated his time, so that even then he was known all over the face of the globe. Simple, unassuming, democratic, he was welcomed by kings, he was loved by plain people.

If foreign nations love him, we in this country give him first place in our hearts. The home without Mark Twain is not an American home.

The Centennial Half-Price Sale Must Close

Mark Twain wanted these books in the hands of all the people. He wanted us to make good-looking, substantial books, that every man could afford to own. So we made this set, and there has been a tremendous sale on it.

HARPER & BROTHERS
Franklin Sq.,N.Y.

Send me, all charges prepaid, a set of Mark Twain's works in 25 volumes, illustrated, bound in handsome green cloth, stamped in gold, gold tops, untrimmed edges. If not satisfactory I will return them at your expense. Otherwise I will send you $1.00 within 5 days and $2.00 a month for 12 months, thus getting the benefit of your half-price sale. World's Work 6-17

But Mark Twain could not foresee that the price of paper, the price of ink, the price of cloth, would all go up. It is impossible to continue the long sale. It should have closed before this.

Because this is the one-hundredth anniversary of the founding of Harper & Brothers, we have decided to continue this half-price sale while the present supply lasts. Get your set now while the price is low.

Send the coupon today before the present edition is all gone.

Name..........................

Address.......................

10% added to price in Canada because of duty

Harper&Brothers
1817-1917
Franklin Square
NewYork

Figure 4.1. This 1917 ad for a collection of fiction by Mark Twain sells the stories themselves.

gentle and soft, while words were used too loosely: "Ideas slide off, slip away, and disappear," as she put it. In advertisements, however, every word counted when thousands of dollars were paid for one magazine ad to run one time only. So she tried writing the sample advertisement in the same manner as the book copy. "Then sentence by sentence, word by word, I softened it, sweetened it, made it sticky with sugar," explains Woodward. "Whenever I thought it was needed, I stuck in a *cute* word."[3]

In 1912 Woodward had also picked up freelance work for the Heinz food account, a client of the Frank Presbrey Agency. Heinz liked her work so much that the agency hired her as a full-time copywriter. Woodward drew on her *Woman's Home Companion* experience, touching on the fears and joys of motherhood to sell baby food and appetizing presentations of food. This now-obvious approach was a novel idea at the time. She also used powerful emotional appeals to advertise insurance, showing a weeping widow with children or a bandaged man in a hospital bed. But ads emphasizing the benefit rather than the disadvantages of owning an insurance policy pulled the best response, like those featuring images of a couple happily receiving a check from an insurance company with a burning house in the background. Such ads for Aetna Life Insurance and Hartford Fire Insurance Company were keyed and couponed to track what copy approach pulled the best. Woodward continued to work happily until 1915.

That year, Woodward decided that she could earn more money on commission than on salary, while still enjoying full responsibility for an account. She proposed to work for the usual 5 percent commission paid to all salesmen who wrote their own copy, and she would write the copy on any account that she brought into the agency. But her proposal was a fairly radical move at the time. The vice president at the Frank Presbrey Agency flatly turned her down: "It isn't businesslike. It isn't dignified to have a woman working on commission." Firms generally excluded women from "contact" or "outside job positions that required face-to-face interaction with manufacturers' representatives." Eventually, the agency allowed Woodward to work on a percentage basis. She found three aspects of this new contract fascinating: "One was this independence; another the sense of risk; the third, a feeling of responsibility," recalled Woodward. "No longer would I hesitate to take long vacations, to go to California or Europe, or come to the office only two or three days in the summer. When a little while later, I was married, this freedom became even more useful."[4]

At first Woodward made only a hundred dollars a week, but she felt more independent than men in the organization who made two to three times the amount. Initially, she worked on advertising books and magazines sold to men. Only later did she manage to get women's accounts—curtains, stockings, fabrics, cosmetics, and perfumes—as men gradually came to see that articles used by women should be advertised by women. For Woodward, writing these ads came easily, as she wrote from her own experience: "When a man wants to write an advertisement about cold cream, first he has to ask his wife and sister-in-law and cousin and stenographer what she does with cold cream and how and when and why, while a woman sits down and writes freely and from the heart about beauty."[5]

Nevertheless, the profession eventually spoiled Woodward's rosy attitudes and made her an outspoken critic of advertising. In 1924, Woodward retired and went to Paris to write her autobiography, *Through Many Windows*. She followed up with other critiques of the industry from within the business, including *Three Flights Up* (1935) and *It's An Art* (1938): "There was no standard of honesty" in the advertising business, according to Woodward, who specifically criticized claims within food, cigarette, beauty product, and medicinal advertisements. "If you were able to put over a trick on the public you did it." She also wrote *The Lady Persuaders* (1960), a critique and historical overview of the creators of women's magazines, describing how advertisers strongly influence the content of magazines.[6]

Paradoxically, successful ad women like Woodward could express a sense of superiority as snobbish as any male dogma. In *Through Many Windows*, for example, she reinforces nineteenth-century notions of women as the naturally inferior sex and as being as difficult to work with as men. From her perspective, women have enough of "some quality different from other people" to make them difficult. "No woman should be at work in the stimulating atmosphere of an office during the first two days of her monthly disposition [menstrual cycle]. No matter how equable she may be ordinarily, or how strong, she is at that time likely to be nervous and depressed." Furthermore, Woodward claims that a woman is "proceeding on the theory that sex is sin and so she is neurotic." Finally, her life is further complicated with responsibilities for housekeeping, no matter how simple, and childcare. Even feminist Jane J. Martin believed women would never achieve equality with men in the business world, because they preferred marriage to a vocation. "A large percentage of women in business are there because of an economic necessity, and you will find true that most business men who object to women, object because they figure she is an economic loss," noted Martin in 1915.[7]

Although ad women like Martin and Woodward may have chafed at being the target themselves of sales pitches based on the prevailing views of gender, they and many other women shrewdly carved out a niche in the consumer mass-market industry, consciously and unconsciously exploited the prevailing ideals of femininity, and refashioned their identity as professionals working in the masculine world of business. These contradictions are even more apparent in the work of Helen Lansdowne Resor, who repackaged age-old stereotypes that women are emotional and projected these images in the national media.

HELEN LANSDOWNE RESOR:
COPYWRITER, THE J. WALTER THOMPSON AGENCY

Copywriter Helen Lansdowne Resor played a signal role in changing advertising to women and was instrumental in opening the advertising profession to women. Over four decades, she and her husband, Stanley Resor, built the J. Walter Thompson Company (JWT) into an advertising powerhouse. During their tenure, the agency grew from a few offices in the states and fewer than one hundred people to a worldwide staff of over seven thousand in twenty-three countries and $360 million in billings, making it an industry leader in total billings.

In everything she did, Lansdowne was committed to women's rights. Her own mother taught her an early lesson in feminism and the importance of self-reliance, which provides some insight into Lansdowne's later focus on a career and redefined what it meant to be a modern woman. When Lansdowne was four years, her mother divorced and moved her nine children to Covington, Kentucky, where she supported the family selling real estate and insurance while working as a librarian. In 1903, Lansdowne graduated from high school as class valedictorian. After a brief assignment auditing bills at Procter & Collier Agency in Cincinnati, she moved on to write retail ads, and in 1906, she worked for a nationally prominent, streetcar-advertising firm. In 1907, Stanley Resor, who had been hired as a Procter & Collier salesman three years earlier, persuaded her to return to the agency as a copywriter. When Resor and his brother Walter later opened the J. Walter Thompson Cincinnati office in 1908, they hired Lansdowne as the agency's first copywriter. Three years later, Lansdowne was promoted and followed the Resors to the New York headquarters.[8]

Lansdowne became the first woman to successfully plan and write national advertising campaigns rather than just working in retail. Her landmark Woodbury Facial Soap campaign first appeared near the end of a major transition in American marketing in 1911, but its fundamental principles closely resemble a modern one. In shaping the sales messages, Lansdowne made assumptions about the gendered nature of the audience and added the essential emotional appeal to the rational sales argument. Once the audience for the facial soap was determined to be women, Lansdowne planned the advertising to initially appear exclusively in the important women's magazines with large national circulation to reach a white middle- and upper-class audience. Lansdowne knew too well that one of American women's fantasies was a man's complete attention and adoration, which she embodied in the selling message and image. The ad featured a painting of an attractive couple and a provocative headline that invited the audience to read further: "A skin you love to touch." Below, the copy outlined a skin-care regimen and closed with an offer for a week's supply of soap, plus the art from the advertisement. Instead of merely selling soap, the ad also discussed the benefits of using the product, suggesting softness, sex appeal, and even romance. Later ads informed women that they, too, could have beautiful skin, even if their skin was colorless, coarse, or excessively oily; each problem could be solved with the Woodbury treatment. Each ad displayed different illustrations of men adoring women (figure 4.2). In this way, sex could sell a lot of soap. Sales of the Woodbury line skyrocketed over fivefold in a five-year period, from $515,000 in 1915 to $2.58 million in 1920.[9]

Lansdowne's work on the Woodbury campaign may also be understood as part of the broader movement of agencies using market investigations, insights from psychology, and copy testing to put advertising on a more scientific basis. On the creative side, Lansdowne developed an "editorial style" look to her ads that resembled adjacent reading material and attracted readers' attention. A typical ad featured an arresting image followed by selling copy that provided specific reasons to purchase the product; the ad closed with a coupon offering free or inexpensive product samples or booklets by mail. Moreover, her words and visuals embraced women's hopes, fears, desires, and dreams regardless of what they did for a living. She then

Figure 4.2. Sex could sell a lot of soap. Woodbury's Facial Soap advertisement, illustrator Neysa Moran McMein, *Ladies' Home Journal*, 1917.

built the advertising around provocative arguments for improving oneself and how to emulate the habits of richer people. This proved much more effective than simply emphasizing practicality and price. In addition to the Woodbury campaign, Lansdowne's distinct editorial style is also evident in her work on Crisco, Cutex nail products, Yuban Coffee, and Maxwell House Coffee. In part, the effectiveness of such ads was the promise. Trust me, the ads would say, in effect, and you will have your heart's desire. "I added the feminine point of view," Lansdowne explained. "I watched the advertising so that the idea, the wording, and the illustrating were effective for women."[10]

In 1916 a group headed by Stanley Resor bought out the retiring J. Walter Thompson agency, and Resor became president. The following year Resor and Lansdowne wed. Together they ran the agency —he concentrated on administration, while Lansdowne tended to the preparation of ads and raising three children. The other part of the creative revolution at the Thompson agency was James Webb Young, who had succeeded Lansdowne as copywriter at the JWT Cincinnati office in 1912. While in New York he met his old hometown acquaintance Lansdowne, who was then working as a JWT copywriter. Upon hearing that Young was moving to the Midwest, she suggested he call her husband, Stanley Resor, who persuaded him to come to work for the JWT Cincinnati office. In 1917, Young became the creative head in the New York office, and eleven years later in 1928, he left to open the JWT branch offices in Germany, Italy, and Egypt, among others.

Just as women advanced the feminine viewpoint, Young's work complicates the prevailing notion that a woman was more qualified than a man to write women-centered copy. As the *pattern-maker*, Young created the first ad, or series of ads, that would set the theme and style for a campaign, and others would then carry out the work under his editing. For Libby, McNeill & Libby canned goods, for example, Young not only wrote copy that appealed to women, but he also wrote *as* the voice of the first "Mary Hale Martin," the fictitious spokeswoman who instructed housewives on what they could do with the food in Libby cans through advertisements, brochures, and company correspondence.

Young also took on the delicate task of selling deodorant, a product that most women thought unnecessary. In those days, women met the problem with rubberized dress shields, which were unpleasant things. By advertising Odorono deodorant, Young exploited another essential emotive appeal—women's fear of social disgrace. By heightening social concerns about offensive body odor, he penned one of advertising's most famous headlines in 1919: "Within the Curve of Women's Arm" followed by a subhead that read: "A frank discussion of a subject too often avoided" (figure 4.3). The ad featured a picture of a man and a woman about to embrace in a moonlit garden, but the copy suggested that the woman had reason to feel insecure. She could be suffering from the "personal handicap" of excessive perspiration without even knowing it. "Anyone who had sat next to Little Eva after her dancing would have smelled out the reason for such copy," explained Young. With this sensational advertisement, Young repositioned Odorono from a proprietary medicine to a beauty aid, enhancing any woman's charms. So powerful was this image that sales of the product more than doubled—and some two hundred readers of the *Ladies' Home Journal* canceled subscriptions in outrage over the "indelicacy" of the advertisement. Before long, many other ads followed with this "your best friend won't tell you" theme.[11]

The Women's Editorial Department

Perhaps Lansdowne's greatest contribution to the field of advertising was her opening up the profession to women. Both Lansdowne and her husband believed that the growth of advertising relied on female consumers. To position JWT as a specialist in selling products to a women's market, or what would later be called *gender-based marketing*, the agency employed more women in creative positions than any other agency at the time. These female executives controlled most of the agency's prestigious soap, food, drug, and toiletry accounts. In 1918, the copy written by the Women's Editorial Department accounted for $2.26 million of the company's $3.90 million billings.[12]

Under Lansdowne's leadership, the Women's Editorial Department specialized in products sold to women. Lansdowne hired, trained, and mothered a group of largely white, middle- and upper-class ad women,

There isn't a girl who can't have the irresistible, appealing loveliness of perfect daintiness

Within the Curve of a Woman's Arm
A frank discussion of a subject too often avoided

A woman's arm! Poets have sung of its grace; artists have painted its beauty.

It should be the daintiest, sweetest thing in the world. And yet, unfortunately, it isn't, always.

There's an old offender in this quest for perfect daintiness—an offender of which we ourselves may be ever so unconscious, but which is just as truly present.

Shall we discuss it frankly?

Many a woman who says, "No, I am never annoyed by perspiration," does not know the facts—does not realize how much sweeter and daintier she would be if she were *entirely* free from it.

Of course, we aren't to blame because nature has so made us that the perspiration glands under the arms are more active than anywhere else. Nor are we to blame because the perspiration which occurs under the arm does not evaporate as readily as from other parts of the body. The curve of the arm and the constant wearing of clothing have made normal evaporation there impossible.

Would you be absolutely sure of your daintiness?

It is the chemicals of the body, not uncleanliness, that cause odor. And even though there is no active perspiration—no apparent moisture—there may be under the arms an odor unnoticed by ourselves, but distinctly noticeable to others. For it is a physiological fact that persons troubled with perspiration odor seldom can detect it themselves.

Fastidious women who want to be absolutely sure of their daintiness have found that they could not trust to their own consciousness; they have felt the need of a toilet water which would insure them against any of this kind of underarm unpleasantness, either moisture or odor.

To meet this need, a physician formulated Odorono—a perfectly harmless and delightful toilet water. With particular women Odorono has become a toilet necessity which they use regularly two or three times a week.

So simple, so easy, so sweet

No matter how much the perspiration glands may be excited by exertion, nervousness, or weather conditions, Odorono will keep your underarms always sweet and naturally dry. You then can dismiss all anxiety as to your freshness, your perfect daintiness.

The right time to use Odorono is at night before retiring. Pat it on the underarms with a bit of absorbent cotton, only two or three times a

week. Then a little talcum dusted on and you can forget all about that worst of all embarrassments—perspiration odor or moisture. Daily baths do not lessen the effect of Odorono at all.

Does excessive perspiration ruin your prettiest dresses?

Are you one of the many women who are troubled with excessive perspiration, which ruins all your prettiest blouses and dresses? To endure this condition is so unnecessary! Why, you need *never* spoil a dress with perspiration! For this severer trouble Odorono is just as effective as it is for the more subtle form of perspiration annoyance. Try it tonight and notice how exquisitely fresh and sweet you will feel.

If you are troubled in any unusual way or have had any difficulty in finding relief, let us help you solve your problem. We shall be so glad to do so. Address Ruth Miller, The Odorono Co., 719 Blair Avenue, Cincinnati, Ohio.

At all toilet counters in the United States and Canada, 60c and $1.00. Trial size, 30c. By mail postpaid if your dealer hasn't it.

> Dr. Lewis B. Allyn, head of the famous Westfield Laboratories, Westfield, Massachusetts, says:
>
> "*Experimental and practical tests show that Odorono is harmless, economical and effective when employed as directed, and will injure neither the skin nor the health.*"

Address mail orders or requests as follows:
For Canada to The Arthur Sales Co., 61 Adelaide St., East, Toronto, Ont. For France to The Agencie Américaine, 38 Avenue de l'Opéra, Paris. For Switzerland to The Agencie Américaine, 17 Boulevard Helvetique, Geneve. For England to The American Drug Supply Co., 6 Northumberland Ave., London, W. C. 2. For Mexico to H. E. Gerber & Cia., 2a Gante, 19, Mexico City; For U. S. A. to The Odorono Co., 719 Blair Avenue, Cincinnati, Ohio.

Figure 4.3. This 1919 Odorono ad so outraged some two hundred *Ladies' Home Journal* readers that they canceled their subscriptions over the "indelicacy" of the topic.

as opposed to a bullpen of male copywriters. Among this creative female staff, women held degrees from Smith, Barnard, Vassar, the University of Chicago, Wellesley, and Columbia. In fact, many of these women writers later became famous in their own right: Aminta Casseres, Peggy King, Frances Maule, and Nancy Stephenson, to name a few. Ruth Waldo, who later held Lansdowne's position managing the Women's Editorial Department in 1929, went on to become the first female vice president at JWT in 1940.[13]

For many of these women, a career in advertising combined their experience in writing, in organizing reform activities, and in promotion of various causes. Work by Jennifer Scanlon on the JWT Women's Editorial Department demonstrates that these women belonged to the Suffrage League, Consumers League, National Women's Party, and the League of Women Voters. Women like Eleanor Taylor, for example, entered JWT with an impressive background as a social worker in the United States Children's Bureau in Washington, publicist for the National Women's Party, and editor of the *Suffragist*. For the same magazine, another feminist, Therese Olzendam, worked as a typesetter and power press operator as well as a circulation manager. And in Maule's personnel file, Lansdowne wrote a note that recommended her for hire, highlighting her suffrage activities.[14] Also an ardent feminist, Lansdowne most likely understood suffragists like Maule, who used "color and dash" to sell their cause and produced spectacular campaigns in large urban centers. "They mastered the modern means of advertising, publicity, mass production, commercial entertainment, commercial design, retailing, and publishing," explains Margaret Finnegan. "They put up billboards and colorful posters; they created artful window displays, they produced movies, pageants, and plays; they hawked suffrage wares through special stores and catalogs."[15]

During the interwar era, the work of this cadre of women writers did more than any other advertising effort to shape the image of the female consumer in national advertising and advance what would become key tenets of normative femininity. Interestingly, Scanlon points out that these female ad writers of the 1910s and 1920s, many of them college graduates and feminists, could hardly be called representative of the *average woman* whom they wrote for, largely the married women at home. For the most part in 1930, the median annual salary of all women at Thompson was $2,200, including those with a college degree. This mirrored the average salary of $1,900 earned by women with a college degree. But some of the Thompson women writers remained single, or if divorced, never remarried; others made their lives with other women. The Thompson agency had also come to similar conclusions about the differences between the writers and their audience: They rarely went to church, infrequently went to Coney Island or similar resorts, never lived at or below the national income, and most employed domestics. Certainly the Thompson writers were not representative of the "average" woman and housewife pictured, "happily waxing her floor in the Wizard mop advertisements," concludes Scanlon.[16]

This was a sensitive matter. The new advertising called for intimacy with consumers, seeing the product from their viewpoint, and imaginatively portraying how it fit into their lives. Certainly Helen Lansdowne Resor assumed that the Thompson female writers, who specialized in selling products to women, shared a common knowledge and appreciation for women, regardless of class, ethnicity, or other differences. From her perspective, effective advertising had to be "made with knowledge of the habits of women, their methods of reasoning, and their prejudices." Ironically, Lansdowne and the ad women had seemingly distanced themselves from consumers by emphasizing their intelligence, training, and the importance of scientific market research over their intuition in gaining insight into the "unformulated ideas" of housewives—their impulses, prejudices, desires.[17]

These differences in class and education occasionally surfaced in descriptions of their work and conveyed a degree of condescension toward the "composite woman." For instance, copywriter Dorothy Dwight Townsend wrote an article titled "Mrs. Wilkins Reads the *Ladies' Home Journal*," in which she describes the typical reader as being far removed from the world pictured in the advertisements. Mrs. Wilkins had put aside two hours that evening to go through a portion of the magazine but saved the fiction to enjoy later. There were the articles, the fashions, and now the pages of advertising began:

> Here was a shopping trip through new and endless department stores but with no tired feet and no embarrassment when you looked too long in the cases and the saleslady asked, "Can I help you?" She looked in at homes she would never dare to enter; studied the get-up of women she never dared stare at in the city. Such smart women—in such beautiful homes—they did things with such an air.[18]

The progressive ad women could claim that educating women like Mrs. Wilkins in how pleasurable it might be to consume tied in with reform rhetoric and the missionary spirit. Women spent a great deal of money and needed professional guidance to spend it well. In selling a product, ad women could educate people in the knowledge of the comforts and conveniences of life, to speed up and eliminate drudgery, and to raise standards of living.

A good case in point is the Women's Editorial Department's work on the advertising of the relatively new product canned milk, introduced by Libby, McNeill & Libby. To encourage women to use more of the product, Libby suggested delicious uses of this milk with recipes in the advertising, explained Lois Ardery, a Thompson writer. Women might not want canned goods or packaged meats, but advertising was telling the "The Woman Who Never Went Out" that she spent too much time setting the table, and she could prepare delicious meals with their products and still have time for other interests—for tea parties, luncheons, and movies with her husband, stopping for a sundae on the way just as they had done when they were engaged. Ardery reasoned that women had certain known wants, and in particular, "certain vulnerable points of appeal—vanity, appetite, economy, health. But women have also another set of wants—unexpressed and unrecognized even by them. *Inarticulate longings!*" A woman may not always be able to express just what she wants, "but she is quite likely to know it when she sees it!"[19]

Despite the enormous efforts made to understand the habits and thoughts of women through scientific research, each copywriter brought her own observations of prevailing attitudes, notions of artistic expression, and interpretation of market investigations. Some well-intentioned ad women like Frances Maule, a veteran of the feminist movement, struggled to envision the "New Woman" and challenged popular clichés of women. In her article "The Woman Appeal," also in one of Thompson's bulletins published for clients, she argued against stereotyping female consumers. She also criticized advertisers for relying too much on the "the good old conventional 'angel-idiot' conception of women, and she urged them to remember the old suffrage slogan—that Women are People." Maule added that "it is just as impossible to pick out a single feminine type and call it 'woman,' as it is to pick out a single masculine type and call it 'man.'"[20]

Instead of one mass market, Maule recognized a variety of women's experiences in modern society, each responding to different appeals: (1) housewives concerned with a well-stocked and well-run home; (2) society women oriented to fashion and leisure, the chief purchaser of fashion, cosmetics, toiletries, and other luxuries; (3) a new class of women interested in the politics of consumption; and (4) the workingwomen, an ever-growing class with an entirely different set of needs, looking for fashion and style at a reasonable price. In trying to broaden the women's market, ironically, Maule created other composites or stereotypes of the female consumer as one who is "susceptible to the atmosphere, the sentiment, the prestige that we throw around our copy."[21]

On another frequently debated topic, Maule had long held that some men could be qualified to conceive of women-centered copy as empathetically as a woman. Thus Maule assumed that the male copywriter had accurately observed women, had the faculty to understand the needs of other people, and had the ability to record his thoughts and observations in words that "glow and live." For Maule, men's background or experience was salient. "If a boy has been around his mother's kitchen from his earliest years, has wiped the dishes for her and set the table, and run errands for the soup ladle, the dish mop, the carpet-sweeper," she writes, "he will have as good a background for writing copy on household things as women with similar training." But most boys didn't have this background or experience, whereas nearly all girls did; they could hardly escape it. Still, practically "every normal woman" has an innate, instinctive sympathy for the needs of the home and of children that cause her to think more deeply on these subjects than do most men.[22]

Though the JWT women were liberated, even by today's standards, they did not have equality. Although the Thompson agency was not unique in hiring women, it organized its copywriters in a separate department, perpetuating the nineteenth-century pattern of separate spheres. Copy styles, accounts, and even the office space were all rigidly segregated by gender. Women's presence immediately raised the issue of how these sexually and socially different workers would be assimilated into an urban office, the male-defined area of business, without upsetting canons of respectability. By separating workers, mandating an open-door policy, and even controlling their personal times such as lunch hours, the agency could remove the possibility of encounters, or at least put them under management's control without elaborate methods. When Barnard graduate Louise Fox came to JWT in 1916, for example, women worked from 8:30 to 5:30 and were allowed half an hour at lunchtime, and some also worked a half-day on Saturday. But women were not allowed in the dining room at the same times as men. "We hardly knew the men at all although the men were right there, the men's copy department," explained Fox. "Only a wall then separated the men's and women's copy groups, but they couldn't look at each other when you're sitting down."[23]

Such gendered workplaces and space practices were fairly common at the time. Department stores, hotels, and banks had separate entrances and facilities for women. Financial offices set men and women workers apart, showing an enormous concern for unbridled sexuality as frequently discussed in the prescriptive literature. Yet management's desire to segregate the sexes, not only in work areas but also during private times like lunch hours, further complicates the issue. It set men and women workers apart in ways that both reflected and justified the distinctions created by salary differentials and gendered work assignments. In the case of Fox, who worked on larger national accounts like Pyrex and Cutex, the agency paid her less than her counterparts in the men's copy department. But Fox did not consider it "suffering," she explains. "I just thought, 'That's a woman's life.'"[24]

Business travel posed other challenges for professional women. When JWT sent Fox and Richard Connell, also a writer for the agency, to survey what Ohio subscribers of the *Christian Herald* thought about the magazine in 1916, Connell could not understand why the company sent two young people who were neither related nor married to stay at hotels together. Fearing disapproval from the conservative magazine readers, Connell said, "I want you called my sister," and he called himself "Reverend Doctor Cornell" when visiting the subscribers. Despite the barriers, they developed more than a working relationship and married two years later, an event Fox called "my greatest achievement."[25]

Nevertheless, there were two jobs women did not do at JWT or many other agencies. Women were neither art directors nor account representatives at major agencies, and few women broke the barriers that kept them from the vice presidency. Lansdowne became a stockholder and the director of JWT in 1924, but she never held the title of vice president. She seldom sought publicity; she gave no speeches and authored no books or articles. Rarely photographed, she turned down numerous requests for interviews by many magazines and newspaper syndicates, and seldom attended industry meetings. Lansdowne also made it clear that she was not part of the agency; rather, she was just a contributor. "But there was a very deliberate thing of keeping her in the background, by him and her," explained Samuel Meek in 1963, head of JWT international relations, "believe me this was a strong policy by—hers too, and his too." Three years after her death in 1967, Lansdowne was honored for her copywriting and elected one of the first women to the Advertising Hall of Fame.[26]

YELLOW WRITING AND PERSONALITY ADVERTISING

The 1920s marked a new high point when mass-produced images in glossy magazines and Hollywood film distinctly and powerfully began to influence men's and, especially, women's self-conception, as they compared themselves to the ideals of beauty, masculinity, and femininity considered desirable at a particular point in time. In order to reach this new audience, the Women's Editorial Department experimented with a wide variety of formulaic advertisements that relied on an intimate, personal style to connect with women's hidden desires to be sought after and well liked and to join the successful middle class. They tested placement of the ads in both the new confession magazines as well as the higher-grade periodicals.

The creative strategy depended on the product being advertised, explains JWT copywriter Edith Lewis in 1923. First, one can place the emotional emphasis on the product itself, as in food, furniture, fashion, and vacation trips, which have in themselves a strong emotional appeal. It is also possible to dramatize the product itself, making it alone seem attractive and desirable, as is done with commonplace articles like rubber boots, kitchen utensils, or household tools. But there are other products that are less likely to appeal to the imagination, such as soaps. The differences between such products, however real, are so intangible that it is difficult to impress anyone with their importance. So the ad maker has to create a situation outside the product to arouse an emotional appeal, such as fear, appetite, humor, love of luxury, desire for economy, and so forth. It is this third type of advertising, where the emotional emphasis relies on some outside situation, that is generally thought of as *emotional writing*, or what has been called *yellow writing*—suggesting the sensational and scandalous news coverage that masqueraded as factual reporting in the late nineteenth century.[27]

Although advertising often gave readers reasons to purchase the product, yellow writing or emotive ads strongly dramatized the social disadvantages of not using the advertised product and the social incentives for using it. Provided the story was well done, the ad women reasoned that people going through the magazines were looking for entertainment in the form of a short story; and so a short, powerful narrative with characters whom readers want to know about would reveal something worth knowing. Lansdowne also added dramatic photographs to the campaigns by signing Edward Steichen, recognized as one of the greatest photographers of the time, as well as Cecil Beaton and Yousef Karsh. Looking at the whole range of advertisements in this era, there are five formulaic ad approaches under which a majority of these ads can be subsumed, which I term: Melodrama, Friendly Adviser, Modern Testimonial, Tabloid Technique, and Celebrity Endorsement.

Melodrama. With the Odorono deodorant campaign as a pattern, the Thompson writers refined a melodramatic style often called *scare*, or *whisper copy*, that incorporated appeals to fear, emphasizing the negative consequence if the consumer would not change a behavior or attitude. Previously, ad makers had used fear-based appeals to address legitimate concerns such as disease, germs, loss of health, or safety issues, while they based others on irrational fears such as the fear of social disgrace or shame. When the ad makers switched from factual copy to incorporate the enormously popular narratives of *True Story* and *True Romances* magazines, they kept copy short, personalized, and intimate, emphasizing romance, tragic adventures, and other dramatic accounts rather than reality.

For example, Woodbury's facial soap ads shifted from an educational approach to reminding women that they were endlessly on display in the 1920s. Caring for one's appearance, ad writers claimed, was part of a larger commitment to women's self-expression and dignity. In a world peopled by spectators, even the most intimate moments were all made visible to the reader, a kiss between two lovers, a scene in the boudoir: "His unspoken thoughts when he looks into your face—what are they?" or "All around you people are judging you silently." The cumulative effect likely reinforced readers' impression of being surrounded by a host of accusing eyes and unspoken comments, leaving them feeling guilty and anxious, worrying about how their friends and acquaintances perceived their personal appearance. Not even the prettiest clothes, charm of manner, or highest character could counteract the first impression of neglect and carelessness about their appearance. By using the product, so goes the melodrama formula, one could not only change her look but also remake herself and her life chances.[28]

Friendly Adviser. The Thompson agency had also found the use of experts, or what Stanley Resor called *personalities*, proved an important element of fostering warmth and a more personal touch. Not a new idea, the face of Lydia Pinkham on her Vegetable Compound package had effectively worked for decades, while more recently Ruth Knox's recipes for Knox Gelatine also proved successful. But the fictitious *Betty Crocker*, invented by General Mills in 1921, has since provided a model for other sponsors to combine instruction with the long promotion of particular products in both print and broadcast advertising (figure 4.4). But not until the 1930s would women be specifically targeted as radio listeners.[29]

With these spokeswomen as a model, the Women's Editorial Department experimented with the creation of a caring friend, the fictitious friendly adviser who spoke to readers with chatty "write-me columns" to promote products. Among them, Libby canned products presented *Mary Hale Martin*, Odorono deodorant featured *Ruth Miller*, Lux Soap Flakes offered helpful advice from *Marjorie Mills*, and Lux Toilet Soap used chatty confidante *Dorothy Dix*. And readers did respond. They wrote for advice, returned coupons, and purchased the promoted products, and the agency measured their responses through sales, personal letters, and coupons. The enormous returns from print advertising convinced the agency that readers wanted a more intimate connection with the manufacturer. Ultimately, the Women's Editorial Department found consumers responded to not only friendly advisers

Figure 4.4. As American society changed, General Mills updated Betty Crocker's portrait to reflect contemporary women, from 1936 to 1986. Since her creation in 1921, Betty Crocker has provided tips, meal plans, and products to American families. *Betty Crocker®* is a registered trademark of General Mills and is used with permission.

but also to other personalities—prominent people, authority figures, and celebrities.[30]

The Modern Testimonial. As early as 1914, JWT took endorsement advertising to another level by persuading well-known and respected women, from actresses to socialites to European royalty, to back the product in advertising. In magazines, advertisements for Pond's vanishing cream and cold cream prominently displayed photographs of actresses, such as Elsie Janis, Frances Start, and Anna Pavlova, among others, who affirmed that it was Pond's that allowed them to maintain the "purity and clearness of the skin." The gentle-selling copy invited other women to discover for themselves "why it is used by more women on the stage than any other cream," with the promise that they, too, could obtain the same effect the actresses so marvelously attained.[31] What distinguished this Pond's campaign from those of its competitor was the way it used celebrity testimonials to reach a broad, middle-class market through the ad's presence in the *Ladies' Home Journal* and *Woman's Home Companion*, as well as the "class" magazines such as *Vogue* that targeted society women. But it would be the Pond's campaign of 1924 that sparked a testimonial craze.

Pond's ads mirrored the beauty editorials features, but they now included *talks*, or interviews with American reformers, socialites, and debutantes on skin care. Alva Belmont, a well-known suffragist who bankrolled the National Women's Party, appeared in Pond's first testimonial, her cooperation secured through Frances Maule's circle of feminist friends. Following Belmont, other prominent women in the world of politics and society appeared in the ads throughout the 1920s and 1930s, including Alice Roosevelt Longworth, Washington hostess and daughter of Theodore Roosevelt, and Mrs. Reginald Vanderbilt. When Belmont agreed to the interview for the endorsement, however, she refused to allow her photograph to appear. Where her portrait would have been was a picture of her library, "an incongruous image for the sale of a beauty preparation," concludes historian Kathy Peiss. "This singular effort to showcase distinguished and newsworthy women was undermined from the start, however, by the need to project an 'image of status and prestige' in order to improve Pond's rank relative to expensive treatment lines."[32]

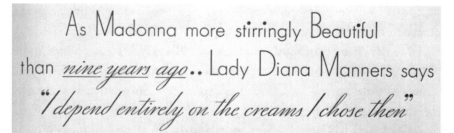

As Madonna more stirringly Beautiful than *nine years ago* .. Lady Diana Manners says *"I depend entirely on the creams I chose then"*

In 1924

Lady Diana Manners, when she first appeared in "The Miracle." Famed as the most beautiful woman of English aristocracy, Lady Diana said: "I know that every woman can effectively accomplish loveliness by using Pond's Two Creams."

Today

Loving audiences are again spellbound by the still beauty, more moving than ever, of Lady Diana Manners, now Lady Diana Duff-Cooper, as she plays the famous rôle of Madonna in the recent London revival of "The Miracle."

"CONTRARY to common belief, women on the stage seek the simplest methods to care for the skin." Lady Diana Duff-Cooper speaks with disarming British candor.

"After all," she declares, "good care of your skin consists only in cleaning it thoroughly with a pure cream, and always protecting it."

That surprises you. As you look at the exquisite loveliness of Lady Diana's complexion, you imagine that she uses many secret and expensive formulas for beauty.

Uses Just Two Creams

"It was in America when I first opened in 'The Miracle' that I discovered Pond's Two Creams. From that time on I have been positively devoted to them.

"I use Pond's Cold Cream constantly (day and night and always after exposure) to cleanse my skin—and it removes make-up perfectly! Also when one's face feels tired a generous patting of Pond's Cold Cream revives and stimulates it.

"And the Vanishing Cream is a hope fulfilled. I should feel lost without it! It is such a glorious foundation for cosmetics. And never do I expose my skin in any climate without first smoothing it on. It is the most enchanting, most protective cream I have ever known. I am always preaching its wonderful efficacy."

Lady Diana Manners adds: "I am delighted with Pond's new Face Powder. Almost unbelievable . . . so exquisite a powder at so moderate a price!"

Lady Diana Manners uses Pond's Cold Cream —To cleanse the skin thoroughly of all foreign particles after every exposure.

"To remove all traces of cosmetics from face and lips."

She uses Pond's Vanishing Cream: "Always as a foundation for make-up. It's simply perfect and holds the powder like nothing else."

"Before every sport and every exposure.

"To smooth chapped and roughened skin if I have been careless.

"Almost every day to keep my hands and arms soft and white."

Pond's Famous Creams and New Face Powder

Many titled Englishwomen use and praise Pond's simple way to beauty. Among them:
The Marchioness of Carisbrooke
The Lady Louis Mountbatten
The Countess Howe
The Lady Violet Astor
Lady Georgiana Curzon

Send 10¢ (to cover cost of postage and packing) for choice of free samples

POND'S EXTRACT COMPANY, Dept. D
107 Hudson Street   New York City
Please send me (check choice): Pond's New Face Powder
in attractive jar, Light Cream ☐ Rose Cream ☐
Brunette ☐ Naturelle ☐
OR Pond's Two Creams, Tissues and Freshener ☐

Name _____

Street _____

City _____ State _____
Copyright, 1933, Pond's Extract Company

TUNE IN on Pond's program every Friday, 9:30 P. M., E. S. T. . . . Leo Reisman and his Orchestra . . . WEAF and NBC Network

Figure 4.5. Pond's Cold Cream campaign used celebrity testimonials to reach a broad middle-class market, 1933.

Nevertheless, the Thompson agency increasingly turned to younger, more beautiful women. In 1925, Thompson's advertising research had shown that the American public preferred European royalty and titled nobility to prominent American socialites, with Princess Marie de Bourbon well on the top. Given this bias for titled Europeans, advertisers set them before the general public as models and advisers not only in *Vogue* for the high-society women but also in *True Story* for the working-class readers (figure 4.5). The Women's Editorial Department concluded that women readers preferred glimpses of the rich to reflections of their own lives. The wealth these people enjoyed, the ads pointed out, enabled them to choose products without regard to their price; their lineage gave them "instinctive" discerning taste; and they were always the first to recognize products of quality. When a woman uses the cold cream of that cosmopolitan grand lady, when she sleeps on the same mattress used by a duchess, she identifies herself with these exalted personages.[33]

Indeed, the powerful appeal to emulation, or the desire to be like others, especially those who occupy an envied position socially or financially, emerged as another one of the great buying forces—what Thompson writer Aminta Casseres called the *snob appeal*: "Snobbery is one of the sweetest, deepest vices of women" (figure 4.6). In fact, Maule went so far as to say that the copying of this character does more. "In the lingo of the psycho-analysts, it ministers to his 'inferiority complex.'" Whether people knew it or not, they were suffering from a sense of "unimportance, insignificance, inadequacy," and a large part of their energies were directed toward making themselves feel important, significant, equal to anything. "This is the 'grand and glorious feeling' which we are seeking all the time," explained Maule.[34]

Figure 4.6. Aminta Casseres, copywriter, J. Walter Thompson Company, from *Printers' Ink*, August 1926.

The Tabloid Technique. The advertising for Fleischmann's Yeast is another variation of how Lansdowne's editorial style imitated the look of the tabloid newspaper and endorsements to give the selling message credibility. Typical of this genre, a bold headline opened the story; the text was broken into four or five sections, each of which had illustrations and dramatic photographs and invited readers to browse the page. The technique can be seen clearly in the agency's work to promote Fleischmann's Yeast as a bountiful source of vitamins and a remedy for acne, constipation, blemished skin, and other ills. Although the American Medical Association warned against professional endorsements of any commercial products with such dubious claims, the Thompson agency found doctors in Europe who would say just about anything about Fleischmann's Yeast for five hundred dollars. Hence, the reading public was offered an endless series of pictures of European physicians from 1928 to 1936 (figure 4.7).

Celebrity Endorsements. Perhaps more than anything else, Hollywood offered the creative department endless possibilities to reach Mrs. Jones, the typical woman buyer with visions of love, romance, riches, and glitter. For her, the movies provided a change from the day-to-day troubles of life. She could imagine herself as glamorous Greta Garbo, and handsome men like Gary Cooper fell in love with her. And through the movies, she also could visit the homes of the wealthy, where the husband is immaculately groomed, children are all charming, and the women wear smart clothes. Thompson copywriters like Mildred Holmes agreed that advertising could be most effective when it makes the best use of glamour, she wrote in 1929. "For imagination is the swiftest approach to the emotions and the emotions are more powerful persuaders than logic."[35]

The Lux Toilet Soap "Hollywood campaign" exemplified this turn to glamour. To promote Lux, Thompson had set up elaborate machinery to make sure Hollywood studios and actresses received a supply of the soap at regular intervals, and they then signed up unknown actresses hankering for publicity. If they became famous, they appeared in Lux ads at no further expense. In 1928, the famous slogan "9 out of 10 Screen Stars Care for Their Skin with Lux Toilet Soap" ran as a headline. However, movies stars like Joan Crawford ("Never have I had anything like it for keeping the skin smooth"), Janet Gaynor ("Lux Soap has a caressing quality"), Clara Bow, and others only appeared to endorse the

University of Brussels, where
Dr. Mayer is professor

Why I have prescribed yeast for 25 years

by

DR. LEOPOLD MAYER

Belgium's Great Surgeon

DR. LEOPOLD MAYER

Knight of the Order of Leopold and of the Legion of Honor; Officer, Order of the Crown of Italy; Professor, University of Brussels; Secretary-General, International Society of Surgery; Editor-in-chief, Brussels Medical Journal; Corresponding Member, Belgium Royal Academy of Medicine; Correspondent, National Society of Surgery, Paris and Rome.

"By reason of its absolute harmlessness, yeast is a remedy of first rank and its wealth of Vitamin B makes it a food of great value. For more than 25 years I have found yeast advantageous in my practice to regulate the digestion of my patients, especially of those affected with chronic intestinal trouble or with biliousness."

[signature]

MANY among the exclusive aristocracy of Belgium are patients of Dr. Leopold Mayer of Brussels. Doctors and surgeons throughout the world know him for his scientific writings.

Like thousands of physicians in America, Dr. Mayer finds constipation one of the great handicaps to health.

For 25 years, Dr. Mayer states, he has given his patients yeast. And, in a recent survey in the United States, half the doctors reporting said they prescribed yeast for constipation and its attendant ills.

This is the welcome answer to all those who still suffer from the headaches, colds, indigestion, bad breath and bad skin due to clogged intestines.

Fleischmann's Yeast is a plant, fresh as any garden vegetable. It helps the colon perform its function almost miraculously.

Eat 3 cakes of Fleischmann's Yeast daily, a cake before each meal or between meals. To get full benefit from yeast you must eat it regularly and over a sufficient period of time. Start now. At all grocers, and many leading cafeterias, lunch counters and soda fountains. Write for latest booklet on Yeast in the diet—free. Health Research Dept.C-123, The Fleischmann Company, 701 Washington St., New York, N. Y.

DO YOU KNOW that from throat to colon is one continuous tube? That is why poisons from clogged intestines can spread through the system. 90% of our ailments start here, and here is where yeast works. For a happy, wholesome body, keep your entire intestinal tract clean, active and healthy with Fleischmann's Yeast.

FLEISCHMANN'S YEAST for HEALTH

Figure 4.7. This Fleischmann's Yeast ad illustrates the tabloid technique. *Literary Digest*, November 17, 1928.

soap. That is, the ad makers strategically placed the captions near their photographs. If they used the product at all, they did not necessarily prefer it to all others (figure 4.8). The campaign worked. Sales for Lux Toilet Soap nearly doubled in 1928.[36]

So successful was the work of the Women's Editorial Department that their formulaic approaches later showed up in some of the era's most successful campaigns. The Lux Hollywood campaign inspired countless soaps, cosmetics, and other toiletries to add the new look of glamour into their advertising. Pond's testimonials inspired endorsement campaigns for Lucky Strike, Old Gold, and Camel cigarettes. Odorono's views of body odor and social disgrace appeared behind whisper copy for *The Book of Etiquette*, Listerine mouthwash, and Pepsodent antiseptic. Indiscriminate use of the fear theme then led to creating new menaces—such as the medical-sounding halitosis (bad breath), tina trichophyton (athlete's foot), comedones (blackheads), and lordosis (poor posture)—many of which advertisers claimed could be prevented or cured by the advertised articles. And, the Fleischmann's Yeast tabloid technique appeared in ads selling everything from automobiles to Ritz Crackers.

Yet for all the talk of social revolution and women's freedom, the Women's Editorial Department and other ad women made few attempts to depict women in the workplace, meeting room, and polling booth. At first glance, the strategy of picturing the modern, attractive girl in advertisements as a model for beauty products but also running vacuum cleaners, operating washing machines, and other appliances may have seemed overdone. Countless speeches, talks, and addresses at ad women conventions, advertising club dinners, and club luncheons criticized such campaigns: From a woman's viewpoint, too many pretty girls are used as *bait* in advertisements. Why not show women with accomplishments or real, everyday women like their neighbors down the street?

Despite all the economic and social changes, market research indicated that the modern woman shared identical desires for beauty and romance and aspired to emulate her betters, just as did the nineteenth-century woman. Even with the attempts to represent women as the diverse and consumer-savvy group they had become, the stereotype of the *happy homemaker* emerged as the dominant image.

Figure 4.8. The "Hollywood" campaign for Lux Toilet Soap effectively used celebrity endorsements, 1928. Reproduced from Julian Watkins, *The 100 Greatest Advertisements, 1952–1958* (1949; New York: Dover, 1959).

Certainly the Women's Editorial Department recognized that women preferred that they carry the illusion further by showing a female beauty in an ad. The whole picture, the whole impression demands an attractive set of characters to preserve the illusion. "The fact of the matter is that women aren't tired of them by a long shot! *They want them!*" Not just men, but women as well. In advertisements, as in fiction, according to Ruth Leigh writing in 1924: "[W]omen demand vicarious experience. They know they are not like the pretty, dainty young housewife in the kitchen cabinet advertisement, but they like to think of themselves in terms of that trim young thing."[37]

CHRISTINE FREDERICK:
BRINGING WOMEN BACK INTO THE KITCHEN

For another group of businesswomen, home economics—not writing—would be their entering wedge into the advertising field. In the Progressive Era, the home economics movement evolved from the Victorian cult of domesticity, which held that a woman's place was in the home as championed by Catherine Beecher, into the reform campaign led by Ellen H. Richards, to create a new field based on applying scientific approaches to social problems in the home.

Around the turn of the twentieth century, Progressives expanded the concept of the word *home* itself to encompass everything relating to family, household, and the woman's sphere; certain middle-class women built significant public careers around the home economics, sanitary reform, and settlement movements, such as Richards, Charlotte Bartlett Crane, and Jane Addams. These social workers, women doctors, and club members traveled extensively among all social classes, protected by their professions. African Americans also had their own version of the movement, which they applied to their schools, colleges, and hospitals. Ironically, these women carved out a highly visible public role in applying their scientific approaches directly to social problems in the home, while they built a career on advocating that a woman's place was in the home, nurturing her children and taking care of her husband.

Moreover, the home economics movement brought business values directly to the home and opened up new marketing opportunities for the mass-consumer industries. A case in point is the electric power industry. Although by 1920 one-third of American homes had electricity and by decade's end that number had doubled, manufacturers had to convince people that the copper wires did more than produce illumination. The utility could also supply power to run small machines that could make their lives easier and for only pennies a day.

When an increasing number of comfortable middle-class families with incomes of $3,000 to $4,000 a year could afford washing machines, electric irons, fireless cookers, gas ranges, and vacuums, manufacturers needed help to create a demand for their goods and to teach women how to use the array of new household technology. But men's traditional misconceptions about what women actually did and how they worked inside the home led to poorly designed and inefficient new domestic appliances. Male engineers pushed such appliances as irons that might be plugged into a light socket but would blow the fuses; while salesmen delivered their presentations in a condescending tone, suggesting that a female homemaker might not be technologically competent to toast bread, make waffles, brew coffee, or even grill a beefsteak. Eventually marketers recognized that female elders, not men, traditionally taught their daughters how to run the household. So they began to use women to cook up recipes on new gas ranges, explain the benefits of home appliances, organize industry information services, develop home economics laboratories, and create advertising programs. The need to wash, scrub, scour, mop, dust, and polish everything in the house week after week also generated a whole industry of household cleaning supplies to lessen women's work—soaps, detergents, waxes, polishes, and other specialized cleaning products.[38]

Thus, home economists came to work for manufacturers as researchers and educators to promote standardized goods, sanitary packaging, and brand names, even as they promoted themselves as gatekeepers of normative domestic practice. Their work in nutrition, health, and household efficiency also connected women consumers to manufacturers, retailers, teachers, and government agencies. Ultimately, these early female home economists had a significant influence on shaping lifestyles, perpetuating stereotypes, and engendering the practice of consumption as a feminine pursuit.

One of these early pioneers was Christine McCaffey Frederick, who represents a transition figure in the larger field of home economics, a cultural mediator between consumers and manufacturers. In this new role, she became an influential efficiency expert and avid promoter of new products for the home. Frederick, like most middle-class American women of her generation, chose homemaking as her life work when she married advertising writer J. George Frederick in 1907 and raised four children. Her husband's career in advertising may provide some insight into Christine's interest in the field. George successively edited *Judicious Advertising*, *Printers' Ink*, and *Advertising & Selling* magazines, but later at Business Bourse, he edited, published, and wrote scores of titles, including the work of his wife, Christine. One among the growing number of women earning college degrees, Frederick graduated Phi Beta Kappa from Northwestern University in 1906 and built a successful business career by promoting domesticity.

Unlike the home economists typified by Richards, however, the scientific management approach advocated by Frederick sought to bring women back into the kitchen rather than carry their reform values outside into the larger community. "Our greatest enemy," Frederick heralded in 1914, "is the woman with the career. . . . Let her find it just as interesting to care for her own children as it is to go down to the east side and take care of Annie Bulowski."[39] Not surprisingly, Frederick's hostility toward the career woman "marked the beginning of a backlash against women's reform work outside the home, paradoxically led by a new group of professional career women like those in home economics," explains historian Sarah Stage.[40]

Frederick conceived of her task as a scientific attempt to upgrade the home, a physical place where women labored, much in the same way her male counterparts worked to streamline factory production and office procedures. Frederick learned firsthand about what she later called "drudgifying" housework compared to her earlier college education and teaching experience. Something had to change. When her husband came home with ideas about Frederick W. Taylor's time management, his accounts so interested Frederick that she recruited her husband's efficiency engineer associates to explain to her how they made industrial practices more efficient and profitable. She then visited several factories to see such principles in action as how manufacturers replaced small nonstandardized coal shovels with large standardized ones to streamline the operation. These principles of Taylorism so impressed Frederick that she set about applying the concepts of scientific management to the home. That is, the one best operation could be achieved when the worker worked at the right height, with the right tools, and under the right conditions in terms of light, ventilation, and comfort.[41]

These ideas appeared in a series of monthly articles titled "The New Housekeeping" in the *Ladies' Home Journal*, for which Frederick served as contributing household editor from 1912 to 1919. She later compiled the *Journal* articles into a book titled *The New Housekeeping: Efficiency Studies in Home Management* (1913), which included two principles for which Frederick was most famous. First, she encouraged women to make sure that the height of kitchen equipment fit their anatomies and published charts of exact measurements to direct women in their kitchen renovations. In addition, Frederick introduced the concept of "routing" in the kitchen, saving steps from endless treks between the cabinet and sink, pantry and table, to prepare for a meal and clean up afterward. Scientific housekeeping promised women more control over the household finances, acknowledged the complexities of their work, and validated their work. Each article stressed that women could have unlimited power in the home, whether as efficient homemakers or as rational consumers. Although the movement bolstered the reputation of women's work, it also encouraged women to learn to live within the domestic arena rather than pursue paid employment.

Frederick's editorial work at the *Ladies' Home Journal* also illustrates the increasingly mutually dependent relationship between magazines and advertising. Changes in her career point to the ways in which advertising subtly and not so subtly organized these publications. In letters to *Journal* readers, for example, Frederick shifts from suggesting that women use new technology to advocating the use of specific brand-name products to modernize their homes. She counsels housewives to lay out money for "every device she can afford" as dishwashers, bread mixers, and electric washing machines would save the family the wages of domestic help. For years she also wrote, lectured, and testified in favor of "price maintenance" during the first half of her career. Frederick argued that honest businessmen could not continue to produce reliable consumer goods if retailers cut their suggested prices. But housewives could help manufacturers maintain reasonable prices by avoiding discounted prices of imitators and buying only the brands of manufacturers of trademarked products, because they have a better basis of comparison. Still, Frederick's frequent assertion that she cared only for the housewife belied most of her efforts, which seem clearly in the interest of business, not the predominantly female consumers. This hidden agenda of women's magazines, which still haunts readers today, with ads for household cleaners placed around editorials about the importance of keeping the house clean, had its roots with Frederick and her contemporaries. They served not only consumers but also manufacturers.[42]

In 1912 Frederick's relationship with manufacturers became more direct when she and her husband moved her family to a rural setting on Long Island and established their country homestead called Applecroft. At the time, Edward Bok, editor of the *Ladies' Home Journal*, suggested that she continue experimenting with new appliances, and she established the *Applecroft Efficiency Station*, later the *Applecroft Experiment* station in her home. The station would test new products and promote domestic routines based on principles of scientific management.

By this time, Frederick's interest in home economics had evolved into a career in advertising. Frederick kept a file on every piece of equipment, and her assessments appeared in advertising pamphlets. "Women know the woman's viewpoint better than a man," wrote Frederick in 1914. "This makes her better fitted to take charge of advertising clothing, foods, household articles, furnishings, household articles, furnishings, etc." For the last five years, she had been testing all kinds of household equipment, and so she began to accept commissions to write booklets and pamphlets promoting a variety of early appliances and processed goods. She spoke from her experience in "You and Your

Laundry" for Hurley Washing Machine; "Come into My Kitchen" for the Hoosier Cabinet, Volrath Company; and "Hershey's Favorite Recipes." The American School of Home Economics also published her *Household Engineering: Scientific Management for the Home*, a twelve-part correspondence course. In this volume, she promoted such brand-name goods as Kitchencraft cabinets, Simplex ironers, and Walker electric dishwashers. Frederick continued this work well into the 1920s.[43]

Perhaps Frederick's main contribution to marketing thought was her book *Selling Mrs. Consumer*, published in 1929. It was one of the first works to enlighten sales and advertising people about women as buyers in the home. Like many advertisers, Frederick believed that women did not simply use rational, economic reasoning in making purchasing decisions. Although logic was a primary tool of business, it had much less use at home. To reach Mrs. Consumer, advertisers had to present their appeals in simple terms rather than elaborate arguments. Frederick, however, based her position on the theory that the average woman could not pass the army intelligence tests any more than her husband. "I really believe that the average woman's vocabulary would be only 1,200 words," wrote Frederick. "Mrs. Average Consumer does not know much more, intellectually than the present 14-year old adolescent, if as much."[44]

Although Frederick became well known as a marketing consultant, she remained an outsider. The larger group of the American Home Economics Association (AHEA) represented by Richards remained deeply ambivalent over the role of home economists who worked for manufacturers and advertisers rather than directing their efforts toward reform and women's issues. Not until the 1920s would another group establish the Home Economics in Business section, following Frederick's lead. When corporations hired in-house economists and formally trained them to sell new products to homemakers in the 1930s, Frederick's career in advertising came to an end; so did her marriage. But Frederick reinvented herself. Though past middle age, she enrolled at Cornell University, where she qualified in housing, home building, and decoration. Eventually she moved to Laguna Beach to work as an interior decorator, where she later retired.[45]

What is significant is that Frederick might have been an efficiency engineer, an advertising executive, or even a manufacturer, but prevailing concepts of her gender governed her activities. As a woman, Frederick chose to apply modernization to the home. Arguably, she used her enthusiasm for technology and keen interest in business to promote homemaking, but she also recognized that a woman's viewpoint would be acknowledged on matters of the home. Thus she mastered the intricacies of scientific management, conferred with manufacturers, and spoke to audiences of businessmen. When the occasion might warrant it, she might refer to herself as a feminist: attempting to alleviate women's work, marching with suffragists, campaigning for women's labor laws, or taking on the consumer advocate role as Mrs. Consumer. Thus Frederick, posing as a housewife, came to epitomize progressive women who built a significant career around the cult of domesticity and strived to convey that housekeeping was the greatest business in the world.[46]

Another paradox emerged when Frederick defended a woman's right to join the Advertising Men's League of New York, which led to her participation in the formation of the first women's advertising organization. When she later told her husband, J. George Frederick, then an editor of *Printers' Ink*, that she wanted to attend a presentation on "Salesmanship in Print" at the league, he said it was impossible: "Why, you couldn't possibly come," he told her, "unless you sit in a box—up above all of us—and let us pull a velvet curtain in front of you so that none of the men will know you are listening." This, too, was impossible. So Frederick responded by inviting about forty women "interested in the field of advertising" to a dinner, and the group appointed an organizing committee that went on to create the League of Advertising Women of New York (now Advertising Women in New York) in 1912. Despite Frederick's lead role in establishing this organization, she never became an *official* dues-paying member, but she did on occasion attend meetings and give presentations. It may be that there had been a mutual agreement of keeping Christine in the background of this organization, an act similar to the deliberate practice of keeping Helen Lansdowne Resor and Rose Markward Knox in the background.[47]

Thus, this generation of ad women would advance, with some ambivalence, a woman's viewpoint on modern consumer culture, an outlook more revolutionary in advertising women-centered products than ever had been. The extensive advertising of housekeeping products created the stereotype of the happy homemaker that confined women to the home, the dominant image from the 1920s through the 1950s, while it also dismantled stereotypes and summoned women to proclaim their liberation from the past by purchasing cosmetics and beauty aids, skirts raised to the knee, and even cigarettes.

NOTES

1. *Printers' Ink*, November 7, 1929. See also "Two Women at the Counter," *Ladies' Home Journal*, March 1929. On "business of femininity," see "Women in Business III," *Fortune*, no. 13, July–December 1935, p. 81.

2. "Girl Graduates Start Climb for $25,000 Jobs," *New York Times*, July 29, 1923.

3. Helen Woodward, *Through Many Windows* (1926; repr., New York: Garland, 1986), p. 160.

4. Ibid., pp. 226–27.

5. Ibid., p. 231.

6. Representative works of Helen Woodward include *Through Many Windows*; *Three Flights Up* (New York: Dodd, Mead, and Co., 1935); *The Lady Persuaders* (New York: Ivan Obelensky, 1960); *It's an Art* (New York: Harcourt Brace, 1938). "Honest work": Woodward, *It's an Art*, p. 10.

7. Woodward, *Through Many Windows*, p. 233. Jane Martin, interview, *New York Times*, June 2, 1915.

8. On the Lansdowne family, see "Real Estate," *Nutmegger*, August 1968, Colin Dawkins Papers, box 3, folder: Helen Resor/her sister Theresa Lansdowne, JWT. On career, see Stockholders Affidavit Helen L. Resor, March 20, 1924. *J. Walter Thompson Company News Bulletin*, January 10, 1964, Biographical Files, box 15, folder: Helen Resor, JWT.

9. The Andrew Jergens Company—Woodbury's Facial Soap: 7, Account Files, Andrew Jergens Company, Account Histories 1916–1926, box 1, JWT. See also "Woodbury's Facial Soap," n.d., Account Histories, 1946–1950, box 1, JWT.

10. Helen L. Resor Affidavit, March 1924, JWT.

11. On Odorono, see James Webb Young, *Full Corn in the Ear* (Coapa, NM: Piñon Press, 1959). *J. Walter Thompson Company News*, February 7, 1964, Colin Dawkins Papers, box 5, folder 1: James Webb Young, JWT. On "Little Eva," see "My Life in Advertising," James Webb Young, February 20, 1928, Colin Dawkins Papers, box 6, folder 5: James Webb Young, Howard Henderson Personal Files, JWT.

12. Helen L. Resor Affidavit, March 1924.

13. Sam Meek, interview by Sidney Bernstein, November 1963, Sidney Ralph Bernstein Company, History Files, box 1, folder: Sam Meek, JWT.

14. Jennifer Scanlon, "Advertising Women: The J. Walter Thompson Company Women's Editorial Department" in *Gender and Consumer Culture Reader*, ed. Jennifer Scanlon (New York: New York University Press, 2000), pp. 208–16.

15. In 1917 Lansdowne marched along Fifth Avenue for women's suffrage, leading a group of JWT secretaries and professional copywriters. "Helen Resor" in *Ad Men and Women: A Biographical Dictionary of Advertising*, ed. Ed Applegate (Westport, CT: Greenwood, 1994), p. 268. See also Jennifer Scanlon, *Inarticulate Longings* (New York: Routledge, 1995). On suffrage and publicity in general, see Margaret Finnegan, *Selling Suffrage* (New York: Columbia University Press, 1999), p. 11.

16. Scanlon, *Inarticulate Longings*, pp. 169–96.

17. Helen Resor Affidavit, March 1924.

18. "Mrs. Wilkins Reads the *Ladies' Home Journal*," Dorothy Dwight Townsend, *J. Walter Thompson Company News Bulletin*, June 1923.

19. "She Wants It but She Doesn't Know It—Yet!" Lois Ardery, *J. Walter Company News Bulletin*, December 1924, JWT.

20. "The Woman Appeal," *J. Walter Thompson News Bulletin*, January 1924, JWT.

21. Ibid.

22. Ibid.

23. Louise Fox Connell, interviews by Colin Dawkins, box 16, Oral Interview Transcripts, folder: Louise Fox Connell, June 1977, July 1979, Colin Dawkins Papers, JWT. On gendered workplace, see Angel Kwolek-Folland, *Engendering Business: Men and Women in the Corporate Office, 1870–1930* (Baltimore: Johns Hopkins University Press, 1994), pp. 41–69.

24. On gendered workplace, see Angel Kwolek-Folland, *Incorporating Women: A History of Women and Business in the United States* (New York: Palgrave, 2002), pp. 106, 122–23. Louise Fox Connell, interviews.

25. Louise Fox Connell, interviews.

26. Although Helen Lansdowne Resor never held the official title, her successor, Ruth Waldo, eventually became JWT's first female vice president in 1945, as head of the women's group. At JWT, Mary McKinnon may have been the first woman illustrator, working on the Lux Flakes campaign in the 1910s. Years later, in 1924, Nedda McGrath became the first woman art director at a major advertising agency, Blackman. On McKinnon, see Cynthis G. Swank, slide lecture to JWT employees, 1983, 5. Colin Dawkins Papers, box 3, folder: Helen Resor, JWT. On McGrath, see *Advertising Age*, November 1, 1930. For an article thought to have been written by Helen Lansdowne Resor, see: "'Doctor? Lawyer? Merchant? Chief?' Which Shall She Be?" with the byline "Harriet Abbot," *Ladies' Home Journal*, July 1920. *J. Walter Thompson Company News Bulletin*, January 10, 1964, Biographical Files, box 15, Helen Resor, JWT. Helen Resor, Sam Meek interview by Sidney Ralph Bernstein, JWT.

27. "The Emotional Quality in Advertising," *J. Walter Thompson News Bulletin*, April 1923, JWT.

28. On Woodbury's Facial Soap advertisements: "His Unspoken Thoughts,"

Ladies' Home Journal, September 1921. "All around You," *Ladies' Home Journal*, December 1922.

29. In the 1920s, radio as a medium for advertising to a mass market was discouraged by the high cost of sets, the number of broadcasting stations, and number of programming hours. Beginning in 1924, Betty Crocker hosted the first radio show. James Gray, *Business without Boundary: The Story of General Mills* (Minneapolis: University of Minnesota Press, 1954), pp. 177–78. See also "Thousands of Cooking Students Are Graduated in Our Homes," *Radio World*, January 23, 1926, p. 31.

30. Young, *Full Corn in the Ear*, chap 5. James Webb Young Papers, box 1, folder: Full Corn in the Ear, JWT.

31. "The Charm Every Actress Knows," advertisement, Ponds, *Ladies' Home Journal*, April 1916.

32. Kathy Peiss, *Hope in a Jar: The Making of America's Beauty Culture* (New York: Owl Books, 1999), pp. 137–38.

33. "How Important Is the Style of Copy?" Aminta Casseres, *J. Walter Thompson News Bulletin*, July 1923.

34. "The Snob Appeal," Frances Maule, *J. Walter Thompson News Bulletin*, March 1923, JWT.

35. *J. Walter Thompson News Bulletin*, August 1929, JWT.

36. Company Meeting on "Personality Advertising," April 4, 1928, Information Center Records, box 4, folder: Testimonial Advertising. Lever Brothers, Account Histories, "History of Lux Toilet Soap 1925–1951."

37. "Do Women Respond to Pretty Girl Pictures?" *Printers' Ink*, November 6, 1924.

38. James C. Williams, "Getting Housewives the Electric Message: Gender and Energy Marketing in the Early Twentieth Century," in *His and Hers: Gender, Consumption, and Technology*, ed. Roger Horowitz and Arwen Mohun (Charlottesville: University of Virginia Press, 1998), pp. 95–113. See also Carolyn Goldstein, "Mediating Consumption: Home Economics and American Consumers, 1900–1940" (PhD diss., University of Delaware, 1994). Sarah Stage and Virginia B. Vincenti, eds., *Rethinking Home Economics: Women and the History of a Profession* (Ithaca, NY: Cornell University Press, 1997).

39. Christine Frederick, "Points in Efficiency," *Journal of Home Economics* (June 6, 1914). For a complete biography of Fredericks, see Janice Williams Rutherford, *Christine Fredericks and the Rise of Household Efficiency* (Athens: University of Georgia Press, 2003).

40. Stage and Vincenti, *Rethinking Home Economics*, p. 32.

41. "Drudgifying": Christine Frederick, *The New Housekeeping: Efficiency Studies in Home Management* (Garden City, NY: Doubleday, Page and Co., 1914), p. viii.

42. For Christine Frederick's ideas on scientific housekeeping, see, for example, Frederick, *The New Housekeeping*. See also Christine Frederick, *Household Engineering: Scientific Management in the Home* (Chicago: American School of Home Economics, 1919). On price maintenance, see "A Woman Buyer's Five Demands," *Advertising & Selling*, June 18, 1921. "Women Buyers, After All, Are Receptive," *Printers' Ink*, May 24, 1934. For examples of the relationship between national advertisers and magazines, see correspondence from *American Weekly*, Press On, Taylor Instrument, and Lawrence H.

Selz to Christine Frederick, 1941 and 1942, Frederick Papers, box 1, folder 7, Schlesinger Library.

43. For booklets and pamphlets 1914–1937, see Frederick Papers, box 12, Schlesinger Library.

44. Christine Frederick, *Selling Mrs. Consumer* (New York: Business Bourse, 1929), p. 21.

45. Obituary of J. George Frederick, *AdLibber*, AWNY Collection, box 2, folder 4, Schlesinger Library.

46. "Career Chronology of Mrs. Christine Frederick," box 2, folder: Advertising Women of New York Collection, Schlesinger Library. "Mrs. Christine Frederick, Author and Lecturer," Frederick Papers, box 1, folder 15. "Mrs. Consumer Speaks Up," New York Rotary Club speech, March 10, 1938, folder 10, Frederick Papers, Schlesinger Library.

47. League of Advertising Women: J. George Frederick to Jo Foxworth, March 3, 1964, Frederick Papers. See also "Founder's Section," Dignam, box 1, folder 15: Advertising Women of New York Collection, Schlesinger Library. Lansdowne: *J. Walter Thompson Company News*, January 10, 1964, p. 10, Biographic Files, box 15, folder: Helen Resor, JWT. Markward: "Women in Business," *Fortune*, September 1935; and "Grand Old Lady of Johnstown," *Collier's*, January 1, 1949.

CHAPTER 5

THE DEPRESSION AND WAR YEARS

RETAIL, RADIO, AND YELLOW WRITING

Tom Verney: "You're a beautiful brain and beautiful clothes. No temperature. No pulse. That's all."

A. M. MacGregor: "Where did you learn about women, Verney?"

Tom Verney: "It isn't a matter of learning. It's instinct."

A. M. MacGregor: "I'm a brain with no pulse, eh? I'm a woman. Verney, more woman than you'll ever know."

I t was the snap and crackle of a romance between two equals that engaged the audience in the 1942 comedy *Take a Letter, Darling*. In the film, advertising executive A. M. MacGregor (Rosalind Russell) hires a struggling painter as her male secretary (Fred MacMurray) as a way to keep the wives of some of her clients from becoming jealous, until she quits her career to travel around Mexico in a trailer with him. Although Russell is cast as the stereotypical, repressed boss-lady who is tamed by love, the film also reflects changes in women's access to entrepreneurship and their more visible role in business. But it remained a troublesome issue, as we have seen, ever since women began to work for wages and entered the all-male office in the late nineteenth century. As the film suggests, new definitions of a woman's place stretched but ultimately did not break traditional notions of the differences between men and women.

The Depression and World War II contributed to an environment that reinforced conservative stereotypes of womanhood, but these events did not end women's involvement in the advertising profession between 1930 and 1945. There is no question that this fifteen-year period witnessed more profound growth and new opportunities for ad women than any previous time. A by-product of the general growth of leisure time was America's demand for popular entertainment, which fueled the development of new recording technologies and the cult of celebrities. This new market for film, radio, and sound recording also opened important business avenues for women, as they virtually took over working as stenographers, typists, and secretaries in these new industries. With clerical work experience, moreover, large numbers of these women then advanced into specialized positions in ad agencies, advertising management, publicity, retail advertising, and fashion promotion.

THE ADVERTISING PROFESSION IN THE 1930s

The bright prospects for women in the advertising world that seemed attainable in the 1920s initially seemed less possible in the 1930s. The stock market crash of 1929 marked the beginning of the worst economic depression in American history, as well as hard times in advertising. Businesses folded, schools cut the length of terms, and employers laid off workers. The number of unemployed Americans reached an estimated one in four of the workforce, the highest unemployment rate in the nation's history.[1]

Virtually all the advertising agencies felt the economic downturn by 1932. The total volume of advertising revenue plunged nearly 70 percent from a 1929 high of $3.4 billion to a low of $1.3 billion in 1933.

To save money, agencies hired fewer prominent artists and copy-writers, and companies set up inexpensive in-house art departments, many staffed by inexperienced workers willing to work for lower pay. Many agencies also eliminated paid vacations, forced staff members to take days off without pay, and slashed salaries and staff. Other agencies simply closed up shop. Even the favored group of business-women and professional workers, who had not generally suffered as seriously from the Depression as the working class, now found their achievements swept away by economic forces. Over half of the women advertising executives surveyed by the American Women's Association reported decreased earnings. Meanwhile, the busy ste-nographer who averaged forty dollars a week in 1929, four years later earned only fifteen dollars a week in 1933, reported the Women's Bureau. Sometimes, the jobs held by two women were combined into one, and the post was given to a man. Companies often fired married women and excluded them from new hires. Older women were also hard hit, since many companies refused to hire women over thirty-five years of age. Between 1933 and 1937, gender discrimination became the rule in most New Deal work programs, when state and federal agencies stepped in to regulate business and ruled that only one member of a family could work in the government service, with the intention to create more jobs for the heads of families.[2]

The Depression also affected women's participation in adver-tising and their business opportunities in many other ways. Ironically, the economic downturn also reinforced their economic importance. Initially, the consumer goods industries and clerical occupations were less affected than the advertising agencies. By the 1930s, the devel-opment of modern marketing was well under way. Certainly poor eco-nomic conditions may have motivated some firms to pursue obvious hard-selling approaches to move products, but shrewd business-people knew very well that they could not afford to alienate cus-tomers with buyers in short supply. They also knew it was more important than ever to understand and to cater to buyers. Advertisers short of money also wanted to know if their advertising brought in sales, and if so, how, when, and why. To fill this need, methods of gathering, measuring, and evaluating market information had improved greatly. For example, A. C. Nielsen Company, a New York research and marketing service, sold the syndicated *Food Index and Drug Index*, a report measuring consumer product purchases in specific categories in food, drug, and mass merchandising outlets. Surveys, store interviews, and test cities also became common agency tools, while George Gallup's magazine and newspaper readership studies subjected advertising to rigorous analytical tests. Such detailed work demanded an ever-increasing number of clerical workers, and women rapidly filled the positions.

In addition to marketing research, a buyer's orientation was also evident in the two most significant marketing developments of the 1930s—the supermarket and the consumer-engineering movement. The supermarket was an instant success in America from the opening of the first stores in the 1930s. Its success had nothing to do with hard-sell practices; rather, the self-service stores offered shopping carts, plenty of parking, and low prices to attract customers and met their need for inexpensive groceries.[3] In addition to the supermarket, other retailing distribution systems underwent rapid changes, including the discount house and the planned shopping center. Such large-scale corporations quickly recognized the advantages of controlling production and centralizing management, as well as assuming marketing and purchasing activities. But the key to business growth became the concept of *consumer-engineering*, which refers to the design of new and existing products in order to meet carefully researched consumer needs.

Even during the economic devastation of the 1930s and emergencies of the war years of the 1940s, this tremendous amount of activity continued to open up unprecedented new opportunities for women in the expanding mass-consumer goods industries, department stores, and service departments of magazines, as well as in broadcasting. Some of the biggest gains came from large numbers of women leaving traditional women's wage work to take marketing and advertising jobs vacated by men during World War II, in which the United States was involved between 1941 and 1945. This scenario was similar to that brought about by World War I twenty years earlier.

Some fabulous success stories came out of these years. Although women's opportunities in advertising agency work would shrink as the economy contracted during the Depression years, women still became involved in many aspects of agency work, as represented by copywriters Ruth Waldo of the Thompson agency's Women's Editorial Department and Dorothy Dignam for the N. W. Ayer agency. At the same time, the new technologies of film, sound recording, and broadcast created entirely new jobs for women, such as radio scriptwriter, taken on by Irma Phillips, Anne Ashenhurst, and Jane Cruisenberry. But it would be retail work that offered the best opportunities for women, as symbolized by the careers of Bernice Fitz-Gibbon and Frances Bemis.

RETAIL ADVERTISING

Local retail work, especially in New York, continued to give ad women their best opportunities during the interwar period. In 1931, nearly half of the New York department and specialty stores had female advertising managers; outside of New York this figure stood at more than one-quarter. These positions offered the allure of an actual chance to be well paid and well traveled with work in glamorous settings. Over time, the field offered unprecedented new opportunities to rise to the top; this type of advancement was exemplified by Dorothy Shaver, who first worked for Lord & Taylor as a comparison shopper before becoming the store's vice president of advertising and promotion, and in 1945, the president of the New York department store.[4] Bernice Fitz-Gibbon and Frances Bemis similarly had not only the obvious qualities of personality, ability in merchandising, and good taste but also a dramatic instinct for publicity. They followed a similar path that many ad women had taken during the last fifty years, stepping from writing the pages of women's articles in newspapers to writing advertising copy.

Bernice Fitz-Gibbon: Be Specific—It Pays

When Bernice Fitz-Gibbon landed in New York in the mid-1920s, she was as poor as "Job's turkey" with $200 to her name. By 1941, her annual income was $90,000, equal to one million dollars in today's take-home wages. She went on to become the highest-paid woman in advertising in the forties and fifties (figure 5.1). Certainly Fitz-Gibbon had struck it rich in retail advertising.

Fitz-Gibbon, or "Fitz," as friends and colleagues knew her, was born in Waunakee, Wisconsin. As a child, her informal education at home on the farm had a distinct influence on her success in advertising. In her book *Macy's, Gimbels, and Me*, Fitz-Gibbon tells of how her father, a teacher and a farmer, expected his children to have a command of language and a keen sense of observation. He created games that encouraged his family to use long, descriptive, and colorful words in their conversations, such as having them describe various rooms in the house, forcing them to develop their powers of observation and see common objects in a new way. When it came to strict adherence of the rules in writing, syntax, word selection,

Figure 5.1. Bernice Fitz-Gibbon. Photo from American Advertising Federation Hall of Fame.

spelling, and punctuation, she credits her training to a convent prep school that convinced her "an error in English was a mortal, not venial sin." Fitz-Gibbon later would demand these same skills from her staff to describe specific items for sale.[5]

After graduating in 1918 with a BA degree from the University of Wisconsin, Fitz-Gibbon taught high school English for two years before writing for the Rockford, Illinois, newspaper. She soon learned that the advertising manager for the newspaper earned double that of the city editor, and she asked to be transferred from society reporter to the advertising department. She left the newspaper to work briefly at Marshall Field's furniture floor in Chicago; spent a summer at Wanamaker's in New York, and eventually worked at Macy's. Ten years later in 1928, Fitz-Gibbon was earning $15,000 a year as head fashion copywriter at Macy's, a fantastic wage at the time, when she coined the famous phrase: "It's Smart to Be Thrifty." By this time, she had already married attorney Herman Block and applied for maternity leave, expecting the first of two children.

When Fitz-Gibbon arrived in New York City though, she considered herself just about the least likely person to rise to the top of the glamorous advertising business. She was even the wrong sex, since advertising still pretty much belonged to the men. "In agencies only an occasional very chic female (a fashion plate who wore her hat all day) was hired," said Fitz-Gibbon, "mainly for window dressing or to impress clients with the fact that the agency was up on the 'woman's viewpoint.'" But Fitz-Gibbon was not chic. A tall, heavy-set woman, she looked practical and businesslike. Her aura of efficiency was heightened by her unfashionable attire, black dresses or black dressmaker suits, such as worn by stout matrons.[6]

The key to Fitz-Gibbon's success was her use of vivid English and keen sense of observation. She placed simple words in a new order to produce a fresh thought, while she could also put herself in the reader's shoes. She asked, what would interest *me* if *I* were "a woman expecting a baby in six weeks? . . . Or she imagined herself a teenager about to buy her first high heels and nylon stockings." Fitz-Gibbon then wrote as if she were actually talking to someone in every ad, as simply as she'd talk to her sister or best friend—a reasonably intelligent person talking to another intelligent person. Instead of detailed, hard-sell copy using words like *item, event,* or *sale,* Fitz-Gibbon's chatty advertisements engaged readers with brief anec-dotes, catchy slogans, and puns revolving around what the product could do for them and nothing else. When Fitz-Gibbon wrote an advertisement for the new strapless evening gown, for example, she started with a provocative question: "How Do You Keep It Up Night After Night?" followed, of course, by specific details on how Macy's strapless gowns stayed up practically by themselves. But some of Fitz-Gibbon's most cherished verses and clever puns passed right over the heads of well-informed readers, such as one ad headlined "Readin', Writin' and Thriftmetic.'" On the other hand, misquota-tions, printers' errors, or mistakes were bound to appear when ad copy came fast off the press. "Macy's, once terrified of such disasters, had come to treat them blithely," wrote Fitz-Gibbon. "When an advertise-ment for taffeta dresses misquoted a wrong passage in *Pickwick Papers,* an apologetic notice from Macy's two days later read: "Great Scott! We slipped up on our Dickens."[7]

Fitz-Gibbon stayed with Macy's for twelve years, until the thought of a pay cut caused her to leave. She was then wooed back to Wana-maker's to take over the advertising department in 1935, and she set out to change the merchandiser's image to compete successfully with other major department stores. Because of the Depression, there was little money for salaries and media, and nothing for art, publicity, and crowd-getting events. Retailers had to work hard to show how their products were necessary or attractive in terms of the price, function, or value, since people felt hesitant to spend money in those hard times. Fitz-Gibbon redirected the ads to feature items specifically of interest to women and then shifted some money from media for promotion and publicity of creative events, such as fashion shows featuring Arthur Murray dance instructors and guest speakers at the store. After four years at Wanamaker's, however, she cleaned out her desk and moved to rival Gimbels in 1940, which more than doubled her earnings.

When Fitz-Gibbon took over Gimbels' advertising department, "Gimbels was just Gimbels—an awkward, rather ugly department store," reported the *Saturday Evening Post.* Thanks to Fitz-Gibbon, it was now "Good old Gimbels, the plain store for plain people, where you get a fifty-carat diamond or a ten-cent pot holder, wrapped in the same brown paper bag." To Frederic Gimbel, Fitz-Gibbon imbued the store with personality and brought in sales—Gimbels' business increased 96 percent from 1939 to 1945, and Fitz-Gibbon became one of the highest-paid women in American advertising.[8]

Many advertising people consider that Fitz-Gibbon's most brilliant work was done at Gimbels. One explanation is that Gimbels gave the copywriter the creative freedom that she desired. Her deceptively simple, folksy style planted the "good old Gimbels feeling" in the minds of the reading and buying public. There she wrote the famous slogan: "Nobody but nobody undersells Gimbels." She also wrote sensational ads, such as the one promoting natural cow manure as the perfect Christmas gift for the gardener. The full-page ad looked very festive, picturing a manure pile in the shape of a Christmas tree and at the very top a rooster instead of a star with the headline: "No Bossy but No Bossy Has Finer Manure than Gimbels." For nineteen dollars, Gimbels would ship a one-ton batch of "Daisy's finest to your door (or the rear door of your barn) . . . But out of the stable now . . . and back to Gimbels Flower Shop, that patch of good green earth in the heart of our new street floor" (figure 5.2). And as Fitz-Gibbon rationalized, "a good headline should cause a disturbance, and since manure is the most wanted and unreceived gift, the whole promotion is perfect." It worked. The ad sold tons of product.[9]

Although the store management felt that only females should write store ads, Fitz-Gibbon strongly disagreed. "Women aren't brighter than men. Men aren't brighter than women," argued Fitz-Gibbon. "No sex—but no sex—is superior to any other sex. And that intuition stuff is malarkey." From Fitz-Gibbon's perspective, if you could write a good ad about one thing, you could write a good ad about anything, and that was why she felt it was pointless to look for a copywriter with fashion experience or one with food experience. "If you can write pickles, you can write about petticoats."

As a manager, however, Fitz-Gibbon was a perfectionist and a stern taskmaster. She hired only Phi Beta Kappa college graduates with high academic distinction in the liberal arts rather than a profes-

Figure 5.2. This Gimbels ad offered to ship a one-ton batch of "Daisy's finest to your door," or natural cow manure, the perfect gift for the gardener. Reproduced from Bernice Fitz-Gibbon, *Macy's, Gimbels and Me* (1951; New York: Simon & Schuster, 1967).

sional curriculum, because they were either willing to work hard or were naturally brilliant. Among them were famed Macy's copywriters Margaret Fishback, Alice Hughes, and Katherine Lowe. Though Fitz-Gibbon encouraged her copywriters to have wild ideas and worked them hard, she also gave them something just as attractive as money: time off—four weeks in the summer and three or four weeks in the winter. She would rather have a good advertising person in the department six hours a day but thinking fourteen hours a day, than having them in the office a conventional eight hours a day and thinking eight hours a day. Reva Korda, who worked as a Gimbels copywriter, summed up her boss in this way: "Working for Fitz was like working for a marine drill sergeant, and the headmistress of an especially rigorous school, all rolled into one."[10]

In 1954 Fitz-Gibbon left Gimbels confident in her ability to be self-supporting and opened her own retail advertising consulting firm on Fifth Avenue called Bernice Fitz-Gibbon, Inc. Ten years later in 1964, Fitz-Gibbon retired. Among her numerous honors, she was given the Woman of the Year in Business award by the women editors of the Associated Press (1955), elected to the Retail Advertising Conference Hall of Fame (1967), and given the American Advertising Federation Hall of Fame award, a month before she died in 1982.

Frances Bemis: Mrs. Barnum of Merchandise

As Fitz-Gibbon symbolized traditional opportunities for women in retail advertising, the career of fashion promoter Frances Bemis represented new opportunities for women in department store and fashion show promotions. The trade journal *Retailing* described the small, dark-haired, attractive woman as "The Mrs. Barnum of Merchandising" for creating glamorous events, attention-getting publicity, and prestigious promotions that drew crowds; building favorable images; and helping sell the department store's merchandise (figure 5.3). Indeed, her promotional work for Hearn's in New York City and Rich's department store in Atlanta calls to mind the general spirit of P. T. Barnum, who harnessed a wide variety of media to publicize his exhibitions in the late nineteenth century.[11]

Fashion promoter Bemis was born in Denver but spent most of her childhood in Atlanta, where she helped to organize its Theatre Guild. At eighteen, she wrote a daily column for the *Atlanta Constitution* newspaper while she studied journalism at Oglethorpe University. It was in New York City, however, where Bemis learned the art of department store promotion. In 1928 she found herself writing pages of copy for newspaper and radio ads with a major emphasis on price at the successful Namm's department store in Brooklyn for sixty dollars a week. But turnover was the pattern in the retailing business, especially when business began to tail off with the onset of the Depression. When the store failed to meet quotas, staff cutting began for those in the higher echelon of pay, and Bemis was let go. She returned to her hometown of Atlanta to write fashion copy for Rich's, the leading department store in the area. When her husband accepted a new position, she accompanied him to New York City. It was here she began a career in retail advertising and promotion in the 1920s.[12]

During her time in New York Bemis never lost her leisurely Southern manner or her drawl, as she had learned that a calm working style proved most productive on her biggest retail promotion projects. At the peak of the Depression in 1933, Bemis worked as a copywriter for Hearn's Department Store, an old New York institution that had declined in prestige and business. She also demonstrated the ability to glamorize and dramatize the selling of merchandise by creating and staging events, presenting celebrity appearances, and working on press coverage.

Key to Bemis's success were her entrepreneurial and public relations skills. When Bemis suggested holding a summer carnival to promote Hearn's Festival Sale with circus acts and other attractions, for example, she offered advertising space to an amusement park owner in order to persuade him to furnish bands, circus acts, clowns, give-away tickets, and even free

Figure 5.3. Frances Bemis, n.d., from Frances Bemis Papers, no. 4, box 1, folder 4, Sophia Smith Collection, Smith College, Northampton, MA.

lemonade, while Hearn's advertised practically give-away merchandise to create an impact. Another successful promotion was the series of Charity Days, at which Hearn's gave 5 percent of the day's gross sales to high-profile charitable organizations that sponsored merchandise for the day. One of the first benefits was hosted by Mrs. William Randolph Hearst (Millicent Veronica Wilson) and featured a galaxy of stars, including singer Kate Smith, silent film actress Francis Lederer, comedian Leon Errol, and Metropolitan Opera singer Giovanni Martinelli. Many other celebrities participated in Hearn's many events for "only the cost of simple hospitality and a few flowers," explained Bemis.[13]

Like Macy's department store, Hearn's became famous for its commercial spectacles during the Depression era. For Thanksgiving, for instance, Bemis staged an outdoor circus on the Mall at Central Park, a forerunner to the opening of the store's Toytown the next day. Hearn's Christmas spectacle became the talk of New York, featuring a real circus with elephants, horses, an Eskimo village, a "Midget" village, rides, popcorn, lemonade, clowns, balloons, and music. In between, Hearn's Little Theatre, conducted free for its customers, featured many of the leading stars of stage, screen, and radio. Hearn's also sponsored one of the first amateur hours on the radio, among other constant running events, attractions, and shows, all planned with but one idea: "To create good will—to help sell goods."[14]

During a period of performing freelance work from 1939 through the war years, Bemis produced and directed a series of fashion shows for the *New York Times*, called the *Fashion of the Times*, that showcased young American designers to promote New York City as a fashion center. When Bemis agreed to produce and direct the two-hour tribute with a cast of over one hundred and twenty-five models, she asked for help from a venue in the downtown theater district and produced the first of a series of shows in scenes with lavish settings. The fact that she insisted that each clothing category had its proper setting and complementary music apparently impressed the audiences.[15]

In the first of the series, *Fashions Then and Now* gave a look at fashions for 1942, as contrasted with the fashions of other war periods in American history. For models in evening clothes, an orchestra in formal dress played classical music; when the tribute featured sports clothes, the scenery changed, and the music was gayer, all the while presenting the fashions in a dramatic way. "I was tired of seeing models walk across a stage with a curtain drop and a potted palm in front of rayon satin curtain," commented Bemis. Another show, *A Living Fashion Page*, brought fashion to life with dramatized episodes, such as one in which a sturdy little boy arrived at the civilian defense office to offer his wire-haired terrier for active duty. The third edition paid tribute not only to the American designers but also to fashion workers—cutters, pattern makers, pressers, finishers, and dyers. One scene showed women's eternal quest for color, presenting twenty-two original costumes, as well as the crowning of the Queen of Cotton. And in 1945, the first peacetime edition of *Fashion of the Times* reflected the American fashion industry and presented new synthetic fabrics for women's apparel, such as DuPont Nylon, rayon—the "artificial silk," and Lastex, the thread-covered fashion. Bemis also staged events for R. H. Macy, the Ford Motor Company, the Celanese Corporation, the US Treasury, and the National Association of Manufacturers.[16]

After the war, Bemis returned to Atlanta. As the director of special events, she handled fashion shows for Rich's department stores and worked in promoting the entire chain-store program; the following year, Bemis returned to New York City as director of feature events for Abrahams & Strauss, the city's second-largest department store, until she resigned in 1954. After a twenty-five-year career in the fashion world, Bemis retired to St. Augustine, Florida.[17]

Certainly the success stories of Bemis, Fitz-Gibbon, and Shaver were testimony to the many opportunities open to women who were willing to work in retailing, who believed in the possibilities of individual effort, and who embraced the values of the new ad woman. But it would be the new technology of broadcasting that would offer women the most revolutionary opportunities in advertising.

RADIO ADVERTISING TO WOMEN

Newspapers and magazines dominated mass communications until radio slowly emerged as a major industry following World War I. Similar to newspapers and magazines, a mass market for the product itself—the radio set—first had to be created; and then after a sizeable listening audience had been built, the medium could be sold to the advertiser. Because of the limited use of broadcasting as a viable advertising medium and the limited number of home radios, broadcasters did not target women as radio listeners until the 1930s. When they created programming that connected with women, so powerfully did radio transmit the spoken word simultaneously into millions of homes nationwide that the new medium eventually surpassed magazines as a source of advertising revenue in 1938.

Early Radio Programming

Men had monopolized the early radio industry as broadcasters, radio engineers, and listeners. The early radio sets required some technical skill to tune once the set was properly assembled, skills many American men had learned as hobbyists and in the armed forces during World War I, and then had passed on to their sons. Of course, some women learned about radio technology, explains historian Susan Smuylan, but the idea "persisted of radio as an evening, family, and father-controlled entertainment." Well into the 1920s, many people perceived new technology as instantaneous as broadcasting an intrusion into the home, unlike newspapers and magazines that permitted screening and could be hidden from children or other sensitive members of the family. Even after radio commercials became commonplace in the 1930s, the Women's National Radio Committee recommended the elimination of certain kinds of distasteful advertising for products such as laxatives and certain patent medicines that made exaggerated or fraudulent claims.[18]

Despite the widespread calls to keep radio programming genteel and limit the types of advertising, the development of weekly programs, rather than one-time efforts, gradually convinced advertisers that the new medium deserved their backing. The key to the success of radio programs was developing a strong personal bond between the listening audience, the artists who appeared on the programs, and the sponsors. While it is logical to say that the executives and the program staff directed the radio station, the listeners largely directed them, in turn.

A good case in point was one of the most popular and long-running programs on radio, *The National Barn Dance*, underwritten by Sears. In 1924 Sears began broadcasting WES in Chicago; the call letters stood for "World's Economy Store." Shortly after, WES changed its name to WLS and its slogan to "We Help Others." One night the station broadcast old-time music rather than the "high-brow" music they had been playing, and the response from Midwest folks was enormous. The station staff received so many enthusiastic telegrams of approval that they got the idea for the first barn dance, which eventually became known as *The National Barn Dance*. During the early years, however, Sears management, aghast by the square dance song on the new station, demanded that the "hillbilly" shows be cancelled. When confronted by the angry executives, the station managers pointed to the fan mail from radio listeners with overwhelming approval, and they changed their minds. The *Barn Dance* served two distinct audiences that met Sears' sponsorship needs: the rural farm audiences as well as city listeners who had come from rural communities. The program's theme gained popularity, and the show expanded from a one-hour Saturday evening program to a three-hour show. So popular had the Iowa show become, WLS moved the audience studio several times, ending up at a forty-two-hundred-seat auditorium to accommodate listeners who wanted to attend a live broadcast, as well as into the local communities for special events and even the Iowa State Fair.

In the era before media rating services, radio stations like WLS sought ways to keep a finger on the pulse of listener interest to make programs more popular. To generate a response, they encouraged their fans, or *radio friends*, to write to the station, or they used offers of small premiums to fans who sent stamped, self-addressed envelopes. Kristine M. McCusker carefully studied hundreds of thousands of such pieces of fan mail and concluded that *Barn Dance* had become part of people's lives on many levels. That is, the radio-home entertainment fashioned a virtual community of radio friends coast-to-coast, as well as local and regional groups of people who interacted face-to-face at the staging of live broadcasts at local auditoriums, community events, and state fairs.[19]

Although popular musical variety programs that played in the

evening hours attracted sponsors, daytime programming proved a
harder sell. Advertisers and broadcasters believed many homemakers
would be too busy to stop and listen to their daytime short instruc-
tional talks on homemaking, childcare, and other topics by representatives for sponsors. But slowly a female audience developed. By
1930, the radio program *Betty Crocker's Cooking School* for General Mills
had proved so successful that many household products were advertised in this manner. As radio time became more expensive, some of
the programs even accepted multiple sponsors, similar to a magazine
selling pages of the publication to interested advertisers. Now many
other companies could afford to buy small blocks of radio time
without the expense of sponsoring an entire program. Women in
these early days of the Depression sought money-saving recipes and
household tips from the cooking and household-advice broadcasts,
but these offerings alone were not enough to sustain listener interest.
For daytime radio to serve sponsors' needs, networks responded with
a new entertainment format that would encourage housewives to
listen during both morning and afternoon hours. By the late 1930s,
the soap opera—the fifteen- or thirty-minute daily serial initially
sponsored by soap manufacturers—had become a popular art form, a
source of significant revenue, and a stimulus for mass consumption.[20]

Moreover, daytime programming opened up unprecedented
opportunities for women in broadcasting as commentators, actresses,
producers, program managers, community and social agency radio
directors, and retail advertisers. Among them, Alice Keith founded
the National Academy of Broadcasting in 1934, where she taught
broadcasting techniques and published *How to Speak and Write for
Radio*. Women also worked in network staff positions. But the "real
glamour jobs" in radio were with the advertising agencies: time and
spot buyers, producers, casting directors, talent buyers, performers,
public relations directors, and writers.[21]

Soap Operas Encourage Mass Consumption

Of all the radio programs, the serials, or *soap operas*, initially sponsored
by soap manufacturers such as Procter & Gamble proved best suited

to meet both the needs of broadcasters who wanted to win high day-time ratings and the needs of advertising to capture the mind and money of the homemaker who was most likely listening in gaps between her chores. Since women could write specifically for the female audience, they readily found sponsors for their material and were well rewarded. At the time, writers of average serials made anywhere from $125 to $500 a week for five fifteen-minute episodes; this at a time when the average doctor made less than $5,000 a year. Among the most prolific and successful soap opera writers were Irma Phillips, Anne Ashenhurst Hummert, and Jane Cruisenberry.

For the sponsors, the soap operas provided opportunities to slip in low-key references to their names or products in a style comparable to radio shows, that is, many times in one program, day after day, week after week—a practice better known today as *product placement*. In addition, the continuing story lines kept listeners turning their radios to the same dial, and loyal listeners purchased the products the characters used. To make programs more popular, radio stations encouraged fan mail by offering small premiums—such as photographs of the radio star, booklets, and recipes—to listeners who would send in a stamped, self-addressed envelope.[22]

The initial reaction to *Painted Dreams* in 1930, generally considered the first soap opera broadcast on the station WGN in Chicago, was not promising until Irma Phillips added a third character and wrote ten scripts to establish the general story line. Phillips, a University of Illinois graduate and speech teacher, fell into radio broadcast writing quite by accident; she had no experience in script writing, advertising, or any other aspect of broadcasting. Her first scripts for the soap opera included poetry, music, and philosophy to appeal to women listeners. In a proposal for Montgomery Ward in 1931, Phillips shrewdly suggested that the value of sponsoring the program was to generate sales, rather than merely to build an image for the store. With this in mind, she planned to combine subtle product plugs with the radio serial—an engagement, a wedding, the planning of a trousseau, and the furnishing of a home to occur on air, opening an avenue to merchandise any article from the nationwide Montgomery Ward stores.[23]

To demonstrate the popularity of *Painted Dreams*, Phillips used a twofold appeal to generate fan mail and to get a finger on the pulse of the radio listener: she offered listeners who sent in a stamped, self-addressed envelope copies of a poem that had been presented on the broadcast; at the same time, she stimulated the listeners' involvement with the story by urging them to also write her about their favorite character. This local broadcast eventually paved the way for the national network programs *Today's Children* and *Woman in White*, as well as *Guiding Light*, which originated in 1937 on radio and was the first serial to move to television. These radio dramas dealt with home-town values and moral issues, such as career versus marriage, love interests, and marital fidelity versus true love. With the help of coau-thors, researchers, and a full-time secretary, Phillips had as many as five soap operas on the air at one time. Clearly, Phillips strove not only to attract listeners but also to develop a program format that met the needs of advertisers. Although Phillips never married, she adopted two children and reputedly became one of the highest-paid writers in soap operas.

While Phillips was mostly a writer of daytime serials, Anne Schu-macher Ashenhurst and her husband, Frank E. Hummert, worked primarily as producers of radio dramas. Before going to Paris in 1926, Ashenhurst met Hummert while working as a newspaper reporter for the *Sun* in Chicago, but within a year she had married and divorced a fellow reporter, John Ashenhurst, and was back in Chicago with an infant son. Failing to get another newspaper job, she became an assis-tant to the widowed Hummert, a former St. Louis newspaperman who had become a famed copywriter and partner in the Chicago agency Blackett, Sample, and Hummert. Although Hummert was two decades older than she, he quickly recognized that his twenty-two-year-old assistant brought such varied ideas and efficiency that he pro-moted her to an agency vice president two years later. The couple married in 1934, a match that lasted until Hummert's death in 1966.[24]

During the 1930s and 1940s, Ashenhurst and Hummert were pro-ducing about eighteen daytime serials for over thirty different sponsors. They created an efficient *factory* in which they relayed their plot sketches and summaries to a group of anonymous writers, script readers, and typists. They expanded and refined the summaries and eventually turned out the final scripts under the couples' supervision. When under a deadline, a writer might be confined to a hotel room and given provisions until the script was done. In particular, Ashenhurst was deeply involved in every aspect of the production and even directed the work of the writers, directors, actors, and musicians. She had a photographic memory and became well known in the industry for her ability to remember each intricate twist and turn of every one of their scripts. Their programs proved so successful that they generated more than five million letters, tangible evidence for the client that the radio program was reaching a large audience. Among them, Kolynos Toothpaste sponsored *Just Plain Bill*, a soap opera about a small-town barber always in financial difficulties; Gold Medal Flour underwrote *Betty and Bob*, and Procter & Gamble's Oxydol Detergent backed *Ma Perkins* (figure 5.4). For their efforts, Ashenhurst and Hummert were each making $100,000 a year from their empire, a luxurious sum at the time. When television began to displace radio, the couple simply retired and traveled.[25]

Ultimately, these soap operas succeeded because the Depression-era audience became devoted to their radio friends on the air and purchased the products they endorsed. The soaps provided a model of real families with whom the audience could identify, and who successfully overcame not only regular everyday problems that any marriage goes through but also traumas—like murder, birth, death, affairs, accidents, divorces, and disease—to attain well-being and happiness.

The fan letters to Jane Cruisenberry, creator of the long-running serial *The Story of Mary Marlin*, provide a vivid illustration of the strong bond between the listening audience, the artists who appeared on the programs, and the sponsors. For instance, one fan wrote that she crocheted a "Mary Marlin bedspread," where each medallion represented a Mary Marlin program, "for when I hear the sweet strains of your theme song, out would come the crochet hook and cotton." When other loyal listeners found that the program and their relationship with their "radio friends" had ended, they stopped purchasing, or boycotted, the product. One such disappointed female fan addressed her letter to the "Meanest Man or Woman in the World, or whoever brought the story of Mary Marlin to a close." For years she had fol-

Figure 5.4. Virginia Payne played Ma Perkins from 1933 until 1960. This photograph, offered as a premium to listeners, was signed: "Your radio friend, Ma Perkins."

lowed the radio drama and even stocked her shelves with the sponsors' soap and Crisco product, but no longer. With such "data" from hundreds of thousands of fan letters, sponsors and broadcasters monitored listener interest in order to make their programs more popular.[26]

In a complex relationship, women's work on radio programming had a significant influence on shaping lifestyles, reinforcing stereotypes, and gendering consumption. Certainly soap operas urged women to consume and to identify themselves primarily as housewives and agents of consumption, reinforcing the status of the housewife. To meet the needs of advertisers, female and male characters both repeatedly affirmed the importance of homemaking tasks, particularly of cooking. In keeping with this philosophy, marriage of the single woman was a major event on the soap opera, and following her wedding the female character gave up paid employment. The radio dramas also validated popular racial stereotypes, as portrayals of African American women on the airwaves were dominated by images of Aunt Jemima, the "Mammy" figure, or Sapphire, the bossy, shrewish wife.

So important had the broadcast medium become that the Rockefeller Foundation started funding the *Radio Project* in 1937. Several universities became involved, and sociologist Paul Lazarsfeld, the founder of Columbia University's Bureau of Applied Research, headed the project to investigate the effects of new forms of mass media on society. The first studies focused on the phenomenon of soap operas. For the 1938 Halloween broadcast of *The War of the Worlds*, for example, the study found that an estimated six million people heard the radio drama about the invasion from Mars; surprisingly, some 25 percent of the people thought it was real. Another effort, *The Little Annie Project*, was a new method developed to measure audience response to the program at any individual moment through a dial, which listeners would turn to express their preferences.[27]

Among the notable members of Lazarsfeld's massive research project was Herta Herzog, who later married him and applied the methods of measuring audience responses to advertising research. But social philosopher Theodore Adorno, another research member, became an outspoken critic of the social effects of mass media. Originating in the 1920s and 1930s Frankfurt School of Sociology, Adorno and other scholars argued that the mass media had the ability to shape public opinion and persuade a mass audience toward nearly any point of view desired by the creator of that particular message, since people were passive and equally susceptible to media messages—what since has been called the Magic Bullet Theory of mass communication. By the 1950s, such fears about the effects of mass media would continue to escalate. Nevertheless, the focus on daytime programs targeted to women opened up unprecedented professional positions for women in the new field of broadcasting, while agency work offered fewer opportunities.

JWT: A HARD SELL FOR A HARD TIME

For better or worse, the Women's Editorial Department at the J. Walter Thompson agency adapted to changing needs and changing times, shifting from gentle selling and pretty art to a harder sell that tapped into the fears and insecurities of the time. After the onset of the Depression, manufacturers placed enormous pressure on their advertising agencies to produce more effective ads for less money. In those years, ad makers worked hard to show how their client's products were necessary in terms of price, function, or value.

Ruth Waldo: Copy Head, Women's Editorial Department

This shift to the hard sell is evident in the work of Thompson copywriter Ruth Fanshaw Waldo, an authority in appealing to women and the firm's first female vice president in 1944. Waldo was reared on a farm in eastern Connecticut, the only daughter of descendants of eighteenth-century settlers. After concentrating on languages at Adelphi College, she received a graduate degree from Columbia University in 1910 and became a social worker in New York City. After four years, she moved on to the Thompson agency as an apprentice copywriter, since the field offered more opportunities for advancement.

Between 1915 and 1930, Waldo established herself as a copywriter, working among the agency's Chicago, London, and New York offices. After playing an important part in the London and Chicago offices as copy head, Waldo returned in 1930 to New York, where she supervised the women's copy for the entire agency. Since decorum was especially important to Waldo, an active Quaker, she instructed her female staff on proper manners, the right and wrong way for a lady to act, and provided a model for women aspiring to management. She also insisted that the female copywriters who worked under her call her *Miss Waldo*, never *Ruth* or *Waldo*, and that they always wore hats at work to avoid being mistaken for one of the female secretaries who did not wear hats at the office. Consumed by her interest in work, Waldo never married and worked until she retired in 1960.[28]

During the 1930s and 1940s, Waldo and her women copywriters created a series of advertising campaigns whose slogans became household words. One notable campaign was for Pond's, one of the agency's oldest and largest accounts, and featured the slogan: "She's lovely! She's engaged! She uses Pond's!" with society ladies and debutantes elegantly endorsing low-priced cold cream intended for the masses. When the Depression began, however, Waldo's images of aristocratic style went by the wayside. When money was so tight, she felt the need to give consumers more specific reasons why they should buy even the simplest products from soap to toilet paper. As the Depression deepened, an edge of fear crept into advertising, and the hard sell gave way to the sensational. Strident copy, gross exaggerations, and pseudoscientific arguments became the new approach at the Thompson agency. In the case of Lux Flakes, a soap product for laundering fine fabrics or washing dishes, the ad makers shifted from using movie star endorsements to a stronger sell: Use Lux for underthings to prevent "Undie Odor." Further installments emphasized that nowadays no girl could take chances with perspiration odor, with a job, romance, or even her marriage all too important to risk. Equally melodramatic, Lux ads for washing dishes promised to prevent "Dishpan Hands." Such ads grimly warned readers: "If you don't buy this product, you will be sorry."[29]

Perhaps the Thompson agency's most aggressive work was for Scott Tissue. Before the agency acquired the account, toilet paper was generally considered a delicate topic to talk about in public. Typical advertising to women used indirect headlines such as: "Feminine ideals of purity, daintiness, and hygiene for their intimate personal requirements are fully rewarded in Scott Tissue." In the hard times of the Depression, the agency set out to find a more aggressive way to sell the paper.

One Thompson market investigation found that only half of American families used toilet tissue, which meant that less wealthy people most likely cleaned themselves with scraps of other paper products and various materials such as rags, wood shavings, leaves, and cobs of corn. The chief competitors were unknown private-label brands of toilet paper that were generally rough and of poor quality; many had chemicals remaining from the bleaching process of the wood pulp. But women were not particularly interested in these qualities or the fact that they might have any medical significance, until prominent urologists, proctologists, and rectal specialists featured in the advertising told them about how inferior toilet tissue was responsible for rectal troubles. In one Scott Tissue ad, masked doctors and nurses looked down grimly at a patient on the operating table over the headline: ". . . and the trouble began with harsh toilet tissue." The copy continued: "A single contact with inferior toilet tissue may start the way for serious infection—and a long painful illness." Certainly this ad and others in the series made the point that hospitalization and even painful surgery could have been averted had the consumer only used the advertised product.

However, Waldo expressed concern that the agency pushed the hard sell a "little bit too far" in 1932. Instead, she suggested using a "more appealing" image of a child as the innocent victim in a hospital bed with this frightening claim: "For two-thirds of the so-called 'brands' of toilet tissue are unfit to use . . . and contain impurities which are actual menace to health. Strong acids, mercury, sand, chlorine—and even arsenic were found." But scientific tests had shown that the extremely soft, absorbent Scott Tissue and Waldorf Tissue were "Medically Safe," "entirely free from harsh irritants," and have always been "approved for safety by doctors, hospitals, and health authorities" (figure 5.5). Although the *Journal of the American Medical Association* criticized the agency's entire health platform—that is, the scientific or medical approach that the agency believed in and practiced—the agency conducted independent clinical tests, and the campaign continued. As a result, sales of Scott toilet paper more than doubled in five years, since the agency took over the account in 1927. One Thompson executive credited the success of the Scott campaigns to fear appeals, "one of the most effective methods of influencing the masses."[30]

Similar negative ads for cigarettes, soaps, sanitary napkins, disinfectants, deodorants, and yeast went beyond previously accepted standards of decency in this era, reflecting an extraordinary preoccupation with bodily flaws, functions, and odors. Such advertising also raised ethical issues that brought women into the consumer movement. One sign of the rising public distrust was a wave of publications written in the interest of the consumer, such as Frederick Schlink and Arthur Kallett's *100,000 Guinea Pigs*. Former copywriter Ruth Lamb's *American Chamber of Horrors* also warned readers of hazardous foods, drugs, and cosmetics on store shelves. On the national level, the

American Home Economics Association focused on securing guarantees of safety concerns of consumer products and lowering the escalating costs of housing and food, while local women's organizations denounced deceptive advertising, packaging, and all distribution costs deemed as nonessential. These groups hosted panels of experts to educate consumers, boycotted food stores charging high prices, and demonstrated against evictions for the nonpayment of rent. They also directed consumer cooperative stores, which functioned as direct distributors from the producer to the consumer, as was done in Europe. In the food field, the actual establishment of cooperatives had retailers alarmed, as they already experienced tough times. And women's advertising clubs nationwide also sponsored a variety of consumer forums.

When these powerful new consumer organizations brought their concerns to the attention of the federal government, Congress passed a flood of legislation to protect consumers. In 1934 the US Food and Drug Administration (FDA) expanded to cover cosmetics and to regulate advertising as well as labeling. Four years later, the Copeland Bill gave new powers over the manufacture and sale of drugs, although the legislation did not call for a grading system for food. The Federal Trade Commission also issued a number of orders to drop deceptive claims and campaigns to companies including Fleischmann's Yeast, Lifebuoy, and Lux soaps. The industry eventually acknowledged that it could no longer ignore the consumer movement's political clout and began the trend toward self-regulation.

New Visions of Women's Beauty

The economic insecurity of the 1930s also became evident in fashion and media images. Strong women became standard figures in movies, comics, popular culture, and the new soap operas broadcast on radio. They looked more mature, confident, and glamorous, with longer skirts and more-defined bosoms shaped by figure-molding undergarments. Perhaps more than anyone else, Greta Garbo personified this new standard of beauty and behavior for American women in the 1930s, a time in which Americans seemed to desire a more mature model of behavior and appearance.[31]

With the popularity of motion pictures, the Thompson agency found that the Hollywood campaign for Lux Toilet Soap in the 1930s proved just as effective as in the 1920s. Although the earlier ads talked about Hollywood stars in general, they now focused on specific celebrities such as Bette Davis, Carole Lombard, and Ginger Rogers. These faces were familiar to the young urban workingwomen who read *fan magazines*, which presented gossip, news, and photographic close-ups of their highly made-up screen stars with glamorous lighting. Historian Kathy Peiss vividly illustrates how men and women were drawn to the latest actresses, particularly influencing how American men and women looked at women. Female fans copied their appearance and gestures driven by the possibility of transformation and hope that most women experience each time they look in the mirror.[32]

Still, it was Helen Lansdowne Resor's campaign for Woodbury Facial Soap that would again challenge what had seemed to be fixed and unshakable codes of decency in the early twentieth century. Although provocative copy had been used before, illustrations had barely hinted at sexuality. Scantily clad women, who had previously appeared only in lingerie ads, began to appear altogether unclad in mainstream women's magazines. This shift began in 1936, when Lansdowne hired the well-known photographer Edward Steichen to develop a series of classical nude studies with a veneer of fine art. The Woodbury woman, an unclothed model, is languidly stretched out next to a swimming pool, her back to us, wearing only sandals. The text below connects the image to the product benefits: the Woodbury Soap formula packed "Filtered Sunshine, nature's source of beauty for the skin!" into every ray to give the consumer "all the benefits of a sun bath." In other ads, a classical column partially obscured the nude, or a model draped over a large urn was shown from the back, unclad from the waist up. By comparison to scenes of passionate romance in Hollywood movies and glossy magazines, the depictions in ads of physical contact between the sexes was still limited to carefully staged variations of caresses and kisses (figure 5.6).[33]

Given that the magazines where Lansdowne placed the ads—*Good Housekeeping, Ladies' Home Journal,* and *True Story*—aimed at both proper housewives and shop girls, Lansdowne understood that the nude female body no longer shocked and offended the reader when it appeared in the context of fine art. Thus far, at least in women's service magazines, nudes in advertising had been confined almost entirely to feminine subjects. Justification for the use of boudoir-style illustrations for such items as skin-care products, underwear, and hosiery grew out of a more sophisticated understanding of consumers' desires. The picture supposedly reflects how the prospect would like to think she would look in such garments or in using the advertised product, rather than the reality. Such images presented an idealized beauty, as could be found in the nudes of Titian, Rubens, Goya, and Gauguin, whose masterpieces hang in galleries for all to

Figure 5.6. This 1936 ad for Woodbury's Facial Soap went far beyond the previous decade's standards of acceptability in advertising.

see. On the other hand, men's magazines of the era routinely reproduced completely nude photographs of women to sell car wax, lubricants, and steel; the same images also appeared on pinup calendars and posters. "Whereas Woodbury's nudes were designed to communicate aesthetic qualities of a beauty brand, images in direct mail, trade ads, and promotional products had a more prurient purpose," explains Tom Reichert.[34]

As in the past, advertising played a significant role in the process of making and remaking ideals of beauty, as well as which forms of maleness and femaleness were considered desirable at any point in time. The Woodbury Nudes campaign reflected the further easing of social and sexual mores, as strong women and sexuality became standard in movies, comics, popular literature, and the new soap operas. But it was the automobile more than any other consumer good that offered women new possibilities for mobility, for leisure, and for socialization.

FORD, FASHION, AND FEMINITY

Similar to the beauty and fashion industry, astute automakers knew it was important to understand and cater to buyers. During the Depression, the percentage of new car sales dropped dramatically when families slashed expenses, put off repairs on the family car, and eliminated luxuries like buying a new automobile, while others simply did without a car. For the US auto industry, consumer engineering emerged as the key to growth, and automakers began to offer cars to meet the needs of an untapped market, women drivers. Until World War I, automakers positioned the electric car with batteries as cleaner and safer for women to handle than more powerful, gas-powered models that could cover difficult terrain and long distances. During World War I, wartime meant putting aside gender conventions, and a number of women learned how to drive gas-powered vehicles for the service of the nation.

When it came to consumer behavior, automaker Henry Ford had yet to learn that women customers did not buy cars or influence their purchase on price alone. At the time, Ford produced his affordable

Model T between 1914 and 1925 ("It's available in any color you want, as long as it is black"). Ford's insistence on the dark hue stemmed in part from his masculine bias, but also because black lacquer paint dried faster than any other color—a design feature that made it more suitable for mass production and keeping lower production costs. In 1923, however, Ford's rival General Motors in cooperation with DuPont chemical laboratories perfected a quick-drying lacquer in a palette of colors. When Ford's low-cost Model T began to lose market shares to Chrysler and General Motors' colorful models with feminine luxury and comfort, he felt compelled to launch new cars with colored body styles and appropriate advertising. "Even Ford would approach the female market in 1926," wrote Virginia Scharff, "with ads depicting stylishly dressed women approving the Ford for being so good looking, easy to drive, and park, reliable, and inexpensive to buy and maintain."[35]

In the early 1930s, Pontiac took the next initiative and ran a fashion ad linking design and styling to their limousine models, further paving the way to the vast women's market. In 1935 a consumer survey on women and cars provided automakers with new insights into the female market. When the *Woman's Home Companion* found that women drove about one-third of all cars, they set out to find how many women bought cars on their own and how many influenced the purchase choice for the family car. Automakers like Ford sensed an opportunity for consumer engineering and pitched to the female audience, appealing to women's growing sense of independence and fashion. But there were still few women in the automotive field; instead it was male engineers, salesmen, and ad makers who took responsibility for devising marketing and advertising strategies to consumers, similar to the electrical appliance industry.

For the essential woman's viewpoint, Ford brought in Dorothy Dignam, an N. W. Ayer copywriter, to direct the campaign and to write all the material for their effort to reach the women's market through dealer programs, advertisements, booklets, magazine articles, and radio programs (figure 5.7). Slim, auburn-haired, and blue-eyed Dignam grew up in a house where advertising shoptalk took place regularly across the dinner table. She was the daughter of J. B. Dignam, a pioneer advertising agent in Chicago, and she was expected to write. When she was only twelve, she edited a children's column titled "Cousin Dorothy" in the fashion-oriented *Dignam's Magazine*; and still in her teens, she worked on the staff of the *Chicago Herald* from 1917 to 1919. Dignam moved on to write for Vanderhoof and Company, later McJunkin Advertising Company in Chicago, and in 1929, she joined the staff of N. W. Ayer in Philadelphia, working at this major agency until she retired in 1962.[36]

Similar to the career path of home-efficiency expert Christine Frederick, copywriter Dignam also specialized in promoting household equipment and food products. In Dignam's career, though, we see a divergence to include a variety of other products directed at the women's market, such as cosmetics, feminine necessities, and fashion. Dignam later went on to take charge of merchandising copy for the Commonwealth Electrical Shops, the largest electrical store in Chicago, selling home appliances and lighting equipment. She also edited all of Commonwealth Edison newspapers and national magazine advertising on electrical power, industrial lighting, commercial refrigeration, and even motor truck transportation. The Commonwealth account even took Dignam overseas over the period of 1921–1928, where she investigated markets for American-made home laborsaving devices. She spent many months learning about housekeeping habits in Europe and reported on London's first electrically cooled florist refrigerator installed at Selfridges department store in *Electric Refrigeration News*, electric devices in French kitchens in *Electrical Manufacturing*, and gas advertising in Europe in *Gas-Age Record*, among others.[37]

To understand automobiles and the automobile market, Dignam studied textbooks, product literature, competitive journals, magazines, and newspapers. For the Ford account, she even took special training at a trade school for motor mechanics in Philadelphia, the

Figure 5.7. Dorothy Dignam, copywriter, from *Printers' Ink*, August 1926.

only woman enrolled. As a reporter, she also learned to keep moving among people, identifying fashion trends, and tying in the style news to interest women. This approach is evident in her Ford campaign for women, where she tied together Ford and style through fashion shows and auto exhibitions to reach the female audience. More important, she approached women in ads by recognizing their self-confidence, responsibility, and independence with a car.

These ideas came together in Dignam's "complete style-plan" built around the upcoming 1936 Ford V-8 automobile. The campaign focused on a series of selling points of particular interest to women. First, Dignam pitched Ford fashion on four wheels: a fingertip gearshift that didn't strain glove seams, deluxe interiors with new upholstery effects and color schemes, and a baked enamel finish that required almost no "complexion care." Similar fashion themes continue through the promotional booklets. The model featured that "trim, lithe sweep of the line that now runs through the fashion world," wrote Dignam, describing the new hood that extended gracefully over the newly designed radiator grille. The horns also had disappeared, because they were just as useful out of sight: "It's like taking a dangling something off a dress and making it much more attractive." For the DeLuxe model, Dignam emphasized the spacious room and the "lounge-like" cushioned seats (figure 5.8). In addition to fashion merits, she also highlighted the ease-of-operation, safety, interior comfort, and dependability as sales points to women. Another ad headlined "Lady Relax" made the point that the ease of handling the new Ford took the trouble out of traffic, the powerful V-8 engine made "molehills out of mountains," and the sturdy brakes brought the car to a "swift, swerveless stop," whereas the "Doors Open at 8 AM" Ford ad recognized women's responsibilities: "When the car doors open at eight in the morning and Mother begins a day of driving-duty, her car is her second home, and should certainly be well-equipped."[38]

Finally, women's understanding of cars and vehicle maintenance continued as a significant advertising theme for the postpurchase automobile market. The theme appeared in Ford handbooks, like "Greetings to a Good Driver," what Dignam called the first driving

Enter, Madam!

Entering some doors is an event in life, and you'll feel something of that same thrill when you step inside the De Luxe Ford V-8 Sedan. • How much bigger it seems! There are extra inches of spacious room this year. The broad, cushioned seats are so luxurious and lounge-like . . . the arm rests with their ash trays so inviting. And all the interior fittings are richer, finer than any Ford has ever had before. • Even the driving of this car seems planned for your *pleasure*. Won't you "Enter, Madam," and enjoy it?

THE   DE   LUXE   FORD   V·8   FOR   1938

April 1938 Good Housekeeping

Figure 5.8. This Ford ad focuses on selling points and fashion themes to interest women, such as the spacious interior and cushioned seats. *Good Housekeeping*, April 1938.

manual. For the monthly company publication *Ford News*, which went to nearly one million Ford owners, Dignam contributed monthly articles on automotive style, fashions for touring, and good driving as evidenced in one regular feature: "A Chat with Women Drivers." Here Dignam explained to her feminine audience that you could help lower operating costs by the way you drove, "just as in housekeeping, it's the little leaks that count." Among some things to avoid: Buy your fuel from a reputable dealer: "You learned that lesson in any kind of shopping." Don't step on the gas; instead use a "gentle toe-touch." Make a smooth "lady-like" stop, instead of jamming on the breaks. Such women-centered advertising established the Ford models as a viable choice for women.[39]

Femininity Is a Business Asset

Women such as Dignam, Bemis, and Waldo became professionals because of the persistent belief that women, even trained copywriters, understood female customers better than men did. They also understood that their own truly *feminine* personalities were business assets, integral to their success in the business world. To compete, these ad women carefully crafted their self-images, creating distinct versions of femininity that resonated with their particular aspirations and social experiences of those they targeted as consumers. Paradoxically, they also learned to *do* as a man and *appear* as a woman. In fact, one Chicago journalist described Dignam as two people: "One is a gay, imaginative little girl, wearing a pink dress with sash, the other a shrewd, hard-headed young woman with her mind concentrated on business."[40]

Another major trend affecting the development of the female professional in advertising was the expansion of women's networks. As women increased their representation as managers and executives, entrepreneurs and workers, successful women like Dignam also presented the bright prospects that seemed attainable. Together Dignam and copywriter Blanche Clair edited *Advertising Careers for Women* in 1939, the first book specifically for women on the advertising profession. It was based on a series of lectures covering some twenty-two phases of the business, presented by successful women in the

Philadelphia area working in the field of advertising, ranging from copywriting to print production work.

As bright as the prospects may have appeared in advertising, Dignam also acknowledged the barriers to women workers, including the ceilings on salaries and limits to promotions. To be professional also increasingly meant that women were required to not only earn a college degree oriented to business skills but also to make a lifelong, uninterrupted commitment to work. The truth be told, wrote Dignam: "The advertising agency is, and probably always will be, a masculine stronghold. Men have built up all the big agencies and still control their management, although wives (behind the scenes) are a factor." Why, then, was the agency any place for a woman to look for a job? "The simple reason is this: women, for the most part, are the buyers of advertised commodities, and one woman knows what it takes to make another spend money," explained Dignam. "Women know women . . . their habits, their wants, and their weaknesses. It is as an interpreter of women and her buying ways that you'll be useful." In the end, Dignam encouraged aspiring ad women to dress well and "keep a stiff upper lip, with some lipstick on it" (figure 5.9).[41]

The same year that *Careers for Advertising* was published, the Second World War began in Europe after Germany invaded Poland, and two years later in 1941, the United States went to war. Production of civilian automobiles, consumer electronics, and appliances came to a halt until after the war.

THE WAR AT HOME AND OVERSEAS

World War II brought profound changes to the American way of life. The war sped up industrialization, and production boomed at aircraft factories, shipyards, ammunition plants, and other critical wartime industries; but the production of consumer items did not reflect this boom. No cars or refrigerators were manufactured during this period. As part of the war effort, the government urged citizens on the home front to conserve power, save fat for explosives, and collect tin cans, paper, and rubber for recycling. Food staples were rationed, the lim-

Figure 5.9. Do you have the makings of an advertising woman?

I. Have you changed your hairstyle at least once in the last five years?
II. When you were feeling very "down" did you ever buy a new hat just to cheer yourself up? (Did it?)
III. In a train, bus, or streetcar, would you rather study the people around you than read even the most exciting book?
IV. Did you ever speculate—just once—on how false eyelashes would look on you?
V. Do you read "Advice to the Lovelorn" in your daily papers?
VI. Do you like women—at least as well as you do men?
VII. Can you think of at least one way to improve the appearance of each of your five best friends?
VIII. Are you as interested in *why* people do things as in *what* they do? (Are you also interested in *what they do?*)
IX. Do you think requited love should be the most important aim of most women?
X. Have you ever, that you remember, spoken to a stranger in an emergency, a shared emotion, a sudden excess of friendliness and enjoyed it?

If a woman answered six or more questions with a "yes," copywriter Elizabeth Colt Kidd of the N. W. Ayer agency suggested that she could earn a living at cosmetics writing, but a score of eight or more meant that she had the makings of a good advertising woman. Source: *Advertising Careers for Women*, 1939, Dorothy Dignam Papers, State Historical Society of Wisconsin.

ited supply of gasoline curtailed auto travel, and the scarcity of fabric forced fashion changes. Instead of purchasing scarce consumer goods, people bought war bonds, paid off old debts, and did something for the war effort—serving on rationing boards, donating blood, and planting "victory" vegetable gardens.

As defense production increased, millions of people left their hometowns to work mandatory forty-eight-hour weeks in factories and on assembly lines to replace the men who had joined the military. Campaigns encouraged women to enter the labor force and take over the many jobs left behind by servicemen, with messages such as "We Can Do It," "Do the Job He Left Behind," and "Soldiers without Guns" (figure 5.10). Almost eighteen million women entered the labor force,

SOLDIERS *without guns*

Figure 5.10. Rosie the Riveter symbolized employed and independent women during World War II, US Army poster.

working on factory assembly lines, running offices, and selling in stores, while still managing the home. The work of Helen Lansdowne Resor for the Advertising War Council captured this era with the image of "Rosie the Riveter," who came to symbolize successfully employed and independent women of the war years. Even the oversized power tool on her lap suggested that she did not require a man for anything.

The unprecedented economic recovery programs of the New Deal did not end the Depression; World War II did. But the long-term impact of the war on the country and the consumer culture would not be evident until the postwar boom of the 1950s. With the defeat of Germany and Japan and a return to a peacetime economy, the United States enjoyed another surge in prosperity.

NOTES

1. The search for jobs affected countless middle-class Americans. In 1929 the "white-collar class" represented about two hundred and fifty men to every one hundred positions and two hundred women for every position. When the slump came in February 1929, the ratio skyrocketed to 1,416 men to 100 positions and 782 women applicants for every position. See "No Women in the Bread Line," *Independent Woman*, October 1930.

2. Lorine Pruette, ed., *Women Workers through the Depression: A Study of White Collar Employment Made by the American Women's Association* (New York: Macmillan, 1934), p. 4. See also Women's Bureau, Bulletin 120, *The Employment of Women in Offices*, 1934, Women's History Subject Collection, box 10A, folder: Employment of Women, Smith College Library.

3. In 1937 the first supermarket in the United States opened in a six-thousand-square-foot garage in Queens, New York, with shopping carts. *Mass Market Retailers* 19, no. 9 (June 17, 2002): 172.

4. On Shaver, see Allen Talmery, "Dorothy Shaver of Lord & Taylor, Unorthodox Store Strategist," *Vogue*, February 1, 1946. Jeanne Perkins, "No. 1 Career Woman," *Life*, May 12, 1947. Dorothy Shaver Papers, Costume Division, American History Archives, National Museum of American History, Smithsonian Institution, Washington, DC. Hereafter, American History Archives, Smithsonian.

5. For Fitz-Gibbon's ideas on teaching yourself and your family all about the English language, see *Macy's, Gimbels, and Me: How to Earn $90,000 a Year in Retail Advertising* (1951; repr., New York: Simon and Schuster, 1967), pp. 42–69.

6. "That's Not Blasting—That's Bernice," *Saturday Evening Post*, November 30, 1946, p. 17–18.

7. Fitz-Gibbon, *Macy's, Gimbels, and Me*, pp. 29–30. On Macy's copywriters, see Margaret Case Harriman, *The Price Is Right* (Nashville, TN: Word Publishing, 1958).

8. "That's Not Blasting—That's Bernice."

9. Fitz-Gibbon, pp. 236–37. For representative advertisements, see Bernice Fitz-Gibbon Papers, reel 1, State Historical Society of Wisconsin.

10. "Fond Memories for a Hall of Famer," *Advertising Age*, March 29, 1982; sec. 2, pp. M–11; Fitz-Gibbon, pp. 247–51.

11. "New Field": "Atlanta Woman Wins Title of Mrs. Barnum," newspaper clipping (n.d.), box 1, folder: Y2, Frances Bemis Collection. "Mrs. Barnum": unpublished autobiography, Frances Bemis, p. 3, box 4, folder 4: Bemis 5, Frances Bemis Collection, Sophia Smith Collection.

12. Autobiography by Frances Bemis, box 4, folder 4: Bemis, Frances Bemis Collection, Sophia Smith Collection.

13. On Bemis's work in merchandising from 1933 to 1954, see her unpublished autobiography, "Barnum in Merchandising," box 4, folder 4: Bemis 3, Frances Bemis Collection, Sophia Smith Collection. On payment to celebrities, see autobiography by Frances Bemis, pp. 4–6.

14. "Dramatizing the Sales of Merchandise," in *The Story of a Store with Heart*

(Hearns, company publication, 1936), box 5, folder 4: Bemis 8, Frances Bemis Collection, Sophia Smith Collection.

15. "She Made U.S. Designs Fashionable," *Jacksonville News*, p. 23, September 1946. See box 1, folder: Y2, Frances Bemis Collection, Sophia Smith Collection.

16. Miscellaneous newspaper clippings from *New York Times*, October 8, 1942; October 21, 1943; October 15, 1944; October 26, 1944; and press release by Frances Bemis, "Fashions Then and Now," January 23, 1942. See box 6, folder 4, Frances Bemis Collection, Sophia Smith Collection.

17. "Frances Bemis Announces Promotion and Public Relations Service," press release, October 12, 1954, box 1, folder 4: Bemis 2, Frances Bemis Collection, Sophia Smith Collection. "Fashion Promoter May Turn Talents to Brightening Ancient City's Allure" (n.d.), box 1, folder: Y2, Frances Bemis Collection, Sophia Smith Collection.

18. Susan Smuylan, *Selling Radio: The Commercialization of American Broadcasting 1920–1934* (Washington, DC: Smithsonian Institution Press, 1994), p. 87. John Irving Romer, "Radio as an Advertising Medium," *Printers' Ink*, April 27, 1922. "What the Women Like and Dislike about Radio," *Printers' Ink*, March 21, 1935.

19. Kristine McCusker, "Dear Radio Friend: Listener Mail and the National Barn Dance, 1931–1941," *American Studies* 38, no. 2: 173–95. See also Kristine McCusker, *Lonesome Cowgirls and Honky-Tonk Girls: The Women of Barn Dance Radio* (Urbana-Champaign: University of Illinois Press, 2008).

20. "Housewives Receptive to Radio in Morn," *Advertising Age*, January 25, 1930.

21. Alice Keith, *How to Speak and Write for Radio: A Manual of Broadcasting Technique* (New York: Harper & Brothers, 1944).

22. On the history of soap operas from radio to television, see Robert C. Allen, *Speaking of Soap Operas* (Chapel Hill: University of North Carolina, 1985). Also, Jim Cox chronicles thirty-one radio serials and their influence on radio programming in *The Radio Soap Opera* (Jefferson, NC: McFarland & Co., 1999). On women listeners as active participants, see Duana Jones, *Ads, Women, and Boxtops* (New York: Printers' Ink Books, 1955).

23. On reference to retailers, see "Plan Presentation Montgomery," memorandum (n.d.), box 4, folder: Painted Dreams 1931, Irma Phillips, Personal and Business Papers (1931–1966), State Historical Society of Wisconsin.

24. Obituary of Anne Hummert, *New York Times*, July 21, 1996.

25. On the Hummert script production system, see Cynthia B. Meyers, "Frank and Anne Hummert's Soap Opera Empire: 'Reason-Why' Advertising Strategies in Early Radio Programming," *Quarterly Review of Film and Video* 15, no. 2 (November 1997): 113–32.

26. Cruisenberry, box 3, folders 9 and 10: Story of Marlin Fan Mail. Jane Cruisenberry Personal and Business Papers, State Historical Society of Wisconsin. See also "What Radio Advertisers Do with 'Fan' Mail," *Printers' Ink*, September 1932.

27. The Radio Project Report: Paul Lazarsfeld and Harry Field, *The People Look at Radio* (Chapel Hill: University of North Carolina Press, 1946).

28. "Ruth Waldo and the Spirit of Thompson," *J. Walter Thompson Newsletter*, September 1975, Biographical File, box 21, JWT. See also Obituary of Ruth Waldo, *New York Times*, September 5, 1975.

29. On Lux Flakes, see Group Meeting, September 30, 1930, JWT Staff Meetings, Minutes of Representatives, box 3. See also *JWT Forum*, November 9, 1937, JWT Staff Meetings, box 6, 7, and 8, JWT.

30. On Scott Tissue, see Representatives Meetings, November 10, 1927; Creative Staff Meeting, April 16, 1932, and September 28, 1932, in JWT Staff Meetings, 1927–1929, boxes 1 and 5, Minutes of Representatives Meetings, JWT.

31. On strong women, see Lois Banner, *Women in Modern America: A Brief History* (Belmont, CA: Thompson Wadsworth, 2005), pp. 120–25.

32. Kathy Peiss, *Hope in a Jar: The Making of America's Beauty Culture* (New York: Owl Books, 1999).

33. On Steichen, see Patricia Johnston, *Real Fantasies: Edward Steichen's Advertising Photography* (Berkeley: University of California Press, 1997). On Woodbury nude series advertisements, see *Ladies' Home Journal*, 1936: April, July, and November. See also *Good Housekeeping*, 1936: April, June, August, October, and December.

34. Tom Reichert, *The Erotic History of Advertising* (Amherst, NY: Prometheus Books, 2003), p. 99.

35. Virginia Scharff, *Taking the Wheel: Women and the Coming of the Motor Age* (Albuquerque: University of New Mexico, 1991), p. 130.

36. "Dignam, Dorothy," *Who's Who of American Women*, Volume 2, 1961–1962 (New Providence, NJ: Marquis, 1962).

37. Ibid. See also "Business Biography of Miss Dorothy Dignam," 1928, Dorothy Dignam Papers, box 1, folder 2, State Historical Society of Wisconsin. For representative articles by Dorothy Dignam, see box 3, folders 21 and 22, Dorothy Dignam Collection. Also see Dorothy Dignam scrapbook: "London Admires Its First Electrically Cooled Florist Refrigerator Installed at Selfridge's," *Electric Refrigeration News*, February 27, 1929. "France Wants American Appliances," *Electrical Manufacturing*, May 1929. "In Munich the Chimney Sweeps Have Become Fireplace Inspectors," *Gas Age-Record*, October 12, 1929, Dorothy Dignam Collection, State Historical Society of Wisconsin.

38. For correspondence, scripts, and papers concerning Dignam and the Ford account, see box 1, folders 1 and 2. For advertisements and booklets, see package 3, Dorothy Dignam Papers, State Historical Society of Wisconsin.

39. "Chat with Women Drivers: Car Economy," *Ford News*, August 1937, company publication, Ford Motor Car Company, package 2, Dorothy Dignam Papers, State Historical Society of Wisconsin.

40. "Business Biography of Dorothy Dignam."

41. On "masculine stronghold," see Blanche Claire and Dorothy Dignam, eds., *Advertising Careers for Women* (New York: Harper and Brothers, 1939), p. 19. "Lipstick": Dorothy Dignam, "Up the Ladder We Must Go," speech transcript, 1933, pp. 6, 12, box 3, folder 19, Dignam Papers, Schlesinger Library.

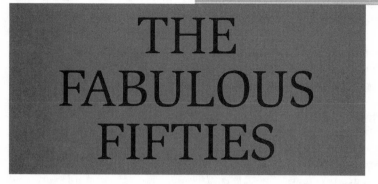

CHAPTER 6

THE FABULOUS FIFTIES

REDESIGNING MR. AND MRS. CONSUMER

I n 1947 developer William J. Levitt started work on a massive, planned suburban community on Long Island called Levittown, and a later one near Philadelphia and New Jersey, by building homes on tracts of land on which had been farms, forest, and countryside. The first homes were originally put on the renters' market for $58 a month in 1947, with an option to buy later, only 5 percent down required for veterans, and repayment over a long period of time (at a time when the average annual income was about $3,000). With the initial purchase price for Levittown houses so modest, buyers kept buying and Levitt kept building more than seventeen thousand nearly identical eight-hundred-square-foot, nostalgic Cape Cod cottages and contemporary ranch homes set on various plots. These communities were connected to cities by trains and freeways and vastly expanded the number of suburban shopping centers.[1]

Before Levittown, the bedroom communities had been the exclusive provinces of the well-off, but after the war millions of returning veterans and workers with wartime savings needed homes for themselves and their growing families. Although the postwar baby boom was a worldwide phenomenon, it was more pronounced in the United States than elsewhere. The birthrate increased 25 percent following the end of the war in 1945 compared to the mid-1930s, and it remained there through the 1950s. The Levittowns offered homes to the working class, because virtually no home construction had taken place since the 1920s; they also helped redefine class by allowing working-class Americans to experience home ownership for the first time in their lives.[2]

Although suburban, working-class residents were mixed by ethnicity and religion more than ever before, they were mostly all white. When African Americans or unmarried women went shopping for a new home in Levittown, the real estate agents bluntly told them that they were not wanted. Furthermore, government loan policies and underwriting policies of local banks now enforced racial segregation, as it also did gender discrimination in lending. Even more overt racism constrained African American consumption in the South: African Americans were simply not allowed to shop in the same stores, eat in the same restaurants, or attend the same private schools, as consumption became more differentially distributed than democratic as conceived in theory. Thus, the long-term economic effects of racial and gender exclusion were that blacks and unmarried women found career ladders, paths to home ownership, and upward mobility largely blocked, which set the stage for the emergence of the civil rights movement and a second wave of feminism more militant than any of its predecessors.[3]

Hence, the postwar era marks a turning point for minorities and women, largely in terms of their own attitudes, aspirations, and expectations, as well as how marketers reconceptualized the American market and further advanced gender-based advertising. At the heart of this analysis is the concept that after the Second World War, modern marketing and advertising evolved into a dynamic, interactive process between producers and consumers, as marketers sought to further differentiate the mass market and understand consumer behavior.

With this in mind, the next two chapters examine this new postwar order. First, I look at how men and women, Mr. and Mrs. Consumer, imagined postwar America as a result of their wartime experiences, the restructuring of residential and commercial centers that accompanied the postwar period, and the evolving marketing thought and strategies to encourage mass consumption, as well as the contradictions that created them. The subsequent chapter focuses on those professional women who worked as cultural mediators, and how they interpreted the currents of culture.

THE BACK-TO-THE-HOME MOVEMENT

The United States emerged from World War II not just a victor but a global power. Far from slipping back in an economic recession as some feared, the nation embarked on a remarkable period of growth powered by massive war spending. The postwar era consisted of two distinct phases. The first period was about catching up, which lasted until the early 1950s. The wartime rationing of shoes, tires, foodstuffs, and so on had come to an end, and returning servicemen clamored for housing and jobs. Manufacturers switched from the production of jeeps, tanks, aircraft, and uniforms to production of consumer goods for the free market. People made up for lost time buying goods that they had denied themselves, put off buying, or that were not available in the preceding Depression and war years, and they acquired multitudes of material goods. Still, there were chronic shortages of goods such as clothing, refrigerators, cars, and stoves as late as 1948.

After Americans had caught up on their long-delayed purchases, corporate profit motives prompted the second phase from the mid-1950s to the mid-1960s, transforming the productive wartime economy into an even stronger consumer economy. For a time, the material affluence and the celebration of the American way of life obscured underlying social tensions of a rapidly changing postwar society.

Catching Up

The Levittowns, large families, modern kitchens, televisions, and enormous chromed automobiles came to symbolize the hopes and possibilities of the postwar era. Men returned from the war to higher-paying jobs, subsidized college education, and wives with accumulated savings. The 1944 GI bill (Servicemen's Readjustment Act) provided veterans returning home from the war with government loans and benefits that meant they did not immediately start jobs. Some took advantage of the opportunity for subsidized education and enrolled in college and professional training programs.

Moreover, the war had dramatically changed how society regarded the education and employment of women. Women who had served in the military were also entitled to the same benefits as male veterans under the GI bill, but colleges that were still the gateway to managerial and professional jobs generally turned down women to admit men. The same process of exclusion occurred in the workplace. Millions of women held heavy-duty industrial jobs and served in the armed services; work that had been perceived as unfeminine suddenly became a patriotic necessity. If there were good, well-paying jobs, they obviously belonged to men who came home from the war to head families; nevertheless, more women held industrial jobs than ever before. Still, the alternative of a wife at home supported by a husband at work became increasingly attractive to some women who had worked during wartime.[4]

Together, the unions and military helped boost employment and wage levels. By the mid-1950s, nearly 60 percent of working people had a middle-class income, almost double the number in the 1920s. The GI bill's low-cost housing loans further cemented the idea in the American consciousness that every family could aspire to a suburban, middle-class lifestyle, with the husband earning enough wages to support a wife at home with their children. After the war, the rates of marriage remained high and family sizes increased compared to the Depression and wartime, when weddings were postponed for reasons of economics or separation from loved ones. By 1963, on the average, women married at twenty; at twenty-two, they were considered old maids. Bridal and baby showers were constant, with consumer goods given to the expectant bride or mother to prepare her for her future role.

The postwar economic boom also uprooted many families, in part to meet the demands of ever-expanding industries and corporations. Military spending helped fuel the growth of such key sectors of the economy as aircraft manufacturing and electronics; it also fostered economic growth and urbanization in the South, in Southern California, and in Seattle, as well as on Long Island. Millions of people living in rural communities poured into cities and their sprawling suburbs to work in factories, offices, and stores. The number of Americans living on farms had dropped from nearly 25 percent in 1940 to below 7 percent by 1964. Between 1940 and 1964, the population of the Pacific Coast states more than doubled, and by 1964 California became the nation's most populous state. This growing suburban population created a demand for new housing, shopping centers, and strip malls; it also offered automobile, home furnishing, and appliance manufacturers an enormous market for their mass-produced goods. Such rising levels of consumption spurred increased production, which in turn generated new jobs.

The Decade of Domesticity

The economic boom reshaped American society, transformed urban ethnics into middle-class suburban homeowners, and changed housing patterns. Advertisements for the massive, suburban housing developments with their four-room Cape Cods and, later, ranches evoked picturesque images and promised: "Your happiness is a 'sure thing' at beautiful Haywood Park" or "A vacation that lasts a lifetime begins here" at Presidential Lakes Development. For the postwar women and men who had suffered tough economic times throughout the Depression and separation from loved ones during the war, indeed the suburban home became a refuge, and family togetherness fulfilled a psychological need. "Owning a house came to be the embodiment of the new American dream," explains author David Halberstam. "As promised by endless Hollywood films, it represented fulfillment and contentment, as well as reinforced the traditional, gendered stereotypes of the confident dads, perky moms, and glowing children, attending good schools and colleges."[5]

At this point it is impossible to underestimate the importance and influence of the transformation of the residential experience, what historian Lizabeth Cohen called, "the reconfiguration of community marketplaces" in the 1950s and 1960s. Suburban housing patterns were designed for a family in which Mom stayed at home, Dad worked in the city, and other relatives remained at a distance. First, it was difficult for women in the suburbs to work outside the home, since jobs in suburbia were limited and domestic help hard to find. With husbands away from home for longer periods because of a long commute to work, wives were left with responsibility for the family. Life in the early suburbs also had few of the social institutions that women relied upon, such as the corner grocery to relieve the burden of shopping, the nearby grandparents for childcare. Now domestic tasks also included the major one of transportation, since schools, stores, and train stations were rarely located within walking distance from home. At the same time, the lower density of the population made these modes of transportation unprofitable. Instead, the station wagon, which could hold children, groceries, and materials for home improvement, became the symbol of suburbia's means of transportation.[6]

Sociologists and other critics denounced the suburbs for breeding conformity and status seeking, as suburbanites tried to keep up with the Joneses by buying new cars and appliances. Among these critics, William H. Whyte's *The Organization Man* (1956)—a study of Park Forest, Illinois—concluded that mindless conservatives and extreme conformity typified the suburbanites. At the same time, a small group of intellectual rebels—or *beatniks*—used poetry and literature to mock the values of the American mainstream. Led by Allen Ginsberg and Jack Kerouac, the beat poets idolized African Americans, especially jazz musicians, and denounced middle-class life, what they perceived as materialism, sexual repression, and spiritual emptiness. While the beats were writing, a separate culture of rebellious teenagers emerged with their distinctive clothing, hairstyles, and rock 'n' roll music. Partly as a result of the popularization of such attitudes, large numbers of middle-class women also began to seriously question the ideological framework that confined them to the home, when other opportunities existed outside this arena. "I was dismayed to learn the average woman feels there is something demeaning about caring for a home and that she feels defeated when she has to write down her occupation as housewife," wrote Bernice Fitz-Gibbon in 1956. "That's feminist propaganda . . . don't you believe a word of it."[7]

When Betty Friedan wrote *The Feminine Mystique* in 1963, she captured this moment in time and raised questions about whether larger opportunities could be available to women. Writing like a housewife, she talked of the emptiness of the suburban lifestyle and criticized the prevailing domestic ideology of the postwar era, a belief system she called the *feminine mystique.* The myth perpetuated by popular women's magazines led millions of women to reject careers for community affairs and seemed aimed at getting women back into prewartime roles as nurturing mothers and servants of men, when many of them did not find it all that fulfilling. Such narrow societal expectations were causing many women to feel useless, depressed, and even suicidal. "Ah, the problem that has no name," as Friedan described the feminine mystique, "is my problem. It's our problem. It's the problem of women."[8]

Yet the sharpest critic of America's celebration of an affluent, classless social order was the racism prevalent in the North and South, shaped by the legacy of slavery, economic structures, and private belief systems. Even after World War II, minorities had far less access to material affluence than white Americans. Private schools, workplaces, and the new suburban communities accepted the white veterans but were not as open to black veterans returning from war. By the end of the 1960s, however, civil rights activists would mobilize public opinion and spark a broad wave of popular activism that called for the full realization of America's democratic promise: the American dream of a middle-class life was attainable for every American.

Encouraging Mass Consumption

Once Americans had caught up on consumption—buying goods not available in the hard times of the Depression and war years—many businesses feared that the shopping spree would end and would plunge the nation into a new economic downturn. This led marketers to search for more sophisticated ways to ensure a constant demand for goods and new ways to create demand for their flood of new products. Marketers experimented with three strategies: (1) design new and existing products to meet carefully researched consumer needs, (2) pricing and credit to increase people's ability to purchase, and (3) planned obsolescence to encourage more frequent consumption.

First, postwar manufacturers shifted from wartime production to producing what consumers would buy. This change came as the new materials, improved technologies, and efficient manufacturing systems developed for the military defense effort were adapted for civilian use. For example, nylon, which had been created to make parachutes, replaced costly silk in women's stockings. The aerosol container, commonly know as a bug bomb, first appeared as a pesticide fogger in the South Pacific. With the addition of a simple spray top, the new cans dispensed everything, including furniture polish, cheese, whipped cream, antiseptics, hairspray, perfume, and deodorant. New light plastics offered convenience and added affordable glamour to everything from squeeze bottles to furniture. Other wartime innovations like adding machines, electric typewriters, and computers streamlined office operations.[9]

Marketers also tried setting sought-after goods like appliances at higher prices to bring in greater revenue, while the increasing availability of credit increased consumers' ability to purchase them. Although a wide variety of goods could be purchased by installment payments since the 1920s, now retailers with both downtown and suburban branches fueled the growth of charge accounts. But the concept of paying merchants with a card provided consumers with a new convenience to consolidate multiple purchases. Diners Club offered the first *charge card* in 1950, authorizing the holder to buy food and entertainment on credit at participating establishments but requiring that the entire balance be paid with each statement. In 1958, Bank of America created a *revolving credit card*, which eventually became the Visa and later the Master Card system; it allows the consumer to make a minimum payment and revolve the balance to the next statement at the cost of having interest charged. Such credit cards expanded women's access to family income from spending the weekly or monthly household allowance to committing the family's future earnings, while they also deepened women's economic dependence on men. Unlike the local store credit system, qualifying for a line of credit with a bank depended on the husband's income, even when women earned their own money, in most cases.

Finally, manufacturers promoted the concept of newness, or *planned obsolescence* to encourage more frequent purchases. Although General Motors chairman Alfred Sloane had outlined this concept back in the 1920s, it was fully realized in the 1950s. Whether it was a two-year-old car, a five-year-old house, or whatever, it was "used," and therefore second-best. But new looks and features had to be visible. It was design intended solely to sell a new product. The kitchen then became a status symbol, displaying the latest appliances with new push-button technology and decorator hues. Even the simple, two-door refrigerator became an exercise in planned obsolescence, with Westinghouse offering as many as fifty color combinations, including Flamingo Pink, Robin's Egg Blue, and Buttercup Yellow. Even as these innovative strategies ensured greater profits, marketers competed in an increasingly cluttered marketplace as business boomed in the postwar era. For every new product, four or five major competitors already existed. In order to sell more, businesses advertised more to the mass market, where consumers shared a similar set of tastes and desires. Advertising now had to contend with more clutter in both print and broadcast media than ever before. As a result, postwar companies found that their core market—the white middle class—had already been developed to the point where additional advertising and selling expenditures yielded diminishing returns.

Just as marketers grafted on to new ideas in the 1920s and 1930s, increasingly sophisticated theories and studies came together that moved them away from assuming a unified mass-consumer market to categorizing, or *segmenting* the market by variables other than gender or class. The growing influence, in particular, of psychology, social science, and anthropology gave practitioners new tools for identifying, classifying, and appealing to distinct groups of consumers. In their estimation, segmented markets would promise greater, steadier profits through expanding the pool of potential customers for a wider variety of products, each designed to meet the distinct needs, wants, and preferences of a distinct community of consumers. From these goals of learning more about the mass market of consumers evolved the kernels for strategies that eventually included segmentation of the mass market, development of new products and line extensions, and advances in brand management.

WHY WE BUY

In the 1950s, a perspective called Motivational Research (M. R.) attempted to bring together the study of psychology and marketing to understand the factors that influence *consumer behavior*, or the acquisition, consumption, and use of products. In short, why we buy.

The M. R. approach was largely based on psychoanalytical or Freudian interpretations with a heavy emphasis on unconscious motives, which a small group of European intellectuals trained at the University of Vienna brought to Madison Avenue in the 1940s. Among them, Ernest Dichter and Herta Herzog both studied under Paul Lazarsfeld, one of the giants of twentieth-century sociology and audience research. There also was Hans Zeisele, who along with Herzog went to work for McCann-Erickson. These researchers devised surveys with hundreds of questions based on Freudian dynamic psychology, using devices to measure audience response, such as hypnosis, role-playing, and Rorschach inkblots. They also invented what we now call the *focus group*, in which a group of people interact and answer questions about their attitude toward a product, concept, advertisement, or packaging. In the commercial area, psychologist Dr. Ernest Dichter emerged as the most prominent motivational research practitioner—as well as perhaps the most controversial.[10]

Sex and Symbolism

Ernest Dichter started his career in motivational research after emigrating from Vienna to the United States. He first directed psychological research for the Stirling Getchell advertising agency in New York before conducting his own research, and in 1946, he formed the Institute for Motivational Research and did consulting for hundreds of major corporations of the day.

Advertising research had been concerned with quantitative studies until that point, basically recording who was buying what and where. Instead of this approach, Dichter advocated the new technique of Motivational Research, which relied on a depth interview, or a long interrogation, to understand the deeper meaning of buying motives.

During the interview, the psychoanalyst (or in this case, Dichter) asked a number of questions about the uses of the products, purposes for buying, feelings about, and beliefs about a particular product. The interpretations usually involved a complex of repressed and forgotten impressions, since Freudian theory heavily influenced Dichter's work. The Austrian psychiatrist Sigmund Freud theorized that dreams are an unconscious representation of repressed desires, especially sexual thoughts. By the 1950s, the mass media abounded with articles on psychology, images of dreaming, and Freudian symbolism in advertisements. In the subconscious world of Freudian analysis, any elongated object could be interpreted as a phallic symbol, such as sticks, tree trunks, and sharp weapons. Women's clothing styles even took on aggressive suggestions of male penetration, such as an aggressively pointed hat, skirts shaped with sharp angles, or other personal items like a lipstick tube or umbrella (figure 6.1).[11]

Dichter, following Freud's theory, suggested that consumers channeled their unacceptable desires into acceptable outlets; in this case, buying consumer goods that signify their underlying desires. That is, the product stands for, or represents, a consumer's true goal, which is socially unacceptable or unattainable. Advertising and design then

the brightest jewel of all can be your lips...

Tangee's newest lipstick shade—BRIGHT 'N CLEAR is the brightest, clearest, most dazzling red on record. It is exactly the color and lipstick America's leading beauty authorities say smart women should wear. And— exciting miracle!—here is an indelible-type lipstick that actually stays BRIGHT 'N CLEAR for hours and hours. It will not dry your lips...will not go dull and hideous even after blotting. So start your BRIGHT 'N CLEAR future today!

Tangee PRESENTS

"BRIGHT 'N CLEAR"

a new shade - a true shade - a just right for you shade !

Figure 6.1. Freudian symbolism suggests that an elongated object such as a lipstick could be interpreted as a phallic symbol.

served to amplify the features of useful things, transforming them into appealing commodities that promised to satisfy emotional as well as material needs—the hopes and desires of the buyers. For example, Dichter hypothesized that people attached great importance to their first car. It is a "puberty symbol," signifying that "at last you can get away from your parents and be on your own," he explained. The findings led to a Plymouth advertising campaign that used the nostalgia theme "Do you still remember when . . . ?" The ads showed an old car linked with very new Plymouth models. In further research for Chrysler, Dichter found that more men bought a sedan even though they were attracted to a convertible because they associated the practical hardtop with their wife. Even men's socks were invested with emotional significance and could inspire passion. When a husband finds an empty sock drawer, he interprets this as a symbol of an empty heart or his wife's neglect, Dichter deduced in another study for DuPont's hosiery section. But an overflowing sock drawer can be seen as visible evidence of his wife's consideration, concern, and love.[12]

When looking for reasons why cake mixes had fallen flat in the 1950s, Dichter discovered that the process of baking also held emotional significance. The main appeal was the convenience; one simply added water to make the batter. But the quick mixes served up anxieties to homemakers, argued Dichter, since women wanted some sense of participation in the making of a cake. If she used a quick mix, adding only water instead of baking from "scratch," she felt unfulfilled in producing something new for her family. Eventually Dichter's insights led to countless ads and magazine articles that emphasized women's overall participation, creativity, and appearance over taste. For modern women then, the real art of baking began after the cake emerged from the oven, putting on their own frosting, spreading fillings between layers, or covering it with glazes. Thus, a huge, lavishly frosted cake became the dominant image in advertising (figure 6.2).

Although some of Dichter's interpretations may not sound plausible, he did reinforce what marketers and advertisers have long known in selling the women's market: "Since buying is only the climax of a complicated relationship based to a large extent on the woman's yearning to know how to be a more attractive housewife, a

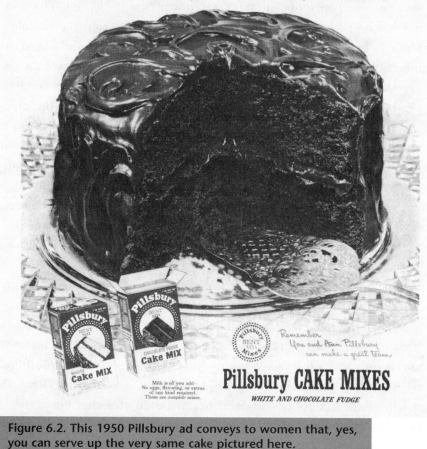

Who...Me?

Yes, Madam, you can make a cake of the very same lush, well-turned-out appearance as the cake you see here. And you do it without raising a single bead on your pretty brow. How do you do it?...

By merely adding milk to either of the two new Pillsbury Mixes... you triumph, you please, you make everybody very, very happy. How about a Pillsbury Mix Cake tonight? How about...YOU?

Remember
You and Ann Pillsbury
can make a great team

Pillsbury CAKE MIXES
WHITE AND CHOCOLATE FUDGE

Milk is all you add—
No eggs, flavoring, or extras
of any kind required.
These are complete mixes.

Figure 6.2. This 1950 Pillsbury ad conveys to women that, yes, you can serve up the very same cake pictured here.

superior mother, etc., use this motivation in all your promotion and advertising." Furthermore, Dichter found that people responded well to products that were sex-typed, because such products solicited the inner hopes and passions of the buyer. By using this approach, Dichter identified masculinity/virility as a major motive for purchasing such products as coffee, red meat, heavy shoes, toy guns, fur coats for women, and razors for shaving. On the other hand, he identified femininity with the major consumption motivations for cakes and cookies, dolls, silk, tea, and household curios. As a result, marketers perpetuated the sex-typing of things, producing boys' and girls' bicycles, toys for boys and girls, and so on. In this social framework, people articulate themselves as *female* or *male* in part through the material objects and images that frame their daily activities.[13]

Despite the sexual themes, Dichter's maverick methods made him and other researchers a fortune. M. R. tended to be less expensive than large-scale, quantitative research survey data, because interviewing and data-processing costs remained relatively small. Though the samples were small, many marketers and advertisers found that their knowledge derived from the research helped developed new products and marketing communications that appealed to deep-seated emotions and thus provided a more powerful appeal to attract consumers. A pilot project with forty to seventy-five interviews concerned with a specific problem cost around $5,000 to $7,500 in 1957; and a full study of a specific problem, $20,000 to $50,000.[14]

Adding further to M. R. theory, other graphic artists, product designers, and psychologists addressed issues of geometry and color combinations in packaging. One example is the graphics on the Procter & Gamble Tide laundry box that features concentric waves of high-intensity, orange and yellow color with the word *Tide* in blue lettering, communicating that the product is powerful yet mild. To differentiate the Cheer brand of detergent that worked in both hot and cold water from the well-established Tide brand, Procter & Gamble simply added blue flakes, advertised them as Blue Magic Whiteners, and positioned the detergent as the modern approach to laundry. These findings about graphics and color still guide contemporary product marketing. But the pioneer in studying people's emotional response to packaging was Louis Cheskin, who began research in the 1930s. He found that certain color combinations could imbue packages with a bold new look or a seductive manner. For example, the look of a package had an enormous impact on crackers' taste, on how soaps are perceived to clean, on how rich and satisfying a beer is to drink. Cheskin also tested symbols for the Betty Crocker logo, recommending the spoon as the most effective image; once added to packaged cake mixes, sales doubled in less than twelve months.

When the Leo Burnett agency of Chicago repositioned Marlboro from a cigarette for women to one targeted at men, it consulted with Cheskin on the packaging, color, geometric design, and symbolism. Traditionally, the market for filter-tip cigarettes had been females who desired a mild smoke; and so in 1924, Philip Morris positioned the Marlboro cigarette for the women's market with the slogan "Mild as May." For years the cigarettes were sold in a dainty white box and featured a red paper "beauty-tip" to conceal lipstick traces. In order to reach an old group of customers—male smokers who were willing to try new cigarette brands—Philip Morris revised the product design, packaging, and advertising. First, the red filter tip was replaced with brown paper, and the dainty package with a convenient, flip-top box that displayed a red-and-white geometric design with black letters. In the world of M. R., the bold design of the pointed crest could also be interpreted as aggressive male penetration. But it would be the gendered advertising campaign for Marlboro cigarettes more than anything else that sold the cigarette to the men's market.

To promote the most masculine cigarette on the market, the Leo Burnett agency made the most masculine symbols in American life central to the campaign. The first ad, which appeared in 1955, introduced a character who was to become a cultural icon—the Marlboro Man. This symbol proved that there was nothing feminine about the filtered cigarettes: "Man-sized taste of honest tobacco comes full through." Other ads featured a wide variety of rugged outdoorsmen—skin divers, football players, boxers, canoeists, and race car drivers—to suggest toughness and virility. These characters also had a tattoo on their hand or wrist to suggest an interesting past. But the campaign eventually returned to the familiar cowboy, the Marlboro Man, riding horseback, rounding up cattle, or relaxing beside the campfire (figure 6.3). This archetypal figure, drawn from American history, apparently hit a subconscious nerve in the public mind. At a time when many Americans feared the extreme conformities of suburbia, the myth of the cowboy evoked memorable imagery of real men in a man's world. Eight months after

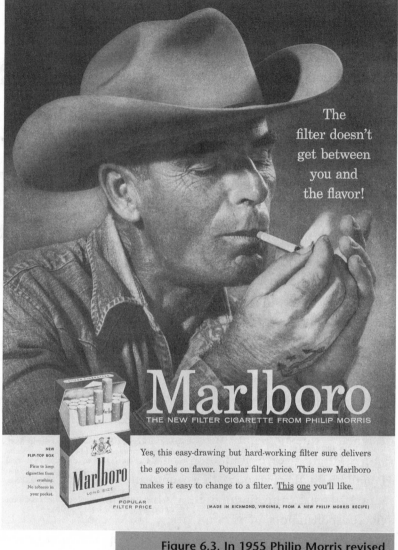

The
filter doesn't
get between
you and
the flavor!

Marlboro
THE NEW FILTER CIGARETTE FROM PHILIP MORRIS

**NEW
FLIP-TOP BOX**

Firm to keep
cigarettes from
crushing.
No tobacco in
your pocket.

**POPULAR
FILTER PRICE**

Yes, this easy-drawing but hard-working filter sure delivers
the goods on flavor. Popular filter price. This new Marlboro
makes it easy to change to a filter. This one you'll like.

(MADE IN RICHMOND, VIRGINIA, FROM A NEW PHILIP MORRIS RECIPE)

**Figure 6.3. In 1955 Philip Morris revised
Marlboro's product design, packaging, and
advertising to connect with the men's market.**

the campaign opened, sales had increased 5,000 percent; now Marlboro
ranks among the world's most valuable brands. Quite obviously the
macho quality of the campaign placed the cigarette "right in the heart
of core meanings of smoking: masculinity, adulthood, vigor, and
potency," explained market researcher Pierre Martineau.[15]

A second school of M. R. thought relied on a combination of qualitative interviews and quantitative research, which gave a more scientific basis to the findings than Dichter's interpretations. Among the earliest researchers in this field, Viennese-trained psychologist Dr. Herta Herzog had worked on investigations of daytime radio and soap opera listeners as part of Paul Lazarsfeld's programs of mass-media research in the 1930s and 1940s. Herzog moved on to work for a small adverting agency called Jack Tinker & Partners, made up of some of the best people from the McCann-Erickson agency. Here she trained dozens of interviewers and sent them out to analyze the psyche of the American consumer. While people spend money based on their motivations, according to Herzog, such actions are also affected by "need priorities." For example, they change their buying behavior when money is tight; similarly, they change with fashion and fads. Here she believed that the quantitative method of M. R. was capable of uncovering the motivating factor and predicting the ultimate effectiveness of that appeal when translated into an advertisement.

The Herzog method is characterized by a series of four steps: (1) Using conventional mass-market research methods, she first located potential consumer markets. (2) She then tabulated the reactions and buying motives of between three hundred and four hundred consumers, using depth interviews and projective tests. (3) She next designed a questionnaire to test out M. R. conclusions on a larger sample, from twelve hundred to three thousand consumers. (4) Having finally discovered a strong motivating factor for a product, she helped translate the findings into advertisements and pretested to selected consumers in various cities. Such research proved useful where products are not distinguishable in quality, performance, or price. For example, Herzog helped select the brand name Oasis cigarettes because her research suggested that the name brought to mind connotations of cool, bubbling springs and would have the greatest appeal to the orally fixated smoker (figure 6.4). Clearly, the increasingly fashionable concept of M. R. contributed to drawing consumers and producers closer together in a collaborative process of inscribing goods with new meanings.[16]

Figure 6.4. This ad for Oasis cigarettes was designed to appeal to the orally fixated smoker.

Group Behavior of Consumers

A third school of M. R. practitioners included psychologists and sociologists, who emphasized the group behavior of consumers and the impact of culture and environment on their opinions and reactions. Traditional market segmentation based on social class revolved around occupation and discretionary income, usually that of the head of the household or chief wage earner, provided one way for categorizing consumers' distinctive tastes, wants, and product preferences. Hence, marketing thought assumed that the upper classes were the first to try new products, which then *trickled down* to the middle class and eventually to the working class. Historically, there had been some justification for this view. For example, the middle and upper classes first adopted new technology such as the indoor bathroom, refrigerator, washing machine, automobile, and telephone. By the 1950s, however, as Americans became more affluent, this process became less apparent in certain segments of society. Now the new *opinion leaders*, or experts on particular subjects, came from certain media messages and information from their friends, families, and peers as part of their everyday relationships.

In this era, several studies provided new tools to help marketers to segment the mass of prospective consumers not only in terms of wealth and power but also on previously ignored aspects, such as consumption patterns, suggesting the growing centrality of lifestyles and working class. Here was a hugely profitable market. Among these researchers, anthropologist William Lloyd Warner applied the techniques of his discipline to study contemporary American culture. During Warner's years at the University of Chicago, his research included important studies of African American communities in Chicago and the rural South, a midwestern community (called Jonesville), and a New England community (Yankee City). In his landmark book, *Social Class America* (1949), Warner divided society into five class categories—Upper Class, Middle-Upper Class, Upper-Middle Class, Lower-Middle Class, and Upper-Lower Class/Lower Class— and pointing out that the last two were considered the working class.

To Warner, American social class was based more on attitudes than on the actual amount of money an individual made. One crucial observation he made of the upper-lower classes was that they might make more money than members of the lower class (for example, a well-salaried factory worker vs. a secretarial worker), but their identity was based on the type of work they performed (blue-collar manual labor vs. white-collar office work). Another finding that he made was that the upper-middle class, though a relatively small group, usually "set the standard" for proper American behavior as reflected in the mass media, echoing nineteenth-century sociologists Theodore Veblen and George Simmel. To marketers and advertisers, "Middle Majority woman is the target you are supposed to hit," claimed Warner. She occupied the combined social classes of white-collar workers, tradesmen, and skilled and semiskilled workers, who made up approximately 65 percent of the workforce. Furthermore, the typical American housewife lived in a very narrow world, tended to accept conformity, and built her whole life around the home. Here was a hugely profitable market that required a thorough understanding of distinct tastes and desires.[17]

With the shift to more elaborate market segmentation after the Second World War, marketers not only differentiated the market by gender with the basic categories of female and male, but they also subdivided these segments into smaller groups by social class. Now interest grew in defining a much more complex group of values and preferences to distinguish one group of buyers from another, shifting from the woman as the purchasing agent for the family to the differences in attitudes and motives of the entire family.

Sophisticated marketers hired sociologists and anthropologists to help them understand what working people wanted, taking into account more than income, explains Lizabeth Cohen. The University of Chicago and the *Chicago Tribune* newspaper, for example, funded the influential and respected Social Research, Inc. (SRI), established by Burleigh Gardner, a social anthropologist and former business professor who worked with Warner. In addition, Sears stores commissioned SRI to undertake a series of comprehensive studies of working-class taste, the most well-known being *Workingman's Wife: Her Personality and Life Style* (1959). Some of the other SRI studies for the *Tribune*'s advertisers included air travel and airline personalities, Chicago women and their clothing, definitions of new shopping centers, how women read price advertising, and men's clothing as a symbolic expression (figure 6.5). And Bernarr McFadden, publisher of *True Story* and other magazines, hired SRI to conduct studies to help advertisers sell more goods to the working-class readership.[18]

In the marketing journals, two other sociologists, Wendell Smith and Pierre Martineau, further advanced the modern concept of market segmentation. In 1956 Smith proposed an alternative to mass marketing in a landmark article in the *Journal of Marketing.* As many companies faced growing product competition in mass markets, Smith advised that the smaller or fringe market segments taken together could yield greater consumer satisfaction, profitability, and a more secure market position. Two years later in 1958, Pierre Martineau, *Chicago Tribune*'s research director and something of a disciple of Dichter, elaborated further on the rationale for isolating unique markets to be sold different products more by taste than the ability to buy.[19]

One key finding was that sociologists found that class differences had as much to say about self-identity, tastes, and attitudes as they did about economic well-being measured by the household's amount of discretionary income. The place one occupies is an important determinant not only of how much money is spent but also how it is spent. For example, an understated way of living is a hallmark of so-called *old money*. People who have had it for a long time did not need to prove they have it. In contrast, the *nouveau riche*, or consumers who are relative newcomers to affluence, might allocate the same money to something different. For example, blue-collar workers with relatively high-prestige, well-paying jobs still tend to identify themselves as working class, even though their wages may be equivalent to many white-collar workers and regardless of whether they were supporting no children or a family of five. More discretionary income did not result in increased status or changes in their consumption patterns, because it tended to be devoted to buying more of the usual rather than upgrading to higher-status products. This fact reinforces the idea that the labels of *working class* or *middle class* are very subjective.[20]

These different perspectives further helped marketers conceptualize buyers as individuals who set different priorities in consuming as lifestyles quickly overtook the more traditional class markers of

Nails lovely
and pliant

Brittleness makes fingernails split, break, difficult to manicure properly. Seven out of 10 women have regained pliant loveliness within 3 months, simply by drinking daily one full envelope of Knox Gelatine (costs about 5¢) in fruit or vegetable juice, bouillon or water.

KNOX
UNFLAVORED
GELATINE

KNOX UNFLAVORED GELATINE

BEAUTY IS PROTEIN. A vital source of beauty is an adequate intake of protein, for the nourishment of one's skin, one's hair, one's fingernails, and one's overall well-being. Knox is useful as a supplementary protein.

Figure 6.5. According to James Witherell, executive director for Social Research Institute, many women objected to extremes in femininity in ads, such as this image for Knox Unflavored Gelatine, from *McCall's*, March 1959.

income and even education and occupation. For instance, working-class consumers tended to evaluate products in more utilitarian terms such as sturdiness or comfort rather than style or fashionability. In contrast, more affluent people are more likely to experiment with new products or styles, such as modern furniture or colored appliances. There was in all this an interactive process between marketers, the cultural mediators, and consumers that accentuated differences among and within social groups, bringing implications that transcended who sold what to whom. But M. R. was not without its critics.[21]

The Hidden Persuaders

Motivational Research had been attacked for two opposing reasons. Some felt that it did not work, whereas others felt it worked too well. Many consumer researchers felt that the method lacked sufficient scientific rigor and validity since the analyst generalized findings to a larger market from interviews with only a small number of people. Moreover, researchers found the interpretations essentially subjective; no two M. R. qualitative studies were likely to reach identical conclusions: you get two different psychologists, and you get two different answers.

For example, Foote, Cone & Belding agency hired both Dichter and Burleigh Gardner of the Social Research Institute to analyze consumer attitudes toward the advertising concepts used by Dial Soap. Dichter found that the emphasis on the deodorizing effect made people unconsciously scared about losing their own distinct body odors and recommended less emphasis on the soap's deodorant features. On the other hand, Gardner found Dial's deodorizing power (hexachlorophene) appealed to consumers, and he advised them to continue the pitch. The agency apparently was not impressed with either analysis but welcomed Gardner's findings to support their own ideas about advertising Dial. The scientific community, too, questioned the findings of such investigations. In reviewing the studies from the 1950s and 1960s, "more than 85 percent of the publications in the field of consumer psychology before 1968 have a low [scientific basis] and are of questionable value," reported J. Jacob in the *Annual Review of Psychology*.[22]

Still, the vague image of nameless experts on a mass scale manipulating consumers was quite disturbing in a culture already fearful of the effects of mass media in the 1950s, especially the possibility that advertising affected people's conscious and even unconscious desires. But the resulting postwar literature had gone far beyond the Frankfurt School of Sociology during the 1920s and 1930s, when Theodore Adorno and other scholars proposed that the new forms of mass media had the ability to shape public opinion and control people's unconscious minds. Freudian psychoanalysis, behaviorism, and motivational research gave credibility to the general fearfulness. Vance Packard's *Hidden Persuaders* provided more evidence that advertising could attach psychological messages to consumer products, embed them in advertisements, and that these commercial messages had become part of our lives. This was an unnerving possibility to the American public.

When James Vicary, a research consultant from New York, announced to the press that he had discovered a new advertising technique in 1956, fears about the effects of M. R. practices escalated. It was feared that M. R. was so powerful that no one could resist it; so subtle most Americans would not realize that their behaviors had been affected. In a controversial six-week experiment, Vicary briefly flashed "secret messages" on the screen—"Drink Coca-Cola" or "Eat Popcorn"—at a speed so fast that apparently none of the moviegoers were apparently aware what was going on during the show at a Fort Dix, New Jersey, movie house. According to Vicary, this subliminal advertising technique proved so effective that sales of popcorn allegedly jumped immediately afterward. Within days after a press conference in 1956, a flurry of newspapers and magazines were full of anguished articles about a new method of "mind control," and television networks passed measures banning the practice. However, this experiment has never been successfully replicated. In fact, Vicary later admitted that he used the infamous "popcorn" experiment as a valiant attempt to save his failing business, and it had no scientific or practical validity.[23]

With the publication of Vance Packard's best seller, *The Hidden Persuaders* (1957), fears about the effects of M. R. practices would reach an even higher pitch. Packard warned the public about M. R. with this message: "Large scale efforts are being made, often with impressive success, to channel our unthinking habits, our purchasing decisions, and our thought processes by the use of insights gleaned from psychiatry and the social scientists." More alarmingly, Packard claimed that two-thirds of the one hundred biggest advertisers were using M. R. and subliminal advertising techniques.[24] Although Packard named few sources, he aptly recognized the work of Vicary, Dichter, and Cheskin as part of a broader movement in advertising to use psychological methods to find out what makes people behave, buy, read, or listen the way they do. Packard also skillfully explained that M. R. used eight "hidden needs" to market everything from appliances to automobiles to cake mixes to celebrities like Liberace—that is, appeals to emotional security, reassurance of worth, ego gratification, creative outlets, love objects, sense of power, sense of root, and immortality.

Today we can recognize that these reasons for consuming are normal features of social and material life. People consume for unconscious reasons—to increase self-esteem, to express creativity, to win affection, and so on. Other reasons for why people buy what they do go far beyond the product utility—commodities are used to mark rites of passages, to provide excuses to see friends, to repay favors, to have a little fun, and so on. These exchange practices are embedded in ritual, emotion, social approval, family, and aesthetics.

Even after Vicary's subliminal advertising experiment was revealed as a scam, Betty Friedan drew heavily on Packard and Dichter in writing *The Feminine Mystique* (1963). She put forth the argument that the existence of markets in the postwar economy required the oppression of women. For this reason, the new culture of consumption needed women to be potential buyers for all the new washers and dryers, pressure cookers, and blenders. Capitalists, in this version of history, seem to control not only the means of production but also the minds of passive consumers to purchase consumer goods far beyond the necessities. Therefore, the claims that advertisers were delving deep into the consumer's unconsciousness and transmitting messages to appeal to *hidden needs* unfortunately became one of the principles held as being true in feminist theory. "Thus, in feminist criticism, it is not uncommon to read that the whole of postwar consumer culture was a conspiracy organized for the specific purpose of keeping women down," explains Linda Scott. "Feminist writings on media, advertising, or the market frequently claim that women, because they are excluded from the ranks of labor, are intrinsically separate from the life of the market and thus are wholly victimized by it."[25]

SEGMENTING THE AUDIENCE

For marketers, a key problem of targeting certain segments of consumers continued to be finding the best method to reach the desired audience. With new insights from group behavior studies by sociologists and anthropologists, many businesses shifted their selling strategy from a broad base of customers into niche markets with the maximum potential. They defined these segments, or target markets, by the key variables of class, gender, race, and age. Still, segmenting by gender was the most pervasive in the development of marketing science, because marketers had envisioned the consumers as female since the early days of mass marketing.

The Women's Market and Women's Magazines

Although there were extensive options of mass media, print remained the most effective way to advertise to women, and for good reason. The basic service of women's magazines was, and continues to be, to help women take care of themselves and their families. As in the 1920s, postwar publishers reshaped the editorials, content, and advertising of a group of magazines to more effectively reach their female audience. The practice of segmentation using variables of gender, race, class, and lifestyle continued to offer opportunities for defining niche markets. At the same time, editors positioned certain magazines to advertisers as the best avenue to reach this audience. They also provided concise directions for editorial development and content to attract more ad dollars. For marketers, then, the magazine pages offered an opportunity for niche advertising for their health, beauty, fashion, and household products.

However, the deeply "gendered infrastructure" of the postwar era had redefined the conception of the consumer that had reigned since the late nineteenth century. In the 1920s and 1930s, marketers had conceptualized women as shoppers, household experts, and purchasing agents for their families, constantly pursuing the consumer perishables of meat, milk, canned goods, and other food in the Depression and wartime period. *McCall's* women's magazine underscored this notion in 1937: "Categorically . . . man is always the producer . . . woman, the consumer." As the nation moved forward into the mass-consumption economy in the postwar era, the critical goods shifted from consumer perishables to consumer durables such as cars, houses, and appliances that men played a larger role in acquiring, explains Lizabeth Cohen. "The gendering of the 'consumer' thus shifted from women to couples, and at times to men alone." Now men accompanied women more frequently on shopping trips and exerted more control with the expansion of credit. Consequently, marketers began to perceive the average household as presided over by a male head of spending unit or a husband-wife dyad, with men doing an additional share of purchasing. Although postwar trade journals continued to promote Mrs. Middle Majority as the average consumer for everything from shaving cream to scouring pads between 1945 and 1950, references to Mr. and Mrs. Consumer also began to appear—a white middle-class audience being targeted by the shopping centers popping up all over the suburbs. They reasoned that this audience had the means to buy the products advertised, whereas working-class people could afford to purchase only a limited range of products. By the 1950s, the emphasis on each family member becoming more involved in every aspect of the others' lives reached a new height.[26]

The ideal fifties woman was to strive for what *McCall's* magazine insistently called "Togetherness." Typical postwar market surveys described such families as having a marriage as partnership in order to establish a comfortable home, equipped with a number of desirable products and home appliances. A shiny chrome automobile in the driveway, a gasoline-powered machine for mowing lawns, workbenches with tools, and an outdoor barbecue became other major consumption items. Furthermore, husbands, wives, and children were encouraged to do everything together. They spent evenings together in their family room where they watched TV, read, or did homework. People who wanted to see a movie bundled their children together and went to the drive-in. Family restaurants like McDonald's specialized in child-friendly menus, and Disneyland provided the ideal family vacation. Wives, then, were supposed to get involved in household matters that had always before been designated as womanly concerns. In this marriage partnership, one thing did not change. The husband continued as the designated leader, working hard to win a better life for his family; the wife was his helpmate on the domestic side, duly appreciative of the immense sacrifices made for her and her children. But the ideal father also took over grilling food outdoors, went shopping for furniture with his wife, discussed the color scheme of the house and the menu plans, and changed diapers, at least in emergencies. Despite the social emphasis on being a *family man*, most American men viewed shopping, cooking, cleaning, and changing diapers as women's work. Consequently, women who did work outside the home were usually left with the burden of housework and childcare.[27]

At this point, it is important not to underestimate the importance and influence of the glossy women's magazines that targeted the white middle-class woman, claims former ad executive Helen Woodward. In her 1960 book, *The Lady Persuaders*, Woodward makes the point that women's magazines comprised the core medium for the new young suburban wives before the coming of daytime television talk shows largely designed for housewives. The periodicals provided comfort, assurance, and information. Women also used them as trade magazines to learn more about their job—homemaking. They offered vital advice, information, and opinions on childcare and medicine, beauty, furnishings, home care, cooking, design, finances, health and nutrition, male and female relationships that affect the way they live. To fill this need, the magazines explained how women's new lives were to be for them, from how to dress and what to eat, to what they should feel about themselves and their children. "To the uninitiated, a woman's magazine may seem merely a powdery bit of fluff. No notion could be more unreal or deceptive. That is just the style in which the magazines express themselves, for if the top layer seems fluffy; the underlying base is solid and powerful," wrote Woodward.

"These publications involve a giant business investment, and have an overwhelming influence on American life."[28]

To promote their effectiveness in reaching women consumers, the periodicals aggressively put their message out to potential advertisers, citing demographic and circulation statistics and promising to make their profits on ads soar. Typical were surveys for women's magazines suggesting that "women buy more than 60 percent of men's shirts and even target percentage of men's ties, robes, socks, and underwear." Such statistics led to a 1954 campaign for *Ladies' Home Journal* headlined: "Never underestimate the power of the No. 1 magazine for women." Similarly, editors boasted that four million women read *Harper's Bazaar*. With such ability to deliver the women's market, service magazines succeeded in filling page after page of ads of not only women-centered products but also men's clothing and underwear, men's grooming products, and even business services such as insurance, personal finance, and travel, because women did much of their spending on behalf of the family.

When the volume of advertising increased, so did the influence of advertisers on the publications themselves. Eventually, magazines, in partnership with publications, provided manufactures and retailers with promises of complimentary editorial content and even special considerations of their national magazine layout and format. Campbell's Soups, for example, advertised so widely and consistently from the 1910s through the 1950s that it was always able to command premium positioning. Month after month, Campbell's ads appeared on the right-hand ad page following the editorial in dozens of publications, such as *Ladies' Home Journal, Woman's Home Companion*, and *Good Housekeeping*. If the advertising was designed to let women know what the newest appliances were and how to use them, then the accompanying articles were designed to show how they could not live without them. But there was an instinctive bias that service magazines were to be about domesticity and that it all was supposed to be upbeat. Ultimately, the articles reminded women that their fulfillment was in a support role. For example, Mrs. Dale Carnegie, wife of one of the nation's leading experts on how to be likeable, advised *Better Homes and Gardens* readers that women must help their husbands decide where they are going and help them succeed. "Let's face it, girls. That wonderful guy in your house—and in mine—is building your house, your happiness and the opportunities that will come to your children," wrote Mrs. Carnegie in 1955. "Split-level houses were fine for the family, but there is simply no room for split-level thinking—or doing—when Mr. And Mrs. set their sights on a happy home, a host of friends, and a bright future through success in HIS job."[29]

When Friedan wrote *The Feminine Mystique* in 1963, five of the top ten magazines in the United States were these women's magazines: *Women's Day, Family Circle, McCall's, Ladies' Home Journal,* and *Good Housekeeping,* in that order. Together they enjoyed a circulation of more than forty-five million readers. Add the pass-along readership to that number, and an estimated half of the American population read the magazines. Another top seller among women was *Better Homes and Gardens,* which along with *American Home* provided hints on interior decorating, remodeling, crafts, food, and family projects. In the end, Friedan's assertion was true that an increasing number of American women were not adequately served by periodicals for the "middle-class, American housewife," when almost half of all adult women were now in the workforce. It was also true that most editors of these service magazines were male in the 1950s and early 1960s. But by the time of the women's liberation movement, a number of women edited major magazines aimed at the female audience: Nancy White at *Bazaar,* Helen Gurley Brown at *Cosmopolitan,* Shana Alexander at *McCall's,* Edith Raymond Locke at *Mademoiselle,* Enid A. Haupt at *Seventeen,* and Diana Vreeland at *Vogue,* among others. And women continued to write their usual staple of articles on diets, recipes, decorating, household management, child rearing, catching and holding men, sex, and health.

Where Friedan had seen stereotyping as limiting women's role in society, the popular image of Mr. and Mrs. Consumer served the media and advertisers well as a means to sum up the complex social reality into one simplified symbol. For men, the American home represented a haven from work, but for women, it had become defined as a site for labor. One only has to think of the traditional typology that recognized the feminine and masculine type—the Happy Homemaker and the Suburban Dad—readily recognized by consumers. A profusion of ads idealized versions of Mom, Dad, Junior, and Sis, and Americans struggled to fill these unrealistic roles. The ads usually portrayed Dad as the strong, decisive father and businessman, equally productive around the home and at the office. Yet Dad was also married to his employer, taking off for distant places at a moment's notice and uprooting his family to new locations. Perhaps the most common stereotype was the dedicated homemaker who sacrificed all personal aspirations to pamper husband, chauffer her children, scrub floors, and teach her daughters to do the same (figure 6.6). Thus, women's magazines filled with advertisements served to both encode the modern female identity with attributes of middle-class femininity and their proper role as consumers.

Men's Market and Men's Magazines

Although the media had a bias toward women as primary consumers in the postwar era, manufacturers, publishers, and advertisers began to court the male consumer not only for cigarettes and automobiles but also for magazines and toiletries. The effort to conceptualize the men's market actively began in the 1930s and 1940s, when magazine publishers and advertisers collaborated to shift from a focus on the women's market to also bring in the male consumers to revive market demand during the Depression and war years, explains Kenon Breazeale.[30]

For example, the stylish *Fortune* magazine was offered to the corporate culture and proved that with the right demographics, a male-identified magazine could attract national advertisers. On the other hand, the editorial format of *Esquire* magazine linked a seductive, middle-class lifestyle with masculinity and included drawings only, not photographs, of voluptuous, seminude women. The lifestyle magazine also served as vehicle for men's apparel and alcoholic beverages, disdained by many other publications. These magazines succeed in transforming many white middle-class male readers into consumers. With *Esquire* as a model, publishers introduced a new generation of men's magazines specifically as advertising vehicles to reach new segments of the lucrative, middle-class men's market, who were ready to buy everything, from clothing and cigarettes, to liquor and automobiles.

In the postwar era, then, the emergence of men's magazines such

Figure 6.6. This ad portrays a common stereotype, the dedicated homemaker who sacrifices all her aspirations to dote on her family and teaches her daughter to do the same.

as *Playboy* (1953) and *Sports Illustrated* (1954) provided important vehicles for male-oriented advertisers. But *Playboy* also symbolized the appearance of a freer sexuality for women, as well an increased objectification that would continue to exist to the present. Hugh Hefner, who had been on the staff of *Esquire*, first published *Playboy* in 1953. The monthly magazine featured photographs of nude women, along with various articles on fashion, sports, and consumer goods, interviews with celebrities from various fields, and short fiction by top literary writers such as Ernest Hemingway, Alex Haley, and Ray Bradbury. The high literary caliber of the articles became responsible for the long-running joke quoted by many men: "I only read it for the articles!" In the following year, the launch of *Sports Illustrated* also proved especially popular with the explosion of spectator sports in the United States, driven largely by economic prosperity and televised sporting events.

Yet mass marketers such as Procter & Gamble and General Foods did not recognize or attach much significance to a man's influence on household purchases, because the tasks related to cooking and cleaning had remained associated with women, not men. Not surprisingly, then, issues of *Fortune* and *Esquire* dating back to the 1930s, as did *Playboy* and *Sports Illustrated* since the 1950s, conspicuously show an absence of ads for kitchen appliances, cooking and cleaning products, and other items for running a home. Until the 1980s, little would be known about the male shopper.[31]

Elaboration of Segmentation

In addition to the men's market, publishers began to reconceptualize the buying public by further elaboration on the variables of gender, age, race, and lifestyle. This new class of publications helped define new audiences and delivered new advertising vehicles for marketers. Among the niche markets were the workingwomen, teen, baby boomer, and black consumer market.

Beginning in 1944, editor Helen Valentine, art director Cipe Pineles, and promotion director Estelle Ellis built *Charm*, the first magazine to position workingwomen as comprising a separate market. The same team also helped develop the teenage market with *Seventeen* in 1944, when Ellis commissioned the first market research studies to establish teenage girls as another economically powerful market. The glossy, teen magazine began an adventurous and sophisticated conversation with its readers. The magazine published literary fiction, dared to admit that teenage girls dated boys, and in prefeminist 1945, even published the pros and cons for coeducation. The magazine aimed to convince advertisers that teens were a vital market force.[32]

Up until the 1930s, most teenagers worked for a living on farms, in factories, or at home. Most Americans did not consider them teenagers yet, or even adolescents, for that matter. The Depression changed all that as the hard times forced many young people out of the workplace and into the classroom. According to teen historian Grace Palladin, this shift helped create the idea of a separate teenage generation who enjoyed the freedom and social life of high school. The rising postwar baby boom generation (or "boomers") could hardly be aware of what their parents and grandparents had endured during the lean years of the Depression and World War II. This new generation had more money to spend than in the past and more time to enjoy it. Teenagers adopted fashions to distinguish themselves from adults. Pony-tailed girls wearing heavily made-up eyes, bobby sox, and saddle shoes were one target of the growing cosmetics and beauty market. As for the new affluent young men, they could afford expressive hairstyling, while "dungarees" became a staple wardrobe for both sexes, and rock 'n' roll provided the beat for the generation. Sales of radios, record players, records, cosmetics, blue jeans, and soft drinks soared (figure 6.7).[33]

Moreover, the baby boomers were the first generation that marketers began to conceive as a generational market. At first, it was just thought that the children were the market, until television came along and gave advertisers a very powerful way to talk to that market. As the boomers have aged, companies have created and marketed prod-

Figure 6.7. This 1950 ad for 7-UP soft drink targeted a new generation of teens, who had more money to spend than in the past.

ucts aimed directly at this group. The baby boom did not name itself the "Pepsi Generation"—Pepsi did that.

Finally, another class of national magazines helped to reconceptualize the African American consumer market. Starting with the publishing of *Negro Digest* in 1942, Johnson Publishing Company produced a series of magazines—*Ebony*, *Jet*, and *Tan*, among others—that not only informed but also helped redefine black Americans and a new generation of advertising vehicles that depended on a new class of subscribers. These publications attracted enough national advertising to support a few pioneering African American ad men to open their own agencies in the postwar era, but they were mostly limited to selling "black" products to black consumers (see chapter 9). From the standpoint of the white, national advertisers, however, the primary market continued to be not city dwellers but white suburbanites—the typical *average Americans* who also appeared in print, radio, and television ads. This well-off group read a lot magazines and watched a lot of television, and many took cues from these media on how they should live. In short, they were ideal targets for advertising. Still, advertising excluded not only African Americans but residents of ethnic neighborhoods, the single, the widowed, and single parents.

As we'll see in the next chapter, women working as cultural mediators applied these new concepts of marketing segmentation and motivational research to advertising in an attempt to imbue not only fashion and beauty products with deep-seated emotions, sex-typing, and even sexuality, but also everyday household products, furniture, or just about anything with which we surround ourselves. When you think about it, it was a radical idea at the time.

NOTES

1. Obituary of William Levitt, *New York Times*, January 29, 1994, sec. Y, p. 11. Also see "Levittown, Pa. Building the Suburban Dream," online exhibit, State Museum of Pennsylvania, at http://server1.fandm.edu/levittown/one/c.html (accessed June 25, 2007).

2. Barbara M. Kelly, *Expanding the American Dream: Building and Rebuilding Levittown* (Albany: State University of New York Press, 1993).

3. On segregation, see David Halberstam, *The Fifties* (New York: Fawcett Columbine, 1993), p. 141. Andrew Wiese, "Racial Cleansing in the Suburbs: Suburban Government, Urban Renewal, and Segregation on Long Island, New York, 1945–1960," in *Contested Terrain: Power, Politics, and Participation in Society*, ed. Marc L. Silver and Martin Melkonian (Westport, CT: Greenwood Press, 1995), pp. 61–70.

4. Before the 1930s, women attended colleges in roughly the same number as men. Men began to dominate campuses during the Great Depression, and their enrollment increased after World War II, partly because of the GI benefits. See "The Homecoming of American College Women: The Reversal of the College Gender Gap," by Claudia Goldin, Lawrence F. Katz, and Illyana Kuziemoko, *Journal of Economic Perspectives* 20 (Fall 2006): 133–56.

5. On suburban housing, see Thomas Hine, *Populuxe: The Look and Life of America in the 50's and 60's, from Tailfins and TV Dinners to Barbie Dolls and Fallout Shelters* (New York: Knopf Books, 1986). On "owning a home," see Halberstam, *The Fifties*, p. 132.

6. Lizabeth Cohen, "From Town Center to Shopping Center: The Reconfiguration of Community Marketplace in Postwar America," in *Gender and Consumer Culture Reader*, ed. Jennifer Scanlon, pp. 257–66.

7. Bernice Fitz-Gibbon, "Women in the Gray Flannel Suit," *New York Times*, January 29, 1956, p. 196.

8. Betty Friedan, *The Feminine Mystique* (New York: W. W. Norton, 1963). The theme of independent women emerged earlier in Friedan's work, on a range of progressive social causes from labor unions to cooperative suburban communities. See Daniel Horowitz, *Betty Friedan and the Making of "The Feminine Mystique": The American Left, the Cold War, and Modern Feminism* (Amherst: University of Massachusetts Press, 2000).

9. On developments in postwar packaging, see Thomas Hine, *Total Package: The Evolution and Secret Meanings of Boxes, Bottles, Cans, and Tubes* (New York: Little, Brown and Company, 1995), pp. 140–74.

10. As early as 1943, psychologist Dr. Ernest Dichter published his ideas on "Motivational Research" in *Printers' Ink*, but it would be another decade until articles regularly appeared examining the value of applying motivational research to advertising.

11. Sigmund Freud, *The Interpretation of Dreams*, trans. A. A. Brill (New York: Modern Library, 1950), pp. 242, 247.

12. "Psyching Them Out: Ernest Dichter Thrives Selling Firms Research on Hidden Emotions," *Wall Street Journal*, November 17, 1972.

13. Jeffrey F. Durgee, "Interpreting Dichter's Interpretations: An Analysis of Consumption Symbolism," in *The Handbook of Consumer Motivation, Marketing and Semiotics: Selected Papers from the Copenhagen Symposium*, ed. Hanne Hartvig-Larsen, David Glen Mick, and Christian Alstead (New York: Taylor and Francis Group, 1991).

14. "What Makes Her Buy?" *Printers' Ink*, October 18, 1957.

15. On Marlboro campaign, see *Esquire*, June 1960. On "core meanings," see Vance Packard, *The Hidden Persuaders* (New York: Pocket Books, 1981), p. 57.

16. "Advertising: 'Depth' Too Deep?" *New York Times*, February 1958, p. 11. See also "Huge Rise Is Seen for Advertising," *New York Times*, October 20, 1955.

17. W. Lloyd Warner, *Social Class of America: A Manual of Procedure for the Measurement of Social Status* (Chicago: Science Research Associates, 1949).

18. Lizabeth Cohen, *A Consumers' Republic: The Politics of Mass Consumption in Postwar America* (New York: Knopf, 2003), p. 311.

19. Wendell R. Smith, "Product Differentiation and Market Segmentation," *Journal of Marketing* 21 (July 1956). Pierre Martineau, "Social Classes and Spending Behavior," *Journal of Marketing* 23 (October 1958). Martineau, *Motivation in Advertising: Motives That Make People Buy* (New York: McGraw-Hill, 1957).

20. Pierre Martineau, "Social Classes and Spending Behavior."

21. Richard P. Coleman, "The Continuing Significance of Social Class to Marketing," *Journal of Consumer Research* 10 (December 1983): 265–80; Stuart U. Rich and Subhash C. Jain, "Social Class and Life Cycle as Predictors of Shopping Behavior," *Journal of Marketing Research* 5 (February 1968): 41–49.

22. J. Jacob, "Consumer Psychology," *Annual Review of Psychology* 28 (January 1977): 331–58.

23. James V. McConnell, "Subliminal Stimulation: An Overview," article accepted for publication, *American Psychologist*, May 1958. On TV networks, see *New York Herald Tribune*, November 8, 1957; November 25, 1957. Vicary admits the experiment was nothing more than a scam, *Advertising Age*, September 17, 1962.

24. Vance Packard, *The Hidden Persuaders* (1957; repr., New York: David McKay Company, 1974), pp. 2, 110.

25. Friedan, *The Feminine Mystique*. See also Linda M. Scott, *Fresh Lipstick* (New York: Palgrave Macmillan, 2005), pp. 234–35.

26. On *McCall's*, see *Advertising Age*, July 12, 1937, pp. 14–15. On gendering the consumer, see Lizabeth Cohen, *A Consumers' Republic*, p. 147.

27. On togetherness, see "*McCall's* Breaks 84-Year-Old Tradition," *Advertising Age*, May 3, 1954.

28. Helen Woodward, *The Lady Persuaders* (New York: Obelensky, 1960), pp. 1–2.

29. Mrs. Dale Carnegie interview, *Better Homes and Gardens*, April 1955.

30. On the trend to legitimate men as consumers as a remedy to the 1930s Depression, see Kenon Breazeale, "In Spite of Women: *Esquire Magazine* and the Construction of the Male Consumer," *Signs* 20 (Autumn 1994): 1–22. On the crisis of the Depression and American commercial culture, see Stuart Ewen, *All Consuming Images* (1988; rev. ed., New York: HarperOne, 1990) and Terry Smith, *Making the Modern: Industry, Art, and Design in America* (Chicago: University of Chicago Press, 1993). On the logic to constantly organize new tastes, see Jeffrey Meikle, *Twentieth Century Limited: Industrial Design in America, 1925–1939* (Philadelphia: Temple University Press, 1979). For a case study on selling toiletries to the men's market in the 1930s, see Kathy Peiss, *Hope in a Jar: The Making of America's Beauty Culture* (New York: Owl Books, 1999), pp. 164–66.

31. Neglected male market: "Male Market: Big, Rich, and Tough," *Printers' Ink*, July 20, 1962, pp. 21–25. On later studies, see "There's a Male in Your Market," *Advertising Age*, May 28, 1973, and Patrick Reilly, "Magazines Beckon 'New Man,'" *Advertising Age*, October 19, 1991, p. S26.

32. Amy Janello and Brennon Jones, *The American Magazine* (New York: HNA, 1991), p. 82.

33. Grace Palladin, *Teenagers in American History* (New York: Basic Books, 1997).

CHAPTER 7

THE FABULOUS FIFTIES

SELLING MR. AND MRS. CONSUMER

The new medium of television presented America with dozens of model wives on programs like *The Donna Reed Show*, *Leave It to Beaver*, and *Father Knows Best*. Television commercials and advertisements in women's magazines then glorified the typical housewife's everyday life and constantly reminded the American woman of everything she ought to be. These images displayed idealized fifties women with freshly shampooed hair, whiter-than-white teeth, fresh breath, and smooth skin that all ended with romance and eventually marriage. Elegantly attired models clad in Dior gowns extolled the virtues of everything from refrigerators to dishwashing detergent, showing how the latest product or new technology removed drudgery from household chores.

What Betty Friedan and other feminist critics later deemed as *sexualizing* American women and *stereotyping* their role in society as mothers, wives, and servants of men was not an all-male development by men's institutions and advertising—that is, solely the work of the businessman and the ad man. For one thing, these commercial images were largely created for women by women. At every level of marketing and advertising activity for the women's market—cosmetics, fashion, food, home furnishings, housewares, and even the key financial services and automotive industries—women had become involved. The very notion of this business of femininity contradicts feminist theories that claimed it was the ad men, acting from their limited ideas of female character and aspirations, who turned women into sex objects and portrayed them in narrow roles. In doing so, they discounted or even ignored significant market-oriented women's contributions in the mass-consumer goods industries.

Certainly women in marketing, advertising, and public relations in the 1950s had a different view of their work from feminist critics. For example, the glamorous Betty Furness recognized the value of her appearance to become a credible television spokesperson. Three of the most famous cosmetic and fashion campaigns of the 1950s were created by women, Kay Daly for Revlon, Mary Fillius for Maidenform, and Shirley Polykoff for Clairol hair coloring, and all used sex as a basis of their appeals. The very appearance of female industrial designers to add the feminine touch to automotive design suggests a broad-based demand for women's sensibilities to reach the expanding women's market. The whole mass-consumer goods industry seemed intent on pushing exaggerated statements of gender. But, in fact, things would never be the same.

THE ADVERTISING PROFESSION IN THE 1950s

In the years since World War II, for the most part, there continued to be a general breaking down of barriers by workingwomen. They especially were welcome in advertising agencies and selling fields to service "female interest" accounts, as the number of agencies tripled in the nine-year period from 1939 to 1948 to meet industry demand, and they were offered a sizeable number of new jobs. By 1950 women accounted for about one-third of the workers in the advertising industry alone (38,859), according to the federal census. This trend would continue in the decades to follow, as women created jobs for women, organized associations, and utilized networks as expressions of solidarity and support.

These numbers revealed just how far the *woman's touch*, or the feminine viewpoint, had progressed. The view that because a woman possessed a certain mysterious quality, ad makers felt that she could facilitate communications between manufacturers and Mrs. Consumer, or the women's market. Hence, agencies and industry hired more and more women to work as writers, artists, and merchandising experts; research workers, media analysts, administrators; models and spokespersons; and people who knew graphic arts, radio, and television production. Women also proved effective in direct sales to the women's market.

To communicate with Mrs. Consumer, these cultural mediators would make use of things they already knew just by being a member of the same gender. They would select the most familiar pictures, the heroines, the best-known narratives, the prejudices, as well as the hopes, dreams, and fears to appeal to other women. However, these cultural mediators also were a product of their own upbringing, so it was not unusual to see some of their personal experience reflected in their communications. Thus, women understand other women much better than men do, so thought the industry; most men did not understand women at all. "Though the largest part of consumer spending is done by women, it is fantastic how little the average businessman understands feminine psychological goals," noted sociologist Pierre Martineau. "We men spend a lifetime associating with women—our mothers, our sisters, our wives, and even our own daughters—yet it never dawns on us that they have fundamentally different motives and interests."[1]

Postwar women who aspired to a career in advertising turned to numerous booklets, books, and other vocational guidance. In 1946, for example, Maureen Daly, an associate editor for *Ladies' Home Journal*, wrote the booklet *Advertising* for the magazine, which provided ideas on how aspiring young women could fit in advertising and what they could earn. In the career guide, B. J. Kidd, then a female vice president for Lewis & Gilman, Inc., and secretary of the Advertising Federation of America, reminded readers: "You are not competing with men with whom you come into business contact. You are complementing them by supplying the one factor they cannot obtain elsewhere—your own femininity." Kay Daly, copywriter for Foote, Cone

& Belding, advised readers that a retail background was invaluable for work in an advertising agency. Other experts like Bernice Fitz-Gibbon reminded women that to be a good copywriter, they should go to college, take "impractical" courses that would give them a rich cultural background, but also learn to type fifty words a minute.

Others turned to Mary McBride's *How to Be a Successful Advertising Woman* (1948), published by the Advertising Women of New York. The book featured the capsule careers of a number of successful women who told one thing—there was no rigid formula for success in the business world, because there were no training programs—at any agency. Nonetheless, a number of ad women filled top executive positions, opened their own agencies, and came to serve as role models for this new generation. McBride herself had become a well-known broadcaster on the radio in the 1930s and 1940s. By the 1950s, more women handled commercials on radio and television than ever before, and they increasingly held positions as copywriters and at the administrative and management levels. Practically every agency of any size also maintained a well-staffed research library, hired researchers on the marketplace, and built in-house television production facilities. In addition, agencies like BBDO, JWT, and the Gardner agency had realized that investments like home economics departments were necessary to ensure complete account servicing (figure 7.1).

Among women in food advertising, perhaps Jean Rindlaub at BBDO was the best known in the 1950s. Before working on Campbell's Soup for many years, she wrote campaigns for Community Silver ("Back Home for Keeps") that resonated as a wartime theme, as well as for General Mills and Artcarved Rings (figures 7.2, 7.3). Instead of focusing on the Campbell Kids for Campbell's Soup, she stressed health claims, fitness issues, good taste ("Mmm good"), and serving suggestions like chilled soup ("Soup on the Rocks"). She also supervised the introduction of Velveeta cheese. In Rindlaub's thirty-four years at BBDO, she became vice president in 1946, the first woman at that level, and in 1954, she became the first woman on the advertising board. The American Advertising Federation named her Woman of the Year in 1951 and in 1989 elected her to its Advertising Hall of Fame (figure 7.4).[2]

Figure 7.1. Advertising Opportunities for Women from A to V, according to Dorothy Dignam in 1949.

A — Account Executive or
        Agency Representative
    Advertising Agency Worker
    Advertising Manager
    Art Buyer
    Artist or Art Director
B — Baby Products Specialist
C — Classified Solicitor
    Clerical Worker
    Commercial Film Writer or
        Producer
    Copywriter
    Correspondent
    Cosmetic Specialist
D — Department Store
    • Advertising Manager or
        Assistant
    • Artist
    • Copywriter
    • Display Designer
    • Proof Girl
    • Publicity & Promotion
        Director
    Direct Mail Producer
    Display Manager or
        Assistant
    Drug & Toiletries Specialist
E — Educational Director
    Electrical Equipment
        Specialist
F — Fashion Advertising Creator
    Food Advertising Creator
    Fund-Raising Expert
G — "Girl Friday"
H — Home Building &
        Equipment Specialist
    Home Economist
    Home Furnishings Expert

    Hostess for Plant Tours
    House Organ Editors
I — Industrial Advertising
        Producer
J — Junior Executive Producer
K — Kodachrome & Black and
        White Photographer
L — Layout Artist
    Lecturer
    Lettershop Owner or
        Manager
    Librarian in Advertising
        Agency
M— Media Buyer
    Merchandising Specialist
N — Newspaper Advertising
        Worker (Service, Copy,
        Space-selling)
O — Outdoor Advertising
        Worker
P — Package Designer
    Photographer's Assistant
        and Prop Girl
    Poster Artist
    Premium Specialist
    Printing & Engraving Buyer
    Printing Salesman
    Production Worker
    Proof Reader
    Publicity Girl
    Public Relations Executive
Q — Questionnaire Interviewer
        and Survey Assistant
V — Vice-presidency, which is
        high enough for any
        girl to aim.

Source: "How to Land That Advertising Job," a 1949 supplement to *How to Be a Successful Advertising Woman*, Dorothy Dignam Collection, Box 3, Folder 19, Schlesinger Library, Radcliffe Institute, Harvard University.

Figure 7.2. Jane Rindlaub. Photo from American Advertising Federation Hall of Fame.

A number of women throughout the mid-century also found business opportunities in sex-typed industries. In 1954, for example, the largest percentage of women who owned their own businesses were in retailing (32.5 percent), compared to only 3.8 percent of the enterprises in printing, advertising, and editorial. This entrepreneurship trend is evidence in the careers of Bernice Fitz-Gibbon and Margaret Hockaday.[3]

After twenty-five years of writing copy for Macy's and Gimbels, Fitz-Gibbon followed the entrepreneurial trend and opened up her own shop—Bernice Fitz-Gibbon, Inc. By concentrating on retail work, the company specialized in institutional campaigns, anniversary celebrations, and openings of new stores. Fitz-Gibbon's agency was small, as were most women-owned companies, since family responsibilities or access to capital often limited the size of such businesses. To keep the overhead low, Fitz-Gibbon relied on freelance talent from her Gimbels, Wanamaker's, and Macy's trainees. The business also allowed flexibility for the demands of motherhood, while providing her with an outlet for her entrepreneurial drive and the poten-

BACK HOME
FOR KEEPS

It's that moment you've dreamed of, longed for, ached for . . . you and *your* man, home for keeps. Take down the stars, turn out the moon . . . you won't need them any more. Your eyes are aglow, your heart aflame. You were cold, you are warm; you were scared, you are safe . . . this is something old, something new, this is *forever*.

For today, tomorrow, and always, too, is the silverware we're planning for you . . . patterns as shiningly right as Community* has ever been, as precious as your dreams of tomorrow. Our craftsmen's hands have kept their skill, our designers' hearts are turning home. *The day will come*, when you'll have your house, *his* heart, and your own beloved *Community!*

TRADEMARK   COPYRIGHT 1945. ONEIDA LTD.

SPEED THE DAY   BUY WAR BONDS!

Community
THE FINEST SILVERPLATE

Coronation Design

If it's Community . . . it's correct

FREE! *If you'd like a full color reproduction of this painting, without advertising, write* COMMUNITY, *Dept. I-3, Oneida, N. Y.*

Figure 7.3. In this ad for Community Silver, the theme "Back Home for Keeps" resonated with the wartime generation. *Good Housekeeping*, May 1945.

> **Figure 7.4.** Founded in 1948, the American Advertising Federation honors advertising leaders who made significant contributions to the advertising industry and its reputation and who made volunteer efforts outside the workplace. Since then eleven women have been inducted as members.
>
> 1952   Erma Perham Proetz, former creative vice president and executive vice president, Gardner agency
>
> 1967   Helen Lansdowne Resor, former executive, J. Walter Thompson Company
>
> 1981   Bernice Fitz-Gibbon, former copywriter, Gimbels Department Store
>
> 1989   Jean Wade Rindlaub, former vice president, Batten, Barton, Durstine & Osborn (BBDO)
>
> 1996   Jo Foxworth, president, Jo Foxworth Inc.
>
> 1997   Gertrude Ramsey Crain, publishing executive, Crain Communications
>
> 1998   Janet L. Wolff, former executive vice president and director of creative services, William Esty
>
> 1999   Mary Wells Lawrence, founder, Wells, Rich & Greene
>
> 2000   Patricia Martin, former director, Marketing Support, Warner Lambert
>
> 2001   Katherine Graham, publisher, *Washington Post*
>
> 2008   Andrea Alstrup, former corporate vice president, Johnson & Johnson
>
> Source: American Advertising Federation Hall of Fame.

tial to earn a lot of money. Fitz-Gibbon also accepted numerous invitations to speak to groups and organizations and wrote numerous articles for women's magazines. Her topics included how to get a job and make money and a woman's place in business.

Although Fitz-Gibbon favored sincerity and clever copy, Hockaday "injected fashion" into retail ads. A Vassar graduate, Hockaday began her career as a copywriter for Marshall Field in 1929 and also spent time as a fashion editor with *Harper's Bazaar*, *Vogue*, J. Walter Thompson agency, and Montgomery Ward stores. As World War II came to a close, she, along with art director Alvin Chereskin, borrowed a small amount of capital, rented space, and opened a little shop in New York City in 1949, and in came the clients. Their inventive and offbeat approach can be best seen in the campaigns for Capezio footwear, Dunbar furniture, and Jantzen swimsuits ("Just wear a smile and a Jantzen"), which featured imaginative copy and modern European graphic design that used universal symbols, dynamic composition, and modern typography (figure 7.5).

Despite all the talk of new opportunities and successes in the profession, the idea that women were moving in force into the upper echelons of advertising agencies was largely a myth, reported *Printers' Ink* in 1960. Although women had made gains in the advertising field during World War II, since then, the journal claimed, they'd done little more than hold their ground. Most women found themselves in positions segregated into women's-only departments and not paid as much as men. Prejudice was one factor, the article explained. The advertising agency was still overwhelmingly a man's world. Women in some agencies like JWT may have outnumbered the men; the great majority were clerical and secretarial workers. There were, of course, a number of women who held top agency posts, but *Printers' Ink* concluded that they were "unusual": In 1960 J. Walter Thompson employed 7 women of 132 people as vice presidents. McCann Erickson's, 6 of 100. Young & Rubicam, 1. Ted Bates, 1 of 45. N. W. Ayer, 1 of 36. And Leo Burnett, none.[4]

Although *Printers' Ink* pointed out, quite rightly, that some of the major agencies had few or no women in higher posts, it vastly understated women's contributions to the soft goods manufacturers, department stores, mail-order, and public relations field that had been hiring women ad executives for many years. These ad women, who had begun work in the 1920s and 1930s, were now coming up through the ranks, having proved themselves as professionals and carved out a niche in the field. In the late 1940s and 1950s, an increasing number of women came to fill executive posts in these industries. Many of them brought extensive experience in mass marketing and retailing to the agencies, particularly in New York and other major cities, where they began to fill positions formerly held only by men. For example, Phyllis Robinson joined Doyle Dane Bernbach (DDB) as a copywriter in 1949, when the initial staff consisted only of Doyle, the account executive; Dane, who handled administration and finance;

DUNBAR

Edward Wormley Designs for Dunbar, Berne, Indiana. Showrooms: New York, Boston, Chicago, Kansas City, Los Angeles, Seattle.

Figure 7.5. After Margaret Hockaday's Dunbar furniture campaign was launched in the early fifties, the chairs turned up in the most unusual places. *New York Times Sunday Magazine*, October 16, 1954.

and Bob Gage, the art director. Here Robinson wrote award-winning copy for Ohrbach, Chemstrand, Acrilan, and Polaroid. At a time when automotive accounts were traditionally considered men's work, Robinson also helped the Volkswagen and Avis brands achieve prominence, which brought DDB major national accounts and moved the firm into the ranks of the top-billing agencies in 1965.[5]

At the major agencies, other notable women included Peggy King, the second female vice president after Ruth Waldo at J. Walter Thompson; Olive Plunkett and Jean Rindlaub, Batten, Barton, Durstine & Osborne (BBDO); Margot Sherman and Dr. Herta Herzog, McCann-Erickson; Mary O'Mears, Young & Rubicam; Reva Fine Korda, Ogilvy, Benson & Mather; Reselou Flanagan, Norman, Craig & Kummel; Beatrice Adams, Gardner Advertising Company; Dorothy Noyes, Noyes & Sproul; Florence W. Goldin, Grey Advertising; Annette Talber, Elizabeth Pike, and Dorothy Whitney, Benton & Bowles; and Bonnie Dewes, D'Arcy Advertising Company. Ad women were strongly, if not unequally, established in the business and impacted the basic promotional appeal for many accounts.[6]

Who, then, was at fault for women being denied opportunities for filling top posts in the advertising industry? Management was just half of the explanation, argued James M. Woolf, a contributor to *Advertising Age*, in 1951. Women were also equally responsible, since they should not attempt to sell themselves merely in the art of the "woman's touch." On the other hand, management was at fault because it could not forget that women are women, hence they are all-around experts in selling the women's market. Therefore, women were engaged by agencies and for this very reason they were often not considered when broader opportunities beckoned.[7]

Still, Woolf neglected to mention that these were the days when many forms of both gender and race discrimination were still legal. If a boss paid a woman less because she was a woman, the boss was unapologetic. If a person did not want to hire a woman for a man's job, he or she just didn't. Expressions of discontent with the industry and government's failure to relieve such racial and social injustice, which had become more noticeable, would dramatically alter the nation, as well as reform advertising in the 1960s and 1970s.

EXPLOSIVE GROWTH OF TELEVISION

Like the medium of radio in the 1930s, the new medium of television provided women with some of the best opportunities during the postwar period. Before the 1950s, television played a small role in American life, and businesses mainly advertised through newspapers, magazines, and radio. In 1946 the nation had fewer than six thousand television sets and only six stations, each of which broadcasted for ten hours a week. But two years later, in 1948, American television began its explosive growth and soon would become the leading medium for advertising.

Television grew more rapidly than radio because the developers of the new medium learned from their early experiences as radio broadcasters. Recognizing that the shoestring operations characteristic of many radio stations were no longer feasible, broadcast developers began to establish networks of affiliated television stations. Initially, the national networks were limited to the big three—CBS, NBC, and ABC. But television usage skyrocketed with the gradual westward expansion of the television networks for various reasons: a drop in the price of sets, increased leisure time, and increased disposable income. As a result, the number of American households with TV went from less than 1 percent in 1946 to 55.7 percent in 1954, and 90 percent by 1962.[8]

By the mid-1950s though, television became the leading medium for advertising. The advertising firms that adapted most readily to television tripled and quadrupled their annual billings. For example, the Batten, Barton, Durstine, & Osborne (BBDO) agency, an early booster of television, moved 80 percent of its media buys to television, and by 1950, the television department had grown from twelve people to one hundred and fifty. The firm went from billings of $40 million to $235 million in the fifteen-year period from 1945 to 1960.[9]

Similar to radio, television networks produced shows like *Milton Berle*, *The Ernie Kovacs Show*, and *The Ed Sullivan Show*. Hollywood got into the act when Disney brought out programs like the *Mickey Mouse Club* and *The Wonderful World of Disney*. By sponsoring programs, advertisers could control when and how commercials were inserted. For example, Philip Morris cigarettes owned *I Love Lucy*, General Mills sponsored *Betty Crocker's Star Matinee*, and Dutch Masters supported *The Ernie Kovacs Show*. And market research assessed the programs that drew the most viewers—that is, potential customers—to determine which programs aired. Sponsors hoped that the shows would create good feelings about their products so people would buy them. As long as producers broadcast commercials on radio only, it was generally thought that a voice was all that was needed, no matter what kind of person was behind it. Many sponsors had the idea that a homemaker busy with housework welcomed a male voice in her isolated world. But when it came to television, they found that credibility was tremendously important in a spokesperson. "It's just not simply convincing for men to be selling some products," *Printers' Ink* explained in 1954. "Credibility demands a woman on household products and other merchandise sold to and largely used by women."[10]

The Lady from Westinghouse

One figure that came to symbolize suburbanization and the explosive growth of television in the 1950s was Betty Furness—the Lady from Westinghouse, America's first full-time product spokeswoman on television (figure 7.6). In 1949, Furness was thirty-three, doing some television acting on the program *Studio One*, where Westinghouse was the sole sponsor. Someone from the ad agency asked her to try out for a commercial, which paid $150 a week—a considerable sum at the time. On each episode of *Studio One*, she had to deliver one three-minute commercial and two one-and-half-minute commercials. At the conclusion of each commercial, she looked at the camera and said: "You can be sure it's Westinghouse." Consumers found her endorsement credible.

By 1952 Furness had become a celebrity spokesperson of significant proportions who exuded confidence as she handled any appliance and promised that each product made household chores downright easy and even glamorous. Of course, mistakes did happen during live broadcasts (videotape recording had not yet been

Figure 7.6. Betty Furness, the Lady from Westinghouse, from *Printers' Ink*, July 2, 1954.

invented). In a classic 1954 commercial, Furness calmly explained why a new Westinghouse refrigerator was easy to use, all while she was tugging on a refrigerator door whose latch stuck. To all sorts of people, she was simply Betty, a caring friend who had been in their homes and helped them out in the kitchen. And viewers did respond. Over an eleven-year period, the sale of Westinghouse appliances boomed, as Furness promoted the ever-fancier and bigger appliances on television, in print advertisements, and in store displays.[11]

Yet Furness had a strong sense of her own identity and controlled her image. When the advertising people wanted her to appear more like a housewife, they pressured her to wear a wedding ring, put on an apron, and take an assumed name, which would make her the living Westinghouse logo, like Betty Crocker for General Mills. But she knew exactly how she wanted to represent Westinghouse. Intu- itively she knew how to look modern, sophisticated, and upbeat without looking too glamorous. She had to be interesting, too. So she bought her own clothes and constantly changed her appearance, rather than let Westinghouse pay for the wardrobe and decide what she should wear. The advertiser's theory was that a girl in a pretty dress working the machine would outpull a commercial with a model standing idle. "That party dress did something else," explained copy chief William E. Pensyl, who wrote washing machine commercials for Furness. "It makes it pretty obvious that you *could* do a wash without looking like a hag if you had to."[12]

After Furness, the perky blonde Julia Meade first appeared for Lincoln automobiles in 1956. Soon she was earning a hundred thousand dollars a year, a sizeable sum at the time, producing convincing spots also for Richard Hudnut hair products and *Life* magazine, among others. Meade soon became the prototype for other carefully coiffed, wholesome women who sold consumer products with their appearance and flawless enunciation. Anita Bryant, Carmelita Pope, and Florence Henderson also constantly appeared as short, sixty-second reminders of everything the American woman ought to be. As expected, viewers became conditioned to seeing glamorous models and handsome actors in commercials effectively deliver the marketer's message of product, brand, or company image. By the mid-1950s, though, many spokeswomen were replaced by hundreds of unknown actresses who portrayed the *little woman* in scenarios believed by the advertising agencies as representative of real-life situations, dramatizing everyday washing machine problems to fighting dirt in any form, reinforcing the traditional stereotype that a woman's place was in the home. But celebrities continued to reflect their fame on some product brands, such as Dinah Shore for Chevrolet, Polly Bergen for Pepsi, and Ozzie and Harriet Nelson for Coca-Cola.

Yet a fundamental and far-reaching change was taking place: the ideal fifties consumers, Mr. and Mrs. Consumer, or the stereotypical Suburban Dad and Happy Homemaker, portrayed in advertising were in the process of being undermined almost as soon as they appeared. A new kind of "liberated" man and woman appeared in the postwar era and brought a wave of sensuality that heralded a new freedom of sorts for young Americans, while the stereotypical images began to lag behind the times. Women entered the workplace, went to professional schools, fought for social emancipation, got the Pill, and changed their fashions. The idea of the bachelor as an alternative lifestyle also took shape in the 1950s, when *Playboy* began publishing renderings of state-of-the-art *bachelor pads*, as unmarried men began paying attention to their homes and spending money on them in ways that only wives used to do.

GENDER-BASED MARKETING: FASHION, BEAUTY, AND STYLE

The increased importance of gender-based marketing—a term that usually applies to marketing that is directed to women—was not about male versus female during the postwar era. Rather, it was about understanding why a consumer buys, what motivates her to purchase, and how a firm's customer wanted to use its product. Although it seemed as if every ad embodied sexual symbols from cake mixes to cigarettes, and a charge of desire pervaded everything from lipstick to brassieres in America, of course, this was not the case. In the 1950s though, sexual content and ideas about motivational research were far more visible even in advertising, compared to the previous decades.

The Fifties Woman

Perhaps the single most important discovery about the fifties woman goes back to Alfred Kinsey's pioneering work, which found a vast difference between what American society believed about sexual behavior and the practices that actually existed in the decade of domesticity. The publication of *Sexual Behavior in the Human Male* (1948) and *Sexual Behavior in the Human Female* (1953) quickly reached the top of best seller lists and turned Kinsey into an instant celebrity. Articles about him also appeared in magazines such as *Time*, *Life*, *Look*, and *McCall's*. His interviews had shown that at least 80 percent of successful businessmen had extramarital affairs. Of the thousands of women that he interviewed, some 90 percent had participated in petting before marriage, while half stated that they had engaged in premarital intercourse, and a quarter admitted to having extramarital affairs. Those women seemed to indicate the possibility of some sexuality, pleasure, and independence for women in a decade of domesticity. "God," Kinsey noted, "what a gap between social front and reality!"[13]

Although Kinsey's critics furiously disagreed with his figures and above all his failure to condemn what he found, other signs of disobedience, a triumph of sexuality, and a shift away from Puritanism soon appeared in women's fashion and popular magazines. In a society of strict gender roles, postwar women were expected to emulate the new look inspired by Christian Dior in 1947. It featured long, full skirts with a defined bosom and waist. Not since the Victorian era had women's fashions been so confining—a girdle molded the body, a "merry widow" corselette cinched the waist, and the conical bra shaped breasts into points. On the big screens of movie houses, all classes of women across America saw portrayals of grand dames and socialites in Dior-inspired fashions, as well as everyday shop girls, secretaries, and housewives with flattering makeup, elegantly coiffed hair, and immaculate, colored nails. By the mid-1950s, however, the look became more sexualized with plunging necklines, bare midriffs, toreador pants, strapless dresses, and tight sheath dresses, in addition to full skirts with cinched waists. Even brassiere and girdle ads of the period became bolder, as they accentuated the form and emphasized women's sexual allure. The illustrations by pinup artists George Petty and Alberto Vargas for lingerie and swimsuits, once common in men's magazines like *Esquire* and *Playboy*, now appeared in the domestic milieu of women's magazines and even mainstream daily newspapers (figure 7.7).

Similar to the fashion trade, this quasi-explicitness also appeared in the editorial material in women's magazines in the 1950s. Instead of articles devoted only to matters of cooking, decorating, and childcare, the periodicals also counseled on how to keep one's mate aroused, as evidenced by such sensational titles as: "My Husband Avoids Making Love to Me" (*Redbook*); "My Husband Wanted Me and the Other Woman, Too. He Needed Us Both!" (*Ladies' Home Journal*); and "Sexual Problems of Beautiful Women" (*Cosmopolitan*). Collectively these articles and fashions seemed to indicate the possibility of some independence for women in a conservative period.[14] This pattern of gradual relaxation of attitudes that Kinsey observed also appeared in advertising.

It was during this time that fragrance, lipstick, hair coloring, and brassieres also became tangled up in the sexual revolution, feminism, and self-esteem. Similar to the 1920s and 1930s, these products were part of the package that women bought as they entered the workplace and battled for social emancipation and power. The ads, then as now,

Figure 7.7. Illustrations by pinup artist George Petty, once common in men's magazines like *Esquire* and *Playboy*, now appeared in women's magazines and even mainstream daily newspapers.

for fashion, cosmetics, and beauty promised happiness, more success, more romance, and more lustrous experience, if women would only let beauty and style into their lives. But what fashion and beauty advertising learned was to sell attitude and fantasy in the 1940s and 1950s, shifting from chaste to evocative images with minimal copy and high glamour suggesting an older, more knowing sexuality.

For example, part of the effectiveness of campaigns for Tabu, a perfume by Dana, was in the expectation of beauty, confidence, and sexuality instilled in women as they viewed and read the ads. Just the name Tabu seems to push the envelope, evoking the word *taboo*. The signature ad for the perfume, which ran for many decades, showed a male violinist lustfully embracing his female piano accompanist, who freely gave into her yearnings, to symbolize the moment when people are swept up in the throes of passion. The captivating ad first ran in 1941 issues of *Vogue* and *Harper's Bazaar* with the tagline "Tabu, the forbidden fragrance by Dana." In addition to the class magazines, it also appeared throughout other women's magazines in the 1950s, 1960s, and 1970s (figure 7.8).

By the late 1940s and early 1950s, ad women boldly embraced what women hoped to get for their beauty dollar by promising better things to come. For cosmetics, copywriter Kay Daly perfected a certain genre of women-centered advertising that did just this, it offered what she called a "little immoral support." The Revlon company, a world leader in fragrance, beauty, and personal-care products, sold women a chance to be fashionable for the price of a lipstick and matching nail polish. Full-scale color promotions began in 1944, which allowed for *total theming* of Revlon's marketing effort, from color spreads placed in the fashion magazines, department stores furnished with window displays, and matching showrooms. But the shade promotion that proved to be one of the most effective ads in cosmetic history was for Revlon's award-winning "Fire and Ice" campaign in 1952.[15]

The central idea behind the Revlon campaign played on a psychological interpretation, the duality of women—there was a little bit of bad in every woman. Among the key people within the company and the numerous agency people who developed the campaign, Revlon's Bea Castle worked with Kay Daly, later vice president and

Figure 7.8. Tabu, the forbidden fragrance by Dana, 1941.

creative director of Norman, Craig & Kummel. They had struggled together to develop names and themes for the color red. But how much can you say about red? As they were talking about what a woman really is, Castle said: "A woman is hot and cold, good or bad, a lady and a tramp . . . a woman is fire and ice." Together they wrote the questionnaire, and the creative process unfolded as they presented glamorous American women in a season when Italian movie starlets like Gina Lollobrigida and Sophia Loren first emerged. But Daly insisted that the ads were also intentionally playful, rather than being just an image common in men's magazines that objectified and demeaned women.[16]

The first ad in the series promoted the new shade "Fire and Ice" with a two-page spread, featured Richard Avedon's photograph of a beautiful model in a low-cut, icy, silver-sequined gown with a fiery scarlet cape; and on the facing page, the headline: "Are you made for Fire and Ice?" You were, the copy said, if you could answer "yes" to eight of fifteen questions about heterosexual romance, but also about women's desire for sensual pleasure, their adventurousness, and their free thinking: "Do you dance with your shoes off? Do you secretly hope that the next man you meet will be a psychiatrist? Would you streak your hair with platinum without consulting your husband?" Since the turn-of-the-century Gibson Girl, women had been "everything nice," but now there was a new American beauty: "She's a tease and temptress, siren and gamin, dynamic and demure. . . . This is the 'Fire and Ice girl' (Are you?)." For another new shade of Revlon red lipstick, "Cherries in the Snow," millions of women read every word of the ad copy like pages from their own diaries. "Who knows the black-lace thoughts you think while shopping in a gingham frock? . . . Who knows the secret, siren side of you that's female as a silken cat?" A reclining woman in a red sheath and billowing ermine was not only a promise of better things to come but a dare to make them happen. And so the playful ads ran. Wear it tonight, the ads promised, and anything could happen. These fifties shades of red lipstick—Cherries in the Snow, Fire and Ice, and Love That Red—remain in the Revlon color line (figure 7.9).[17]

Hence, confident, sexually charged women appeared in ads for

Figure 7.9. Kay Daly's campaign for Revlon's "Queen of Diamonds" lipstick and nail polish combined the appeals of dignity, class, and glamour. *Vogue*, November 1954.

beautifying products for the makeup regimen and marketing beauty. Trust me, these kinds of ads would say, use this product and you will have your heart's desire. Their advertising also carried a powerful and redemptive message—an immediate and affordable means of transformation. You could be whatever you want to be, from the good girl to the bad girl, a lady or a vamp. Similar to Kay Daly, Mary Fillius for Maidenform brassieres and Shirley Polykoff for Clairol hair also captured the female sensibilities of the day. "To be socially attractive, to be attractive, and to win a husband, to keep a husband, a women had to look sexy, free, and available," wrote historian Carol Hymowitz of the new woman.[18]

Mary Fillius: Maidenform "I Dreamed"

Similar to the Revlon ads, the Maidenform campaign brought a sexual playfulness to woman-to-woman advertising. The print advertisements, which pictured Maidenform brassieres, stressed the fit, comfort, and shaped the advantages that the product could make in a woman's appearance and confidence. But the images also showed a glamorous woman in control of her environment, and an altogether different woman behind her social or professional veneer ran for decades. They first appeared as half-page, black-and-white ads in women's magazines, but within one year, full-page, four-color ads appeared and ran for decades.

Starting in 1949, a tastefully bejeweled, barefoot young woman floats through a surreal sketch of a grocery store on a serious shopping spree. As she arches her back and lifts her arms, however, she exposes her bare midriff and reveals the Maidenform "Alloette" brassiere. The reader is brought into the fantasy: "Asleep . . . but it all seemed so real. Leafing through lettuce, browsing through broccoli . . . all eyes gave my figure a big 'aye' . . . And all because of my Maidenform brassiere." Although the theme of shopping may have been a natural one for women's roles, such a fantasy ad was daring in 1949. But the agency had no problem placing the ad, except in the *New Yorker*, which wanted to censor every ad.[19]

The dream theme had been created by copywriter Mary Fillius, a Smith College graduate and one of Bernice Fitz-Gibbon's trainees at Gimbels. While working at the Norman, Craig, & Kummel agency, Fillius first presented the idea to a lingerie house, which turned it down. The agency then brought it to Maidenform, which came to use the theme. Throughout the 1950s, ad women Mary Fillius, Kay Daly, and Kitty D'Alessio would think of themes and write them on three-by-five-inch cards, narrow them down to four or five ideas, and then determine how to produce the concepts before making their presentation to the company. Each "I dreamed" theme had to connect with the audience, pitch to the current fashions, and adapt to the particular line that Maidenform was producing. The final decision on the themes was determined in conferences with Ida Rosenthal, the founder of Maidenform, her daughter Beatrice Coleman, vice president in charge of design, and the advertising agency.[20]

For more than twenty years, the Maidenform Woman appeared in everyday and fantastic situations, such as drifting in a hot air balloon, propelled in a roller coaster, and floating over the crowds at the opera, stressing freedom of movement in the company's undergarments.

Despite the stay-at-home mom image popular on television, the scantily clad Maidenform model also appeared working outside the home not only as a student, artist, and dress designer, but also as a firefighter, cowboy, railroad engineer, police officer, lawyer, and a boxer (figure 7.10). The Maidenform Woman even turned up on a barge down the Nile, in medieval times; later in the 1960s, she appeared in Europe on a Paris rooftop, in a castle in Spain, and in a gondola in Venice. Long committed to print, the campaign appeared in magazines with newspapers secondarily. The ads appeared in *Vogue*, *Bazaar*, *Glamour*, and *Mademoiselle*, and even a teenage campaign for *Seventeen*. But Maidenform drew the line with television. With men and children as viewers, they deemed the medium as not appropriate. The Maidenform campaign was fun in women's magazines but bad taste on tele-

I dreamed I stopped them in their tracks
in my *maidenform bra*

New Sweet Music' bra by Maidenform... spoke-stitched cups for gently rounded contours—the new, naturally you way to look! Snug fitting, all elastic band keeps you comfortable, laminated undercups never let you down! This and 6 other styles, from 2.50.

Figure 7.10. The "I dreamed" theme for Maidenform was based on what motivation research later concluded was women's conscious or unconscious exhibitionist tendencies.

vision; acceptable for women but not for men and children; lovely on the dance floor but not in a nightclub. Thus, delineating appropriate images based on medium, time of day, activity, age, and circumstances had become crucial to drawing the fine line between propriety and a projection of a sexual being.[21]

Every Maidenform model had to meet certain strict standards, instructed the advertiser. She was to be "healthy, unmarried, twenty-six, and more fulsome than a 34-B cup," which was the average size of the Maidenform consumer in 1961. Maidenform girls dreamed in white bras, because most women wanted their bras white, unlike men, who preferred them to be black. But here again the key was the art direction that made photos more comic than erotic and that were shot in high contrast by such well-known photographers as Richard Avedon, Irving Penn, and others. "We tried to inject fashion as well as some humor, so that the ad would be fun," recalled Kitty D'Alessio. "People looked for them because they were campy . . . people thought about them, remembered them, and looked for the next one."[22]

Ultimately, Maidenform paid little attention to the reaction of some dismayed women readers and kept on running the campaign. Research found that women readers were twice as likely to read and remember a specific Maidenform ad than an ad of any competitor. The campaign had struck a chord with women. One explanation for this came from motivational research that suggested that any woman is basically a born exhibitionist, desiring to look more appealing—and, sometimes, sexy—to the interested observer. In a dream or fantasy, of course, women readers can safely act out their innermost desires to appear scantily clad or undressed to a make-believe audience and arouse a man's emotions. Dreaming also played an important role in the 1950s. "Whether it was a dream house, Dream Whip, dream kitchen, dream cake, or 'Dream Lover,' the opulence and technology of the decade optimistically suggested that many of these dreams could come true," explains Barbara J. Coleman.[23]

When Maidenform began offering cash prizes of up to $20,000 for other original dream sequences in 1955, the public helped articulate what was, in effect, a collective fantasy that allegedly spoke to the repressed needs of middle-class American women. In 1957 the first prize for this effort was "I dreamed I danced the hornpipe with Sinbad the Sailor in my Maidenform bra"; the second: "I dreamed I was a silhouette until I was spotlighted in my Maidenform bra"; and the third: "I dreamed I played the violin at Carnegie Hall without strain in my Maidenform bra." The contest aside, entrants also submitted a twenty-five-word essay on why they liked their Maidenform bra and proof of purchase of their product. Women readers participated in this fantasy by imagining that they, too, were confident and attractive enough—sexual enough—to appear in public exhibiting their own Maidenform bras. They even sent scores of unsolicited photos of themselves in endless *I dreamed* scenes in their Maidenform bras. Thus the Maidenform Dream campaign uplifted not only the female anatomy but also her spirit. When the ads no longer appealed to younger women, the fantasy theme was dropped in 1969, as more women opted to pursue careers and make their dreams a reality.[24]

Shirley Polykoff: Clairol "Does She . . . or Doesn't She?"

As the lone female copywriter at the Foote, Cone & Belding advertising agency, Shirley Polykoff had another take on how to portray the modern woman (figure 7.11). When she took over the new Clairol account in 1955, few American women dyed their hair. At the time, women who colored their hair were mainly models, actresses, and members of elite café society.

To make hair coloring popular in mainstream America, Polykoff made it clear that respectable women colored their hair. So she insisted that models in the Clairol ads resemble the girl next door, who's a little prettier, wears cashmere sweaters, and lives in a slightly nicer house than yours, instead of glamorous women. The print ads also included a child with the mother to make it clear that suburban, tastefully dressed matrons were using Clairol, not just "fast women" or glamorous actresses (figure 7.12). The copy was friendly, soft with caring overtones, as if two women were having a conversation, talking about a third woman whom they both knew—the woman featured in the ad. In the middle of the conversation, the copy would switch to the topic of the reader's own hair and how Clairol could improve her

Figure 7.11.
Shirley Polykoff.
Photo from
American
Advertising
Federation Hall
of Fame.

looks and outlook. Almost overnight her slogan "Does She or Doesn't She" caught on, and soon dyed hair became fashionable. Despite the fact that male executives at *Life* magazine turned down a ten-page Clairol layout, the ad theme ran for the next eighteen years until Polykoff retired from FCB, and the number of American women coloring their hair jumped from 7 percent to more than 40 percent.[25]

Similar to selling cosmetics, Polykoff promoted hair coloring to women as a way not only to change their appearance and boost their morale, but also to continually experiment with, and renew, their looks. As in most hair color ads, there was the message to women that you look younger when you eliminate that gray hair. For Clairol Loving Care, a nonpermanent color designed to cover gray hair, the campaign ran with the slogan, "Hate that gray? Wash it away," as well as the tagline "Makes your husband feel younger too, just to look at you!" But it was Polykoff's promotion of the Lady Clairol cream-and-bleach combination that brought silver and platinum shades to

Does she...or doesn't She?

Hair color so natural only her hairdresser knows for sure!™

On a clear crisp day, in brightest sunlight, or in the soft glow of a candle, she always looks radiant, wonderfully natural. Her hair sparkles with life. The color young and fresh, as though she's found the secret of making time stand still. And in a way she has. It's Miss Clairol, the most beautiful, the most effective way to cover gray and to liven or brighten fading hair color.

Keeps hair in wonderful condition—soft, lively—because Miss Clairol carries the color deep into the hair shaft to shine outward, just the way natural hair color does. That's why hairdressers everywhere recommend Miss Clairol and more women use it than all other haircolorings. So quick and easy. Try it yourself. Today. MISS CLAIROL

Even close up. Miss Clairol looks natural. The hair shiny, bouncy, the gray completely covered with the younger, brighter, lasting color no other kind of haircoloring can promise—and live up to!

MISS CLAIROL HAIR COLOR BATH is a trademark of Clairol Inc. ©Clairol Inc. 1962

Figure 7.12. Shirley Polykoff promoted Clairol hair color as an immediate and affordable means of personal transformation.

Middle America: "Is It True Blondes Have More Fun?" and "If I've Only One Life to Live, Let Me Live It as a Blonde." With her ads, Polykoff had created something iconic about not only blondes but also redheads: "Every woman should be a redhead . . . at least once in her life." Thus, Polykoff's ads for Clairol transformed women's views on hair dye. They gave women the license to think of hair coloring as they think of lipstick, one shade one day, and another shade the next.

Polykoff knew firsthand about how hair color provided an immediate and affordable means of transformation. As with many other women of her era, it appears she was caught up in the first stirrings of feminism—to pass as one thing, when deep inside you were something else. Born Shirley Polykoff, she was the daughter of Russian Jewish immigrants living in Brooklyn who had come to America with only a few items. She also knew the value of appearance. As a child growing up in Brooklyn, she dreamed of crossing the bridge to Manhattan, and her values were shaped by the advertisements in glossy magazines. When Polykoff was fifteen, she began to lighten her hair, turning herself into the kind of person that she believed did not go with brown hair. "If you asked my mother, 'Are you proud to be Jewish?' She wasn't trying to pass," says Polykoff's daughter, Alix Nelson Frick. "But she believed in the dream, and the dream was you could acquire all the accoutrements of the established affluent class, which included a certain breeding and a certain kind of look." It was this image of the kind of woman that Polykoff thought she ought to be that was embodied in her Clairol advertisements. "My mother wanted to be that woman in the picture," Frick continued. "She was wedded to the notion that a suburban, tastefully dressed, well-coddled matron was an adornment to her husband, a loving mother, a long-suffering wife, a person who never overshadowed him."[26]

Yet "Shirley Polykoff wasn't really that kind of woman," writer Malcolm Gladwell points out. "She always had a career. She never moved to the suburbs." And she was a very flamboyant, very dominating type who had brilliantly succeeded in a man's world.[27]

Starting at *Harper's Bazaar*, Polykoff began work as a secretary to the circulation manager, making twenty-three dollars a week during the Depression. When she stepped in to write a *Harper's* advertisement for

Good Housekeeping magazine, which would not run the ad unless they received the copy that day, she inadvertently misspelled several authors' names that appeared in the ad. Rather than being praised for her initiative, she was fired. To find a new job, she created a portfolio and made the rounds, showing her book to the advertising departments of large retail stores. Soon she established herself in retail advertising, first for department and variety stores, including Bamberger's and Kresge's in Newark, then for various New York agencies with retail accounts. However, Polykoff's first agency job came with Peck Advertising, where she worked for ten years until eventually moving on to a smaller agency that specialized in retail and manufactured shoe brands. With twenty years of advertising experience, Polykoff next moved to Foote, Cone & Belding in 1955. As the agency's only woman copywriter, she brought the feminine viewpoint to her work on Playtex women's foundation garments, the Perfume Institute, and Savarin Coffee accounts.[28]

Another way Polykoff resolved the contradiction between the kind of woman she was and the kind she felt she ought to be was through a kind of useful fiction. At the age of twenty-five, she married George P. Halperin, the son of an Orthodox rabbi, with whom she later had two children. But she kept her maiden name at the office, since she had already established a reputation, though she used Polly (a short version of Polykoff) Halperin at home. One of the stories Polykoff told was that she put her husband and family above her career, going so far as to limit her Foote, Cone & Belding salary to $25,000 so as not to earn more than her husband. After he died, the agency raised her salary to be commensurate with her position and promoted her to a vice president of the agency, but that was also part of her legend. After eighteen years at Foote, Cone & Belding, Polykoff retired in 1973 as senior vice president, and ten years later in 1983, she was elected to the Advertising Hall of Fame.[29]

Certainly Polykoff, Fillius, and Daly succeeded in making other women feel that hair coloring, lingerie, makeup, and fragrance were an essential part of the package for women to maintain their self-confidence and identity. Such rebelliousness in beauty campaigns continued well into the following decade, giving the impression of an increasing freedom of sexual expression for women.

GENDER-BASED MARKETING: AUTOMOBILES

In 1956 *Fortune* magazine published some unexpected facts about women's place in American economic society in an article titled "You Can Only Estimate the Power of a Woman." Recent market research had found that women had far more purchasing power than estimated: more than twenty million women were employed, about one-third of the workforce. Women bought 90 percent of all household purchases, 62 percent of all hardware, and 89 percent of home remodeling. They held 65 percent of all savings accounts, and accounted for 62 percent of individual stockholders of large corporations. Women also purchased or influenced the acquisition of most automobiles. Finally, women not only outnumbered men, they also outlived them. Thus, *Fortune* concluded, "Who said this was a man's world?"[30]

To key industries like the automotive industry, women represented the largest, most powerful market in the world. Wartime pushed millions of women to take up driving for the service of the nation. Suburbanization also made public transportation inconvenient; mothers raising children in bedroom communities had to get around and so took on the role as family chauffer. Considering that nearly twenty million American women drove cars, and some eight million of them were part of two-car families, the time had long passed when the automobile belonged exclusively to the man of the house. In the postwar years, the emergence of a new generation of suburban homemakers presented an unprecedented opportunity for car manufacturers.[31]

Automobiles offered the suburban woman more than a means of transport and independence; they also suggested a lifestyle. They provided a visible statement not only about a woman's status but also her sexuality and sexual identity. The concept of a car as a status symbol had long been a central theme of General Motors' marketing strategy, suggesting that when you arrived, you bought a Cadillac. In turn, consumers used the vehicles not only for transportation but also to create identities; cars represented people's ideas about themselves to others in a society in which looks, display, and goods are pervasive and inescapable. As consumerism rose to new heights in the 1950s,

Ford Motor Company, Chrysler, and General Motors dramatically shifted the concept of many automobile models from a masculine theme—more power and performance—to a household appliance with fashion, color, and style.

The hiring of women industrial designers largely known for their feminine sensibilities in the 1940s and 1950s coincided with these broad changes in the automotive market. Through female designers and other cultural mediators, the automotive industry came to understand what mattered most to Mrs. Consumer. She wanted to know what it would take to make things for her easier, quicker. To her, color harmony in cars had become as important as body styling and engineering. That brought about brighter colors, trim lines, and upholstery that was more pleasing to the eye and stayed clean longer. Changes in windshields, luggage space, seat adjustments, power steering, power brakes, and power windows also came about, as did station wagons, because automakers had their eye on the women's market. In addition, the steering wheel was lowered, and door buttons and armrests were even redesigned so they wouldn't break women's fingernails. Today the car-buying public not only accepts these improvements and annual model changes, but also has come to demand them.[32]

In these early days of gender-based marketing, marketers and advertisers often missed their mark. "Marketing to women should be transparent, not pink. Companies who want to reach women need to really show that they're sensitive to the needs of this market and that they're taking it seriously," explains Martha Barletta, president of the TrendSight Group. "Because if they think that it's all about décor and all they need to do was paint their brand pink, that will backfire on them 99 out of a hundred times."[33]

Many of them did just this. They not only painted the brand pink, some automakers even went to the extremes of gender typing, painting the product itself pink. For example, Chrysler Corporation introduced the 1954 Le Comte and La Comtesse—the former bronze and black, the latter pink and pale gray—his and hers show cars. The following year, Chrysler produced a fun, high-end model for the fine ladies of the day—the Dodge La Femme in 1954 and 1955. It symbolized Detroit automakers' idea of femininity with two-tone exteriors painted in Heather Rose and Sapphire White or a lavender and white option. Furthermore, they designed the model to be a conversation piece aimed at the wives of doctors and bank managers who would drive it around town, in an era when most families had just one car. But the crowning touches were its feminine accessories with compartments to stow a woman's essentials, including a matching rose-colored leather shoulder bag to hold a cigarette case, lighter, and a compact and lipstick case. The 1955 model also featured a seat cloth with little rosebuds and a rain ensemble with folding umbrella to match. The dealer brochure heralded the new model: "Never a car more distinctly feminine than La Femme, the first fine car created exclusively for women!" Chrysler produced only one thousand models; the demand for the model never justified mass production.[34]

During this period, Harley Earl, General Motors' vice president of the styling division, actively recruited women designers, and they became known as the "Damsels of Designs," often participating in company promotions, television appearances, and public lectures. General Motors had hoped the women designers would bring a distinctly feminine approach to automotive design rather than a masculine stamp. Although the opulent Cadillac model appeared to belong exclusively to the man of the house, the women designers fashioned the Cadillac Eldorado, the Seville Baroness, and a series of other less expensive models to appeal to the modern woman, such as the Chevrolet Impala Martinique. They also introduced slipcovers to change with the seasons, chic color combinations to match dresses, luggage to match the interior, and removable cosmetics cases. Women-oriented ads reinforced the theme with women in evening gowns and female interest situations, such as a mink stole and a box of orchids dropped on the backseat.[35]

When GM showcased its new 1959 Cadillac, the strategy was an obvious attempt to convey luxury, success, and femininity. The new model came in a choice of feminine colors: classic white, powder blue, and, of course, chic pink. A series of ads featured scenes with a mother and daughter wearing coordinating dresses that matched with the shade of the automobile. In one early ad for the pink Cadillac, the text opened with "One of the special delights which ladies find in

Cadillac ownership is the pleasure of being a passenger." Danger-ously approaching condescension, the ad addresses the prospective woman consumer as a passenger or subordinate rather than as a driver taking control of the wheel of a luxury car. To cosmetic entrepreneur Mary Kay Ash, however, the new pink Cadillac was highly valuable for a very different reason. Since she gloried in selling femininity, she promoted the pink Cadillac as a sales incentive to consultants and sales directors who reached and maintained their sales goal achieved from selling Mary Kay Cosmetics at home parties. Today, the car incentive program continues with an expanded fleet, but the pink Cadillac remains the highest honor.

Today, the debate over gendered marketing veers between the poles of stereotyping to self-invention. Gender-based marketing remains a risky undertaking for most companies. Get it wrong, and their audience would be offended. Miss the mark, and their audience would ignore them. Either way, they were looking at a very costly effort, when the general revival of feminism would strongly admonish the advertising business for never quite catching up with the times.

REPRESENTATIONS OF AD MEN AND WOMEN

Achieving the American Dream became inextricably linked with business success after World War II, as an increasingly affluent America learned to define the middle class through possessions, status, and lifestyle. Not surprisingly, best-selling novels and popular films in the postwar era reflected the country's fears of increasing materialism and the promotion industry's expanding impact. Best-selling novels like *Please Send Me Absolutely Free* (1946), *The Hucksters* (1946), and *Aurora Dawn* (1947) portrayed the ad man as a soulless antihero. The *Space Merchants* (1952) took place in the future and went so far as to portray a time when advertising agencies literally ruled the world. In the United States, senators and congressmen were elected not by the people but by corporations controlled by the advertising agencies, and each representative had voting power in proportion to the annual billings of his group.

The popularity of advertising men as heroes, or antiheros, of American life alerted Hollywood to the rich potential such a subject had for major films. Similar to the novels, popular films also perpetuated long-held stereotypes about the ad man as crass, materialistic, deceptive, and interested only in appearances. "They were said to dress more stylishly than the mere businessmen they served. They lived somewhat unconventional even racy lives and were supposedly torn between guarding the public good and using their great gifts to manipulate people for profit," observes David Halberstam. "In effect, it was seen to be a profession where young men traded their ideals for an even higher life-style, with luxurious suburban homes in Greenwich and Darien."[36]

By and large, however, ad women in popular films were portrayed in narrow roles, working behind the scenes in several ways: (1) beauties living a more conventional life guarding the public good or the good of the family, or (2) the voluptuous, earthy model showing off her body. For example, the film version of Frederic Wakeman's novel *The Hucksters* features a scene in which the virtuous Deborah Kerr tells Clark Gable that he does not have to sell out, rather, he can be an honorable man in advertising: "Why don't you be one of those who sells only what he believes in? Sell good things, things that people should have, and sell them with dignity—and taste. That's a career for any man, a career to be proud of."

Other films of this genre include the 1947 film *Her Husband's Affairs*, in which Lucille Ball plays the enterprising wife of an advertising executive played by Franchot Tone. Though the ad man is successful, his wife can't help but feel that he would be more successful if she were to take an active part in his business affairs. In another not so subtle swipe at radio and television advertising, the 1950 film *Pretty Baby* features Betty Drake as an enterprising young woman who always ensures herself a seat on the subway by carrying a doll wrapped in baby bunting. Through a series of complications, Drake's bosses, advertising executives Dennis Morgan and Zachary Scott, assume the baby is genuine and hope to use the little darling to win a baby food account. And in the 1957 film *Will Success Spoil Rock Hunter?* based on a successful Broadway play, ad man Tony Randall hopes to convince blonde bombshell Jayne Mansfield to endorse his product, Stay-Put Lipstick. It pokes fun at everything from advertising, consumerism, and celebrity to sexual mores and success mentality.

When a film portrayed a woman as an advertising executive, typically she was struggling with her career and unfulfilled, as seen in two fluffy comedies, both starring Doris Day. In *Lover Come Back* (1961), the plot revolves around sleazy ad man Rock Hudson, who advertises a nonexistent product called "VIP" just to feature his girlfriend in TV commercials. Meanwhile, rival advertising agent Doris is trying to get the same account with true professionalism. It is not about Doris protecting her virginity from Rock, rather, it is about Doris protecting her autonomy, which makes her an early feminist, as some critics have noted. And in *The Thrill of It All* (1963), housewife Beverly Boyer (Day) happens by chance to impress Rock Hudson with an honest appraisal of one his products, Happy Soap. Working as the new spokesperson for the soap, Beverly becomes an advertising sensation, but her husband has to deal with the social consequences of his wife making more money than he does and how her new career infringes on her duties as a housewife. As this film demonstrates, the main character's career disrupts her private life and the prevailing ideal that a woman's place is in the home.

Thus, advertising is represented as a white-collar profession for men, where traditional family-oriented women are shown in a comedic way trying to make a career of it. Nonetheless, these films also reflect the increasingly active role of middle-class women, including the confusion about the impact of an advertising career on romance, marriage, and sexual propriety. Although the films tried to warn young women of the pitfalls of careerism, they expressed this era's growing anxiety over sexual imagery, explains film historian Jack Boozer. Ultimately, "the American sex revolution that began by the late 1960s was predicated in part on the very prominence over the last ten years of the sexual appeals imposed by modern advertising."[37]

NOTES

1. "You Can Only Estimate the Power of a Woman," *Fortune*, August 1956.
2. Obituary of Jean Wade Rindlaub, *New York Times*, December 22, 1991.
3. Business Professional Women's Survey, see Angel Kwolek-Folland, *Incorporating Women: A History of Women in Business in the United States* (New York: Palgrave, 2002), p. 157.
4. "Women Veeps at McCann," *Printers' Ink*, February 26, 1960.
5. Ed Applegate, ed., *Ad Men and Women: A Biographical Dictionary of Advertising* (Westport, CT: Greenwood, 1994), pp. 273–78.
6. "Advertising Power That Can't Be Skirted," *New York Times*, February 22, 1959. Also see Stephen Fox, *The Mirror Makers* (New York: Vintage Books, 1984), pp. 292–94.
7. James M. Woolf, "Is It True That Women Are Denied the Bigger Opportunities in Advertising?" *Advertising Age*, December 17, 1951.
8. Erik Barnouw, *Tube of Plenty: The Evolution of American Television* (New York: Oxford University Press, 1990).
9. "TV Arrives and the Future Begins," *Advertising Age*, July 31, 1995. On BBDO, see Martin Mayer, *Madison Avenue, USA* (New York: Harper, 1954), p. 11. On the history of early TV commercials, see Jonathan Price, *The Best Thing on TV: Commercials* (New York: Viking Press, 1978).
10. "Are the Gals Taking Over Radio-TV Commercials?" *Printers' Ink*, July 2, 1954.
11. David Halberstam, *The Fifties* (New York: Fawcett Columbine, 1993), pp. 496–99.
12. "Ah, There Mrs. O'Rourke," *Printers' Ink*, June 26, 1953.
13. Cornelia V. Christenson, *Kinsey: A Biography* (Bloomington: Indiana University Press, 1971), pp. 117–18.
14. Ivor Williams, "Pious Pornography," *Playboy*, October 1957.
15. Andrew Tobias, "Fire and Ice and Everything Nice," in *Fire and Ice: The Story of Charles Revson—The Man Who Built the Revlon Empire* (New York: William and Morrow Company, 1976).
16. Ibid., p. 292.
17. Ibid., chap. 8.
18. Carol Hymowitz and Michele Weissman, *A History of Women in America* (New York: Bantam Books, 1978), p. 292.
19. Barbara J. Coleman, "Maidenform(ed): Images of American Women in the 1950s," *Genders* 21 (1995).
20. Bernice Fitz-Gibbon, *Macy's, Gimbels, and Me* (1951; repr., New York: Simon and Schuster, 1967), p. 264. Interview with Kitty D'Alessio, August 3, 1990. Maidenform Collection, box 1, folder 21, American History Archives. Also see "Maidenform's J. A. Coleman," *Madison Avenue*, November 1960, Maidenform Collection, box 1, folder 6, American History Archives, Smithsonian Institution.
21. On censorship, see "Maidenform's Dream Marks Its 20th Year," *Women's Wear*

Daily, March 20, 1969. After Maidenform moved away from the "I Dreamed" theme, the advertisers began in-depth television advertising in 1972. Company publication, *Maidenform, the Golden Dream 1922–1972*, Maidenform Collection, box 1, folder 12, American History Archives. "Maidenform's J. A. Coleman," *Madison Avenue* (November 1960).

22. On standards, see *Maidenform, the Golden Dream 1922–1972*. See also Interview, Kitty D'Alessio.

23. In 1962 Gallup and Robinson research found that twenty-nine out of one hundred women readers recalled a particular Maidenform ad in 1952. See "Maidenform's 40th Birthday," *Maidenform Mirror*, July–August 1962, Maidenform Collection, box 1, folder 12, American History Archives, Smithsonian Institution. "Maidenform Dreams Big," *Sales Management*, April 5, 1963, p. 11. On dreaming, see Coleman, "Maidenform(ed)."

24. "Latest Press Reaction to the Dream Contest," Maidenform Collection, box 1, folder 12, American History Archives, Smithsonian Institution.

25. Shirley Polykoff, *Does She . . . Or Doesn't She? And How She Did It* (New York: Doubleday, 1975).

26. "Polykoff Put Herself in User's Shoes," *Advertising Age*, October 14, 1985. On Frick, see Malcolm Gladwell, "Annals of Advertising: True Colors," *New Yorker*, March 22, 1999, pp. 70–73.

27. Gladwell, "Annals of Advertising."

28. Robert M. Thomas Jr., "Shirley Polykoff, 90, Ad Writers Whose Query Colored a Nation," *New York Times*, June 8, 1998.

29. "Polykoff, Shirley," *Encyclopedia of Advertising* (Chicago: Fitzroy Dearborn Publishers, 2003).

30. "You Can Only Estimate the Power of a Woman," *Fortune*, August 1956.

31. "Sell a Woman, Sell Her Family," *Printers' Ink*, July 5, 1957.

32. On women automotive designers, see Pat Kirkham, ed., *Women Designers in the USA 1900–2000* (New Haven, CT: Yale University Press, 2000), pp. 281–82.

33. "What Women Want," *CMA Management*, December/January 2006, http://www.managementmag.com/index.cfm/ci_id/1165la_id/1 (accessed July 10, 2006).

34. Internet site provides historical information on Dodge La Femme, including how to tell if you own a La Femme, restoration, and worldwide registry, http://www.dodgelafemme.com/info.htm (accessed December 23, 2007).

35. Kirkham, ed., *Women Designers*, pp. 281–82.

36. Halberstam, *The Fifties*, p. 501.

37. Jack Boozer, *Career Movies: American Business and the Success Mystique* (Austin: University of Texas Press, 2003), p. 178.

CHAPTER 8

THE SECOND WAVE OF AD WOMEN

THE FORCES OF FEMINISM

T he song "I Am Woman" penned by Helen Reddy topped the music charts in 1972, boosted by the feminist movement that gained national prominence in the late 1960s. Not since the Progressive Era of the early twentieth century had so large a movement on the behalf of women's rights been seen in the United States.

To describe their efforts, women took over the word *feminism*, a term used occasionally since the 1920s. To distinguish from the women's movement of the 1960s, the new term *second wave* was added. Moreover, feminism was reborn and impacted two generations of women. Middle-class, educated women were, as it turned out, still struggling for better-paying jobs, equal pay for equal work, childcare, and abortion rights. It is crucial to also remember that another generation of young women born between 1948 and 1954 were college girls at this time; they could be characterized as more radical, rebellious, and playful than their predecessors. Although the gulf between their parents and this generation was legendary, for the first time, large numbers of women from both groups began to seriously question the ideological framework that confined especially middle-class women to the home, when other opportunities existed outside the home.

The forces of feminism would gain momentum, and by 1970, they reflected a broader conception of reform in four ways: (1) Feminism would increase society's awareness that women did not have the choices and opportunities that were available to men. (2) Feminists' battle to remove inequities based on gender resulted in higher wages, created new opportunities, and made it easier for enterprising women to establish their own business. (3) The importance of the feminine viewpoint on the basic promotional appeal for women-centered accounts became more important than ever before. And (4) perhaps the most visible result, feminism would increase society's increasing awareness of sexism in advertising images.

REBIRTH OF FEMINISM

Just as the generations of feminists before them emphasized the need for intellectual equality and personal fulfillment, the "New Woman" of the 1960s and 1970s would be at odds with the ideals and practices of conventional family life. But their solutions went beyond personal and individual rejection of marriage, as did those of their predecessors. They embraced complex grassroots mobilization, countercultures, and identity politics, while they gained more opportunities to express their individuality and community through their choices as consumers. In challenging the social order, identities, political preferences, and consumer preferences became inextricably linked through a wave of civil rights, the student antiwar and women's movements, the sexual revolution, and environmental concerns. In this turbulent era, feminist writings would express the ethos, aspirations, and dreams of many women while alienating others.

Feminist Writings

The diverse ideas of Betty Friedan and Helen Gurley Brown laid the groundwork for the second wave of the women's movement. Through their works and other feminist writings, American women become more attuned to the oppression in their everyday lives and their sexuality.

One could certainly say that Betty Friedan's *The Feminine Mystique* (1963) spoke to the lives of middle-class, suburban women far more than it resonated with the lives of other women; that is, poor women and working-class women who had always worked, if not full-time then part-time. But Friedan had touched a sort of raw nerve with an enormous number of women, many of whom were college educated, had worked for wages, and had found their own satisfaction in the workforce. Although many of these women had been content with their roles as homemakers, many others had been moving toward dual roles, working both inside and outside the home since World War II. For many, this wartime experience raised their expectations of what life could be like for them both inside and outside the home. It provided a certain satisfaction despite the domestic ideology that told women they belonged at home.

By the time Betty Friedan challenged women to combine motherhood with a career in 1963, Helen Gurley Brown's *Sex and the Single Girl* (1962) was already urging women to postpone or skip marriage and simply enjoy a fulfilling sexual life. The popular book guided single women through everything from beauty and budgeting to career planning, encouraging them to pursue whatever could give them a richer, more exciting and glamorous life. Brown also told her own story, describing herself as a "mouseburger" who never gave up, advanced in her chosen career, and then married the man of her dreams. Two years later, she followed with a racier advice manual, *Sex in the Office* (1964).[1]

Brown's family lived in Little Rock, Arkansas, until her father died when she was ten years old. Her mother was left to raise two daughters, and the family moved to Los Angeles, California. In high school, Brown set about working hard to escape the life laid out for her, working on school publications and graduating at the top of her class. She attended Texas State College for Women and Woodbury Business College before returning to Los Angeles. In the workforce, she worked at eighteen different secretarial jobs before she was twenty-five. A major career move came in 1948, when she became the first woman to hold a copywriter position at Foote, Cone & Belding, a major Los Angeles advertising agency. She went on to work for Kenyon & Eckhardt, a Hollywood advertising agency, as an account executive and copywriter. She became one of the highest-paid copywriters on the West Coast. In 1959, at thirty-seven, she married 20th Century Fox studio executive David Brown, who later coproduced such films as *Jaws*, *The Sting*, and *Cocoon*. They had no children.[2]

Building upon the success of her books, Brown and her husband developed a plan for a magazine aimed at the eighteen- to thirty-four-year-old, single, liberated career woman. In 1965 Hearst Corporation accepted their idea, and Brown became editor-in-chief for *Cosmopolitan* for the next thirty years (figure 8.1). Although advertising executives had long targeted women as leading consumers, now Brown was urging her middle- and upper-class readers to have it all—sex, love, career, and money. *Cosmo* celebrated women's beauty and power, while the editorial thrust called for young women to have careers, to be adventurous, and to take their sexual lives in their own hands. Moreover, Brown's ideas mirrored Hugh Hefner's sexually permissive, playboy philosophy and offered an alternative, hedonistic lifestyle. After all, women had the equal right to enjoy themselves while waiting for Mr. Right. But her logic was both in touch and at odds with the feminine spirit of the 1960s sexual revolution.[3]

For a small number of feminists, the beat culture offered a seductive escape from a conventional life with an apron. The terms *beat generation* and *beats* originated with writers like Jack Kerouac in 1948 and continued in popular usage through the 1960s, describing a counter-culture philosophy that combined antimaterialism with a *soul-searching* ethos. From the late 1950s on, thousands of women descended upon the bohemian life of New York's Greenwich Village and San Francisco's North Beach in search of poetry, folk music, and sexual experiences. When the federal government approved the use of the birth control pill, the sexual revolution shifted into higher gear,

Figure 8.1. Beginning in 1965, Helen Gurley Brown edited and oversaw the covers for *Cosmopolitan* magazine. Photo courtesy of Sophia Smith Collection, Smith College.

and a significant number of young college-educated women embraced the *swinging singles* lifestyle in large urban cities. They took jobs as airline stewardesses, teachers, editorial assistants, or office workers, filling thousands of new clerical and secretarial jobs that had been created by expanding corporations and government agencies, though most of them expected to marry after a few years.

For millions of American women experiencing discrimination at this time, the civil rights movement came to provide a model of social reform. When President Lyndon B. Johnson pushed through the Civil Rights Act in 1964, the legislation aimed at abolishing racial discrimination in employment and places of public accommodation, protecting voting rights, and further advancing school integration. It also had a ripple effect. An extraordinary number of people came to see the same ways in which gender and sex had also been the basis for discrimination. And so millions of women, especially college-educated, white females who had been raised to think of themselves as having minds equal to those of men, set out to organize to change society and their lives.

By then, the emerging counterculture had reached a critical mass and had become a visible phenomenon that challenged the "establishment"—the government, powerful businesses, and conventional hierarchies of authority—as domestic conflicts erupted and more and more Americans were dispatched to a seemingly futile war in Vietnam. Young people, not surprisingly, gave enormous spirit and energy to the social movements. In the early 1960s, the postwar baby-boom generation came of age, and nearly half of America's population was under age twenty-five. When these baby boomers moved into the nation's institutions of higher learning, enrollment more than doubled over the decade. At the same time, the beats had recast themselves as high school– and college-age hippies, the vanguard of a new counterculture that advocated increasing sexual freedoms. The hippie lifestyle culminated in 1967 with the "Summer of Love" in San Francisco; and in the summer of 1969, music fans flocked to Woodstock to celebrate rock music, sex, and drugs. *Do your own thing* became the slogan of the day, spurring a liberation in music, fashion, and art. While the counterculture continued demands for equal rights and an end to the lingering war, the economy had slipped into a recession by 1969. The post–World War II boom had come to an end. But the women's liberation movement was just beginning.

A series of incremental social changes were reaching a critical mass. When small opportunities became available, questions were raised about whether larger opportunities could be obtainable to women. By the 1960s, millions of women entering the workforce—both singles for the first time and married, middle-class women who sent their children to school—were on the cusp of being able to contribute to society, only to discover that the prevailing domestic ideology told them they could not or should not participate. But the numbers of women in the workforce had increased so dramatically that the pressure to break down the age-old barriers had simply grown too large. As recently as 1971, most women still kept house as a primary occupation. Within two years, however, the tide turned when a majority of women (51 percent) had jobs away from home. The workingwomen had become the new norm and spearheaded the women's liberation movement—the search for what's come to be called equal opportunity in the workforce. They strove for equal access to jobs, credit, fair taxation, and economic independence.[4]

The Women's Movement

The most visible symbol of the women's movement—what's come to be called equal opportunity in the workforce—was the creation of the National Organization for Women in 1966. Once NOW was founded, other organizations appeared, and the new feminism quickly spread throughout the nation. Notably, in 1968 academic and professional women formed the Women's Equity Action League (WEAL) to end sex discrimination in employment and education. As a result, courses on women in every field were added to the college curriculum, and multidisciplinary women's studies programs were also soon established. Job counseling for women, such as Catalyst in New York, also appeared. What's come to be called equal opportunity in the workforce had become the slogan of the women's movement.

At this point, it is crucial to recognize that women continued to face real discrimination in all areas of American life in 1970, fifty years after they earned the right to vote in national elections. Hundreds of state laws were still on the books that often excluded women from serving on juries and limited their rights to make contracts and to hold property. In many states, regulations prohibited many women from working more than eight hours a day or forty-eight hours a week, so they were denied opportunities to earn substantial overtime wages or promotion to jobs requiring overtime. State laws also did not permit women to enter certain occupations for industries deemed detrimental to their morals, health, or capacity for motherhood. It was also a time when women still had no rights to rent an apartment or hotel room in innumerable locations. Women regularly encountered extra difficulty when making large purchases or getting bank loans, mortgages, or credit cards; her gender was bad collateral. Women were hired and paid by a second standard. Even when they were qualified for better-paying jobs, they were paid on the average 60 percent less for doing the same work in virtually every occupation.[5]

Discrimination in countless other ways limited women's ability to travel, conduct business, and network. In 1967, for example, an executive flight left from Chicago to New York every night at six, but Mary Wells, one of the most successful women in advertising, could not get on it. Neither could legendary ad woman Shirley Polykoff; Jean Simpson, vice president at N. W. Ayer; and Jane Trahey, president, Trahey/Wolf, Inc. The flight was for men only. This was indicative of the sexist attitudes that women were still fighting. Women could not join the local men-only organizations of their profession. They were also not allowed to enter numerous bars and restaurants without a male escort, as well as other city and country clubs reserved for men with no comparable facilities for women.[6]

In the suburbs, as well as in the large cities, women shared their life stories in consciousness-raising sessions, novels, position papers, essays, and new forms of artistic expression. In 1969, for example, Kate Millet's *Sexual Politics* became a best seller. It was followed by Shulamith Firestone's *The Dialectic of Sex* (1970), Robin Morgan's *Sisterhood Is Powerful* (1970), and Germaine Greer's *The Female Eunuch* (1971). "These sessions resembled those of Heterodoxy, the major women's organization in Greenwich Village in the 1920s," explains women's historian Lois Banner. "They inspired the women who participated in them to both participate in the feminist movement and to establish feminist organizations in their own communities."[7]

To publicize their views and gain media attention, feminists moved from living rooms to stage performances in the streets. One of the most memorable guerilla theater presentations was the bra-burning performance outside the 1968 Miss America Pageant in Atlantic City, New Jersey. In their event staged for the media, the feminists threw items of women's beauty culture that they perceived as oppressive—bras, curlers, makeup. Like beauty pageants, bridal fairs also became a favorite target of the women's movement. Feminists argued that bridal fairs "add to the sales itch for crystal and furniture and the bride herself, becomes a commodity." Thus, women's liberation groups targeted the marketers of gowns, wedding pictures, caterers, furniture, appliances, and honeymoon trips for turning marriage into an excuse for "conspicuous consumption." They also plastered thousands of stickers urging other women to join them in their protest against bridal fairs on both coasts. Their signs mockingly declared: "Always a Bridesmaid. Never a Person," "Here Comes a Bribe," and "Ask Not for Whom the Wedding Bells Toll." Anything that seemed degrading to women, especially the media and advertising, became a target for feminist protesters.[8]

The publishing industry did not take long to repackage feminism and try to sell it back to women. A flurry of new magazines reached women who otherwise never would have read feminist materials. For example, *Ms.* magazine offered a political slant, while four years later, *Working Woman* enlightened women on negotiating for themselves, getting a good deal, working out work situations fairly, and dealing with husbands and men. And *Cosmo* continued with feminist updates on contraception to promote the equality of the sexes with articles such as: "The New Pill That Promises to Make Women More Responsive" (management removed the words "to men" to avoid censorship); "Girls Guide to Unions"; and excerpts from feminist exposés. Even as the women's movement continued with its perceived characterization of men as the enemy, *Cosmo* continued to encourage women to find satisfying relationships with a man (or men) and to be glamorous with their short skirts, push-up bras, and high heels.

Perhaps more than anything else, affirmative action policies and guidelines opened up access to education and employment for women. In 1967 the original 1965 executive order was amended to make up for past discrimination, specifically requiring organizations accepting federal funds to take affirmative action and to increase employment of members of preferred racial or ethnic groups and women. By the mid-1970s, women were scoring impressive victories through commissions, class action suits, hearings, and protests.

The 1972 passage of the Equal Rights Amendment (ERA) in the Senate marked a milestone for women. Women's entry into the professions began in earnest shortly after the enactment of Title IX in the same year, when the federal legislation mandated equal access to education; it also denied federal funds for men's sports programs unless an equal amount was provided for girls' and women's athletics. In the same year, Congress also extended the Equal Pay Act, which was extended to cover administrative, executive, and professional personnel, requiring equal pay for equal work in industries producing goods for commerce. One year later, in 1973, the Supreme Court ruled in *Roe v. Wade* that abortion was constitutionally protected by a woman's right to privacy. In 1974 Congress passed the Equal Credit Opportunity Act, which allowed married women to obtain credit in their own names for the first time, and the Educational Equity Act, which was designed to eliminate sexist curricula and achieve equity for all students regardless of their sex. And in 1980, the Equal Employment Opportunity Commission added sexual harassment to its Guidelines on Discrimination, redefining unwelcome sexual advances as a violation of women's rights. In the process, this legislation introduced the term *sexism* to challenge everything from women's economic and political inequality to sexual double standards and sex-role stereotypes. The subject of affirmative action, sexism, and sexual harassment conduct suddenly burst into public consciousness in the form of national hearings, trials, and scandals.

Still, equality of women's rights under the law was far from guaranteed. In 1982 the ERA fell three states short of the three-fourths majority needed for adoption. Despite oppositions and setbacks, women became better educated and more socially and politically aware than the previous generation. The number of women enrolled in college rose 45 percent between 1970 and 1975. Women also entered professional schools in record numbers, and by the end of the decade, they were earning 24 percent of all professional degrees—up dramatically from 7 percent in 1970. With higher education now widely available to women, an enormous number of women had more choices than ever before. Some women decided to settle for a comfortable, less demanding job, while many others delayed having children until reaching their thirties and established themselves in their careers. They went into the professions, academia, and business enterprise. Although many women held jobs in such traditionally female fields as secretarial, sales, teaching, and nursing, the nation also saw its first female firefighters, airline pilots, construction workers, and telephone lineswomen. More and more women joined the professional ranks of engineers, doctors, and lawyers. They also expanded into new opportunities in the media, banking, real estate, insurance, and even stock selling.

THE ADVERTISING PROFESSION IN THE 1960s AND 1970s

The affirmative action policies were intended to promote access to employment aimed at minority men and women of all races. But in advertising, circumstances made women a special case somewhat different than that regarding the subordination of blacks and other minorities (see chapter 9). White women had long worked in a wide range of situations in the advertising profession, including in the areas of consulting, agencies, corporations, retail, and public relations. Ad men and the trade journals claimed that advertising treated women better than most other businesses or professions. When public relations and advertising expanded in the 1960s and 1970s, the field naturally opened up for more women to develop the women's market. As a result, the number of women in advertising dramatically increased by one-third over the eight-year period from 1960 to 1968, and for the first time in 1983, more than half of the people employed in advertising were women. These accomplishments fueled the optimism that many ad women shared at the beginning of the twentieth century.[9]

But the possibilities for ad women were tempered by the realities of the advertising profession. Women continued to face gender discrimination, racial discrimination, access to capital, and the struggle for balance between work and family. The term *businesswoman* was itself misleading. In this new era of supposed equality between the sexes, women regularly employed in business still did not convey the female equivalent of the male corporate executive or entrepreneur. Instead, it referred to the growing numbers of women who worked in sex-segregated office positions as stenographers, typists, or clerks. Similar to office work, the overall creative development of advertising campaigns continued to be largely gendered. The initial strategic advertising plan was performed by a man, who gave the assignment to the creative team, an art director (male) and copywriter (male or female), who came up with a concept. As in the past, women typically had most success in writing women-centered copy—good jobs, good pay (but less than a man at most shops).

Mary Wells: Madison Avenue's Golden Girl

In this new era, perhaps no other woman symbolized the creative revolution in advertising more than Mary Georgene Berg Wells Lawrence. Mary Wells embodied the optimism, self-confidence, and dreams of young ad women in the 1960s and 1970s and set a new standard for what was deemed possible. Although Wells had a marketing-oriented mind, a sense of business politics, and the appearance of an haute-couture model that was contrary to the feminist movement, unfortunately she, like other women of this period, found unfairness still existed in the business.

Born in Youngstown, Ohio, Wells's early years focused on dancing, drama, and theatrical elocution, as a possible escape from the fate of marrying a steelworker—a common scenario in the region. At seventeen, she left for New York and enrolled in the Neighborhood Playhouse School of Theater. After two years, she left for Pittsburgh to attend the Carnegie Institute of Technology, where she met and married Bert Wells, an industrial student. Her advertising career began at the age of twenty-three in 1951; she began work as a copywriter at a department store in Youngstown, and one year later she was back in New York on the fast track. First she worked as the fashion-advertising manager for Macy's, the next year she accepted a position as a writer and copy group head at McCann-Erickson, where she remained for three years. Finally, she moved into the limelight as associate copy chief and head of new products development during her years with Doyle Dane Bernbach (DDB). For seven years Wells worked on DDB accounts and honed her creative skills on award-winning campaigns for Volkswagen and Avis Rent-a-Car.[10]

In 1964 Wells was thirty-five years old and had risen to lauded copy chief and vice president of Jack Tinker & Partners, a branch of Marion Harper's Interpublic, a prestigious advertising conglomerate with over fifty overseas offices. Her agency work was praised for television commercials that gave Alka-Seltzer a personality and direction, offering the catchy theme song: "No matter what shape your stomach is in." They also updated the communications style for Braniff Airlines with "The end of the plain plane"—a concept that suggested a

Figure 8.2. This ad for Braniff International shows the "air strip"—airline hostesses changing their uniforms in flight. *Life,* February 25, 1966.

fun, sexy, modern approach to air travel by repositioning the airline's image with colorful exteriors in all the planes, restyled interiors, and the sexy "air strip" idea of stewardesses changing their Pucci uniforms in flight (figure 8.2). When Harper called to say that he was coming by to talk with Mary Wells in 1966, she assumed that he had decided to make good on his promise to make her the president of Jack Tinker & Partners. "Instead, when we met he offered to pay me as if I was the president [$1 million paid over ten years], to give me the authority of the president," recalls Wells, "but he said he could not give me the title of president, because he was certain that would limit the exciting growth of Jack Tinker & Partners." The world was not ready for women presidents, explained Harper.[11]

Wells resigned and left to establish her own agency with two talented young men. The trio, all in their thirties, each invested $30,000 and arranged $100,000 in backing from one of New York's major banks and moved into a seven-room suite in a dignified Fifth Avenue hotel; her mother answered the phones. When Wells Rich and Green opened its doors, Mary Wells was president and chairwoman of the board. In less than six months of the agency's launch, the young firm had enlisted an impressive roster of clients with billings of $28.5 million, putting it among the fifty biggest ad agencies in the country. Wells's tenure also proved to be lucrative. In 1969 she was making $225,000 a year, the highest-paid woman in the world. That year she was also inducted into the Copywriters Hall of Fame, and *Advertising Age* lauded her as advertising's most publicized "symbol of glamour—success—wealth—brains—and—beauty." She was also named one of the Ten Most Successful Women in American Business and in 1971 was honored as Advertising Woman of the Year by the American Advertising Federation, among other awards.

As Wells's professional life changed, so did her personal life. In 1965, after twenty years of marriage she divorced Bert Wells, who was then an art director at Ogilvy & Mather; two years later in 1967, she married Harding Lawrence, whose company, Braniff Airlines, she had turned around. After marrying Lawrence, Wells began using his name professionally and personally (though "Wells" is used throughout this chapter for continuity). Between them, the Lawrences had five children: Mary's two teenage daughters adopted by Harding at the time of their marriage, plus his two sons and daughter. "The one sacrifice I suppose I've made is this, I've given up a personal social life. I really don't have girl friends," reflected Wells in 1978. Since both she and her husband did an "intense amount of entertaining for our clients—we don't see people of any sort on a regular basis."[12]

Still, it was a complicated time for women, particularly for those female equivalents of the ad man or male corporate executive. Others, especially women, began to take issue over Wells's paradoxical role as a powerful woman who promoted no women to the board of directors or to top management and who associated mainly with men away from the workplace as well. "The idea about American men trying to keep women down in business is hogwash," was Wells's opinion of women's lib, though she believed in equal pay for equal work. "I've never been discriminated against in my life, and I think the women who have would have experienced it anyway—no matter if they were men or cows or what have you." Wells was not without her critics. When copywriter Amelia Bass accepted the Advertising Woman of the Year Award in 1970, she berated Wells as "the perfect example of the kind of woman who should be leading women," yet she offered few views on the women's movement or the advertising industry's treatment of women. "I can well believe Miss Mary never got discriminated against. There is no privileged class in the world to compare with beautiful women. . . . It's difficult to tell if success has spoiled Mary Wells; but, boy, is she ever spoiling success!"[13]

Invariably, the "first women" in the feminist movement who achieved high profiles hid many truths about women's lives. Wells's story is a good example of the way many career women learned to give the right answers to reporters trying to capture and cover these tales of individual success that began to appear during the early 1970s. Typically the "the first woman narrative" noted a woman's appearance, frequently with a photograph, and described her marital and parental status. Invariably, the first women learned how to answer journalists' predictable questions. "No, being a woman had never harmed them, nor had it helped them. No, they had no connection with 'women libbers.'" They also downplayed any hostility in the workplace, explains historian Ruth Rosen. They also rarely admitted to having any difficulties juggling their domestic and work responsibilities. But how to achieve balance between work and family life continued to present a challenge for women, regardless of what type of business they were in or in what era they lived.[14]

Balancing Work and Family

In the early vision of women's liberation, the 1960s feminists had argued that they could both work and have a family. The new title of *Ms.*, which had been devised to end categorizing women as a married *Mrs.* or a single *Miss*, also made a woman's marital status as anonymous as that of men. They also insisted that men share family responsibilities and that the government provide childcare services and other assistance to workingwomen. Once again, women had identified a pivotal issue faced by their predecessors—marriage and career lay at the intersection between their professional and personal lives.

Marriage, of course, had the potential to alter radically the direction of a woman's professional life. Some gave up their work after they married. Others rejected this view, believing that a woman could be both a wife and a career woman. For instance, McCann-Erickson named Margot Sherman Peet as senior vice president and assistant to the president in 1964, and she later became the first woman to serve on the agency's board. "I'd like to point out that, with a female, her marriage and family come first. If my husband had to move out of town, I'd go," stressed Peet. "On the other hand, if McCann wanted me to move to Chicago, I wouldn't go." Another married woman who believed being a wife and mother was an asset was Reva Korda, who raised two children in the early 1960s while working full-time as an advertising executive at Ogilvy & Mather before her appointment to executive creative director in 1973. At Ogilvy, she wrote copy for Schweppes, Dove, and Pepperidge Farm.[15]

Other women changed their priorities and took advantage of the unique freedom that the advertising profession offered talented people. Consider Phyllis Robinson, who gave up her position as copy chief and vice president at DDB in 1962 when her first daughter was born. She continued to write part-time for the next twenty years. When she wrote, location wasn't important, explained Robinson. "I write copy here, at home, in the bathtub, on the New Haven Railroad, although I try to have regular working habits." In 1968 Robinson was inducted into the Advertising Writers of New York Copywriters Hall of Fame, having written award-winning copy for Ohrbach, Chemstrand, Acrilan, and Polaroid. And in 1982, she retired from DDB to become her own boss and opened a consulting firm. It's not surprising, perhaps, that Robinson had already helped numerous women get started in the advertising business in the 1950s and 1960s. Among the talented group of women that Robinson supervised were Mary Wells and Paula Green, who both later opened their own agencies, as well as copywriters Judith Protas, Lore Parker, and Rita Selden.[16]

ENTERPRISING WOMEN

Behind these individual stories of success were thousands more ad women who took advantage of the freedom offered by the advertising profession and managed to work without shortchanging their children or their employer. When women could not move up in an agency overwhelmingly dominated by men, many achievement-oriented women left mainstream agencies to freelance, pursue other creative pursuits, and work in boutique agencies—small, flexible idea houses that emerged in the late 1960s. Bolstered by the belief in equality and meritocracy and the new access to capital and credit, women expanded beyond agency, corporate, and retailing work and made their way into mainstream business enterprise.

Women were encouraged by the increasing perception that to start up a boutique agency, all they needed was an office, a typewriter, and ideas. Now success was equated not with size but originality. Add the fact that women could now easily obtain bank loans and credit cards, and much of the barrier to entry for enterprising women was removed. In these smaller agencies across the country, a number of women served as partners, treasurers, corporate secretaries, and creative chiefs. In fact, the last quarter of the century witnessed a dramatic expansion of business ventures started by women. In 1977 women owned just 7 percent of all businesses in the United States; but ten years later, in 1987, this number had increased fourfold, and women accounted for about 30 percent of all American establishments, twice the number of businesses started by men.

These agency owners were as diverse as the constituency of the women's liberation movement with lovers, husbands, and children— or expectations of having a few of each. While the story of Mary Wells reflects much of the progress in the history of ad women—the opening of traditionally male areas of business to women and the expansion of business opportunities—Jane Trahey, Jo Foxworth, and Shirley Polykoff symbolize the continuity that links ad women of the past, such as Helen Resor and Dorothy Dignam, to those of the present. Their market is women; their business is advertising; and their new agencies would specialize in food, fashion, and home furnishings—the modern expression of the enduring feminine role. Here are their portraits:

Jane Trahey was the first woman to achieve major success with her own agency in New York, being the first woman to earn $1 million annually in the advertising industry. From 1958 until 1978, Jane Trahey Associates and later Trahey/Caldwell and Trahey/Wolf were all closely identified with fashion and cosmetics. Clients included Elizabeth Arden, Calvin Klein, Bill Blass, Princess Marcella Borghese, Charles of the Ritz, and Yves St. Lauren. In 1943 Trahey graduated from Mundelein College with a bachelor of arts degree, and in 1975, she earned an MFA from Columbia University. She began her career in advertising as a copywriter for the Chicago-based department store Carson, Pirie, Scott. Two years later, Neiman Marcus, a specialty store in Dallas, hired her as assistant advertising manager and copy chief before she progressed to advertising/sales promotion director, where she remained until 1955. She moved to New York as advertising director for Abraham Feinberg, CEO of Kayser Corporation, where she took over the advertising and created an in-house agency. Two years later, she decided, "If I could make money for Abe in his shop, then I could make money for Jane in her shop."[17]

Trahey began her business with $200,000 in billings promised by her former employer, Kayser Corporation. Among the many recogniz-able advertising campaigns she created was one for Blackglama, which included Richard Avedon's photographs of famous women, each wearing a coat of Blackglama mink. The name of the celebrity did not appear anywhere in the ad, only the copy line "What becomes a legend most?" Some of the well-known women who appeared in this campaign included Joan Crawford, Maria Callas, Judy Garland, Barbra Streisand, and Diana Vreeland, among others (figure 8.3). She also created the well-known campaigns and slogans "Danskins are for Dancing" for Danskin's women's bodywear; "The Echo of an inter-esting woman" for Echo scarves; and "It's not fake anything, it's real Dynel" for a Union Carbide textile. In 1978, after twenty years as the president of her agency in New York and Chicago, she sold the agency to one of her vice presidents, Peter Rogers.

In addition to these achievements and contributions, Trahey wrote over sixteen books, screenplays, and plays, as well as regular columns for a wide range of publications. During the 1970s, she also became more involved in the women's movement and spoke often on the topic of equal pay for equal work. Her advice to those women who wanted to change things was to educate their daughters and to start them thinking about a career early. Her highly acclaimed nonfiction book *Jane Trahey on Women and Power* (1977) provided women with a simple, no-nonsense approach on how to "play with the big boys," stand your ground, move forward, and enjoy yourself while doing so.[18]

Jo Foxworth also emerged as one of the nation's foremost advo-cates for improving career opportunities for women within the corpo-rate management structure (figure 8.4). In 1941 Foxworth graduated with a degree in advertising from the University of Missouri School of Journalism. She worked for a while selling advertising for a newspaper and later started an in-house agency for Jackson department store. But her ambition eventually led her to the advertising scene in the East. In Philadelphia, she acquired valuable experience as an adver-tising and sales promotion director for a fashion house; here she estab-lished herself as a fashion commentator by conducting a series of fashion shows. In 1955 she moved to New York and landed a job as a copywriter at McCann-Erickson, when the executive ranks on

Figure 8.3. This 1977 Blackglama ad features legend Diana Vreeland, editor of *Vogue.*

Madison Avenue remained almost exclusively male. Eventually she worked for sought-after clients like Buick, Coca-Cola, Liggett & Myers, Nabisco, Nestlé, Owens-Corning, and Westinghouse.[19]

Foxworth rose to vice president at McCann-Erickson and held

Figure 8.4.
Jo Foxworth.
Photo from
American
Advertising
Federation Hall
of Fame.

senior positions with its parent, the Interpublic Group of Companies. But in 1968, she went her own way as the president of Jo Foxworth Inc. to specialize in food, fashions, and home furnishings. She set up business in the loft of a D'Agostino market and brought widespread recognition to the chain with her unique light touch that one didn't generally associate with supermarket ads in newspapers or on radio. For example, one print ad headlined: "If there's no D'Agostino near you . . . move!" And few New Yorkers could have escaped her radio ads, a tuneful plea from shoppers in deprived neighborhoods, "Please, Mr. D'Agostino, move closer to me." In fact, she handled the account and devised the advertisements for the D'Agostino chain for more than thirty years.

Since its founding in 1968, the Jo Foxworth advertising agency had grown and moved to loftier quarters on New York's East Side. Also included on her client list were the divisions of J. C. Penney, Shiseido Cosmetics, and Chiquita Banana, but later she cut back in 1980, retaining only D'Agostino as an advertising client. In addition to her agency work, Foxworth also authored three books that address the career interests of women. Her book *Boss Lady* (1978) was a hit on college campuses and in corporate offices. She followed up with *Boss Lady's Arrival and Survival Plan* (1986), and later *Wising Up* (1990). She was elected to the Advertising Hall of Fame in 1997. Clearly Foxworth succeeded in portraying the image of the contemporary ad woman as a person who knows what she is doing, who is effective, and who has achieved an identity of her own.[20]

Other well-known woman agency owners in this era included Shirley Polykoff, Jacqueline Brandwynne, Janet Marie Carlson, Faith Popcorn (who wrote *The Popcorn Report*), Adrienne Hall, Joan Levine, and Lois Geraci Ernst, while African Americans Barbara Procter, Joyce Hamer, and Caroline Jones also opened up successful shops. Together, these women, along with Mary Wells, Jane Trahey, and Jo Foxworth, all personify what appeared to be limitless possibilities for a new generation of ad women. However, as many women succeeded in advertising, others fumed at what they perceived as insulting ads.

SEXISM IN ADVERTISING IMAGES

Anything that seemed degrading to women became a target for feminist protests, especially the all-important media. They charged that sexist images of women were projected in the mass media hourly and daily by the newspapers, women's magazines, fiction, radio, television, and films, which portrayed them in narrow roles and as subordinate to men. Few women hosted television programs, especially during the evening hours. Few documentaries aired about serious social issues that women were concerned about. And there were few positive images and role models of intelligent, successful women to inspire young women. Instead, they had the scatterbrained housewife Lucy on *I Love Lucy*, the nose-twitching witch Samantha on *Bewitched*, and Archie Bunker's wife, Edith the "dingbat," on *All in the Family*— all television shows where women were subordinate to men in the home. But more than anything, feminists claimed that advertising continued to address women in terms of narrow, gendered roles and limited women's chances of achieving their full potential.

By the early 1970s, there appeared at least a fifteen-year gap between what appeared in commercials and what happened in real life. Ironically, an appreciable amount of advertising aimed at selling supplies for household work depicted males in the role of instructing professionals, though housework was the exclusive domain of women. These ads portrayed women as unable to balance a checkbook or manage a household. One of the most successful fantasy television commercials was for Ajax detergent. In 1964 the Ajax White Knight—supposedly every woman's dream—clad in silver armor and mounted on a white steed galloped down neighborhood streets; with the touch of his magic lance, he zapped laundry pure white. The ad ran for five years, followed by Mr. Clean, the Janitor-in-the-Drum, and other strong men sent to the rescue of a damsel in distress. Other ads used such contemptuous phrases as *the weaker sex* and *the little woman*, or consistently showed women waiting on men but never vice-versa, among other sexist and gender stereotypical content. But the ad industry was slow to recognize that such fantasy-filled advertising was no longer appropriate to communicate with the many women who did not accept that they had to get married, start a family, and dedicate themselves to homemaking. Nor did these women accept that they had to be pretty, sweet, and demure.

Thus feminists argued that most advertising aimed at women both distorted and degraded their role in postwar modern society. From a feminist point of view, offensive advertising can be grouped into three main categories: (1) women stereotyped in housework roles; (2) women portrayed as sex objects; and (3) ads that used the jargon of the women's movement but didn't change the real message.

Feminists, the First Call to Action

To improve the status of women, feminists applied pressure to other advertisers through demonstrations, mail and telephone campaigns, and in some cases, national *girlcotts* of products marketed with a sexist image. One of the first organized protests against the representation of women in advertising occurred in 1969. The feminist group staged a protest in front of Macy's department store in New York City, in response to a Mattel ad in *Life* magazine promoting its line of toys for the Christmas season: little girls dream about being a ballerina or a young fashion model, while boys were born to build, learn, and find science fun. Feminists claimed that Mattel's campaign reinforced narrow gender roles because it implied that mind-enriching toys were for boys, not girls.[21]

Other protests raised public consciousness about representations of women as sex objects to sell more products and services. Ironically, the whole swing of selling air travel through sex appeals may well have begun with Mary Wells, who back in 1964 commissioned the designer Pucci to garb Braniff International hostesses in sexy dresses, rather than uniform-style work attire to advertise the attractiveness and friendliness of the stewardesses. By 1971, however, National Airlines "Fly Me" campaign reached a whole new level, promising passengers that they would fly like they never had before. One of the ads pictured a stewardess and the headline: "I'm Cheryl. Fly me," followed by "I'm a girl. I'm an airplane. I'm a fresh way to get you where you want to go!" Other ads in the series introduced "Margie," "Karen," and "Eileen," among others (figure 8.5). During this campaign, all stewardesses were required to wear a button with the same slogan, "Fly Me," but feminists believed the idea was not a commercial proposition but rather a blatant sexual proposition. Taking the position that the advertisers were sexualizing women, NOW filed a complaint with the Federal Trade Commission and claimed that National's ad claims were deceptive, because most of the airline ads referred to stewardesses who clearly did not perform any of the duties mentioned.[22]

Feminist criticism would not abate until the advertising industry recognized its insensitivity to its prime audience—women. And so they joined forces to hold sit-ins and confrontations with magazine publications and broadcasting stations such as *Ladies' Home Journal*, *Playboy*, and Columbia Broadcasting System. In fact, NOW and *Ms.* magazine confronted the agencies themselves. "Advertising is a very important form of education," explained feminist Gloria Steinem, echoing Friedan. "It is estimated that 40 percent of all of our subcultural intake comes from advertising." Ads like Shirley Polykoff's

Figure 8.5. Despite the inroads made by the women's movement, this 1971 ad for National Airlines used sexist—and sexually suggestive—appeals.

I'm Margie.   I'm Margie.

Fly me.

I'm a girl. I'm an airplane.
I'm an airline.
I'm a fresh new way of getting you where you want to go (New York, Miami, New Orleans, Los Angeles, San Francisco—even London).
My name is Margie. Chances are you'll meet and fly Carol, Sally, Michelle and Gayle, too. Chances are you won't meet Leroy, Don, Peter or Lee, because they're working for you behind the scenes. But you'll be flying them all the same.
And soon you'll be able to fly Barbara, the first of our new fleet of DC-10's. She's this year's airplane. This winter she's joining her sister ships, National's 747's, with the only DC-10 service between New York and Florida and between Florida and California.
The idea is to make your next flight a nice personal experience, person-to-person.
So next time you're going someplace, give us a call. And call us by our first name: National.

Fly Margie. Fly National.

National honors American Express, BankAmericard, Carte Blanche, Diners Club, Master Charge/Interbank, UATP and your own card and cash.

Clairol spot ("Does she . . . or doesn't she?") received a NOW "Bare-foot & Pregnant" award. Another prize went to a Geritol ad in which the man stated: "My wife, I think I'll keep her." Another award went to Procter & Gamble's ads for Folger's Coffee, in which the young woman makes good coffeecake but bad coffee, while her husband and Mrs. Olsen chide her incompetence. Feminists also placed "This ad insults women" stickers on billboards, recaptioned posters, blacked out offending pictures, and distributed "Plastic Pig" awards to companies that portrayed women in a demeaning manner.[23]

As women's lib fumed at insulting ads, many ad women took a middle-of-the-road position in the media. They stressed that advertising had done much to liberate women. Certainly it helped make the best of their looks, made housework easier, and provided a higher standard of living than their counterparts in other countries. Perhaps one of the reasons they did not want to appear all that radical or militant was that many of their accounts involved women's products, such as cosmetics, fashion, food, and household products. In 1972 though, Paul Green claimed that the reason advertising was often insulting to women was that almost "all advertising directors are men." Feminists also frequently cited this reason, and so the story goes that the ad man, acting from his limited ideas about women's character, responded with representations of demeaning stereotypes and narrow roles. Nonetheless, partners Marcella Rosen and Olivia Trager of Trager-Rosen Inc. received one of NOW's "Barefoot and Pregnant" awards for an ad that they created for Spa Health Clubs. It showed a shapely young woman and read: "How would you like a wife with firm, young breasts, a Scarlett O'Hara waist, and a derriere, like a just ripe pear (or apple, or peach)?" So the feminists couldn't blame all the offending ads on men, concluded the *New York Times*.[24]

First Response: Repackage Feminism

Initially, the women's movement had a minimal visible impact on advertising. Whereas advertising lagged behind, television, popular music, and the press responded far more quickly to the women's movement with television programs such as *Julia* in 1968, starring Diahann Carroll as a young African American widow working as a nurse and trying to raise a young son alone. Starting in 1970, *Mary Tyler Moore* and its spin-off, *Rhoda*, depicted the emerging paradox of American culture: the growing freedom for women (and men) to shape their own lives, accompanied by a new sense of limits and a loss of optimism. Artist Helen Reddy's hit song "I Am Woman" climbed to the top of the music chart two years later in 1972, with its lyrics of how the numbers of women were too large to ignore. And sexologist Nancy Friday's *Secret Garden* became a best seller in 1973, followed by *Forbidden Flowers*, both of which explored female sexuality, relationships, and the idea of fantasy from the woman's point of view.

For a large part, the first ads that changed seemed to co-opt the women's liberation theme that had already become evident in the popular media. From a feminist viewpoint, these changes were not necessarily an improvement. In some cases, the ads used the liberated women theme to sell products that were in many cases contrary to feminism. For example, the Massengill Feminine Hygiene Deodorant sold with the bold caption "The Freedom Spray," representing an industry that many feminists believed was created around an artificial need. Similarly, copywriter Shirley Polykoff heralded the new Kotex sanitary pad as the "New Freedom" with the slogan "Free to be myself all of the time."[25]

Perhaps the liberation-themed advertising that angered feminists the most was a series of ads for American Telephone & Telegraph (AT&T). This campaign designed counterstereotypes to suggest that the advertiser agreed with at least some of the social aims of the women's movement. One ad in the series appeared in *Ms.* magazine and portrayed one of its first female installers. It read: "The phone company wants more installers like Alana MacFarlane" (figure 8.6). Another AT&T ad pictured a woman executive with the headline "The phone company wants more division managers like Blanche Read." Although AT&T created these ads to show the company as an equal opportunity employer, the Equal Employment Opportunity Commission ranked it as the worst oppressor of women and minorities in employment practices.

Still, there were some advertisements that changed in a positive sense. For the most part, they reflected the message of feminists concerned with gender issues in advertising. Don't treat us as stupid, weak, trivial, or as sex objects. Don't always cast us as wives and mothers. Don't put limitations on our daughters. And above all, don't exploit our movement. In response, some ads just dropped their sexist advertising appeals. Others changed by merely adding women to the scenarios. For example, Dewar's Profiles, an advertising campaign that previously gave only profiles of men who drank their premium Scotch whisky, now depicted women in a variety of occupations. Another direct response to the women's movement was Benson & Hedges' introduction of Virginia Slims, a 100-mm cigarette (slimmer than the usual smoke) packaged in a purse-sized pack specifically targeted to women buyers. To promote the new product, the Leo Burnett Company in Chicago created one of the longest-running, most successful campaigns in advertising history. With its slogan "You've Come a Long Way, Baby" and comparative photographs, the campaign contrasted women of today with those of earlier eras (figure 8.7).

The phone company wants more installers like Alana MacFarlane.

Alana MacFarlane is a 20-year-old from San Rafael, California. She's one of our first women telephone installers. She won't be the last.

We also have several hundred male telephone operators. And a policy that there are no all-male or all-female jobs at the phone company.

We want the men and women of the telephone company to do what they want to do, and do best.

For example, Alana likes working outdoors. "I don't go for office routine," she said. "But as an installer, I get plenty of variety and a chance to move around."

Some people like to work with their hands, or, like Alana, get a kick out of working 20 feet up in the air.

Others like to drive trucks. Some we're helping to develop into good managers.

Today, when openings exist, local Bell Companies are offering applicants and present employees some jobs they may never have thought about before. We want to help all advance to the best of their abilities.

AT&T and your local Bell Company are equal opportunity employers.

Figure 8.6. AT&T created this liberation-themed campaign to show the company as an equal opportunity employer.

Nevertheless, the most serious challenge to marketers was not the objection to stereotypical portrayals in advertising but the radical feminists who called for the abandonment of beauty products traditionally aimed at women. As the beauty industry sales declined, new marketing and advertising strategies had to be developed not only for cosmetics and perfumes but also for everything from cigarettes to household cleaning products.

The turning point came with the Revlon's 1973 campaign for Charlie Perfume that struck a balance: a woman can be feminine and a feminist. It displayed confident, pantsuited young women pursuing traditional male activities (figure 8.8). In the same year, Clairol replaced the "Does she . . . or doesn't she?" campaign with depictions of mothers to show them as jockeys, artists, filmmakers, doctors, and politicians with the new slogan "To know you're the best." L'Oreal

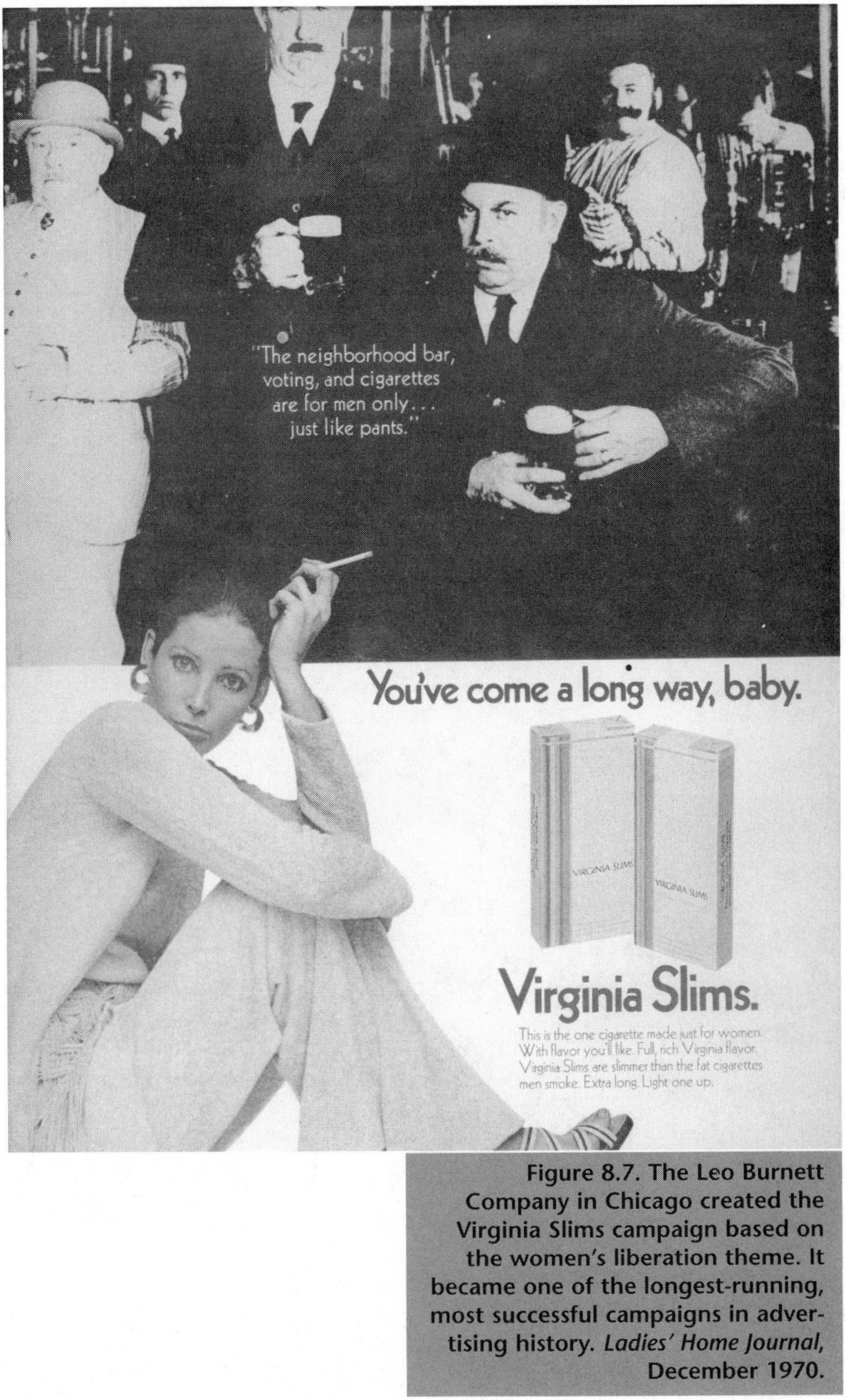
"The neighborhood bar,
voting, and cigarettes
are for men only...
just like pants."
You've come a long way, baby.
VIRGINIA SLIMS
VIRGINIA SLIMS
Virginia Slims.
This is the one cigarette made just for women.
With flavor you'll like. Full, rich Virginia flavor.
Virginia Slims are slimmer than the fat cigarettes
men smoke. Extra long. Light one up.

Figure 8.7. The Leo Burnett Company in Chicago created the Virginia Slims campaign based on the women's liberation theme. It became one of the longest-running, most successful campaigns in advertising history. *Ladies' Home Journal*, December 1970.

Preference then challenged Clairol's dominance in the hair-color market with the memorable "Because I'm Worth It," rather than writing an ad about looking good for men.

But other marketers missed the mark and took gender-based marketing to the extreme. A superb example is Maidenform, which had a sincere desire to show real people using the product in believable ways. Eleven years after their "I dreamed" campaign was dropped in 1968, the Maidenform Woman reappeared in dream sequences in 1979. Now she appeared pursuing male activities, such as reading the *Wall Street Journal* or working as a lawyer or an animal trainer but clad in only her matching bra and panties—and all with men in the pictures. The explosive campaign generated the kind of attention that sent Maidenform sales soaring. But the company also received scorching reviews from various women's organizations,

Figure 8.8. The turning point came with Revlon's 1973 campaign for Charlie Perfume, which showed that a woman can be feminine and a feminist.

which said that the campaign suggested that the Maidenform Woman had achieved her enviable position on the basis of her sexuality rather than her actual competence.[26]

Second Call to Action

Although many ads had been modified or redesigned to appeal to a savvy, female consumer, the degree to which advertising images demeaned women was extensively documented in the 1970s.

Among the influential studies, Alice E. Courtney's *A Woman's Place* (1972) analyzed roles portrayed by women in magazine advertisements. Courtney also teamed with Thomas Whipple to write *Sex Stereotyping in Advertising* to show how advertising divided women into working and nonworking home-based contexts and found that advertising increasingly sexually objectified women. In 1958, for example, workingwomen appeared as secretaries; twelve years later in 1970, however, most workingwomen appeared as entertainers, and two years later, most appeared as decorative objects. Courtney and Sarah Lockertz also found that magazine advertisements rarely depicted women in important activities outside the home and limited them to making decisions only about food, cosmetics, and cleaning products. On the other hand, advertisements sold men more expensive household products, while banks, industrial manufacturers, and institutions also featured men in ads. In addition, Erving Goffman's *Gender Advertisements* (1976) claimed that ads often portrayed women as subordinate to men involved in what he called the *ritual of subordination*, or physically placing themselves in some form of submissive position. Instead of standing upright, women were often shown in ads reclining or lying down on beds, or down on the floor scrubbing bathtubs or cleaning kitchen tiles before the viewer. In still another study, "Media Images: Madison Avenue Brainwashing—The Facts," Alice Embree debunked a prevailing myth that new innovations created leisure time for the woman consumer; rather, the many products locked her into an elaborate routine of home care.[27]

With these and many other gender studies confronting the advertising agencies, the industry eventually began to pay attention to feminists' concerns with gender issues. By 1975 advertising found itself closely policed both within the industry and outside by government agencies, consumer protection legislation, and consumer groups. Notably, the National Advertising Review Board (NARB) released a study that examined industry practices and complaints. The NARB issued a list of recommendations about the portrayal of women that urged agencies to monitor potentially sexist and gender-stereotypical content in their ads. Questions included: Does my promotional campaign imply that creative, athletic, and mind-enriching toys and games are not for girls as much as for boys? Are the women in my ad portrayed as being stupid, unable to manage without the help of outside experts, particularly male ones? And, is there a gratuitous message in my ads that a woman's most important role in life is a supportive one? The industry's own self-regulating organizations also advocated tighter controls on advertising directed toward children.[28]

Yet there was another underlying dynamic that changed the images in advertising that went beyond the feminist protests, regulations, and legislation. Women now held key marketing and advertising positions; they also impacted the basic promotional appeal on many more accounts.

BREAKING THE MOLD

One had only to turn to Lois Geraci Ernst, founder of the agency Advertising to Women, to see that women had achieved a level of professional success. Ernst is largely credited with breaking the mold of selling to women ages nineteen to forty-nine.

The key to her success was finding out what people were thinking. With insights from market research, she developed campaigns that drew attention to the underlying drives that contribute to women's buying actions and established emotional ties with consumers. While at Foote, Cone & Belding, for example, Ernst changed the "Hate that gray, wash it away" theme for Clairol Loving Care to "You're not getting older. You're getting better!" (figure 8.9). The ads showed women in a variety of roles. As early as 1970, Ernst set out a

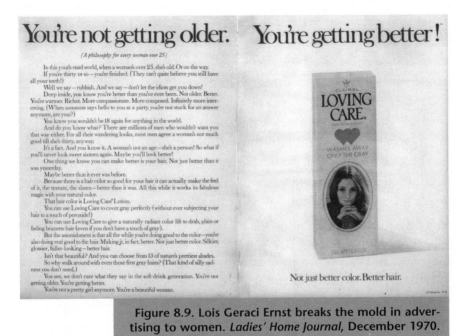

Figure 8.9. Lois Geraci Ernst breaks the mold in advertising to women. *Ladies' Home Journal,* December 1970.

philosophy in a *Ladies' Home Journal* ad: "In this youth-mad world, when a woman's over 25, she's old. Or on the way. If you're thirty or so—you're finished. . . . We say rubbish." Looking back, Ernst recalled that she really reflected on what people in this age group were thinking. "Yes, I'm not 21 anymore, and maybe I do have some gray hair, but I've learned a lot, I'm an interesting person."[29]

In 1975 Ernst opened her own largely female-staffed agency Advertising to Women powered by the argument that it takes a woman to sell a woman. Within five years she built it into a thriving agency billing nearly $50 million from three sizeable accounts—Charles of the Ritz, Gillette Personal Care Products, and RJR Foods—in addition to *Good Housekeeping* magazine. The agency also acquired the reputation of having a finger on the pulse of middle-American women.

Advertising to Women produced a number of success stories. For Jean Naté fragrance, Ernst's campaign featured a female jockey with the caption "Take charge of your life." The ad stressed the stimulating, can-do quality of the after-bath splash to attract young, active women to a product that had been a favorite among older women. In the first half of 1979, sales for the fragrance rose 30 percent. Another success story was the perfume Enjoli, for which Ernst created the now-famous jingle: "I can bring home the bacon, fry it up in a pan, and never ever let you forget you're a man. 'Cause I'm a woman." For another Charles of the Ritz fragrance, she featured a housewife provocatively peeling off her dishwashing gloves, transforming into a brazenly sexual woman, dressed in an alluring negligee with makeup, coiffed hair, and a spray of fragrance. She greets her husband at the door, and his eyes light up with approval as this memorable song plays in the background: "I've been sweet and I've been good, I've had a full day of motherhood, but I'm gonna have an Aviance night tonight." And to reach an altogether different independent woman for Rive Gauche perfume, Ernst featured a contemporary woman, who was having too much fun to marry, tearing through the night in a sports car and arriving at the beach for the first morning light.[30]

Thus Ernst repositioned hair color and fragrance as tools that empowered women in every facet of their modern life, rather than as something that enhanced their attitude or made them feel better as housewives. Although Ernst attempted to make certain not to omit any area of a woman's life, from cooking and cleaning to career and romance, feminists still took issue with the feminist agency's work. Some critics fumed that the Aviance ad treated women as sex objects, while others pointed to the Enjoli campaign as damaging to women, arguing that the ad burdened women with the unrealistic demands of work and home.

Ironically, Ernst and other advertisers who were attempting to break the mold ended up creating a whole new stereotype of women—the *Superwoman* or *Supermom*: an army of suited, briefcase-toting women who balanced career and family, yet who bore little resemblance to ordinary women and the problems they faced daily. Not only did the ideal woman hold down a full-time, high-powered career, advertisers also told the public that she kept a spotless house, raised perfect children, cooked gourmet meals, and lavished affection on her man. Just watching her made many women feel inadequate, if not totally exhausted. At a time when women worked in a diverse range of occupations from laboratories to factories, advertisers often made the mistake of showing images of employed women carrying briefcases and wearing very tailored suits, as codified in John Molloy's *Women's Dress for Success* published in 1977.[31]

Nevertheless, the activism of the 1960s and 1970s women's movement provoked a storm of criticism, what Susan Faludi later called the backlash of the 1980s. Women's search for economic opportunity and equal rights had created enormous social change. They raised all kinds of questions about the nature of family, and particularly of men's role within the family, challenged traditional workplace structures, and wondered whether gender relations could continue segregated and separate. So it is not surprising that there were many people in the 1980s who wanted to go backward or pause to reflect changing social conditions. Particularly formidable was the antifeminist, or *pro-family movement*, which contended that men should lead and women should follow, especially within the family, and that women should stay at home and raise children. The conservative backlash became an increasingly powerful political force with lawyer Phyllis Schlafly's *Stop ERA* campaign in the late 1970s and the *New Right*. The social-conservative Reagan-Bush administration found a substantial base of support from women who had felt left behind in their kitchens, while their sisters entered the workplace. Despite the progress of feminism in forming a second wave of organizations, generating legislation, and changing images in advertising, the New Right defeated the ERA for women in 1982.[32]

Still, a predominant segment of American women wanted to have children and all that encompassed, and advertisers continued to encourage her to fulfill her role. She first had to become a bride, then mother, and then a homemaker. Nevertheless, the recognition of advertisers that women could be interested in a career, in their families, and in their own hobbies, all in the same lifespan, revolutionized advertising to women. The powerful voices of people of color also had a major impact on the advertising industry as the next chapter will illustrate. Although they challenged employment practices and images in advertising, they often seemed more victimized by racism and poverty than middle-class white women were by sexism in the

For women who go to work

and also do their own cooking and cleaning:

You need more than sympathy. You need help. Especially with the tough chores like cleaning a miserably dirty oven. Try Jifoam. It makes the job almost easy. Jifoam sprays on, uses the oven's own heat to dissolve burned-on dirt and grease. Five minutes later, wipe with a damp cloth or paper toweling and the oven will come clean. It works where other cleaners won't. Takes a lot less out of you. Lets you save your energy for other things. That may not seem like much, but it helps.

Would you like a 15¢ coupon toward your next purchase of Jifoam and a booklet on how to use aerosol products correctly? Just send your name and address to Shelco, Dept. J, Wellesley Hills, Mass. 02181.

Jifoam Spray Oven Cleaner

professions or career advancement. They would offer an alternative vision of advertising as well as reform the industry.

NOTES

1. Helen Gurley Brown, *Sex and the Single Girl* (New York: Bernard Geis, 1962) and *Sex in the Office* (New York: Bernard Geis, 1964).

2. Lucille Falkof, *Helen Gurley Brown: The Queen of Cosmopolitan* (Ada, OK: Garrett Educational Corp., 1992). Helen Gurley Brown, *I'm Wild Again: Snippets from My Life and a Few Brazen Thoughts* (New York: St. Martin's Press, 2000).

3. While editor for *Cosmopolitan* magazine, Helen Gurley Brown authored: *Outrageous Helen Gurley Brown's Single Girl's Cookbook* (New York: Bernard Gels, 1969), *Sex and the New Single Girl* (New York: David McKay Co., 1970), and *Having It All: Love, Success, Money Even If You're Starting from Nothing* (New York: Simon and Schuster, 1982).

4. "Advertisers Home in on Working Women," *Adweek*, July 7, 1986, p. 44.

5. In 1968 the average wage for a man in the United States was $7,664; the average for a woman was $4,456 or less than 60 percent compared to men's wages. The main reason for this difference was occupational segregation; throughout the labor force women held nearly 75 percent of the lower-paying clerical jobs.

6. "Less Women at the Top," *Television Age*, November 20, 1967, pp. 22–23. For an example of the places where women were banned in the early 1970s, see "Places in Detroit: Where Women Can't Go," *Detroit* magazine, *Detroit Free Press*, February 7, 1971.

7. Lois Banner, *Women in Modern America: A Brief History* (New York: Harcourt Brace Jovanovich, 1974), p. 170.

8. Ruth Rosen, *The World Split Open: How the Modern Women's Movement Changed America* (New York: Penguin Books, 2001), pp. 201, 205.

9. On women in advertising, see John C. Athanassiades, "Myths of Women in Management," in *Readings on Contemporary Business*, ed. David Grainger et al. (Hillsdale, IL: Dryden Press, 1976), pp. 115–22. On number of ad women from 1960 to 1968, see US Department of Labor, Bureau of Labor Statistics: *Employment and Earnings*, July and August 1968. On number of ad women in 1983, see "A New Day Dawns for Women in Advertising," *Advertising Age*, September 20, 1986.

10. Ed Applegate, ed., *Ad Men and Women: A Biographical Dictionary of Advertising* (Westport, CT: Greenwood, 1994), pp. 214–22. See also "Mary Wells: A Blond Image Maker," *Los Angeles Times*, October 29, 1967; "Explaining the Enigma of Mary Wells Lawrence," *Adweek*, May 1968; "As the World Turns on Madison Avenue," *Fortune*, December 1968; and "If It Isn't Terribly Well Done, I'm a Little Miserable," *Advertising Age*, April 5, 1971.

11. Mary Wells Lawrence, *A Big Life in Advertising* (New York: Knopf, 2002), p. 44.

12. *Advertising Age*, June 2, 1969, p. 1. See also "The All-Out Attractive Style of Mary Wells Lawrence," *Vogue*, February 1978.

13. Mary Wells quoted in *Advertising Age*, April 17, 1967, p. 86. Amelia Bass quoted in *Advertising Age*, December 7, 1970, pp. 48, 50.

14. Rosen, *The World Split Open*, p. 303.

15. Obituary of Margot Sherman Peet, *New York Times*, August 14, 1977. On Korda, see "Some Supermoms Who Led the Way," *New York Times*, August 23, 1984, p. C-1. On career, see "Advertising New Creative Chief," *New York Times*, June 6, 1973, p. 74.

16. Applegate, *Ad Men and Women*, pp. 273–78. See also "Comments of a Copy Chief," *Advertising Age*, July 15, 1958, pp. 47–48.

17. Applegate, *Ad Men and Women*, pp. 325–34. See also "The Low Priestess of Madison Avenue," *New York Sunday News*, October 22, 1972, pp. 12–15.

18. "On the March for Still What They Haven't Got," *Life*, September 4, 1970, p. 21. Jane Trahey, *Jane Trahey on Women and Power: Who's Got It? How to Get It* (New York: Rawson, 1977).

19. Advertising Women of New York, nomination for Advertising Woman of the Year, Jo Foxworth, March 30, 1965, Advertising Women of New York Collection, box 2, folder 21, Schlesinger Library. See also Elsie S. Hebert, "Jo Foxworth," in Applegate, *Ad Men and Women*, pp. 146–50.

20. Obituary of Jo Foxworth, *New York Times*, February 7, 2006.

21. Lucy Komisar, "The Image of Woman in Advertising," in *Woman in Sexist Society: Studies in Power and Powerlessness*, ed. Vivian Gornick (New York: Basic Books, 1971), pp. 207–208.

22. "Airline's Ad Encounters Some Turbulence," *Life*, October 29, 1971, pp. 75–76. "National on the Offensive," *Newsweek*, November 15, 1971, pp. 96, 101. On NOW's legal action, see NOW press release, February 3, 1975, Women's History Subject Files, Employment, folder: Advertising, Sophia Smith Collection. On sex in travel advertising, see "Sex and the Single Airline," *Air Travel, Official Airlines Guide*, July 1970.

23. Quoted in *Advertising Age*, May 22, 1972.

24. "Women's Lib Fume at Insulting Ads; Ad Gals Are Unruffled," *Advertising Age*, July 27, 1970. "Today's Woman Explodes Yesterday's Ad Dream World," *Advertising Age*, December 25, 1972. "On Madison Avenue, Women Take Stand in Middle of the Road," *New York Times*, July 3, 1973, p. 28. "Women in TV Ads: The Old Image Lingers," *New York Times*, May 16, 1978.

25. "Do It NOW," *National Publication for National Organization for Women*, December 1972. "NOW Says: TV Commercials Insult Women," *New York Times*, May 28, 1972, p. SM-12. See also "You Haven't Come a Long Way, Baby: Women in Television Commercials," in *American Mass Media Industries & Issues*, 3rd ed., ed. Robert Atwan et al. (New York: Random House, 1986), pp. 66–74.

26. Maidenform discontinued the "I Dreamed" campaign featuring the Maidenform Woman when the fantasy was judged inappropriate for the realities of the 1970s; but she reappeared eleven years later in 1981. See Carol Moog, *Are They Selling Her Lips?* (New York: William Morris, 1990), pp. 21–35. Also see "The Maidenform Woman Returns," *New York Times*, June 1, 1980, p. 3-3.

27. Matilda Butler, *Women and the Mass Media: Sourcebook for Research and Action* (New York: Human Sciences Press, 1980), pp. 163–66. Erving Goffman, *Gender Advertisements* (New York: Harper & Row, 1976). Erving Goffman, "Genderisms," *Psy-*

chology Today (August 1977), pp. 60–63. Alice Embree, "Media Images: Madison Avenue Brainwashing," in *Sisterhood Is Powerful: An Anthology of Writings from the Women's Liberation Movement*, ed. Robin Morgan (New York: Random House, 1970), pp. 175–97.

28. "Federal Trade Commission Staff Report on TV Advertising to Children," *Advertising Age*, February 27, 1978.

29. Clairol advertisement, *Ladies' Home Journal*, December 1970.

30. "Shop's Theory: It Takes a Woman to Sell One," *Advertising Age*, July 21, 1980.

31. On superwoman stereotype, see *Atlantic*, May 1977, p. 180. On business fashion, see John Molloy, *Women Dress for Success* (El Monte, CA: New Win, 1977).

32. Susan Faludi, *Backlash: The Undeclared War against American Women* (New York: Crown Publishers, 1991). For an earlier focus on the diversity of women in the New Right, see Rebecca E. Klatch, *Women of the New Right* (Philadelphia: Temple University Press, 1988).

CHAPTER 9

THE WOMANISTS

ALTERNATIVE VISIONS
IN THE TWENTIETH CENTURY

During the last century, Aunt Jemima, the symbol for Quaker Oats' pancake syrup, became one of the most recognized trademarks in the world. She also represented an unflattering portrayal of minority women, particularly older African American women. Her character evoked the mythic Southern past and the good-natured, smiling "Mammy" who was willing to serve her masters and mistresses both as an indulgent cook and a nurturer for white children. In 1989 Aunt Jemima turned one hundred years old. To keep pace with the changing times, Quaker Oats updated her portrait to reflect a more positive image of minority women. The Mammy character slimmed down, discarded her bandana head covering, and was given a Betty Crocker hairstyle. She also donned such feminine touches as small pearl earrings, a lace collar, and makeup. Aunt Jemima now looked like a modern working grandmother.

Yet the legacy of the 1960s and 1970s was far more than a new wave of feminism and representations of women in advertising as symbolized by Aunt Jemima. Cultural diversity also became a potent force. The spread of new social values had begun to transform the workplace, creating new demands for equal rights and promotion of African Americans and other ethnic groups. Although advertisers continued to fantasize about a mythical middle America populated by white people and guided by traditional values, such cultural homo-geneity had never existed. Following World War II, vast numbers of blacks had migrated from southern to northern states. Extremely reluctant to develop ties with African American consumers, the adver-tising industry began to focus on the black consumer market only after the civil rights movement demanded racial integration. The reality was that white businesses spent very little advertising money on the African American community despite information that this was a profitable market. When they did use black images in ads, they were comic or stereotypic characters used to target the white consumer.[1]

When economic and social forces finally forced the civil rights issue, the advertising industry eventually changed its practice of regarding African Americans as invisible—just as the media had done. To understand how such factors affected advertising history, this chapter will first describe the powerful influence of contemporary black feminism and civil rights activists outside the advertising industry. As early participants in the civil rights movement, many black ad women practiced what they believed by trying to establish their own views on how the black consumer should be defined in the media and portrayed in advertising. Sources, however, are limited, and it is impossible to document all aspects of these black women's lives, particularly in the advertising profession. Nevertheless, the fol-lowing representative portraits of black female professionals docu-ment that within the African American community there also existed a construction of gender that was deliberately designed to enable women to transcend the multiple barriers for working-class women of race, class, and sex. The strategy involved encouraging and providing for high levels of achievement and then linking that individual suc-cess to community development.

Socially responsible black women in the advertising profession—such as Barbara Burrell, Caroline Jones, Barbara Gardner Proctor, and Carol Williams, who first went into business in the 1960s and 1970s—provide examples of how women impacted the making of American consumer culture. Similarly, women of color also used advertising for community building among Latino and Asian American women.

BLACK FEMINISM

Contemporary black feminism grew out of feelings of discontent with both the civil rights and the feminist movements of the 1970s. Not only did the struggle for civil rights focus on the oppression of black men, but many black women also experienced severe sexism within civil rights groups, such as the Students National Coordinating Committee. Whereas the women's liberation movement narrowly focused on the problems of white middle-class women striving for work and self-fulfillment outside the home, black feminists had long been working for reasons of economic necessity. Furthermore, racism in the women's movement led to a growing focus on black women's resentment toward white women's history of patronizing them as domestic servants. By speaking for all women, white women did not share many of their concerns. To black women, as historian Paula Giddings put it, Betty Friedan's advice to find a meaningful career "seemed to come from another planet."[2]

Because white feminist concerns did not relate to the black women's experience, many black female activists disappeared from the women's movement. Thus emerged the need to develop a distinctive black feminist agenda that spoke to issues specific to African American women on the importance of empowerment in everyday life. Out of this growing sense of disenchantment with racism in both the civil rights and the women's movement, numerous black women began to state their concerns as women in the black press, novels, and scholarly writings. Among them, Toni Cade Bambara's publication of *The Black Women: An Anthology* in 1970 marked the beginning of the contemporary feminist agenda that raised issues specific to black women. This was followed by Toni Morrison's novel *The Bluest Eye* and Alice Walker's novel *Meridian*. Historians also began to ground their research in the lives and experiences of women, while black scholars began to shape these diverse sources into black feminist theory.[3]

While many theorists began writing, black feminist groups were forming that built on themes that had long guided African American women's actions. Twentieth-century Americans had inherited racist attitudes established over three centuries that had hardly been eradicated by the abolition of slavery. Economic institutions and political and social systems based on race in America, as opposed to class, limited blacks from achieving economic equality. Even as slaves, African women were socialized to be independent, self-reliant, and resourceful. Thus, they shaped institutions that allowed them to preserve their dignity and humanity. They formed societies, supported abolitionist newspapers, lectured, wrote books, and worked within the Underground Railroad system to destroy slavery. At the same time, they developed supportive and empowering female networks, nurtured extended families, and worked within traditional black organizations like churches, sororities, and black women's local groups. Others devoted their efforts to black community developments such as the National Association for the Advancement of Colored People (NAACP) and the Urban League. However, African American labor continued to carry a different status than white labor, and few blacks worked as managers in white corporate America until after the civil rights period.[4]

This legacy of struggle and its resulting humanistic vision differentiated black feminism from white feminism in the United States. The foundations laid by early black feminists encouraged African American women to become agents of social change because of the needs of their race, as they fought for abolition, suffrage, and civil rights.

The process produced some notable leaders among black women, resulting in far-reaching consequences in and beyond African American communities. Black feminists addressed the concerns of black women through the National Black Feminist Organization founded in 1973. Other black feminist intellectuals used their writings and teachings as a vehicle to deal with race and class in their push for gender equity. Among black professionals, women dominated the professions of nursing, social work, and teaching. Other African American women used their public office to advance black women's humanistic vision of community and equality for all. By the 1980s, members of other ethnic groups joined in, and a movement emerged to substitute the terms *womanists*, or *women of color* as more appropriate terms for *minority women*, or those who are racially underprivileged, because it includes other ethnicities.

Within the African American community there existed a construction of gender, deliberately designed to enable the members to transcend the multiple barriers for working-class women of race, class, and sex. The strategy involved encouraging and providing for high levels of achievement and then linking that individual's success to community development. In the process, the civil rights movement, the expansion of the black media, and the women's movement all tied directly to the entrance of black women into the advertising profession. Thus, the African American woman's experience in the advertising profession cannot be subsumed and generalized in the context of the white experience.

REDESIGNING THE BLACK MARKET

Since the early twentieth century, black newspapers offered national marketers well-developed advertising vehicles to reach urban African Americans, what was then called the *Negro Market*. For white national advertisers, one of the earliest reports on the market potential of black consumers came in 1928, when *Advertising and Selling* published an article on the attractive sales possibilities in Harlem, New York. Other market investigations soon followed. For the first time, in 1932, Paul K. Edwards, professor of economics at Fisk University, compared black and white southerners' spending habits, concluding that blacks were particularly concerned about quality products, brand names, and their personal appearance. In addition, the National Negro Business League conducted the first national study of blacks' income and living habits in the 1930s, subsidized by Montgomery Ward, Lever Brothers, and Anheuser-Busch; it estimated the overall spending power of this consumer group at $1.65 billion. This led to companies beginning to add black advisers and salespeople to their staffs as marketing consultants to better understand how to advertise to the Negro Market.[5]

The Negro Market underwent changes in the 1940s and 1950s as evidenced in the population migration patterns and the civil rights movement. During World War II, large numbers of African Americans had moved north and west to find work in defense plants, while midwestern and eastern GIs were exposed to reading material and music styles that had not yet become popular in the North. In fact, three times as many blacks left the South than in the decade before for better-paying jobs in the 1940s. As a result, this population migration created areas with dense populations of blacks who had enough money from wartime earnings to establish themselves as an identifiable consumer group. Naturally, it was in the interest of publishers and businesses to introduce a new class of media with black appeal to reach this new working-class and middle-class audience. Gradually, this led to some corporations hiring black advisers and salesmen to develop a systematic means to advertise to this group.

When World War II ended, the black press had established a loyal cadre of readers based on their strong coverage of the war. In 1947 the four leading newspapers directed toward African Americans were the *Pittsburgh Courier*, the *Afro-American*, the *Chicago Defender*, and the *Amsterdam News*. The war had also boosted interest in racial issues, and the black press had a virtual monopoly on this situation. It was an escapable fact that if a national marketer wanted to reach the black consumer, the black press was the only vehicle. But many national white marketers were reluctant to invest in the Negro Market until after the civil rights era, fearing that they would lose their white buyers.

The experience of World War II had given a fresh impetus to the struggle for civil rights. For much of the century, African Americans in the South had been denied the right to vote and to own land. They also had been forced to attend different schools, take rear seats or even stand on public transportation, use separate restrooms, and eat only at designated restaurants. During the war, African Americans served in the armed forces to preserve the ideals of freedom and equality. They returned from the war with a new sense of self and challenged segregation with lawsuits and boycotts. In 1947 Jackie Robinson broke Major League Baseball's color line by starting for the Brooklyn Dodgers. The following year President Harry Truman ordered the military to integrate, and in 1954 the Supreme Court banned segregated schools.

This black militancy combined with wartime labor shortages opened up new places for African Americans. When black employment in the war industry increased, women held 60 percent of the jobs. But the end of the war threatened these gains as both African American men and women were pushed out of their new jobs. In spite of these postwar setbacks, World War II was a watershed for black women's employment, opening up jobs in factories and offices. Between 1930 and 1960, the number of black women employed in manufacturing jobs almost doubled, while the share in clerical and sales jobs grew eightfold. These changes finally allowed black women to move out of domestic service in private households, while other blacks raised their standard of living as they moved from tenant farming in rural areas and into the cities.

Although the possibility for the American dream—symbolized by the home in the suburbs, family, television, and shiny automobiles—was painted as attainable for every American, the reality was that blacks, women, and other minorities had far less access to the same kinds of opportunities. They found career ladders largely blocked, including entrance to prestigious liberal arts colleges that were still the gateway to managerial and professional jobs. The higher-paying jobs accepted whites and returning veterans, but the positions were not as open to blacks. Since African American labor continued to carry a different status from white labor, at the time, few blacks worked as managers in white corporate America. Even more overt racial segregation was enforced by government loan policies and underwriting policies of local banks. When African Americans were not wanted at Levittown, they moved to historic black enclaves or new suburban developments specifically marketed to the black middle class, such as North Amityville's Ronek Park in Long Island, a community of some one thousand three-bedroom homes. This pattern of segregation shaped the black consumer market.[6]

Even so, the education and income of African Americans was on the rise. Their purchasing power accounted for a remarkable $16 billion by the early 1950s, and it continued to steadily increase decade after decade. Gradually corporate America could no longer ignore the growing purchase power of the black consumer, and efforts to organize the Negro Market continued. African Americans also commissioned numerous studies to assess the markets in Milwaukee,

Omaha, Washington, DC, Baltimore, and Philadelphia. During the mid-1950s through the early 1960s, market studies stressed black consumers as brand conscious and brand loyal, as they frequently purchased certain brands in their search for status and prestige. Blacks resented appeals that characterized them as different. In 1958, for the first time, *Printers' Ink* reported on distinct social classes among African Americans, explaining that upper-class Americans respected security and status, while the lower class valued conspicuous consumption and splurging. But a mid-1960s study showed that African Americans spent less on automobiles than whites of the same income level. These findings proved widely opposite of stereotyped ideas about black consumers as having little spending power and making purchase decisions based only on price. It also led to the mass media reconceptualizing African Americans as a consumer group based on income, class, and interests.[7]

Against the backdrop of World War II and the civil rights movement, John H. Johnson, owner of the largest black-owned publishing company in the world, shifted the focus of the black press from a fight against segregation and discrimination to positive coverage of black participation in society and national advertising. The shift began in 1942, when Johnson introduced the periodical *Negro Digest*, and three years later, the premiere magazine *Ebony*. With picture story after picture story, *Ebony* gave middle-class blacks their first intimate glimpse of black entertainment stars, sports heroes, politicians, and entrepreneurs. More important, it showed how blacks, in spite of the pervasive racism, were able to achieve in virtually every category of American life. It also carried similar advertisements found in *Life* and the *Saturday Evening Post*. The magazine proved an immediate success and continues to be the circulation leader among black magazines, a position it has held until this day. Next, Johnson launched *Tan* (1950) and *Jet* (1951), which pulled for the working class, was sized to fit into a worker's pocket, and covered news with tabloidlike features. The success of Johnson Publishing Company also provided his wife, Eunice Johnson, who served as secretary-treasurer of the firm, opportunities to give back to the African American community. She later took charge of the annual *Ebony* Fashion Fair to benefit the United

Negro College fund and other scholarship endeavors—today, the world's largest traveling fashion show.[8]

Compared to publishing though, television, film, and to a lesser extent radio were more capital-intensive industries. These media required huge sums for production. It was for this reason that white entrepreneurs owned the first black radio stations that devoted their entire formats to programming and advertising messages designed to reach African Americans in the major metropolitan radio markets. Ironically, the first radio stations to switch over to black-appeal formats were located in the South. Beginning in 1947, station WDIA in Memphis replaced its classical musical format with black air talent and records by blues artists, religious broadcasts, public affairs, and women's programming. The first radio program by and for black women was *Tan Town Homemakers*, broadcast on WDIA Memphis in 1949 and hosted by Willa Moore, the reigning diva of Memphis's African American social elite. The program featured a mix of soft ballads, favorite recipes, homemaker hints, women's news, and interviews with prominent African American women. Moreover, the success of the program paved the way for more women's programming and female broadcasters. In 1954 the signal could be heard all over the South and had the potential to reach 10 percent of the country's entire African American population.[9]

Although network radio emerged as the most pervasive mass medium in the United States during this period, racial barriers still limited opportunities for blacks in broadcasting. The few black Americans working in radio were the musicians, comics, and entertainers who occasionally appeared on network radio, since network sponsors and national advertisers tended to invest in shows that avoided both racial characters and issues. When they did agree to sponsor a network show with black subjects, like Pepsodent toothpaste for the *Amos and Andy Show*, they preferred white actors or actresses who specialized in "Negro dialect" in those roles. Furthermore, the network neither hired blacks as announcers, broadcast journalists, or technicians, nor did it allow blacks to become producers or executives in the national operations.

As alternative media systems developed, the stereotyped image that many white Americans held of African Americans also emerged inside the mainstream framework of national and public television. For the most part, the dominant white-influenced media and corporate America controlled the content and images that appeared inside mainstream pages of *Saturday Evening Post, Ladies' Home Journal,* and *McCall's* aimed at the American consumer market. Dramas showed few well-developed black characters. Comedies picked up threads of white superiority and blacks as contented servants. Variety shows portrayed the dominant image of blacks as entertainers—totally at odds with the black experience or African American concerns. Like the other commercial media, national television gradually began to include racial minority groups.

Despite the potential of the Negro Market in terms of listeners, readers, and consumer dollars, following World War II national advertisers still were reluctant to invest in black-appeal media, mostly because of the product-identification stigma. That is, they felt that if they directed their message to the African American audience, they would lose more white buyers of their product than they would gain among blacks. As a result, radio and television shows featuring black performers found it difficult to attract sponsors, and other minority group members rarely appeared. From the standpoint of the white advertiser, the prime market continued to no longer be the urban city dwellers but shifted to the white suburbanites—the typical average Americans who also appeared in national television, radio, and print advertisements. This well-off group appeared to read a lot of magazines and later to watch a lot of television, from which they took cues on how they should live. In short, they were ideal targets for white advertisers. Thus, white advertisers continued to treat the Negro Market differently from that of the "average" American consumer.

THE ADVERTISING PROFESSION

African Americans were excluded from employment not only in mainstream mass media but also in the advertising profession until the 1960s and 1970s. Before World War II, in fact, trade journals and annual reports from major agencies showed no photographs of African Americans as copywriters, art directors, or account executives, reported Roland Marchand. The advertising industry changed its policy of totally ignoring African Americans only after there was evidence that doing so would bring them large profits. But even when there were clear indications that targeting black consumers would profit the ad industry, its policy remained unchanged until the late 1970s.[10]

Postwar Era

The activity of the black media encouraged a few pioneering African American ad men to start their own agencies as specialists in the black consumer market. Among them, David Sullivan set up shop in New York City in 1943. Agencies emerged, such as Fusch, Young & Powell in Detroit, and in 1948 the New York–based Brandford Advertising agency announced its incorporation and gained recognition as the "first Negro agency with complete facilities, including merchandising and public relations, art, production, and model services, for service of any nature for the benefit of manufacturers through newspaper advertising." Still, these agencies were limited "to selling black products through black media to black consumers," concluded historian Stephen Fox. "At the major white agencies apparently no black held a significant position until the 1950s. Few were hired, so few applied, so few were hired."[11]

In the postwar era, Batten, Barton, Durstine, & Osborne (BBDO) was the first agency to form a unit of African Americans selling to the black special market. In 1955 Young & Rubicam hired Roy Eaton, probably the first African American at any major agency to work in a creative function not limited to ads and products for African Americans. White agencies and white clients allocated few dollars to reach black consumers, whom they usually declared were no different from the white market. Hence, the advertising industry remained largely unreceptive to black consumers and practitioners. Until the 1960s, the sponsor and advertising industry's attitudes toward social concerns largely went unquestioned. Before then the industry was seen as having no motivation to make changes and appeared to divorce itself from the nation's social issues, until the civil rights movement forced fundamental changes in the attitudes of marketers, advertisers, and manufacturers.

By the 1950s, the civil rights movement was gaining momentum. In 1954 the Supreme Court ruled in *Brown v. Board of Education* that racially segregated education was unconstitutional. A year later, Rosa Parks's refusal to give up her bus seat prompted the Montgomery Bus Boycott, and the Rev. Dr. Martin Luther King Jr. rose to national prominence. Black students faced furious mobs to attend schools, while others endured insults and threats to take seats at white-only lunch counters. As the fight for civil rights was slowly won with the Civil Rights Act in 1964, an image of Black Power rose up. Black nationalists advocated that African Americans find their own schools, businesses, and, ultimately, their own nation. They also proposed alternatives to the term *Negro*, including *black*, *Afro-American*, and simply *African*. They reexamined their heritage and searched for a connection to their African past. Rejecting white standards of beauty, African Americans began to style their hair in Afros or braids, and many wore African jewelry, headgear, and other native garments. "Black is beautiful" became a common theme, as did "Be black. Buy black."

Yet television shows featuring black performers still found it difficult to attract sponsors. Many national advertisers avoided controversial and political issues because they feared breaking the color line represented by the institutionalization of segregation, or for reasons of their own racism. In 1964, for example, General Motors threatened to withdraw its sponsorship of the popular Western television series *Bonanza* should an episode feature an African American guest star. Under pressure from the NBC network and the NAACP, as well as facing considerable negative publicity, the automaker later reversed its position. As late as 1968, Chrysler also complained openly about *Petula*, a variety show that it sponsored. Chrysler did not approve when the show's star, the popular British singer Petula Clark, held the arm of her guest star, black singer Harry Belafonte. Chrysler had deemed it far too intimate a pose to appear on camera. By decade's end, several shows eventually starred African Americans that met with unprecedented approval, including *Julia*, *The Bill Cosby Show*, and *The Flip Wilson Show*.[12]

Similar to feminism, the degree to which blacks were excluded from the mainstream has been extensively documented. For example, Harold Kassarjian's analysis "The Negro in American Advertising" examined the content of twelve national magazines from 1946 to 1965 and found that black models appeared in less than 1 percent of the ads. In a second investigation, the New York City Commission on Human Rights monitored commercials from forty agencies for a one-year period from 1966 to 1967 and found that blacks appeared in only about 4 percent of the commercials. Such studies led to the federal Equal Employment Opportunity Commission (EEOC) hearings and investigations of the number of minority group members in advertisements. All of this eventually contributed to an increase in the number of African Americans appearing in mainstream ads and broke other color barriers in advertising.[13]

A few national advertisers had mounted specialized campaigns aimed at blacks prior to this era. Advertising campaigns used by white companies to attract black consumers simply adopted campaigns for white-oriented media by substituting nonwhite models and running ads in black-oriented media such as *Ebony*. In fact, this technique is still used today. Or, if the campaigns were aimed at a mainstream audience, the ads often featured images of blacks integrated with whites, but this only after market research assured advertisers that their white consumers would not be offended. For instance, Clairol developed an entirely new market for their hair-coloring products by targeting the African American market with two shades—black velvet and sable brown—and ran ads with its famous "Does she . . . or doesn't she?" line with an attractive black model (figure 9.1). When Clairol began to target this audience with fashionably lighter tones of hair coloring, however, it made more sense to create a new theme specifically for this market: "If you want to . . . why not?" The pictures still showed black models but now with hair colored from light brown to blond.

Following the civil rights and Black Power movements, the advertising industry finally began focusing on the task of bringing more minorities into the advertising profession in the late 1960s and early 1970s. Ironically, agencies spent more time recruiting minorities into advertising than they did putting them to work. Still, it was a time

Figure 9.1. Clairol developed an entirely new market for its hair-coloring products by targeting African Americans.

when assigning black professionals to a serious piece of business was unthinkable, because the client would not accept these individuals. Although Benton & Bowles and Ogilvy & Mather had undertaken special efforts to recruit blacks in the early 1960s, few African Americans worked on Madison Avenue in any capacity, professional or clerical. In 1966 the EEOC surveyed sixty-four New York ad agencies and found that only 2.5 percent of white-collar employees were African Americans and even less—1.9 percent—at thirteen large agencies. In both cases, blacks held fewer positions than in the broadcasting and communications field. In response to these findings and pressure from concerned organizations like the American Advertising Federation, the racially unbalanced industry created new training programs and white-collar positions.[14] Despite being pushed into action, at only a few agencies—J. Walter Thompson, Young & Rubicam, Ted Bates, Compton, BBDO, and Ogilvy & Mather—was any minority hiring going on in the late 1960s and early 1970s. A few agencies actually ventured on black college campuses, but they tended to recruit educated black men and women from mostly white colleges and universities. By 1969 minority employment had risen to only 10.5 percent at the fifteen largest New York agencies.[15]

Nevertheless, a growing number of companies made a special effort to target the lucrative black consumer market, which in 1969 spent an estimated $30 billion a year. In particular, department stores, cigarette companies, and cosmetic makers turned to black advertising agencies to develop a separate identity to connect with the black consumer. But it would be the vision of Vince Cullers who would change the way advertising was created for blacks.[16]

Black-Owned Agencies

In 1956 Vince Cullers Advertising, Inc., opened out of necessity and became the first black agency to actively target the African American market. It also achieved success in winning accounts from white corporate America.

When Marian Cullers went into business to help her husband manage the administration, she knew little about the industry. At this time, there were not many opportunities for her husband, Vince, who had studied at the Art Institute of Chicago, to work in the ad agencies in Chicago; they did not hire blacks. Vince ran into the same problem of discrimination in New York City, so eventually he started his own Chicago-based agency with just one employee, and as time went on the business grew. At first Vince found it difficult to find black employees with much advertising experience, so he had no choice but to be both employer and mentor. For years, the agency functioned as a training ground for many young students who began work in the ad industry for the first time. While building the business, Vince brought in his wife, his two sons, and his daughter-in-law Carmelita for key roles in the organization.[17]

In 1968 the increased attention to the black consumer market opened the door for national advertising to Cullers, when Newport, True, and Kent cigarettes contacted the agency, followed by Johnson Products and Bristol-Myers. Cullers had approached corporate America with the idea that rather than integrating black people into a white concept of advertising, advertisers needed to create messages that specifically connected with black people. For a line of black hair preparations for Johnson Products, Cullers took a bold move, filling his ads with attractive, proud dashiki-clad African Americans. At the time, Black Power was at its height, and blacks across the country had adopted the dashiki, a traditional African outfit, as a symbol of their unity. The ads carried the tag line "Wantu Wazuri," Swahili for "beautiful people" (figure 9.2). This was quite a change from the unflattering stereotypes of blacks as cheerful cooks, shuffling servants, and minstrels. "The target audience was clearly black," remarked Ken Smikle, then president of *Target News*. "But the message didn't have to be as black as Vince made it. It was a bold move on his part."[18]

Figure 9.2. Ads for AfroSheen carried the tag line "Wantu Wazuri," Swahili for "beautiful people."

The agency grew quickly, adding white clients such as Ameritech, Amoco, Kellogg's, Pizza Hut, and Sears. In 1973 Cullers's billings had risen to $2.5 million, and by 1950, $20 million. Hence, Cullers demonstrated that the black market had immense potential and also sparked the formation of other African American agencies, some of which would go on to become far bigger enterprises than his agency ever had been.[19]

By the 1970s, over a dozen black agencies had opened and were pitching to white companies that only a black firm could conceive and execute advertisements with the specific needs of blacks in mind. Similar to Cullers's campaigns, many of these black agencies not only emphasized black pride, they were also not the least self-conscious about using black dialect in their ads. For instance, New York's Zebra Associates for All-Pro Chicken created a radio commercial aimed at low-income groups of all colors; one hip version featured the line "Good-lookin', don't shout. Go 'head on. Tell me 'bout it." This same sense of black pride was found in the ads of the Chicago-based Burrell Advertising (now Burrell Communications Group), headed by the husband and wife team Thomas and Barbara Jones Burrell. Founded in 1971, the Burrell agency has since grown into the nation's leading black advertising agency. Thomas Burrell also believed that ads targeted to African Americans must reflect their culture, and he pioneered the concept of "positive realism," showing images of blacks as average Americans with families and in professional and managerial occupations. The agency's clients included Crest toothpaste, Ford, Quaker Oats, Jack Daniels, Coca-Cola, and McDonald's.

Unlike Vince Cullers's postwar experience, the Burrells found that the advertising industry had slowly begun to open up to blacks in the 1960s. Over a ten-year period, Burrell worked in three major advertising agencies—Leo Burnett, Foote, Cone & Belding, and Needham, Harper & Steers—while he kept honing his business plan to run his own agency. While working for Needham, he met his future wife, Barbara, who knew a little about the advertising industry, having worked as a media estimator for several years before serving as the secretary-treasurer of Burrell Advertising, beginning in 1974. Since then, the company grew from a staff of 2 to 114, and from billings of

$500,000 to nearly $80 million. Barbara now serves as vice chair-woman of the Burrell Communications Group with her ex-husband, company chairman, Thomas Burrell; this group includes the sub-sidiaries of Burrell Advertising, Burrell Public Relations, and Burrell Consumer Promotions to meet their clients' total communications needs and includes clients McDonald's, Coca-Cola, and Polaroid.[20]

The black media also changed the face of African Americans in mass communications, as it escalated efforts to develop new adver-tising vehicles. Among the new lifestyle magazines targeting the growing black middle class, *Essence* reached the women's market and *Black Enterprise* spoke to professionals, while Black Entertainment Television achieved success in inspiring African Americans to realize more fully their aspirations. At the time, however, the largest carriers of black advertising were the approximately three hundred radio sta-tions that spun soul music predominantly for the black audience; their radio commercials reached the ear of modern blacks under forty.[21]

Perhaps the most noticeable reform involved the role of African Americans portrayed in ads. Instead of presenting demeaning, stereo-typed images, a growing number of advertisements and television commercials cast blacks in a wider range of occupations and tasks. When a distinct African American culture began to make its mark on the general American culture, however, white corporate America also began using black models on magazine covers, black celebrity spokespersons, as well as black-based rhythm and blues music in many of its ads. In this era, Naomi Sims broke the color barrier as the first black model to be published on the covers and pages of *Life*, *Ladies' Home Journal*, and *Cosmopolitan* (figure 9.3). Black model Bev-erly Johnson appeared on *Vogue*'s cover in both 1974 and 1975 to clear the magazine of any implications of racial bias. Popular black celebri-ties also successfully pitched products in larger campaigns to the mainstream, including entertainer Lena Horne for Sanka coffee and comedian Bill Cosby for Jell-O, Coca-Cola, Ford, Ideal Toys, Kodak, and Texas Instruments. By the 1980s, Chevrolet used singing groups Martha and the Vandellas and the Four Tops in its ads, while Michael Jackson, Lionel Ritchie, and Ray Charles sang for Pepsi (figure 9.4), and Whitney Houston for Diet Coke.

LIFE

Black Models Take Center Stage

Top fashion model
Naomi Sims

Figure 9.3. Naomi Sims broke the color barrier as the first black model used on a *Life* magazine cover, October 17, 1969.

OCTOBER 17 · 1969 · 40¢

THE BLACK BUSINESSWOMAN

When affirmative action policies and their guidelines began to open up doors for women in the late 1960s and 1970s, black business-women began to appear in the fields of banking, stockbrokerage, and advertising. Heeding the demands of social responsibility, many corporations tried to fill managerial posts with blacks or women, reported

Figure 9.4. In 1991 Ray Charles and the Uh-Huh girls sang the praises of Diet Pepsi.

Time magazine in 1971. The "rarest breed of women" were the black businesswomen who could meet the demands of both the NAACP and Women's lib. They were practically nonexistent in major corporations since they contended with issues of both racism and sexism. "When white businessmen look at us, they still see a female, and how far up the ladder can a female go? That's the thing that is scary. Women cannot get beyond the middle-management level," said Shirley Barnes Kulunda, then a black account executive with J. Walter Thompson in New York City. Thus, preconceived notions about women in business complicated the problem for minorities applying for professional positions.[22]

In this era, Caroline Jones, Barbara Proctor, and Carol Williams symbolize the ad woman who found that being a black female had its advantages. These ad women seized the opportunity to learn the advertising business inside and out, but they also found a strong resistance to putting more positive black images into advertising. So the few black women in the ad business found themselves fed up with the racial politics in the industry, and they decided to start their own agencies that specialized in the growing black consumer market. In so doing, they provided role models for other women facing the difficulties of finding financial backing and being accepted by the business world. More important, the work of these black ad women in the late 1970s coincided with corporate America's move to look at untapped markets for growth, as the consumer market had increasingly become racially and ethnically diverse. Here are their portraits:

Caroline Robinson Jones, president and creative director of Caroline Jones Advertising in New York, helped pioneer multiethnic marketing, offering advertising, public relations, direct marketing, and special events promotions to domestic and international clients. "Ironically, because I am such a rarity—a black female advertising professional," explains Jones, "I have come to believe that this combination, or 'double whammy,' is the best set of credentials one could possess today."[23]

When Jones was growing up in the small town of Benton Harbor, Michigan, she excelled in school. At an early age, she also learned how to make her own money. "In the summer, I picked berries for money," recalls Jones. "I also sold magazine subscriptions, greeting cards, pot holders, and cosmetics." Although she seemed to be preparing for her future career in advertising, following high school graduation Jones decided to become an orthopedic surgeon. Though she enjoyed most of her science classes and did very well at the University of Michigan, in her sophomore year she changed her major to liberal arts. Of this abrupt change in direction, she recalled an early anatomy course. "I fainted at the sight of a dead cat on the examination table in the lab." Still, she continued to take science classes and earned her bachelor's degree in 1963 with a double major in science and English.[24]

"Mortuary science or pharmacy" was what a career counselor advised when Jones decided not to pursue medicine. Instead, she packed her bags and headed to New York City, taking the "first and only job" that was offered. Just before graduation, Jones met a representative from the J. Walter Thompson agency at a recruitment event and was invited to come to New York City for an interview. She landed a job in the secretarial pool. Despite being, in her own words, "a horrible typist," her first big opportunity came barely a month after her hiring when she was promoted to secretary for one of the firm's biggest creative directors. Then came training as a researcher for the new consumer research department, and eventually a position as a copywriter—the first black person to achieve the title. She remained at Thompson for five years as a junior copywriter, working on accounts including Prince Matchabelli, Ponds, Listerine, and Scott Paper, among others.[25]

During the heyday of the black movement, Jones fought to use more black faces in Thompson's campaigns. For example, there were the famous shampoo ads of the time, which Thompson managed, and she wondered if they could use a black woman as the Breck Girl to sell more product—only to be told that were no "black blondes." When the company launched a product for brunettes, she protested again when no black or Hispanic models appeared in the national campaign. At the time, many major agencies like Thompson rarely followed the supposed rule in the ad business that each ad with a party or crowd scene should show a black or Hispanic, because they represented one-tenth of the population at the time.[26]

Frustrated, Jones left Thompson in 1969 to join Zebra Associates, the nation's first fully integrated, full-service advertising agency owned by blacks. But the challenge of starting up an ad firm and balancing a marriage and family proved difficult, so she resigned. Now married and with a young son, Jones left the upstart Zebra for a position as a more senior copywriter for an already established firm, Kenyon & Eckhardt. Here Jones honed her television skills, and in 1972, she left to join the Black Creative Group as creative director and established herself as a pioneer in the field of black consumer marketing. Her advice and expertise were widely sought after.

Five years later, in 1977, Jones moved on to the position of vice president and creative group head of the internationally acclaimed Batten, Barton, Durstine, & Osborne (BBDO), where she was the first black woman ever elected vice president of a major advertising agency. At BBDO, Jones helped create successful campaigns for such clients as Campbell's Soup that for the first time targeted black consumers. Although Campbell's Soup ads had never previously included people, Jones insisted that in order to pitch to the black press, they would have to start showing a black family. For radio advertising to reach African Americans, she developed ads that used black actors and music arranged by black musicians. Still, Jones found it difficult to bring in a black family in a Campbell's television ad since black consumers liked specific soups but not necessarily the overall brand.[27]

Despite her fast climb in the advertising world, Jones felt she was still not in a position to really change the racial politics in the industry. In 1977, along with prominent black advertising executive Frank Mingo, Jones formed Mingo-Jones Advertising. The firm made major advances toward integration of blacks in advertising. When many advertisements featured only highly successful blacks and celebrities, Mingo-Jones showed it was all right to show regular people in campaigns geared for the African American community. As the creator of such well-known slogans as "Because I'm Worth It" for L'Oreal hair products and "We do chicken right" for Kentucky Fried Chicken, Jones established a solid reputation. After Mingo's death, the company split into the Mingo Group and Caroline Jones Advertising, Inc., a full-service advertising agency. Jones's agency opened its doors in

1987 with the following mission: "To sell products, through advertising and promotion, by accurately reflecting the colors and cultures of the consumers who use those products." Over the years, her company represented Anheuser-Busch, American Express, Clorox, McDonald's, Toys "R" Us, and the US Postal Service. In many cases, the clients were making their initial forays into marketing to black consumers through a black agency.

Not only did Jones use her agency to further diversify advertising, but she also helped people in a myriad of ways. She was sought after as a role model both for the black woman in a traditionally white, male industry and for the secretary who climbed to the upper echelons of her profession. For many years, she presented lecturers at business symposiums and universities, hosted business television shows, including "Focus on the Black Woman" and "In the Black: Keys to Success," and provided business strategies to emerging African governments. Among many honors, she received the 1990 Advertising Woman of the Year Award. Jones died at the age of fifty-nine in 2001, after battling cancer.[28]

Barbara Gardner Proctor left her position at a white agency in 1970 and became the first black woman to form the nation's second-largest black ad agency, Proctor & Gardner, Inc., based in Chicago. At this time, the Burrell Advertising Group ranked number one in billings among black agencies.

Proctor was born in 1933 in the mountains of North Carolina to a single mother. Her maternal grandmother and uncle raised her in extreme poverty, with no electricity or running water. As for her success, Proctor credits two sources. First, her grandmother, a household domestic, instilled early determination by constantly telling her: "You're not cute, but you're smart, and some day, you're gonna amount to something." She believed her grandmother, studied hard, and won a scholarship to Talladega College in Alabama, though she really wanted to get married. After graduation, she began using her writing skills in the music field as a freelance jazz feature writer and critic. Some years later, she became the international director for a record company, with a company car, expense account, and a world-travel schedule. Shortly after, she met Carl Proctor, who then was a road manager for jazz singer Sarah Vaughn, and decided to marry him after knowing him for only a brief time. It did not work out. "I was well known as Barbara Gardner; people called him Mr. Gardner," she said in 1979. "He wanted the stability of marriage and home, I needed a more flexible lifestyle." After two years, she left both the marriage and her job, because they both were in the same business.[29]

The second motivation behind Proctor's success was the necessity of providing for her son, the result of a marriage that ended after only two years. At the age of thirty-one, Proctor went into advertising, working for three different firms between 1965 and 1970 in Chicago. She recalled finally landing the first job with Post-Keyes-Gardner, the "first black in advertising in Chicago," before moving on to Gene Taylor and Associates, and eventually serving as a copywriter for the North Advertising Agency. But she decided to launch her own business when she was fired for refusing to work on an advertising campaign that she found demeaning to both women and African Americans. The campaign parodied the civil rights movement and featured protesting women running down the street and demanding that their hairdressers foam their hair.[30]

In 1971 Proctor launched her own business, Proctor & Gardner Advertising in Chicago. Her first application for a small business loan was turned down for lack of collateral. She applied again, this time armed with three statements from advertising agencies of what they would pay her as an employee, and she convinced the lender to give her an $80,000 loan with her professional reputation as collateral. In a time when not many women, let alone black women, ran agencies, Proctor shrewdly named the business Proctor & Gardner, which combined her maiden name and ex-husband's name, so that potential clients would assume that the mythical Gardner was a male partner behind the scenes. Moreover, the timing was right for Proctor's business to succeed. In advertising, the black market was just beginning to be understood, giving Proctor's agency a virtually untapped resource. She focused on this niche and presented a positive picture of the African American community. "I try to tell white businessmen that black is now, black is profit, black is here to stay," said Proctor in 1971. And so, she argued, American tastes originated in the black community and spread to more affluent whites. Therefore, she advised her clients—including the Jewel supermarket chain and Sears—to aim their ads in the black-oriented media not only at black families but also the white students attending colleges in predominately black communities (figure 9.5).[31]

Proctor's innovative ideas aimed at the black consumer market paid off, as more corporate giants joined her client roster. By 1983 Proctor's billings amounted to $13 million from several national accounts, including Alberto-Culver, Kraft Foods, and the E. J. Gallo winery. Proctor maintained a diverse staff of twenty-five, including many women and minorities, as well as her son, Morgan. By the 1990s, sales had slowed, however, and Proctor & Gardner Advertising restructured. In 1996 Proctor dissolved the advertising agency and started a new company, Proctor Communications Network, which offered expertise on Internet marketing and Web site design.[32]

Especially noteworthy of Proctor was her deep sense of responsibility to her work, evidence of the influence of black feminism that linked the individual's success to the community and the larger trend toward a social "conscience" in advertising. She insisted on high standards and would turn away business if she felt it reinforced negative stereotypes of blacks or women. As a result, she did not work for cigarettes or liquor accounts that used dubious advertising pitches aimed at women and minorities.

Carol H. Williams experienced a meteoric rise in the advertising field but had started out on a different path. While pursuing a career in medicine at Northwestern University, she wrote a play that attracted the attention of an advertising executive, who offered her a student internship. The work she performed during her internship resulted in several job offers. She joined Chicago-based Leo Burnett Advertising in 1969, and in 1971, she graduated from night school with a liberal arts degree.

Within seven years, Williams went from working as a copywriter to being named the first black female creative director at a major agency in 1976. In the following year, the agency named her as its first woman vice president. While at Leo Burnett, she created the campaigns "Strong enough for a man . . . but made for a woman" for Procter & Gamble's Secret antiperspirant deodorant (figure 9.6) and "Say hello to

Over the bridges
and through the hoods.

Ways to get
there may have
changed;
coming to share
Thanksgiving
hasn't.

Family and
friends from
near and far
share warm
memories.

If Jewel
can help with
the good times...
We give
thanks, too.

Jewel
Food Stores

Together,
we're
good food
people.

Figure 9.5. This Jewel supermarket ad presents American tastes. *Ebony*, November 1978.

Poppin' Fresh Dough" for Pillsbury. In 1979 Williams left Leo Burnett to accept a senior vice presidency and head the creative department at Foote, Cone & Belding in San Francisco. "Within a year, Williams says, she slammed into a glass ceiling," reported *Essence* magazine. "So she resigned, got married, and started a family."[33]

When Williams began freelancing in 1984, she did not intend to build an agency. She first acquired Pacific Bell as a client, and other companies eager to target the black community soon approached her. As business boomed, Williams decided to write a formal business plan. She used $60,000 of her freelance earnings and found investors through her old business contacts to launch her own agency, Carol H. Williams Advertising in Oakland, California. She was fortunate to have the financial support of her husband, Tipkins Hood, an orthopedic surgeon, so she did not have to draw a salary for the first two years and put every penny earned back into the business. By 1990 Williams had a staff of forty-six people and annual billings of over $60 million.[34]

Like many enterprising women, the key to the success of Carol Williams, Caroline Jones, and Barbara Proctor was not only having the desire to strike out on their own but also knowing *the* point. That is, the point in time when they had learned everything they could from working inside a company and realized that pursuing their entrepreneurial dreams was something that they had to do. Having their own business taught women like Williams that they could provide for themselves financially and they did not have to rely on the corporate structure. To be a business owner also gave them other freedoms on different levels. They could decide on how to spend their time, whether it was deciding to go to work, to a spa, or even to Europe. On the other hand, they continued to struggle with the balance between family and work. "I always wanted five like my mother, but I couldn't get to it," say Williams, mother of one daughter. "My initial years, when this business was younger, my daughter spent more time in my office than in play yards. That's hard."[35]

Despite the collective growth in the billings of the black advertising agencies, these enterprises also had to deal with a shifting industry as well as competitive pressures from larger, general-market agencies. Although national advertisers had begun to court the

Figure 9.6. This Secret deodorant ad assures readers that the product is strong enough for a man but made for a woman. *Ladies' Home Journal,* 1978.

expanding African American, middle-class market, the extent to which advertisers cultivated the black consumer remained relatively small in relation to the efforts to influence the white audience. As a result, the success of black agencies appeared minimal compared to white advertising agencies. In terms of gross billings, the six leading black agencies had sales of $155 million in the mid-1980s, compared to the leading white agency, J. Walter Thompson, which had billings over ten times that amount from its US accounts alone.

With desegregation there also arose another question as to whether black institutions like the press and ad agencies were needed to reach special markets any longer. African American culture had become hip to a new generation of many Americans, the baby boomers—both black and white. Moreover, the federal government had begun to relinquish its support of affirmative action, and white corporate America responded by turning over advertising accounts previously held by black agencies to white agencies, which expanded with divisions to handle black and ethnic specialty markets. Therefore, dollars once earmarked for campaigns to reach African American consumers now started shifting to the growing Latino market.

THE ETHNIC MARKET

Similar to the Civil Rights Act, the Immigration Act of 1965 led to a more culturally diverse working- and middle-class society. Millions of people of color came to the United States, inaugurating a period of new immigration from Asian countries, Mexico, and South America. Dramatic changes in the American economy led to an American working class of incredible ethnic diversity. In the 1970s and 1980s, huge numbers of Asian and Hispanic immigrants flocked to America to fill the millions of new service, retail, clerical, and light manufacturing jobs. Between 1983 and 1992, America experienced one of the heaviest floods of immigration in its history. As many as 8.7 million came to live in this country, the highest number in a ten-year period since 1910, and an estimated 5 million more newcomers slipped across the border without documentation.

Like the immigrants of the 1890s and 1900s, those with modest incomes would begin the process of upward social mobility that has been a feature of modern American life. For many of these people, even minimum-wage work in America paid five or ten times more than they could earn in their homeland, and by the 1980s their children would be attending college. As the foreign-born pursued their American dream, they re-created the sights and sounds of their homeland in self-contained, self-supporting communities similar to the African Americans in their segregated communities. By this time, marketing to minorities became ever more critical as the buying power of racially and ethnically diverse consumers increased.

Although agencies like Caroline Jones Advertising, the Burrell Group, and UniWorld helped pioneer multiethnic marketing, the number of such firms had grown in response to this demographic shift. According to the 1993 *Standard Directory of Advertising Agencies*, some 105 firms specialized to some extent in minority markets. Among them, Teresa Zubizarreta opened Zubi Advertising in 1976, now one of Miami's largest Hispanic advertising agencies.

Zubizarreta had left Cuba with no more than a secretarial degree, and her first job in the industry was for the advertising agency McCann Marschalk. After this experience, she left work for a real estate developer, learning every aspect of the business. But eventually the workload and frequent travel left her desiring more time with family, so she decided to open her own shop, Zubi Advertising, to service the increasingly affluent Hispanic market. With the help of friends in the industry who loaned her a spare room, a table, and a typewriter, she began a new career working exclusively on real estate advertising services in the early 1970s, creating copy for print campaigns to promote new buildings and designing their logos. After reading a December 1975 *Time* magazine cover story stating that Hispanics would be the largest US minority by the 1990s, she shifted her business to focus exclusively on advertising to this rapidly growing market.[36]

Similar to the black press that specialized in the Negro Market, agencies like Zubi Advertising could reach the Hispanic American audience through a well-established media system more easily than any other ethnic group. Although Hispanic Americans represented many nationalities—Mexican, Puerto Rican, Cuban, and so on—these groups were also linked by a common language through the Spanish International Network, which included Spanish-language television, radio stations, and publications. Univision emerged as another television network operating in major markets such as Miami, Fresno, San Francisco, and Phoenix. But few national campaigns were targeted directly at Asian Americans, because they represented not only a variety of nationalities but also languages, traditions, and dialects, including those of Chinese, Koreans, Pacific Islanders, Filipinos, and Vietnamese. To tap the Asian market, Eleanor Yu launched the San Francisco–based Adland in 1984 with an investment of $3,000; this was the first major advertising agency targeted specifically at the Asian American market, with billings in 1993 exceeding $16 million. She also published *Marketing Focus*, a trade magazine covering the demographics of the Asian American community. Since then, Adland has expanded into an international agency with offices in Hong Kong, Sydney, and Toronto.[37]

Clearly, the advances made by these women of color and their white counterparts paved the way for the next generation of women bringing change to the advertising field, from the ground floor to the boardroom in the late twentieth and early twenty-first centuries. Government legislation had opened up new opportunities for women in the economy, business schools opened their doors wider than ever before to females, and both agencies and corporations admitted them to the highest echelons of corporate management. Still, another sea of change awaited this third wave of feminists. Although many ad women still continue to advance the woman's viewpoint to sell products aimed at the women's market, others would strike out in new directions, going where they recognized opportunity, regardless of the lure of the gendered marketplace.

NOTES

1. For a comprehensive history of black enterprise, see Juliet E. K. Walker, *The History of Black Business in America: Capitalism, Race, and Entrepreneurship* (Independence, KY: Twayne Publishers, 1998).

2. Paula Giddings, *When and Where I Enter: The Impact of Black Women on Race and Sex in America* (New York: Morrow, 1984).

3. For a significant synthesis on African American women's history, see ibid. Other historians of African American women's experiences include Jeanne Noble, Sharon Harley, Rosalyn Terborg-Penn, and Darlene Clark Hine. Noteworthy examples of contemporary black feminist theory include Angela Davis's *Women, Race, and Class* (1981), bell hooks's *Ain't I a Woman?* (1981), Alice Walker's *In Search of Our Mother's Gardens* (1983), and Barbara Smith's *Home Girls: A Black Feminist Anthology* (1983).

4. Walker, *The History of Black Business in America*.

5. Raymond A. Bauer and Scott M. Cunningham, "The Negro Market," *Journal of Advertising Research* (April 1970): 3–13. See also Paul K. Edwards, *The Southern Negro as a Consumer* (New York: Prentice Hall, 1932).

6. Andrew Wiese, "The Other Suburbanites: African American Suburbanization in the North before 1950," *Journal of American History* 85, no. 4 (March 1999): 1495–1524. Andrew Wiese, "Racial Cleansing in the Suburbs: Suburban Government, Urban Renewal, and Segregation on Long Island, New York, 1945–1960," in *Contested Terrain: Power, Politics, and Participation in Society*, ed. Marc L. Silver and Martin Melkonian (Westport, CT: Greenwood Press, 1995), pp. 61–70.

7. Bauer and Cunningham, "The Negro Market," pp. 3–13.

8. "From *Negro Digest* to *Ebony*, *Jet* and *Em*—Special Issue: 50 Years of JPC—Redefining the Black Image," *Ebony*, November 1992. See also "Reflecting Black America: Black African Salutes Trail-Blazing Johnson Family Empire," *Detroit News*, June 23, 2006.

9. William Barlow, *Voice Over: The Making of Black Radio* (Philadelphia: Temple University Press, 1999), pp. 121–24. On mass media, see *Split Image: African Americans in the Mass Media*, ed. Jannette Davis and William Barlow (Washington, DC: Howard University Press, 1990).

10. On employment policy before World War II, see Roland Marchand, *Advertising the American Dream: Making Way for Modernity, 1920–1940* (Berkeley: University of California Press, 1985), p. 35. On policy remained unchanged after World War II, see Davis and Barlow, *Split Image*, p. 184.

11. On the first "Negro agency," see Walker, *The History of Black Business in America*, p. 350. Also see Stephen Fox, *The Mirror Makers: A History of American Advertising and Its Creators* (New York: Vintage Books, 1984), p. 279.

12. Fred J. MacDonald, *Blacks and White TV: African Americans in Television since 1948* (Chicago: Nelson-Hall, 1992), pp. 88–89.

13. Harold Kassarjian, "The Negro and American Advertising," *Journal of Marketing Research* 6 (February 1969): 29–39.

14. EEOC study, 1966: *Advertising Age*, January 22, 1968. EEOC study, 1967: *Advertising Age*, October 30, 1967.

15. On minority employment, see *Advertising Age*, October 28, 1969.

16. "The Black Man in the Gray Flannel Suit," *Time*, June 27, 1969.

17. On Marian Cullers, "Women in Advertising," *Essence*, January 1, 1990.

18. "Remembering an Advertising Pioneer," *Black Enterprise*, http://www.blackenterprise.com/ExclusivesEKOpen.asp?id=534 (accessed February 18, 2007).

19. On Vince Cullers, see obituary of Vince Cullers, *Chicago Sun-Times*, October 10, 2003. See also *Advertising Age*, October 13, 2003; *Black Enterprise*, December 2003; and *Jet*, October 27, 2003.

20. "Barbara Burrell," *Who's Who among African Americans*, 16th ed. (Detroit: Gale Group, 2003).

21. *Time*, June 27, 1969.

22. "The Rarest Breed of Women," *Time*, November 8, 1971.

23. Jones quoted in Bradley Morgan, *Advertising Career Directory: A Practical One-Stop Guide to Getting a Job in Advertising* (Detroit: Visible Ink Press, 1992), p. 33.

24. Quoted in Robert Fleming, *The Success of Caroline Jones Advertising, Inc.* (New York: Walker and Company, 1996), pp. 6–7.

25. Caroline Jones, speech, "1990 Advertising Woman of the Year Awards Luncheon," Caroline Jones Collection, box 2, folder 12, American History Archives, Smithsonian Institution.

26. Fleming, *Success of Caroline Jones Advertising, Inc.*, p. 14.

27. "Oral History Interview with Caroline Jones," Campbell Soup Oral History Project Interview 31, Campbell Collection, box 4, folder: Caroline Jones, April 17, 1990, American History Archives, Smithsonian Institution.

28. Caroline Robinson Jones, biographical essays: Ashyia Henderson, ed., *Contemporary Black Biography* (Farmington Hills, MI: Gale Group, 2001) and *Notable Black American Women* (Farmington Hills, MI: Gale Group, 2002). See also obituary of Caroline Robinson Jones, *Jet*, July 23, 2001.

29. "Proctor Takes Gamble and Hits the Jackpot," *Working Woman*, August 1979.

30. Ibid.

31. On "black is profit," see "Black Capitalism: The Rarest Breed of Women," *Time*, November 8, 1971.

32. Barbara Proctor, profile in *Notable Black American Women*, ed. Jessie Carney Smith (Detroit: Gale Research, 1992). On Proctor & Gardner agency, see "I Made It because I'm Black and a Woman," *Ebony*, August 1982. See also "Ad Whiz Was on Her Way with Her First SBA Loan," *New Orleans Time-Picayune*, April 30, 1984, "Where Are They Now?" *Forbes*, May 18, 1998.

33. "Women in Advertising," *Essence*, January 1990. See also "Not Just an Ol' Boys Club: Carol H. Williams Advertising, Company Profile," *Black Enterprise*, June 1, 1999.

34. "Life at the Top—3 Successful Black Businesswomen," *Essence*, October 1999.

35. Ibid.

36. Teresa Zubizaretta, biographical essay in *Notable Hispanic Women*, vol. 1 (Farmington Hills, MI: Gale Research, 1993).

37. Eleanor Yu, biographical essay in *Notable Asian Americans* (Farmington Hills, MI: Gale Research, 1995). See also "A Young Lady with a Big Idea," *Adweek*, Western ed., July 24, 1989; "Adventure: Agency Taps Asian America," *San Francisco Business Times*, February 19, 1993.

CHAPTER 10

THE THIRD WAVE OF AD WOMEN

Tradition has dictated that a woman wait for a man to give her a diamond ring. No more. In 2003 ad agency JWT, formerly the J. Walter Thompson Company, launched the *Women of the World Raise Your Right Hand* print campaign to encourage women to think of DeBeers diamond rings in a new way. The premise of empowering women was the main thrust of the campaign that targeted women aged thirty-five to sixty-four—the evolved, affluent, fashion-savvy woman who needs no one's permission to indulge herself. The ad copy encouraged women to think of diamond rings on their right hands as expressions of personal style for the independent, worldly, assertive side of their personality. "Your left hand says 'we.' Your right hand says 'me,'" read one ad. "Your left hand declares your commitment. Your right hand is a declaration of independence," claimed another (figure 10.1). As brilliant and expensive as an engagement ring that says "we," the promotion of the "Me-Ring" as a symbol of independence and freedom connected with many women. Sales of right-hand rings were up as much as 10 percent in the first six months of the campaign.[1]

On another level, this diamond campaign is emblematic of a larger, ongoing discussion in American society about the nature of women's economic independence and identity—a third wave in feminist

Figure 10.1. This J. Walter Thompson campaign encouraged women to think of DeBeers diamond rings in a new way. *Vogue*, November 2003.

thinking. Called the *New Feminists*, or the *postfeminists*, they emerged on the scene in the 1980s and generally speaking fell into the categorization of Generation X, born between the late 1960s and the early 1980s, as well as those who separated themselves from the preceding wave, or *Old Feminists*, with their emphasis on oppression that made women into "victims." This third wave viewed using makeup and wearing provocative clothing as liberating, not confining. They learned martial arts for self-defense and power, while they reveled in their sexuality and used it boldly to get what they wanted. They also could be economically independent of the men in their lives. This image of the modern, individualistic woman, which appeared in advertisements like the DeBeers diamond ad and the popular HBO television show *Sex and the City*, was attached to a particular group of professional women with new freedoms and their own income.[2]

Instead of molding American women of all backgrounds into a single stereotype, advertisers recognized that there has never been only one female ideal in American culture, or even only two; there are many. Emphasis on the multiplicity of ideals and cultural diversity emerged in the 1980s and 1990s. This meant that far more attention would be given to the contributions of women, blacks, Latinos, gays, lesbians, and other minority groups in American society. In order to reach an increasingly diverse audience, advertisers had to face the challenge of drawing authentic images around particular groups, or *subcultures*, which spoke to different races, genders, ethnicities, and lifestyles, rather than trying to impose a rigid archetype—a single ideal. It was in this context that the third wave of ad women appeared and built upon the gains of previous generations.

Today, women are more powerful even on men's terms than ever before in the advertising world and the world at large. Most of the people working in advertising, fashion, retail, and mass media are women. In 2005 women accounted for over half of those employed in advertising and related services (52.2 percent), management of advertising and promotions (56.1 percent), and advertising sales agents (50.2 percent).[3] But the difference between what they were doing with their lives compared with the previous generation of Old Feminists is one of the most distinctive features of the last few decades.

Instead of focusing on the oppressive aspects of the marketplace, women now were in a place to positively impact the media, as well as the promotional appeal and imagery of ads, explains Linda M. Scott. "As a result, the dialogue that began in the 1970s between those who criticize advertising and those who are in a place to positively, actively affect the content of ads, has long since gone quiet."[4]

FROM MASS CULTURE TO NICHE CULTURES

From the perspective of the twenty-first century, the multiplicity of female ideals can be seen as a reflection of the modern values of individualism, through which women identify themselves and their groups, such as the New Feminists. The most enduring aspect of the cultural rebellion of the 1960s and late 1970s, when American men and women challenged established institutions of the nuclear family, religion, and trust in government, was an even more radical form of individualism, a *new individualism* that emphasized personal happiness and the freedom to choose. This movement also shifted the focus from social activism in the sixties to an emphasis on personal fulfillment. No longer limited to freedom of religion or politics, this view included the freedom to buy consumer goods of one's own choice, to earn as much money as one possibly could, or to do what one desired in his or her private life as well. In sum, people should *do their own thing.*

Thereby millions of Americans believed that they could achieve happiness and sought to construct their own identities to fit their own individual needs. During the 1970s, Americans increasingly turned away from society and sought support from self-help books like best sellers *Looking Out for #1, I'm Okay—You're Okay*, and the *Complete Book of Running*. In particular, the white middle class looked for greater control over their lives and greater personal fulfillment in areas besides their jobs or community. They became converts to charismatic religions, vegetarianism, drug use, psychotherapy, all-night dancing at the disco, or physical fitness. As they experimented with new kinds of community, no longer did traditional sources of cultural authority—family, religion, ethnic customs, and the past—dominate their lives. The nation's shared common culture split into dozens of subcultures, but their lives became more intertwined with consumption as a form of self-expression and personal fulfillment, as well as images and messages from advertising, the movies, popular music, sports, television, and later the Internet.

Greed Is Good

Encouraged by the relaxation of government regulation, tax reductions, and a soaring stock market, the making and spending of money became integral components of the mainstream culture. "Greed is good," declared Gordon Gekko, a real estate and stock speculator in the 1987 movie *Wall Street*, as young money managers became heroes of popular culture. With a resurgent economy, a wave of new products, and an enthusiastic consumer base, many Americans enjoyed an aura of prosperity throughout the 1980s. Defense spending, foreign investment, and the maturation of the baby-boom generation sent the real estate, finance, retail trade, and high-tech manufacturing industries soaring. The huge sums spent on publicity and financial speculation also generated thousands of high-paying jobs for young bankers, lawyers, MBAs, and stockbrokers. As long as the market kept going up, baby boomers apparently would enjoy splendid prosperity, except, perhaps, those employees of corporations that were restructured or broken up. In 1984 it was estimated that the twenty-five- to thirty-five-year-old age group controlled an astonishing 23 percent of the country's disposable income.

At the outset of their careers, these baby boomers became a new social phenomenon—*yuppies*, the young, single urban professionals, and *dinks*, married couples with double income and no kids. In 1980 *Black Enterprise* magazine coined the word *buppie* to describe the 21 percent of college-educated African Americans who lived in suburban areas and had upscale tastes in food, fashion, and lifestyles. A decade later, nearly thirty-two million African Americans had an estimated purchasing power of between $170 and $300 billion, and by the year 2000 that amount would almost triple to $889 billion.[5]

The beneficiaries of the new wealth reveled in their status in the 1980s. They not only built large tract houses—what later critics called *McMansions*—and high-end vacation homes, but they also bought expensive luxury items. These well-heeled, well-traveled young professionals seemed to have an unlimited appetite for consuming premium goods—that is, the best money could buy. They drank Perrier, ate Hagen Daaz ice cream, and worked out in exorbitantly priced designer sweats and athletic shoes. Every jacket, polo shirt, and pair of jeans seemed to be stamped with a designer logo. But it was primarily BMW, Mercedes, and other costly automobiles that became badges of success. Such successful brands spoke to the core identity of their customers by allowing them to acquire material symbols of personal and social identity, created for the most part by advertising, merchandising, and publicity.

The prototype for this lifestyle brand was Polo created by Ralph Lauren. The retail stores reflected an upper-class lifestyle with luxurious wood paneling, while the advertisements featured pictures of attractive and wealthy people. With these images, Ralph Lauren created an implicit brand promise: If you buy our products, you, too, can aspire to this lifestyle. Not surprisingly, the not-so-wealthy became caught up in the quest to "have it all." Many people wanted to at least look as if they were rich and powerful, and so the upscale trend trickled down to department and discount stores, which built strong fashion elements into their merchandising. For example, J. C. Penney promoted a private-label polo shirt sporting a fox emblem and claimed parity at a better price than the best-selling Izod line stamped with an alligator logo. Model Cheryl Tiegs lent her name to a clothing line for J. C. Penney, and actress Jaclyn Smith did the same thing for Kmart; Martha Stewart endorsed a line of lifestyle accessories.

But by the 1980s, mass media was fragmenting the nation's mass market into an endless array of subcultures. No longer was the public limited to watching the same programs on three network stations (CBS, NBC, and ABC). Instead, cable television tailored shows to special audiences: MTV broadcast music videos, CNN showed news around the clock, the Cartoon Channel entertained children, Black Entertainment Television reached African Americans, and ESPN engaged sports enthusiasts. Subcultures developed around special lifestyles that were built around leisure activities and interests. For example, people might join together in an enthusiasm for golf, foods, foreign travel, history, and any number of interests. By the end of the twentieth century, the expanding consumer capitalism and the six-ties-style pursuit of personal fulfillment were inseparable. Following the currents of culture, advertisers tied their products to immediate gratification, distinct lifestyles, youth, and sexuality.

THE MOVING TARGET

Although the revived feminist movement opened up a far larger choice of opportunities for women, it also resulted in an enormous shift in the professional and educational activities of women. The number of two-income families increased and expanded the opportunities made avail-able by an expanding consumer economy. Spurred on by affirmative action, employment opportunities for women, especially in the profes-sions, increased sharply, while the number of homemakers dropped. In 1982 women accounted for 43.5 percent in the labor force; many profes-sionals attained significant success and most made modest gains. Still, the question of how one should balance career and family continued to confront every professional woman who embarked on a career.

Similar to the civil rights movement of African Americans, the feminist movement also provoked a traditionalist counterattack, what Susan Faludi termed a cultural backlash. Lawyer Phyllis Schlafly's affirmation of ages-old gender roles received a warm response not only from traditionalist men but also from many religious orthodox women, working-class women, and homemakers, many of whom shared few of the values and experiences of the middle- and upper-class leadership of the feminist movement. Three states short of rati-fication, the Equal Rights Amendment died quietly in 1982. Although gender discrimination continued despite the organized feminist movement, the gains on behalf of women during the sixties and early seventies were by no means lost. Even if the ERA had been passed, by that time nearly all the sex-differentiated laws would have been wiped out.[6]

The Invisible Woman Becomes Visible

Looking back, popular culture was the most visible expression of the abrupt, enormous shift in the educational and professional activities of women since 1970. By the 1980s, the career woman had become a popular articulation of feminism in the mass media—brave and chic. For example, staunch feminist Anne Tolstoi Wallach of Grey Advertising wrote the Madison Avenue novel *Women's Work* in 1981. Drawing on years of ad women's hard-luck stories and spicing it up with sex, power, and success, she told the story of Domina Di Santis Drexler, who worked as a creative director at a leading advertising agency in the early 1970s. In addition, television programs of the 1980s and 1990s showed the professional female figure prominently, in such sagas as *Dallas* and *Dynasty*, as well as *Murphy Brown*, *Moonlighting*, and *Ally McBeal*. In other programs, such as *Who's the Boss?* and *Melrose Place*, women played the role of agency senior executives. This new heroine reflects a perspective on the independent, single career woman who also remains much more dependent than men on success in romantic relationships as a primary source of social identity and self-worth.[7]

In terms of images created by the mass media, what it meant to be a feminist had shifted from involvement in a network of women advocating social, political, and all other rights to being a *superwoman* or *supermom*. Two generations of women raised their education achievements and poured into the labor force. The Superwoman was the model of the new individualist who enjoyed all the pleasures of sexual freedom, marriage, and motherhood. She dressed in a power suit, carried an attaché case, and held a baby in her arms; she supposedly had it all and did it all. Not only did a career offer women individualist opportunities for self-fulfillment and liberation—so did consumption. Instead of demanding general social equality, she was driven by personal success. An example of the new individualist, the modern Superwoman turned to the marketplace, a career, and consumption for her opportunities for fulfillment and liberation. But the stereotypical, career-minded woman who swapped a briefcase for an apron was not nearly so common in real life. What we had in the mass media was a new set of clichés of women.

What Do Women Want?

In this era, marketers became increasingly perplexed about what women wanted, from financial services to cars to household items—and how to sell these things to them. Perhaps the work of Rena Bartos was the most influential in solving these problems and changing marketing to women. In 1982 Bartos, then a senior vice president and director of communications at the J. Walter Thompson Company, had written a book, *The Moving Target*, in which she analyzed the changing patterns of consumption and feelings toward consumption among women, as well as ways to reach it. Born in New Jersey, she studied at Rutgers University and did graduate work in sociology at Columbia University. After working in research at McCann-Erickson, she joined JWT in 1966.

According to Bartos, marketers generally tend to stereotype women as being married, but the reality, obviously, is that not all women are wives. Hence the aim of her book was to convince advertisers that women's role in the market is diverse and ever-changing, and a more realistic approach was needed for a changing and unpredictable marketplace. For marketers communicating with women, Bartos advised that it was particularly important to base their strategies and communications on an understanding of the attitudes and perceptions of the consumers themselves to avoid the danger of alienating valuable prospects.

Using demographics, Bartos studied populations in terms of characteristics such as age, income, and occupation. But she also recognized that many factors beyond simply age and gender came into play. Using a new form of market research called *psychographics*, which emphasizes the understanding of consumers' activities, interests, and attitudes, Bartos identified four new segments of the women's market: (1) the stay-at-home housewife, (2) the plan-to-work housewife, (3) the just-a-job workingwoman, and (4) the career woman. She also studied two other vast but largely unexplored markets: unmarried adults and people over age forty-nine. Among her findings, Bartos showed that the career woman and plan-to-work homemakers actually buy more products than stay-at-home moms, while career women use fragrances, cosmetics, and toiletries far more than just-a-job women. Another important finding revolved around changing representations of men. Bartos showed that women favorably responded to imagery of new lifestyles that presented men in domestic roles—a father trying to make breakfast for his son or diapering an infant—rather than the usual office or factory stereotype.[8]

Even so, for the most part the advertising world assumed that the woman's world revolved around the man, due in part to the lack of women in both senior management on the client side and on the agency side. But that situation was changing partly because the marketplace was changing. By this time, a new generation of female college graduates of the late 1960s and early 1970s had entered advertising, despite their revolutionary friends' criticism of the advertising world, large corporations, and other issues. Although money was rarely cited as the motive, these aspiring ad women often listed glamour, strong interest in creative activities, and a desire for challenge as reasons to enter the profession. Others wanted to make a difference, suggesting that advertising could serve a useful purpose.

Nevertheless, discrimination toward women continued to be an inherent part of the late twentieth century. For the most part, the advertising profession was still segregated by sex, which meant continued wage discrimination, and women continued to encounter barriers to senior management positions. While the ranks of women in management continued to expand, they held only 2.5 percent of senior executive positions. African American women had even less representation. In 1992 *Advertising Age* ran an article titled "The Ad Industry's Little Secret." The story reported that African Americans filled only 5.2 percent of all the positions in the nation's advertising, marketing, and public relations companies; and among managers and professional-level employees, the figure was a minuscule 2.1 percent. In addition to race, other barriers remained for women trying to achieve senior executive positions. Some experts explained that it was the client, not the ad agency, who shut women out of the senior posts, to the extent that there remained a prejudiced view that women did not work on accounts for certain products, such as automobiles or industrial products. "Ninety-five out of 100 of the major clients are men. Most of them are not going to be comfortable with a woman at the top.

The idea of traveling with them, socializing with them, they're just not comfortable with it," explained an executive recruiter in 1986.[9]

For many other women though, a move from heading an office to heading an entire advertising agency was not a question of gender; it was a question of sacrifice. If women wanted to move to the top, they would have to be willing to give up their family. But many women rejected this view, choosing to work full-time and raise a family. Others left the traditional road to success and became consultants and free-lancers, positions that would enable them to balance a career and a home. Still others opted for lives as traditional stay-at-home moms. For these reasons, the surge of women into jobs eventually shattered the notion that the female consumer market was one unbroken segment.

THE DECADE OF DECADENCE

As the purchasing power of workingwomen increased, some advertisers tried to go beyond the old stereotypes and redefine the way they advertised to women purely for economic reasons. Much of the new advertising catered to the career woman because she had more disposable income and remained loyal to specific brands.

For example, advertising agency Ogilvy & Mather created the 1985 American Express "Interesting Lives" campaign for both female and young male professionals, aiming to position the American Express Card as a symbol of people with interesting and multifaceted lives, people with unusual hobbies or unconventional careers. The American Express Card, the ads indicated, gave these holders the opportunity to indulge in their varied interests, to be spontaneous by going to an estate sale or even the Australian Outback, for example. Rather than featuring celebrities, the ads showed confident independent women using the American Express Card to take their husband to dinner or their kids to lunch, bantering with a flirtatious man in a bookstore, or checking into a hotel with suitcases and scuba diving gear. They also were planning surprise weekends, as in the case of a television commerical that pictured a woman taking her husband to a luxury inn, where they both jump on the beds like five-year-olds.

Figure 10.2. American Express went beyond old stereotypes and featured confident, independent women with interesting and multifaceted lives. *Rolling Stone*, May 9, 1985.

"The American Express Card," the tag line says, "it's part of a lot of interesting lives" (figure 10.2).

The ad campaign connected with women, and soon the number of female applicants doubled that of men. By 1984, 27 percent of American Express cardholders were women, compared to 10 percent in the late 1970s. Using the self-fulfillment theme, the ads no longer described why American Express was better or different than other credit cards; it simply was. Powerful images alone were expected to evoke confidence in the brand.

All the marketing to traditional stay-at-home moms and working-women did not necessarily apply to the entire woman's market. Advertisers recognized that there were other consumers out there. The values of independence and personal fulfillment also began to assert themselves in sexually charged ads for everything from perfumes to blue jeans.

Sex and Symbolism

Whereas sex in advertising in the 1950s used a gorgeous girl in a tight sweater, expressed messages with double entendres, and was discreetly sensuous, there emerged an even greater use of sexuality in advertising in the 1980s. It can be traced to the sexual revolution, when Helen Gurley Brown's *Cosmo* magazine came out with its first male centerfold in 1972, a nude Burt Reynolds. In the following year, the new magazine *Playgirl*, which explored women's sexual fantasies with photos of male nudes, emerged as a counter to *Playboy*. These magazines paved the path for more sexualized ads in the 1980s and 1990s.

To enhance the allure of products, few advertisers explained the unique features or gave consumers a rational reason to buy the product. Beauty and fashion ads simply hinted at an experience showing fantasy or dream sequences resulting from using the product. This sexual adventurism is best represented with the work of Rochelle Udell, who captured the attention of women consumers. Although Udell worked as an art director on magazines such as *Gentlemen's Quarterly*, *Self*, and *Vogue*, she did her most striking work in advertising. By the time she reached the age of forty in 1985, she had created some of television's most sensual and provocative advertising for Calvin Klein and Chanel fragrance. Udell also headed the in-house advertising agency for Calvin Klein and later became senior vice president and creative director for Della Femimina, Travisano & Partners.

After graduating with a bachelor's degree in art and education, Udell earned a master's degree in painting from Pratt School of Design. She began her career as a high school art teacher and helped her husband with his graphic design work on the weekends. To be of greater help, she took Milton Glaser's ten-month night school design course and later left teaching to start work as an art director in publishing. By 1976, after five years of working at *Vogue* and now divorced, she left and continued to work with one of her clients, fashion designer Calvin Klein. In 1980 she married Douglas Turshen, then art director with *House and Garden*, with whom she had worked.

In 1981 Udell suggested that Calvin Klein start his own in-house agency, since she felt outside agencies did not listen to him. He took her advice, launched CRK Advertising, and signed her to a two-year contract as chief executive. While pregnant with her first child, she began to create a series of Calvin Klein ads that shocked America's moral majority. To introduce the designer jeans, both Klein and Udell eventually agreed on a series of ads featuring five different types of American women, including white model Andie McDowell, teen star Brooke Shields, and black actress Shari Belafonte. Each ad was designed around the individual model. The result was sexy ads and commercial spots, such as fifteen-year-old Brooke Shields wearing a shirt and jeans while whispering: "You know what comes between me and my Calvins? Nothing." Three network-owned stations in New York banned the ads. Nevertheless, sales of the expensive jeans jumped nearly 300 percent following the first wave of commercials. The once humble "dungarees" had become big fashion.[10]

This foray into sexual adventures continued with advertising primarily aimed at women. With the understanding that women frequently bought fragrance for men, in 1984 Udell launched Calvin Klein Fragrance for Men in women's magazines and suggested that an erotic fantasy awaited them (figure 10.3). The following year, the launch of Obsession perfume for women took the erotic fantasy to another level,

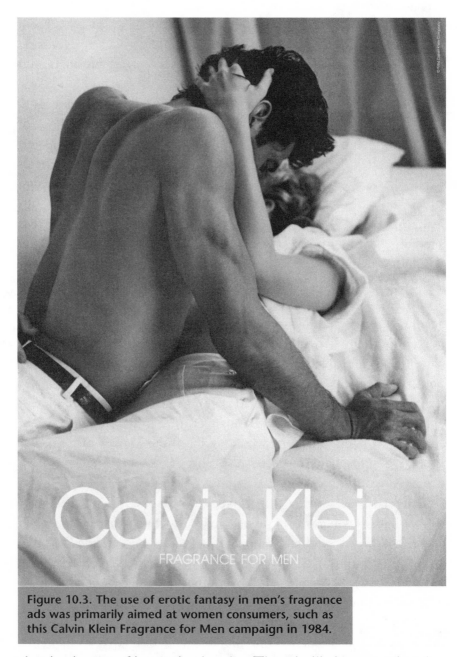

Figure 10.3. The use of erotic fantasy in men's fragrance ads was primarily aimed at women consumers, such as this Calvin Klein Fragrance for Men campaign in 1984.

showing images of intertwined nudes. The scintillating campaign shot the unknown Obsession perfume to the top of the market within months. The firm spent $17 million to launch Obsession, and within one year, it was selling $40 million worth of the perfume (figure 10.4).

Figure 10.4. The promotion of Obsession suggested an erotic fantasy world awaited consumers, 1985.

Many people found the sexual candor refreshing, even healthy, as long as it did not portray women in demeaning ways. In ads that were an expression of the product—soaps, lotions, cosmetics, lingerie, fragrance —sensuality worked. Much to the surprise of her many sister feminists, Gloria Steinem approved Calvin Klein's Obsession campaign for *Ms.* magazine, which she founded and edited at the time. "Sexuality and nudity are a part of life, and if it's appropriate, fine," explained Steinem. "There's a difference between women in tight jeans—where the ads are aimed at pleasing men—and ads like the Calvin Klein Obsession ad, where a man and woman are in positions of equality."[11]

So provocative, so distinctive, and so consistent have these images been, that sex and the Calvin Klein brand have virtually become one and the same. But what was the effect of more explicit and more pervasive sexuality in advertising? Sex had become part of the consumer culture.[12]

After decades of selling products by depicting women as sex objects, the image of a nude or nearly nude man as a prop became standard fare in magazine ads and television commercials for the women's market. Of this trend, business writer Jennifer Foote observed that advertisers had switched "bimbos," going from depicting women as "anxious half-wits and sultry sex objects" to "it's his torso, stripped and moist, promoting everything from Calvin Klein underwear to Kodak film." Not only did ads show more skin, but another set of provocative ads revolved around sexual fantasies with women in control.[13]

"The most risqué copy I have ever seen was for Paco Rabanne men's cologne," said David Ogilvy in 1983. Called *Man in Bed*, one of television's sexiest thirty seconds opened with a French-accented man stirring himself awake as the telephone rang. "Hello," he yawned into the phone. "You snore," a woman's voice informed him. "And you steal the covers," he responded jokingly. As the conversation continued, paintings and discreet camera angles hid his nudity; viewers never saw the woman. In a gender-role reversal, it was now the woman who rose at daybreak to go on a business trip, leaving the lovesick man in bed. A print and promotional campaign also ran; sales for Paco Rabanne went up 24 percent.[14]

This evolution of images of men was the result of the sexual revolution of the 1960s coupled with the breakthrough thinking and sexual candor of a new generation of feminists. The gains women had made in the workplace had actually made them more receptive to ads that represented their desires, or desirability, concluded marketing researchers. In the narratives of these ads, the source of women's power may have been her money or beauty and sensuality; nevertheless the man was under her domination. "Women like it when they're portrayed as taking charge of a situation," noted Rena Bartos. "It implies power."[15]

GLOBALIZATION

By the 1990s, economic realities combined with changing demographics and lifestyles created massive shifts in consumer behavior and buying patterns. Global competition had put American corporations under pressure to restructure, consolidate, and simplify, while the overall US economy shifted from an industrial base toward one rooted in information technology and services. Firms pared down their organizations to an essential core, slicing away layer after layer of the workforce through right-sizing, reengineering, and downsizing. In place of large corporate staffs, firms hired temporary workers on a project-by-project basis. Though the economy stabilized and even improved by 1995, the recession drove home the message that the seeming abundance was in fact finite.

Elaboration of Market Niches and Specialized Media

The classic American dream that hard work brings rewards was fading in the 1990s. For the first time, it seemed that a generation might not surpass or even match its parents' standard of living. Skyrocketing real estate prices vastly inflated the financial worth of many older Americans and placed home ownership out of the reach of many younger people. These emerging trends also coincided with the baby boomers settling down and starting families of their own, as well as often shouldering the burden of caring for their aging parents. Surveys showed couples divorced, entered short-term relationships, and experimented with joint households rather than live in the mythical American family in which the husband works and the wife stays at home with the children. In order for middle-class families to maintain or slightly improve on earlier income levels, increasingly husbands and wives had to work for additional money to pay for childcare, activities for children, and ownership of a second home. At the same time, costs for healthcare, housing, and college soared—all at a time when better jobs were moving overseas. Moreover, the baby boomers represented perhaps the last dominant WASP generation, as America also became more racially and ethnically diverse.

Given the confusion and complications of American culture, it had become almost impossible to speak to women in any single voice, their lifestyles had so dramatically changed with the economy and work world over the last thirty years. Now consumers might be baby boomers, New Feminists, Generation Xers, teens, older Americans, gays, lesbians, African Americans, Latinos, Asian Americans, and so on. And, all these different groups are composed of people with highly different lifestyles and values.

In recent years, skilled marketers merged information on where people live with the US Census Bureau demographic data to produce a form of market segmentation, or *geodemographics*, that identifies neighborhoods by zip codes with similar lifestyle characteristics throughout the country. Such systems like PRIZM provided powerful tools to marketers because they were able to tell what type of segment existed in a particular region or even country—for example, middle-income, urban office workers. Other advertisers continued to use insights from psychographics to segment markets based on lifestyles—consumer activities, interests, and opinions, such as the VALS 2 system developed by SRI International, which organizes the market into eight lifestyles.

Hence, advertisers addressed the new realities of the American family, pitching long-lasting, valuable time-saving features and rock-bottom prices, as well as wholesomeness to health-conscious parents. But consumers increasingly were tuning out televised sales pitches with remote controls, videocassette recorders, and DVD players; or they used software programs to block advertising from showing up on Internet Web sites. They had become too smart, too quick, and too elusive for the slow-moving conventional advertiser. Across all income groups, consumers were also more selective in their buying behavior and were opting for discounted, private-label goods instead of nationally advertised brand names. But images of workingwomen ironically became even scarcer than they had been during the great women's movements of the 1920s and 1970s, even though the two-paycheck family had become the norm. It seemed that the working-woman had become such an integral part of American social and economic matrices that perhaps the advertiser and society took her work and independence for granted.

Third-wave feminism emerged out of this new generation, and feminists clashed over issues relating to sexuality, women's bodies, and cultural representations. Pop singer Madonna personified the postfeminism of this younger generation that was brought up on television, video games, and personal computers. Cars, magazines, music, and clothing—it was hard to name a product marketers were not trying to sell to this prized audience. Advertisers more and more cast off sexual restraint, and pornography moved out of movie theaters and onto the Internet, videos, and later, DVDs. Fashions in clothing became more revealing. Increasingly, marketers began targeting preteens and teens, a group that became known as Generation Y and wielded enormous purchasing power by supplying schools with everything from branded refrigerators and school buses to athletic gear and computers.

Yet Generation Xers had little in common with their boomer parents, who came of age in the reactionary 1960s. These younger adults watched less network television, read different magazines, and were frustrated that the American dream seemed out of their reach. A dollar simply wouldn't buy as much as it had for their parents twenty or thirty years earlier. These young people, who made up 23 percent of the workforce in 1993, earned nearly one-third less than their parents at the same age. In 1973 the typical man age twenty-five to thirty-four earned nearly $30,000 a year; in 1993 he earned only $21,604 in inflation-adjusted dollars. Advertisers recognized the marketing message had to be one of long-lasting value to help consumers justify their purchases in these tight times. For these consumers, quality, durability, and reliability dictated their buying decisions. They also expected advertisers to represent products truthfully and to provide generous warranties that would be honored.[16]

Since too much diversity existed in the needs and preferences of these groups of consumers, further segmentation based on other demographic and lifestyle variables was called for before an appropriate target market could be located. So it had become popular for marketers to choose a relatively small group of consumers with a unique set of needs and who typically were willing to pay a premium price for goods and services that met those needs. An approach called *niche marketing* then grew in popularity, as the mass media continued to splinter into a more complex and narrowly defined array of special advertising vehicles.

Although television was one of the most striking examples of the dramatic shift from a national culture to subcultures, the use of the Internet exploded in the 1990s and the early years of the twenty-first century. The new media had become the ideal marketing tool to identify and access market niches. Millions of Americans logged onto specialized Web sites where they could participate in an enormous array of chat groups, play games, and read newspapers and magazines that replaced the mass-circulation periodicals. The rush was on to create interactive multimedia advertising. With this new medium, advertisers could customize their message. Since Google has become a household word, it has become easier to sell billions of dollars of advertising services and to deliver ads to those people most likely to be interested in the messages without buying expensive broadcast or print campaigns.

THE EMPOWERMENT WAVE

Although a power shift from women to men had already started in the 1980s, in the 1990s women were at senior levels in sufficient numbers to break into the top layer of management. Women with far stronger credentials than ever before—graduate degrees, sales and marketing experience, and client contacts—moved into editorial, publishing, marketing, advertising, publicity, merchandising, and broadcasting fields, where the most plentiful, lucrative, and accessible positions appeared. They came to oversee the creation and the management of the world's largest ad campaigns. They moved into executive suites to hold senior posts and accounted for 65 percent of the entry-level and lower-middle-management jobs in advertising agencies. Corporations also sent thousands of women overseas to introduce goods all over the world, as they began to discover that the client was finally accepting them, since not only were more men willing to work with women, but the number of women had also risen on the client side.[17]

The Year of the Woman—1992

The *Year of the Woman* became a popular label attached to the year 1992, after the election of four female senators in the United States. Never before had four women been elected to the Senate in a single election year. The hotly contested Senate confirmation hearings for

Supreme Court nominee Clarence Thomas then heightened awareness of the issue of sexual harassment in the workplace, coupled with
the Hillary Clinton phenomenon and a resurgence of feminism that
generated more women's involvement in political activity.

This heightened awareness of sexual harassment led Americans to
make a connection between sexist advertising and more serious
offenses within the workplace. The allegedly satirical television commercials for Stroh's Old Milwaukee Beer, from Hal Riney & Partners,
crossed the line for many viewers in 1991, when a group of attractive
young women in bathing suits—dubbed the Swedish Bikini Team—
canoed, parachuted, and climbed mountains to deliver beer to male
beer drinkers. Consumers not only complained about the scantily clad
women, but also five employees of the Stroh Brewery Company
claimed that the company's sexist advertising campaigns communi-
cated a tolerance for sexual harassment in their workplace. The
volume of complaints had become a force inside the industry. By this
time, women were suddenly saying, "It matters to us what your company is saying and how you're portraying women—if we don't like the
message, we'll buy elsewhere," explained Barbara Feigin, then Grey
Advertising's head of research. Still, there were other external forces at
work in the marketplace that generated more women's involvement.[18]

When Charlotte Beers became the new chairwoman and chief
executive of Ogilvy & Mather Worldwide in 1992, she became the
most powerful woman in the advertising business. No woman had
ever headed an ad company this large before. Five years later, she
relinquished her responsibilities as chief executive to another woman,
Shelley Lazarus, a long-time Ogilvy executive who capped her career
by later heading J. Walter Thompson, another advertising behemoth.
Louise McNamee served as agency president with Della Femina,
McNamee WCRS; Mary Moore became president of Wells Rich
Greene; and Jane Newman was appointed president of Chiat/Day's
New York office. Among other women in such prestigious positions
were Cheryl Greene, Deutsch, Inc.; Nina DiSesa, McCann-
Erickson's first female executive creative director; Donna Weinhem,
BBDO; Linda Kaplan-Thaler, Wells Rich Greene; Mary Louise
Quinlan, N. W. Ayer; Helayne Spivak, Interpublic Group's Amierati

& Puras-Lintas; and Anne Tolstoi Wallach, vice president/creative director at Grey Advertising, among others.

Whereas many women found success in agency management, another group became highly visible in the media business. Just as radio in the 1930s and television in the 1950s had created new opportunities for women, the Internet did so in the 1990s. A new generation of computer technology and electronic communication networks transformed the visual communications field, and the World Wide Web, the graphical portion of the interconnected computer networks, emerged as the fastest-growing portion. Publishing companies, restaurants, music stores, television networks, florists, airlines, and other companies soon recognized the advertising possibilities and began creating Web sites that provided information about services and products.[19]

Although advertisers proved willing to experiment with the new medium, the absence of a system measuring the effectiveness of Internet advertising remains an issue. The online ad system has yet to devise a universally agreed-upon definition for standard measures, such as *hits* and *page views*.

Less than a decade ago, the sole source of women's and teen magazines were the stacks of slick, paper-based magazines filling mailboxes: *Good Housekeeping*, *Parents*, and *Woman's Day*. For teens there was *Teen Beat*, *Bop*, and *Seventeen*. Those days are gone. The 1995 launch of online magazines, or *e-zines*, or *zines*, such as *HotWired*, *Vibe*, and Time Warner's *Pathfinder*, provided advertisers with a way to reach a new generation of young, affluent consumers who had access to the Internet. The insurgence of cheap, fast, and easy publishing on the Web also spawned *iVillage*, one of the most successful online communities for women, while other new Web sites featured *grrrl-zines* for the younger woman, such as *Wench*, *Smile*, *Act Nice*, *Bust*, and *Hipmama*. In theory, this new women's culture embraced not only Web sites and magazines but also books, films, television series, and online magazines that circumscribed and catered to women's interests ranging from cosmetics to childcare, from personal grooming to personal relationships. Women could easily move from browsing to shopping and buying what they wanted, all without even having to get dressed.

Underneath this new media that seemingly gave women what

they wanted was a newly visible group of female CEOs and marketing consultants who were positively and actively affecting relationship marketing. For example, Candace Carpenter, a cofounder of *iVillage*, and Geraldine Lavbourne, chairwoman of Oxygen Media, combined a cable TV and Internet network into an entertainment and marketing conglomerate intended predominately for women. Another group of enterprising female entrepreneurs set out to reach women in their teens and twenties. Among them, twenty-four-year-old Heidi Swanson launched in 1998 *ChickClick*, a community of young, female-oriented zines with links and excerpts, with her sister, twenty-one-year-old Heather, who worked at Imagine Media. The site includes free e-mail, discussion forums, and personal homepages with the aim of creating a virtual community. Within one year, *ChickClick* had evolved into a large network consisting of over 2.5 million registered users and generating tens of millions of page views a month. In fact, it has become one of the highest-trafficked properties aimed at young women on the Internet, with many name-brand advertisers and sponsors supporting the site. Clearly, modern ad women not only survived, they thrived in a rapidly changing world.[20]

Celebration of Women's Power

We are now at a point where the daughters of the feminist mystique generation appear to be continuing the aspirations that increased the number of professional women over the last thirty years. Marketers who understood the boomer and postboomer women's markets quickly changed their fashion, beauty and cosmetics, and even automotive advertising. For many of these brands, the first step was reducing the images that offended feminine sensibilities and addressing women as active, confident, and professionally accomplished.

The most visible changes in women's product advertising began in early 1992, coinciding with the start of women's greater political activity in the campaigns for Congress. The bold new advertising campaigns celebrated feminism, as evidenced in a series of underwear campaigns, at that time a $2.7 billion market for men and women. Historically, advertising for women's underclothing not only

showed a seminaked, stiffly posed model, it often relied on stereotypes of women as sex objects and slaves to fashion. As a family business, the Jockey Company did not want to promote sex. The philosophy behind real people as models for its underwear campaign was
that the people shown were not the sports heroes or the Marilyn
Monroes. Research had shown that idealized models were being
viewed with increasing skepticism, and consumers reacted more
intensely to people like themselves, people with freckles, moles, and
blemishes. Instead, women readers were seeing female airline pilots,
dentists, and a truck driver in these ads, but often their unsightly
bulges and blemishes were airbrushed out (figure 10.5). Susan Small-
Weil, former director of Warwick Advertising, who worked on the
Jockey campaign, explained that the real-people themes were a
careful attempt to appeal in a specific way to a specific type of underwear consumer. "You can either forget that your body looks the way
it does, and want to look like Cheryl Tiegs," she said, "or you can
feel you're doing more with what you have." The advertisements
also generated publicity, and hundreds of people wrote letters
inquiring about being models.[21]

Citing new research that said women would not buy products
whose ads offended their feminine sensibilities—and that they
expected companies to reflect their values in ads, Maidenform relied
on an antistereotype campaign developed to cast off their outdated
sexist image. Under the direction of Rochelle Klein of Levine,
Huntley, Vick & Beaver, a New York agency, the selling message was
that Maidenform was a company that supports women and knows that
there is not just one way to be a woman. The new campaign poked
fun at the notion that women had to conform to society's picture of
them. One ad showed a Barbie doll, a tomato, and a fox, with the new
tagline "A helpful guide for those who still confuse women with
various unrelated objects." Another spot in a series of television commercials showed multiple images of women bound in corsets and bus-
tles, with a female voice-over saying, "Isn't it nice to live in a time
when women aren't being pushed around so much anymore?" The
Maidenform bras and panties are notably absent.[22]

This is a dramatic departure from Maidenform's long-running

"I enjoy the freedom of the open road ahead, and the total comfort of Jockey For Her underwear."

Monica Schappaugh
Truck Driver
Pekin, Illinois

So Comfortable
JOCKEY
For Her

For Pantyhose That Fit . . . Wear Jockey For Her Pantyhose with LYCRA

WOODWARD & LOTHROP

Figure 10.5. This ad was one in a series that used "real people" as models for the Jockey underwear campaign.

campaign from 1949 to 1969, featuring the scantily clad "Maidenform Woman" who had many dreams and actually had achieved some of them. When the Maidenform "I dreamed" campaign no longer appealed to younger women in the 1980s, Maidenform launched the "Dream Men" campaign in 1990, which did not even show the underwear. Instead the celebrity ads featured actors talking about women they have known (figure 10.6). But the campaign was not without its critics. The detractors argued that such images implied women buy underwear just to please men and that the ads risked offending women simply by reminding them of the prevalence of sexism.[23]

Ironically, a campaign from Kirshenbaum & Bond made sexism the theme for another lingerie campaign. They poked fun at slang terms to describe women's breasts by picturing a set of headlights, doorknockers, and melons—all ridiculous images men have used to describe women's breasts—with the tagline "Bamboo Lingerie, a company owned by two women. Put that in your pipe and smoke it." Some women's empowerment ads were far more explosive. Body-Slimmers lingerie by Nancy Ganz showed a sexy woman from the neck down wearing a one-piece undergarment; the copy read: "While you don't necessarily dress for men, it doesn't hurt, on occasion, to see one drool like the pathetic dog that he is" (figure 10.7). Of course, all women did not share this mind-set, so ad makers continually faced the challenge of how to reach a new balance, adjusting approaches in favor of women and following the currents of culture.

But it was the Wonderbra that *Time* magazine called one of the top ten products of the year in 1994. The push-up bra featured several strategically placed pads to enhance a women's figure, and marketing positioned it as a tool to empower women. Advertisements showed models wearing only the Wonderbra, with slogans underneath such as "Who cares if it's a bad hair day," "Look me in the eyes and tell me that you love me," and "Live it up" (figure 10.8). With a suggested retail price of twenty-six dollars, the bras began selling at a rate of one every fifteen seconds, and stores could not keep the bras on their shelves. But many feminist groups voiced their opposition, saying the advertising message was that women should focus on their breasts for attention. Sara Lee Corporation countered these criticisms with the

"*A friend of mine says she has better luck in choosing her lingerie than in choosing her dinner companions.*

"*Perhaps there's just a better selection of lingerie out there.*"

Maidenform offers women over 150 ways to express themselves. Obviously people are listening.

MAIDENFORM

Figure 10.6. Maidenform's campaign "Dream Men" featured celebrities such as Pierce Brosnan talking about women they have known, 1990.

argument that the campaign was created by women and therefore could not possibly exploit women.

Gradually—some might even say reluctantly—magazine advertising began to more subtly convey an understanding of women's lifestyles and priorities, communicating a "We know what you're

While you don't necessarily dress for men, it doesn't hurt, on occasion, to see one drool like the pathetic dog that he is.

BODYSLIMMERS™ by NANCY GANZ

going through message." One reason for this heightened sensitivity to the women's market was women themselves. Now more women held marketing and advertising positions and positively impacted the basic promotional appeal for many accounts. They took the lead in the development of many campaigns to ensure that women were treated fairly and respectfully. Rejecting the traditional fantasy-and-romance approach to advertising, they drew attention to the underlying drives that contributed to women's buying actions and developed campaigns that established emotional ties with consumers. These ads creatively addressed such women's issues as maintaining

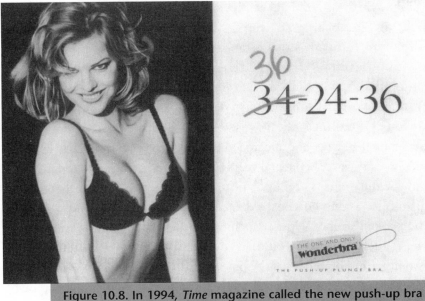

Figure 10.8. In 1994, *Time* magazine called the new push-up bra one of the top ten products of the year. *Vogue,* March 1995.

control without being a superwoman, combating fatigue, balancing family and work, and so on.

For example, the creative team Janet Champ and Charlotte Moore were partners in the creation of the groundbreaking Nike print campaign for women in the 1990s, an inspirational campaign that not only generated hundreds of thousands of responses from women but also spawned a larger debate about the portrayal of women in advertising and the method in which they were addressed. The Weiden and Kennedy copywriters were selling Nike athletic shoes, but first and foremost they were creating a small public forum for talking about women, their bodies, their feelings, their self-images, and self-esteem. What they said so eloquently was that women are often measured by nothing more than their bodies. Instead of saying, "I'm more than what I look like," they said, "I'm strong and I dream and I want to be fantastic." They also celebrated women in sports, as evident in a 1995 commercial titled "If You Let Me Play." The ad featured young girls talking about the benefits society reaps when females participate in sports, such as higher academic performance by girls in school, fewer teenage pregnancies, and reduction of male violence targeted at women. Such athletic shoe advertising to women proved inspiring, uplifting, and even empowering. It also served as a new model for developing campaigns that established emotional ties with women.

Other advertisers attempted to jump on the soulful bandwagon. Similar to Nike, Levi's blue jeans also offered a nurturing message. When Foote, Cone & Belding launched Levi's award-winning "Women in Motion" print campaign, they used abstract illustrations to demonstrate the fit of the jeans and created the most sensitive campaign ever for female jeans wearers. Several years later, stunning television commercials brought the drawings to life. The animated spots had virtually no copy, no voice-over, and no slogans. Instead, they simply conveyed emotional truths about women's lives, touching on such hot buttons as men, love, pain, and food. Pop-up titles included "Women Not Feeling Blue," "Women Finding Balance," "Women Finding Love," and "Women Getting Things Off Their Chest." Many women identified with this type of product advertising that did not use the too-perfect model (figure 10.9).

Men Become the Babes

As women became more comfortable with their professional success, the emphasis on sexuality and gender-bender stereotypes in advertising continued to flourish. In earlier decades, role-reversal ads revolved around the theme of male emasculation as reflected in the stereotypical househusband, who was unrealistically childlike or ludicrous in the traditional domain of women—the kitchen, the nursery, and the living room—often dressed in frilly aprons and struggling with the simplest of household tasks. The message to women was that the advertised product made the task so simple that even a man could do it in those little emergency situations. By the 1980s, the role-reversal version revolved around a *boy toy*, a term that referred to a generally sexually attractive man who is controlled by a woman. However, the emasculated male began to be replaced by the androgynous male in the last years of the century (figure 10.10). Such changing pictures of romantic partnership reflected the changing ideals of American masculinity as well as changing expectations of women.

Over the years advertisers may have exploited images of women

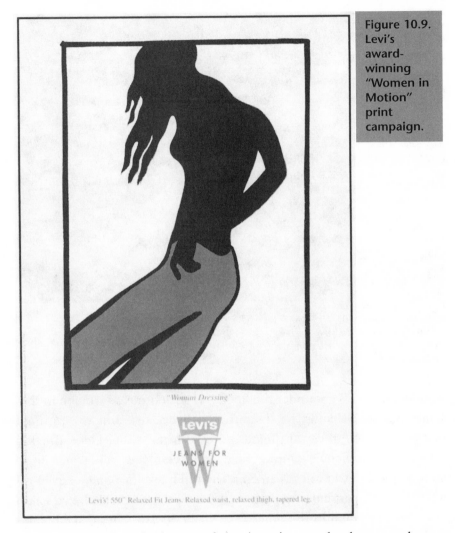

"Woman Dressing"

Levi's
JEANS FOR WOMEN

Levi's 550™ Relaxed Fit Jeans. Relaxed waist, relaxed thigh, tapered leg.

in advertising, but the image of the American male also served marketers well. After consumers complained about the Swedish Bikini Team for Old Milwaukee Beer, a new genre of role-reversal ads emerged to objectify men in the 1990s—that is, *reverse sexism*. In a much-talked-about Hyundai ad called "Parking Lot," for example, two women scoff at men who drive racy sports cars, arguing that they buy powerful cars because they are worried about the size of a certain appendage, whose name is never spoken. "Must be overcompensating for a . . . shortcoming," one says. When a handsome man drives up in an economy Hyundai Elantra, the second woman muses: "I

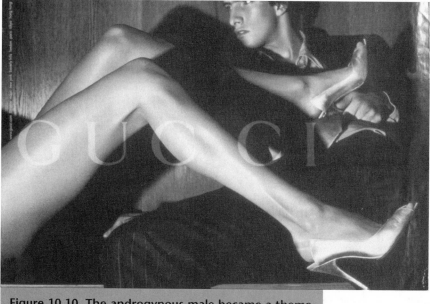

Figure 10.10. The androgynous male became a theme in advertising during the late 1980s and 1990s, representing the discarding of manly stereotypes.

wonder what he's got under the hood." If ads portrayed women in the same manner, it could be definitely called sexist. But the turning point in the role-reversal theme came with the "Diet Coke Break" television commercial. Rather than portraying the strong man in a stereotypical power role, as an emasculated househusband, or even as a boy toy, this particular ad portrayed the man as a sexual object. Like clockwork, women in the office take an 11:30 a.m. Diet Coke break. Only they do not drink the soda. Instead they race to the window to watch, with unabashed admiration, a sweaty, muscular construction worker who strips to his bare chest and refreshes himself with a cool Diet Coke. As they stare down from the window, they fill their imaginations with all sorts of fantasies. At the end of the break, the women, seemingly fulfilled, move away from the window but not before saying, "Same time tomorrow?" to their colleagues. The idea, of course, is a twist on the stereotype of male construction workers ogling women as a spectator sport. Why the turnabout?

On one level, these images were far more than mere sexual fantasies for women; they were statements of women's assertiveness and power. For example, on HBO's *Sex and the City*, the episode "Hop, Skip and a Week" featured sexy public relations specialist Samantha Jones (Kim Catrall) making a deal for her latest love interest to appear nude in a provocative advertising campaign called *Absolut Hunk*. In the episode, Samantha's campaign is a huge success; the ads are appearing all over New York City, and an impressive display on a giant billboard in Times Square shows him nude with his modesty hidden by a strategically placed bottle of Absolut vodka. Yet for all the talk of equality, such sentiments may reflect how much political correctness has overevolved. "The more de-babed we get," explains media critic Barbara Lippert, "the more men have to become the babes because we need babes in advertising."[24]

Gender-Free Advertising

As the distinction between male and female segments of the consumer market began to blur, marketing strategies increasingly turned away from gender-based marketing of products, which focused on one sex, toward dual marketing or *gender-free* advertising. In some ads for products traditionally targeted at women, no images of women even appeared. Commercials for Motrin IB, for example, mirrored the trend that fathers were participating in childcare. Ads for Cheer laundry detergent used a middle-aged, bald man to demonstrate the product's cleaning power. With the exception of some categories like feminine hygiene and cosmetics, the idea of gender began to disappear.

The big winners in this period were attuned to the middle-class American feminist movement and followed the currents of culture. By reviewing their products and services in a serious, consistent way, a number of companies repositioned them as tools that empower a woman rather than as something to enhance self-esteem or make her a better housewife. They also sought to find advertising messages that would resonate with reality and that were not condescending. In so doing, advertisers at this level attracted consumer's interests and the brand loyalty that came with such audiences. With the aging of the baby boomers, a generation of women now in their peak earning years were making the financial decisions in their households. Women were buying houses by themselves and purchasing everything from golf equipment to life insurance products—items that were once almost exclusively advertised to men.

Probably one of the most common arguments against gender-based marketing was that targeting female consumers might alienate the male market. In fact, what women wanted often turned out to be what men also wanted, but no one ever bothered to ask them. Take Home Depot, for example. The hardware retailer had known for some time that, while women accounted for half of the company's sales, their influence on overall purchases was even higher. Recognizing that women focused more on projects and less on products, Home Depot installed design showrooms that presented a focus on decor, trained its sales associates to double-check with customers that they had everything they needed for a project, and made its stores brighter, cleaner, and less cluttered. Although the improvements particularly appealed to women, they also benefited their male customers, because the motivations for home improvement were the same, whether you're a man or a woman. It's about pride of home.[25]

Another reason against marketing differently to the sexes was that young people in their twenties were erasing the lines between traditional male and female roles in education, athletics, and family life. For example, the Citadel, the Military College of South Carolina, was all male until 1996; in the same year, the Women's National Basketball Association was formed as the women's counterpart to the National Basketball Association. Furthermore, some younger husbands have voluntarily pulled back on their careers (or quit entirely) to care for kids and live off their wives' income. Though the number is small, many economists think the number is growing. But the last couple of decades have not been enough to make a difference after centuries of clearly defined roles for men and women.

Despite far-reaching social changes over the last century and men's increasing participation in childcare, studies show that women continue to do most of the cooking, shopping, and cleaning.[26] So, although a growing number of companies are repositioning their products and services as tools that empower women, the majority of advertisements continued to show women in two different worlds. The traditional one was a rerun of the 1950s that lingered past reality with images of apron-clad homemakers and devoted stay-at-home moms putting dinner on the table, caring for the children, and cleaning the house; while in the real world, women took on additional roles outside the home. Nonetheless, such ads for household cleaners, foodstuffs, and over-the-counter medications were still effective for the modern workingwoman, for whom the tableaux mirrored real life. Or, they showed a modern world with workingwomen planning their next mutual fund investment, taking husbands away for the weekend, or buying diamond rings.

Still, there was a constant interplay between consumers and manufacturers, and advertising made it easier to communicate with prospective customers. As markets and consumer identities changed, popular stereotypes, marketing strategies, and advertising messages shifted to connect with well-defined groups of consumers. With women a more powerful force than ever before in the marketplace and workforce, the feminine viewpoint became the nexus connecting consumption, manufacturers, and advertising in modern America. This symbiotic relationship among the consumers, the mass-consumer industry, and advertising has created the greatest consumer market in the world, one in which women themselves played a pivotal role.

NOTES

1. The wedding ring is worn on the left hand because people believed that a vein of blood ran directly from the fourth finger to the heart. So, matrimonial procedure dictated that a wedding ring be worn on this finger, which had supposed magic power.

2. The second-wave feminists criticized the new industrial economy, mistrusted advertising, and made sweeping claims, as evidenced in the late 1970s' *Decoding Advertisements*, a book by Judith Williamson, and *Killing Us Softly*, a series of videos produced by Jean Kilbourne. In the 1980s, examples include Susan Bordo's *Unbelievable Weight*, Diane Barthel's *Putting on Appearances*, and Naomi Wolf's *The Beauty Myth*. On an analysis of the feminist critique, see Linda M. Scott, *Fresh Lipstick* (New York: Palgrave, 2005) pp. 316–26.

3. Statistical Tables 11 and 14, *Women in the Labor Force: A Databook* (Washington, DC: US Department of Labor, Bureau of Labor Statistics, 2006), pp. 28, 31, and 43. See http://www.bls.gov/cps/wlf-databook2006.htm (accessed January 23, 2008).

4. Linda M. Scott, editors' introduction, *Advertising & Society Review* 4 (2003).

5. Julia Baker Woods, *Advertising and Marketing to the New Majority* (Belmont, CA: Wadsworth, 1955), p. 22.

6. Susan Faludi, *Backlash: The Undeclared War against American Women* (New York: Crown Publishers, 1991).

7. Some people speculated that Anne Tolstoi Wallach's book described the J. Walter Thompson Company (JWT), where she served as a vice president/associate creative supervisor before moving on to Grey Advertising. See "One Who Broke the Mold," National Recruitment Survey, *New York Times*, October 11, 1981, p. 31. See also book reviews of *Women's Work*: *Adweek*, August 24, 1981, p. 18, and *New York Times*, August 21, 1981, p. D-13. On the new heroine, see Dorothy C. Holland and Margaret A. Eisenhardt, *Educated in Romance: Women, Achievement and College Culture* (Chicago: University of Chicago Press, 1990), especially chaps. 11 and 12.

8. Rena Bartos, *The Moving Target* (New York: Free Press, 1982), pp. 116–30, 247–52.

9. "The Ad Industry's Little Secret," *Advertising Age*, June 16, 1992. "The Executive Suite: Still a Men's Club," *Adweek*, July 7, 1986.

10. "Making Ads That Sizzle," *Advertising Age*, July 18, 1985.

11. Ibid.

12. "It's Becoming Part of Our Culture," *Forbes*, May 5, 1986.

13. Eric Clark, *The Want Makers: Inside the World of Advertising* (New York: Penguin Books, 1989), pp. 114–15.

14. David Ogilvy, *Ogilvy on Advertising* (New York: Vintage Books, 1983), p. 23.

15. Quoted in Gail Bronson, "King Leer: Sexual Pitches in Ads Become More Explicit and More Pervasive," *Wall Street Journal*, November 18, 1980.

16. "Getting Your Slice of the Pie," *San Francisco Chronicle*, October 14, 1994.

17. "Divas Madison Avenue," *USA Today*, June 12, 1995.

18. "You've Come a Long Way Maybe," *Advertising Age*, February 1, 1993, p. C-23.

19. "In the Beginning," *Advertising Age Special Issue*, vol. 71, no. 16, 2000.

20. "Chick Power," *Adweek*, January 25, 1999.

21. "Real People Are Models for Jockey," *New York Times*, May 15, 1989.

22. On antistereotype campaign, see *Advertising Age*, December 10, 1990; "Sending Up the Bra," *Adweek*, December 17, 1990; and "Maidenform Casts Off an Outdated Sexist Stereotype," *New York Times*, November 17, 1991.

23. "Maidenform Focuses on Stereotypes," *Wall Street Journal*, December 10, 1990.

24. Quoted in "Going One Step Ogle the Line," *Newsweek*, March 14, 1994.

25. "What Women Want," *CMA Management Magazine*, December/ January 2006.

26. "Women: Out of the House but Not out of the Kitchen," *New York Times*, February 24, 1988, p. A-1. See also, "Exactly How Much Houseowork Does a Husband Create?" University of Michigan News Service, April 3, 2008.

AD WOMEN ON TOP

Looking at the twentieth century from the perspective of 1869, when Mathilde C. Weil first sought entry into the advertising profession, women have certainly played a more complex role in the formation of modern consumer culture than historians have attributed to them. Each generation of ad women created new opportunities for the next generation of women. First-wave suffragists fought for women's citizenship and challenged traditional patriarchies, but only rarely did professional women advance as rapidly as men, while other women settled for positions far below their talents and training. Second-wave feminists questioned nearly everything, transformed much of American culture, and expanded the idea of democracy to include women's right to pursue professional careers and to achieve personal success. Their greatest accomplishment was to change the terms of the debate, so that women mattered and gradually assumed many key marketing and advertising positions. As a result, they have impacted the basic promotional appeal for many accounts. They drew attention to the underlying drives that contribute to women's buying actions and developed campaigns that established emotional connections with consumers by insisting that advertising for women had to include the realities of women's lives.

Survey data, employment trends, and statistics all document enormous gains in women's participation in college education, the advertising profession, and entrepreneurship. In a closer look at the advertising industry, the representation of women employed in advertising and related services or as advertising agents has tripled since World War II. In 1940 only 18.1 percent of advertising workers were women. By 1974 the number rose to 44 percent. And in 2006, women accounted for 53.9 of advertising and promotion managers and 52.9 percent of advertising sales agents. They also made up 37.5 of professionals employed in marketing and sales management and 64.8 percent of public relations specialists.[1]

Today, women fill marketing courses. They account for more than two-thirds of the college students majoring in advertising, and nine out of ten students in public relations programs are women. Such educational choices will lead an increasing number of women to move into the fields of editorial work, publishing, marketing, advertising, publicity, merchandising, and broadcasting, where they will shape truly global brands, develop positive advertising campaigns, and persuasively sell consumer products and services. This new breed of workingwomen, the university-educated, middle-class career woman, who first emerged in the 1970s, will have the opportunity to impact not only traditional women's accounts in such areas as food, fashion, beauty and cosmetics, and home furnishings but also traditionally masculine strongholds such as automotive marketing, financial services, insurance, and other industries all over the world. As I have tried to show, every food introduced into daily life, every new style of dress, beauty aid, home appliance, financial service, and even automotive design is largely influenced and managed by women. A lot of the evidence that I have turned up supports the idea that the woman's point of view matters in this kind of work. What I also found, consistently, was that the woman's viewpoint was more complex, problematic, and insightful than this book allowed.

Over the last century, paradoxically, many of the professional and managerial women found themselves reinforcing prevailing sexist images of gender and consumption, as they carved out a niche in the mass-market industries. Although the period from 1920 to 1940 saw more varied images of women than the prior decades, it also ended by reinforcing narrow gender stereotypes of both women's and men's roles in society as they drew upon an array of existing images representing modern American industrial society. Men ran the offices or worked at the factories, while women created the home as a retreat from the stresses of the man's world and built a haven in which to nurture the children. Within these boundaries, ad women challenged the traditional role of women, as they portrayed the sporting woman, the actress, the socialite, and the clubwoman, among others. But for all the talk of social revolution and women's freedom, the range of these roles quickly narrowed and became more conventional, inspiring what would become key tenets of normative femininity in the twentieth century. To succeed in the modern world, beauty and style provided women with a competitive advantage. The advertising campaigns illustrated throughout this book show that the pretty woman has long been a prevalent and potent visual device in advertising, and the happy home-maker was rarely shown as anything but attractive, regardless of the demanding chore in which she may be engaged.

⟨≈⟩⟨≈⟩

Whereas many feminists blamed men's institutions and institutional power for American women's preoccupations with beauty, a great deal of other women subscribed to a different perspective. Women found power in women's beauty and fashion, like Dorothy Dignam, Shirley Polykoff, and Rochelle Udell. Other women found power in their own ethnicity, like Caroline Jones, who fashioned positive images of African Americans, Mavis Codero of Hispanics, and Eleanor Yu of Asian Americans. Others like Charlotte Beers found power and identity in managing multinational companies. Moreover, younger women, who in the 1980s separated themselves from previous generations of feminists, argued that women should embrace their power and become more like men, using their electoral, financial, and political authority to boldly get what they wanted. The Superwoman stereotype became the essence of this new individualist who enjoyed all the pleasures of sexual freedom, marriage, and motherhood. Not only did a career offer the quintessential individualist opportunities for self-fulfillment and liberation—so did consumption.

By the close of the century, awareness of the growing, changing men's market also affected promotion appeals, packaging, and advertising media. At this level, the popular media shaped the image of a new man who was just as strong and secure in his masculinity as his predecessor but far more diverse in his interests. A sense of style, sophistication, and self-awareness was also becoming a defining factor of the modern man with intelligence and sensitivity. An eruption of trendy lifestyle magazines (*Maxim*, *FHM*, and *Stuff*) vied for the attention of young males, while *GQ*, *Details*, *Men's Health*, and *Men's Journal* aimed at the market of professional men with middle to upper incomes. In the popular media, images of men as construction workers, cowboys, successful businessmen, sophisticates in tuxedos, and musclemen represented countless conscious—and often unconscious—decisions by ad makers about what men look like, say, and even think.

But it was the *metrosexual* that came to define the new man who combined a masculine style with attention to clothes, cosmetics, and fashions. Since the once-great divide between straight men and gay men has lessened considerably in recent years, one of the defining characteristics of the metrosexual is that he is not necessarily gay or straight or bisexual. In this way, the mass media helped break various expectations of manly stereotypes, such as what clothes a man is supposed to wear. As early as the mid-1990s, writer Mark Simpson coined the term for this new masculine idea. According to Simpson, "The typical metrosexual is a young man with money to spend, living within easy reach of a metropolis—because that's where all the best shops, clubs, gyms, and hairdressers are."[2]

Since the British newspapers first identified British soccer player David Beckham as the official prototype of the modern metrosexual, other image makers groomed male celebrities to fit this new ideal, including famous names like Brad Pitt, Sting, and Justin Timberlake, among others. This movement pointed the way for *Queer Eye for the Straight Guy*, a popular television show that features gay men who show straight men how to decorate their apartments, what clothes to wear, and how to style their hair and care for their skin. Because of this trend, a whole new range of cars, fashion, grooming products, restaurants, and sports clubs has been launched with a flood of advertising to cater to this modern man, encouraging him to buy more. Even in this age of market segmentation, when men are addressed as style-conscious, the association of femininity and consumption remains nearly seamless.

⊲⋐⋑⊳

By the end of the twentieth century, consumer capitalism and the sixties culture of rebellion had become inseparable. Advertisers had co-opted the individualistic lifestyles, youthfulness, uninhibited instinct, and sexual liberation. As never before, a new class of well-to-do Americans bought cars, home appliances, large-screen televisions, computers, and countless luxury items. Indeed, popular culture and consumer culture were powerful agents that worked to make Americans all alike. Whether first-generation immigrants, feminists, gays, lesbians, African Americans, Latinos, Asian Americans, or Anglo-Saxons, Americans were increasingly buying the same kind of goods, listening to the same radio programs, watching the same movies, and reading the same magazines, newspapers, and books.

We are at the point where some observers believe that such forces of modernity, especially the mass media and consumer capitalism, are even creating a common global culture. So James Twitchell in *Living It Up* concludes that the mass consumption of luxury is actually doing more to promote unity and peace than any religion, culture, political movement or ideology has done.[3] But the influences of modernity also went in the other direction. When the nation moved into a postindustrial economy, rapidly changing technology such as computers, automated assembly lines, and robots replaced workers. Periodic economic downturns and the continuing restructuring of the economy have caused insecurity, while the new immigrant residents are producing a multicultural society with stresses for the population and tensions between the ethnic groups themselves. And, surveys show that only one out of five Americans continue to live in the mythical nuclear family, in which the husband works and the wife stays at home with the children.

America is a deeply divided nation. James Davidson Hunter's *Culture Wars* describes this dramatic polarization that transformed American politics and culture. The war revolves around a number of defining issues: affirmative action, abortion, gay rights, environmentalism, funding for the arts, the public school system, multiculturalism, censorship, and the role of religion in American life. Essentially the "hot topic" issues divided society primarily not by religion, ethnicity, social class, or even political affiliation, but rather by ideological worldviews. In short, we are reorganizing the social milieu around the magnitude of dislikes that groups of people have for one another. Hence, culture war.[4]

These dividing lines evolving in American culture create economic groups that are of special interest to marketers and media people, who face an increasingly fragmented audience. For a number of years, the economy and consumer tastes have been growing increasingly ethnocentric in the choices groups of people make to respect (and purchase) and reject. For instance, consumers organized the first "Buy Nothing Day" in 1992 to examine the issue of overconsumption. Five years later, in 1997, Buy Nothing Day was moved to the Friday after Thanksgiving, which typically is one of the busiest shopping days in the United States and a global phenomenon. Moreover, advertisers find that core promotional ideas may be radiating positively with some consumers but are denounced by others. For example, Coca-Cola was boycotted to protest the war in Iraq, and Wal-Mart faced protests, legal action, and boycotts in its efforts to open stores in California. In sum, these commercial messages carry the coded language and metaphors of the culture war.

For those who were listening, these events and messages spoke loudly, and they spoke to shared beliefs and impulses of certain people, while the distaste for the preferences, values, and symbols of other groups emerged as more hostile. In any case, one message won't work for all people. The culture war encourages the taking of sides, and new generations of consumers are organizing around values, social class, and age. As a result, they are becoming increasingly fragmented and reacting differently to commercial messages by many-sided hostilities rather than uniting in a common purpose. Each

construct or hot topic reflects potent forces for binding groups of
people in the form of a discrete *tribal affinity group*, or persons who
share the same interest or mutual distastes.

This goes for media behavior, too. Media choice is tribal. The
content of preferred media will respect the group's beliefs. Likewise,
media will be rejected when its content carries contrary points of view
and challenges prevailing beliefs. Thus, the traditional evening news,
national magazines, family television programming, and radio no
longer deliver one mass national market to advertisers.

There is no end to this story. The trends that began in the late
nineteenth century continue into the early twenty-first century. As in
the past, the progress of industrialization complicated the selling
process, as marketers faced an increasingly fragmented audience and
diverse emerging markets. Advertising, too, was no longer a Western
phenomenon; it was now global. The themes also encompass the
growing power of mass media and the enormous success of brand
names; the expansion of the economy and certain occupations within
it identified with women (such as clerical work), as well as technological advances and more leisure time, which accompanied changing
attitudes and behaviors in sexual expression and marriage. During the
course of history, discrimination toward sexual, racial, and ethnic
groups continues as an inherent part of American culture, as well as
movements to end such injustices.

⊰⊱

Today, American consumer culture continues to be radically transformed by women's growing economic power. In the United States,
women manage more money than ever before. "Women control the vast
majority of what America buys from cars to computers to healthcare to
hamburgers," wrote Fara Warner in 2005. Women bought 94 percent of
all home furnishings, 62 percent of all hardware, and 89 percent of home
remodeling. They bought 60 percent of cars and trucks. They held 65
percent of all savings accounts and accounted for 62 percent of individual stockholders of large corporations. And of the three million
people earning more than $500,000 a year, 40 percent were women.[5]

Certainly women are a more powerful force than ever before in the marketplace and workforce, too. Their buying power did not go unnoticed by the media industry, which introduced a new generation of magazines that elaborated on the women's market. For example, *Forbes* introduced *Life Executive*, a glossy quarterly magazine that targets senior-level businesswomen to attract advertisers of luxury items. Another monthly business periodical, *Executive Women*, aims at the market of women executives, while *Pink* and *Working Mother* target midlevel managerial women who do not want to sacrifice work or family life.

In the workplace, women continue to make difficult choices to stop working altogether, work only part-time, or take their chances with a glass ceiling in promotion. Nationally, women in their twenties made a median income of $25,647, compared with $28,532 for men in 2007; but one-third of all these women earned more wages than their husbands who have earnings. If and when they do marry, they are bringing with them far more power than any generation before them, shifting the balance of power in families as well as in society. For many couples, some counselors predict that switching in and out of the role as the sole wage earner may become a routine part of life, since careers will involve more moves between industries and more time out of work as a result of retraining or downsizing. So, many couples will be taking turns, one as the primary breadwinner and the other managing the childcare and housework, as their careers ebb and flow. Some experts use the phrase *alpha earners* to describe high-income female providers who are the primary breadwinners for more than 10 percent of American families, and data suggests that women's economic power will only grow. Maybe the balancing act will work this time.[6]

But the creative process hasn't changed much at all. Centuries-old ideas that worked for newspapers, magazines, and broadcast media have now been applied to an enormous range of media, from the Internet to cell phones, movie screens to shopping centers, though there is an age of generational element at play. It seems that advertisers continue to primarily target people in their thirties, forties, and older with traditional media, whereas teenagers and twenty-somethings are basically of a generation that grew up broadcasting the details of their lives on social networking sites, such as *YouTube*,

MySpace, and *FaceBook*, where users can upload, view, and share video clips and blogs that may include journal entries, commentaries, and recommendations by the user. Now these sites have proven the concept of low-cost video broadcasting technology and how it can draw together an audience. It will be interesting to see how these sites fare in developing advertising and what comes next.

As America becomes more divided around separate identities than a common core culture, it is for a new generation to redefine marketing, advertising, and the media in this rapidly accelerating society, which must continually adjust to the currents of culture. Still, as more women are earning more than their husbands, the same questions face today's marketers and advertisers about gender—how much to emphasize it or tone it down.

No one can say yet confidently whether the trends of the late twentieth century and early twentieth-first century were the final stage of modern American consumer culture or the transition to the beginnings of a new one. It is also difficult to predict what the future holds for the woman's viewpoint in business and women in the advertising profession, since there are many factors involved. Regardless, it is clear that Americans in the late twentieth century carried consumer capitalism about as far as it possibly could be taken. No earlier generation in America embraced more fully the idea of making money and consumption as an important component of everyday life. Regardless, women no longer monopolized family buying. Men and youth, especially teenagers, joined in shopping as a form of leisure. In the world of twentieth-century America, mass consumption became equally important to the nation's market-driven economy as corporate capitalism. It was this culture revolving around consumption—a culture in which ad women had significant impact on what we want, need, and buy—that the world came to see as the very heart of American life.

NOTES

1. On 1940 data, see Advertising Occupation Classified as Both Advertising under Business Services and Advertising Agents, Statistical Abstract of the United States, 1950, no. 75, US Department of Commerce. On 1974 data, see Advertising

Occupation Classified under Miscellaneous Business Services, US Department of Labor, *Bureau of Labor Statistics: Employment and Earnings*, May 1974, and Monthly Labor Review, May 1974. On 2006 data, see Advertising Occupation Classified as Both Advertising under Business Services and Advertising Agents, US Department of Labor, US Bureau of Statistics, 2006.

2. Michael Flocker, *The Metrosexual Guide to Style: A Handbook for the Modern Man* (New York: DaCapo Press, 2003).

3. James B. Twitchell, *Living It Up: America's Love Affair with Luxury* (New York: Columbia University Press, 2002).

4. James Davison Hunter, *Culture Wars: The Struggle to Define America* (New York: Basic Books, 1990).

5. Fara Warner, *The Power of the Purse: How Smart Businesses Are Adapting to the World's Most Important Consumer* (New York: Prentice Hall, 2005), p. 3.

6. "For Young Earners in Big City, a Gap in Women's Favor," *New York Times*, August 3, 2007. On wives who earn more than their husbands, see *Women in the Labor Force: A Databook* (Washington, DC: US Department of Labor, Bureau of Labor Statistics, 2006), http://www.bls.gov/cps/wlf-databook2006.htm (accessed January 28, 2008). On alpha earners, see "She Works, He Doesn't," *Newsweek*, May 12, 2003.

INDEX